The American Mafia

Sociology Series

John F. Cuber, *editor*
Alfred C. Clarke, *associate editor*

The American Mafia
Genesis of a Legend

Joseph L. Albini
Wayne State University

APPLETON-CENTURY-CROFTS
EDUCATIONAL DIVISION
New York **MEREDITH CORPORATION**

To my brother Salvatore
who has always inspired me in the
pursuit of truth and knowledge

Preface

This book concerns itself with an analysis and description of syndicated crime in the United States. The major purpose of the work is to describe the functional aspects of criminal syndicates in American society itself. Information was obtained from police and from informants in the underworld, and both these points of view bring into focus that individual without whom syndicated crime would not exist—the American who consumes illicit goods. With this as its major theme, this work goes on to describe how syndicates have developed and continue to exist in order to meet this customer's needs.

The research for this work has taken a period of four years. If it serves to stimulate a reconsideration of many of the unfounded assumptions concerning the origin and nature of syndicated crime in the United States, then this time and effort shall not have been in vain. In my research, I have been fortunate in having the cooperation of many, and I wish to extend my appreciation to the following:

I cannot begin to find words capable of expressing my thanks to Marie Wilt, my assistant throughout this project. Her patience and care in typing and editing the manuscript are deserving of appreciation.

Vincente W. Piersante, Chief Investigator, Organized Crime Division, Michigan Attorney General's Office, deserves a special note of thanks. It was Mr. Piersante who kindly helped me to make the necessary contacts with many of the law enforcement officials interviewed in this project. I turned to Mr. Piersante for help throughout this project.

I also wish to express thanks to others who graciously offered their help in the beginning phases of this work: Lieutenant

Robert S. Earhart of the Michigan State Police; Charles Siragusa, formerly Executive Director of the Illinois Crime Investigating Commission; and Ralph F. Salerno, formerly of the New
York City Police Department.

To the following the author extends his heartfelt thanks for
their help in this project: Albert Shapiro, formerly Deputy
Chief of Detectives, Detroit Police Department; Francis C.
Grevenberg, formerly Superintendent of the Louisiana State
Police; Superintendents John T. Howland and Herbert F. Mul-
loney of the Boston Police Department; Director David W.
Craig and members of his staff of the Department of Public
Safety, City of Pittsburgh; Lieutenant Louis Kulis and Captain
George Sperber of the Cleveland Police Department; Mr.
Dwight S. Strong, formerly Executive Secretary of the New
England Citizens' Crime Commission; Inspector James Bannon
of the Detroit Police Department; and James P. Mullins, Chief
of Police, City of Tampa, Florida.

I wish to thank the following for providing reports, papers,
bibliographical and other material: Dr. Rudolph J. Vecoli, Director of the Center for Immigration Studies, University of Min-
nesota; Virgil W. Peterson, Executive Director of the Chicago
Crime Commission; Charles H. Rogovin, Chief, Criminal Di-
vision, Department of the Attorney General, Massachusetts; the
Honorable Magistrato Salvatore Giallombardo, Associazione
Nazionale Magistrati, Rome, Italy; the Honorable Thomas J.
Graham, Magistrate, The Ontario Police Commission, Ontario,
Canada; Myles J. Lane, Chairman, State of New York Com-
mission of Investigation; Ray Brennan and the staff of the
Chicago Sun-Times; and the Wisconsin Historical Society.

For their help in various phases of this project I wish to
thank T. Col. Dott. Ottavio Mannelli, Instituto Geografico
Militare, Firenze, Italy; Professor Armand L. DeGaetano, Wayne
State University; Nick Gatz, Superintendent of Administration
and Research, Adult Parole Authority, State of Ohio; Adnan
Aswad, The University of Michigan; and Dr. Helen Hause,
Wayne State University.

A special note of thanks is extended to Donald C. Ewing and
his staff of the General Library, Wayne State University.

To Professor Charles M. Unkovic, formerly Director of the Correctional Training Center, Cleveland State University, and to his staff members Joe Maloney and Paula Matthei, I wish to express my gratitude for their help.

To those police officials who gave invaluable information but requested that their names be withheld and to the informants in this project, I extend my deep-felt thanks.

So too, I wish to thank my colleagues and students at Wayne State University who, far too numerous to mention by name, will nonetheless always be remembered for their valuable contributions.

It goes without saying that the ideas and opinions expressed in this work are mine alone, and do not necessarily reflect the beliefs of those individuals who provided me with information.

J. L. A.

Contents

Preface   vii

1 Syndicated Crime:
   A Prelude to Its Conceptualization   1

2 Types of Organized Crime:
   A Plea For Clarification   21

3 The Social Locale of Syndicated Crime   55

4 The Mafia and The Camorra: Prelude to the
   Analysis of American Syndicated Crime   83

5 The Genesis and Development of Criminal
   Syndicates in the United States   153

6 La Cosa Nostra: The Question of the
   Existence of a National Criminal Organization   221

7 Syndicated Crime:
   Its Structure, Function, and Modus Operandi   263

8 The Life of the Syndicate Criminal:
   Some Social and Psychological Aspects   305

9 American Syndicated Crime:
   A Summary of Its Past, Present, and Future   319

Bibliography   331

Author Index   349

Subject Index   353

The American Mafia

1

Syndicated Crime: A Prelude to Its Conceptualization

On October 29, 1967, *The New York Times* carried two stories which quickly bring into sharp focus the question of the existence as well as the problems centering around the study of organized crime or, more specifically, syndicated crime on a national and international basis. One story referred to the statement of a New York State Supreme Court Justice that organized crime was just a "bugaboo" and except for a negligible amount in Las Vegas, there was very little elsewhere.[1] A few pages later we find the statement of a New York clergyman to the effect that if the fight against organized crime is to be successful, the American public must be made aware and convinced that the "Mafia is a guerilla army in our midst" and will continue to exist so long as the public desires its existence.[2] Not only do the statements of these two sources reflect the wide span of current thinking concerning the existence of organized crime; they also exhibit the vast extremes in beliefs regarding its style, ranging from virtually no organization in the State Supreme Court Justice's opinion to the clergyman's warning of the existence of a "guerilla type" organization known as Mafia. This clergyman is certainly not alone in his belief in the presence of an organization known as Mafia, but in calling it a "guerilla army" he

1

adds to the multitude of descriptive phrases used to characterize this organization.

The descriptions of Mafia range from a group of loosely knit criminal associations found only in Sicily to a world-wide criminal syndicate with branches in virtually every city, whose ultimate and final purpose is eventual world-wide domination. Chapter 4 is devoted to a detailed analysis of what Mafia really consists of, but we wish to highlight here some of the contradictory views that have been expounded about this organization, in an effort to emphasize the general confusion that exists about organized crime and, more precisely, about its most celebrated locus—"La Mafia."

Andrew Varna describes this organization as a secret society of Sicilian origin whose members have not only managed to become powerful in Sicily but have established a world-wide network of branches by immigration into such areas as the United States, Tunisia, French North Africa, Argentina, and Cuba, where they resort to blackmail and violence in an attempt to gain and keep control over the most remunerative criminal enterprises.[3] Renée Buse, manifesting a very moralistic tone, equates the Mafia to a sinister octopus whose greedy tentacles reach out across the world.[4] There is no doubt that if Buse were a sociologist he would be classified as the purest of the pure bio-organismic theorists. Harry J. Anslinger, with Will Oursler, in *The Murderers,* states that it was he and the Bureau of Narcotics that "revealed" the existence of "the Mafia" against a background of critics who said that such an organization with rituals and punishments was merely a myth.[5] Anslinger and Oursler then continue by citing the Sicilian origins of the Mafia, which brings them into a series of contradictions that they leave unexplained. In an attempt to support their proof that there is a "Mafia," the authors point out that the underworld does not deny its existence, indicating that even Charles "Lucky" Luciano admitted to a friend that "the Mafia" was real.[6] Six pages later, however, the authors state that the existence of "the Mafia" is always denied by its members because of their attitude of "silence."[7] Anslinger and Oursler restrict their use of the term *Mafia* to refer only to organized syndicated activities in the area of narcotics.[8] It is interesting to note, however, that Anslinger, writing about narcotics traffic, in a work published eight years prior to *The Murderers*, makes no mention whatsoever of a "Mafia" organization but merely refers to the international drug traffickers as "gangsters."[9]

In vivid contrast to Anslinger and Oursler's statement that some members of "the Mafia" openly admit to its existence, the late Senator Estes Kefauver found the exact opposite behavior among these members. In fact, he used this behavior as his basis of proof for the presence of "the Mafia" in American society. Rather than discovering the existence of "the Mafia" during his now famous Senate investigation of organized crime, it seems that he merely assumed its existence and then set out to offer proofs to reinforce this assumption. Thus when several witnesses, whom other witnesses had identified as prominent Mafiosi, refused to admit that they were members or had even heard of the organization "Mafia," Kefauver interpreted this as their unwillingness to talk about it because of the society's code of silence. Hence, in Kefauver's reasoning, for a witness to remain silent on the subject or to deny the existence of "the Mafia" was in itself proof that he was a member. Referring to such witnesses, Kefauver concluded—"None of these vaunted tough boys wanted to admit any knowledge of the Mafia. But the Mafia is there all right."[10] One must agree with Kefauver that it is highly unlikely that these witnesses, some Sicilian by birth, had never heard of "the Mafia," which is a household term among Sicilians. However, this behavior in and of itself does not constitute proof of its existence. Carrying this argument even further, Daniel Bell notes that the entire testimony collected during the Kefauver hearings revealed no real evidence of the existence of Mafia.[11]

One of the more journalistic approaches to the topic of "the Mafia" is found in the popular but poorly documented works of Ed Reid. In his book *Mafia*,[12] Reid presents a haphazard history of the origin and growth of the Mafia after which he concludes that the U.S. Treasury Department has evidence that "the Mafia" is a secret society with interconnections between Sicily, its place of origin, and the United States. He further states that it has a code of rules that include strict obedience to a chief, absolute secrecy about names and activities, and an oath that each member repeats while burning the paper image of a saint after having first wet the image with drops of blood drawn from his right hand.

In another book describing the New York Mafia, Reid maintains that syndicates in large cities in the United States are under the domination of a national crime cartel controlled by Mafia chieftains.[13] He goes on to tell us that this organization has vice-presidents in charge of certain cities or sections of the country as well as group leaders.[14] In New York, he tells us, these leaders are chosen at secret meetings usually held in Brooklyn.[15]

Closely paralleled to Reid's conception is that of Edward J. Allen who in a very moralistic conception views "the Mafia" as an international, sinister, shadowy organization lurking behind America's organized criminal activity.[16] Originating in Sicily, "the Mafia" came to America, where after prohibition, it changed its syle of clothing from wide-brimmed, cocked hats to a more sophisticated manner of dress, but Allen warns, the "wolf" is still concealed under the "sheep's" clothing.[17] As in Sicily, "the Mafia" in America is composed of leaders referred to as "Dons" and their underlings, all of whom abide by the code of silence—*Omerta*.[18] He points out that certain "Mafia" members pretend not to understand the English language when they are asked to testify before legal agencies. He refers to this as the "no capish" (a vulgarization of the Italian phrase, (*Io non capisco*—"I don't understand")) method and gives an example of how an alleged member of "the Mafia" from Cleveland used this device to avoid answering the questions put to him by the Kefauver Committee.[19] On the same page, however, Allen states that this alleged member was "almost illiterate." Yet for some reason Allen does not seem to allow for the possibility that an "almost illiterate" immigrant may in fact have found difficulty speaking and understanding questions in English, a strange language in which he was not fluent.

In another, contrasting conception, Frederic Sondern, Jr. states that oaths as well as a formal structure do not exist in "the Mafia"; rather, it is a family affair.[20] "The Mafia" in Sicily and in America, he maintains, is composed of individuals drawn from the families and relatives of those who participate in its activities. The selected sons or nephews undergo a certain amount of training, after which they are brought into the organization that Sondern states is not a rigidly organized secret society, but rather a loosely-knit organization held together by two centuries of Sicilian history and tradition.[21]

Describing "the Mafia" in Sicily, Gavin Maxwell states that "Mafia" status is hereditary and goes on to note that "the Mafia" in Sicily can be broadly defined as a "protection racket." Its American counterpart he simply defines as a "new kind of Mafia,"[22] which he does not clarify. In a slightly different view, Hank Messick, who is primarily interested in describing the Cleveland syndicate, seems to define "the Mafia" as the Italian segment of the syndicate that is composed primarily of Jewish, Italian, and Irish counterparts,[23] although the interrelationship of these groups is never, in this author's opinion, clearly explained.

Giuseppe Prezzolini states that "the Mafia," in the form of a society, does not exist in the United States; instead, he argues, one could say that there are several "Mafias" in the United States, some composed of Sicilians, others composed of other nationality groups, but certainly not one sole "Mafia" that commands all the others.[24] Finally Alson Smith gives a most sinister description of "the Mafia" when he states that this society is, above all, a mystical organization that has weird ceremonies, secret oaths, secret handshakes, with each member being "a sort of eternal guerilla."[25] He goes on to note that this secret society has branches in Europe and the United States with a "super chief" sometimes referred to as "the High Priest," who resides in Palermo, Sicily. Its present "super chief" (speaking for the time period around 1954) is "75 years old and nearly blind."[26] "The Mafia," he concludes is "as tightly and efficiently organized as the Methodist Church."[27]

Such then, in brief, is the confusion regarding "the Mafia," but if this were not sufficient, many writers have muddled the area further by unclear positions taken in regard to other organizations in the United States that have been likened to and equated with the Mafia. When Joseph Valachi testified before the United States Permanent Subcommittee on Investigations in 1963, he added a new name—"Cosa Nostra"—to an already existing array of confusing terms. Reid simply equates Cosa Nostra with Mafia.[28] In 1965, however, the participants of the Oyster Bay Conference rejected the term "Cosa Nostra" because they maintained that it implied exclusive Italian membership in organized crime and because it was known to be used only in the New York City area.[29] Varna maintains that "the Mafia" is also known as "the society of the Black Hand."[30] Sondern, however, holds that "Mafia" extortion gangs simply used the imprint of a black hand to accompany warnings and ransom notes; that, in reality, the Black Hand was never a society.[31] According to Thompson and Raymond, the American version of "the Mafia" was the "Unione Sicilione."[32] Feder and Joesten offer a variation of this theme in stating that "the Mafia" became the "Unione Siciliano" in the United States only after the purging of the original "Mafia."[33] What this purging consisted of is never explained. Smith on the other hand maintains that the "Unione Siciliano" was founded in the United States in 1895 and functioned as a mutual-aid and benefit organization for Sicilian immigrants, until 1920 when it was turned into a bootlegging enterprise whose control became the aim of several criminal factions.[34] Anslinger and Oursler maintain simply that "The Black Hand" was what the Italian immigrants referred to as "Mafia" back in Italy.[35]

Turkus and Feder[36] are highly critical of the Kefauver Senate Crime Investigating Committee for formally stating that "Mafia," "Black Hand," and "Unione Siciliano" are one and the same organization. "The Mafia," they maintain, is a clannish society while the "Unione Siciliano" cooperates with other mobs. "Black Hand," on the other hand, they maintain, is a term used to describe a form of extortion practiced upon immigrants in the United States and its existence as a society was merely a myth perpetrated by the Sicilian "Mafia" and a Neopolitan criminal society known as "Camorra."

Giovanni Schiavo, highly critical of Turkus and Feder's position, questions the source of their information and points out that the "Unione Siciliana" was, in reality, simply one of many Italian fraternal organizations established in the United States and that "the Black Hand," although not an organization, did exist but existed only in the United States, not in Sicily.[37] Schiavo also points out (correctly) that the various spellings— "Unione Siciliano" and "Unione Sicilione"—are incorrect, the correct spelling being "Unione Siciliana."[38]

Fred Cook,[39] in contrast both to Turkus and Feder, and to Schiavo, argues that whether one calls it "The Mafia," "Cosa Nostra," "Unione Siciliano," "The Syndicate," or "The Combination" is irrelevant. They all refer to an invisible government that rules organized crime in America, that has international ties, and whose structure and heritage can be traced to the "Sicilian Mafia."

In short then, the literature reveals a multitude of contradictions that reduce the lay reader, as well as the researcher of organized crime, to a state of almost complete confusion. These contradictions are not confined to broad conceptualizations such as organizations and their origins. We find that in the literature on this subject even birth and death do not remain absolute. Thus Alphonse Capone, the renowned personality of Chicago's gangland era, was born, according to his biographer, Fred Pasley, in Naples, Italy.[40] Walter Noble Burns, on the other hand, cites Brooklyn, New York as his place of birth,[41] while Kenneth Allsop maintains that Capone was born at Castel Amara, Italy, a town near Rome.[42]

About Salvatore Lucania, the notorious underworld figure more commonly known as "Charlie 'Lucky' Luciano," the literature seems to have been consistent regarding his place of birth— Lercara Friddi, Sicily—but not so in reference to the place and the cause of his death. Cook[43] maintains that Luciano, after having been interviewed by the Rome police, died of a heart attack at the Rome Airport where he had gone to meet a motion-picture executive. According to Cook an Italian detective had accompanied Luciano to the Rome Airport and had stayed with him, being present at the time of Luciano's death. Norman Lewis, on the other hand, states that Luciano died while waiting to board a plane at the airport in Naples.[44] Instead of a detective being present, Lewis maintains that the narcotics bureau of Interpol police were making ready to approach Luciano at the airport, but by the time they arrived he was dead. Lewis goes on to tell that, although officially the reason for death was heart failure, the Italian press seized and perpetuated a rumor that Luciano had been killed by his criminal associates who poisoned his coffee. Michele Pantaleone, in contradiction to Lewis' belief, states that the F.B.I. believes that Luciano was really poisoned just at the time when important arrests and revelations about drug traffic were to take place.[45]

Needless to say, when we delve into the area of interpretation of "cause-effect" relationships, the literature in organized crime has its share of conflicting theories. Thus Courtney Ryley Cooper maintains that Al Capone did not invent "gangdom" or its methods; rather, he believes that it was brought to the United States from China through gangs known as "tongs."[46] Dillon argues the exact opposite; that is, that the Chinese "took hoodlumism" from the Americans.[47]

Suffice it to say then that the question of whether or not organized crime exists as posed in diametrical opposites by the State Supreme Court Justice and clergyman mentioned at the beginning of this chapter is one that is blocked and stilted by confusing literature, confusing concepts, and confusing levels of interpretation. This book is directed toward a clarification of this confusion through analysis and evaluation of historical and new data.

There is no question that much of the material written in the area of organized crime thus far is not scholarly in nature, all too frequently falling into the medium of the journalistic and sensation-oriented style of writing where documentation of sources is either at a minimum or completely absent. Too often these writings are value-laden resulting in outright distortion of fact and, in many cases, the creation of utter nonsense. The lack of objectivity in these writings often manifests itself in selected use of adjectives that present criminals as true Lombrosian "criminal types" while law enforcement personnel emerge as modern urban versions of Wyatt Earp. Without realizing it, these writers, whose aim seems to be that of curbing or eliminating organized criminal behavior, have probably served to aid rather than curtail it. Their use of undocumented material followed by absurd and unfounded conclusions have served to alienate a large part of the academic community and the more sophisticated segment of the general public. By the same token these writings have helped stimulate unfounded fear in the minds of the lay public and those who have either a need or desire to perceive conspiracies in every sector of society.

No observation was more strongly revealed to this author while collecting data than the fact that individuals who have no basic knowledge of organized crime have one thing in common —they display feelings of anxiety if not outright fear of the syndicate criminal. However, the interesting aspect is that, in the majority of cases, when questioned further about the basis of this fear, these individuals seemed to find it difficult to focalize or locate the exact reason for it. Before long, they began to refer to "the Mafia," "gangsters," bodies in trunks of cars, and assorted other versions of gangland-type brutality. There is no doubt, as we shall later discuss, that these activities do occur as part of the modus operandi of criminal syndicates. Violence, as we shall see, serves a vital function in the activities of criminal syndicates. However, once its role is understood within the context of syndicate activity, it becomes obvious that the average citizen, speaking in terms of probability, and in terms of violent crime, stands a far greater chance of becoming the victim of the petty and habitual criminal than he does of being brutally victimized by a participant in syndicated crime. Thus, as expressed by Benjamin "Bugsey" Siegel, himself a participant and later a victim of syndicate crime, "We only kill each other."[48]

Violence then, like many of the other methods employed in syndicated criminal behavior, has, in the modus operandi of syndicated crime—a rationale. This rationale, however, cannot be understood until one is ready to assume and accept the premise that syndicated crime is a functioning part of American society. As Emile Durkheim noted in his classic essay on the nature of crime, criminal activity in any society is an integral part of that society and its presence as well as its elimination fall into the realm of the "collective sentiments."[49] Organized or, more precisely, syndicated crime exists because, using the now familiar concept of Robert K. Merton, it performs a function.[50]

Those writers who attempt to isolate organized criminal activities to select groups such as "Mafia" and "Cosa Nostra" are merely camouflaging the reality that there is in American society a need for illegal products and services. The attempt to provide these needs has given rise to a social group position that Eric Wolf, writing in a different but related contextual framework has come to refer to as "brokers."[51] Serving as an intermediary source between the legal normative and the social normative systems in society, the syndicated criminal dedicates his energy and skills toward erecting a structure that, although illegal, then becomes a functioning part of the social system within which it operates.

As Eric Wolf[52] observes, it is not necessary for the systems that provide illicit needs to be integrated into the political or economic structure of a society; in fact, as he notes, they often are "supplementary or wholly peripheral" to the entire social system. Wolf further notes that within these peripheral spheres there often emerges a competitive attempt on the part of several organizations who strive to achieve control. It is this "peripheral" position of syndicated crime in the United States that seems to account for the fact that although the "professional gambler" may have a high status within his own criminal system, or as Wiley suggests, within the lower class subculture,[53] he has virtually no status in the hierarchy of legitimate statuses recognized by American society. It is only by accumulation of wealth or other means that he is permitted entrance into the legitimate status hierarchy.

This book then concerns itself with an analysis and description of the social system of syndicated crime in the United States. Defining a social system as "any unit of social organization viewed as a functioning mechanism composed of a set of working parts and a complex pattern of operation"[54] this work will attempt to show how syndicated crime functions and has functioned as such a system in American society.

The study of this system is obviously sociological in nature as

well as method. As a sociologist, the author has approached this
study within the framework of a structural-functional method
of analysis. Since the goal of this work is to describe the structure of the criminal syndicate as well as how it performs its
functions, this method appears to be the most appropriate. More
specifically, however, the data in this study consists of archival
material in the form of historical works, government publications, and newspaper and journal articles, written in Italian as
well as English. Analysis of these data was an essential part of
the background for this study.

However, archival materials are not in themselves sufficient
to a complete understanding of the topic. The author interviewed law enforcement personnel, from private detectives to
patrolmen and inspectors. Some of the interviewees were nationally known for their work in the area of organized crime;
others, although not directly involved in duties relating to vice
activities, were able to provide insights into some of the problems of law enforcement and syndicated crime. As well as personal interviews, the author conducted taped interviews with law
enforcement personnel who were not accessible because of
distance and time. In these cases, the author mailed the inter-
viewee a list of questions and a tape which was in turn completed and returned to him. Interviews were also conducted with
informants who had and were participating in syndicate criminal
behavior at the time of this study. As Cressey[55] notes is true of
any research in the realm of organized crime, this presented
the author with some methodological and ethical problems.

These informants did not come from the upper echelons of
syndicate personnel, although among them were some relatives
of important syndicate members. Furthermore, for the most part,
these informants were requested to give and were themselves
willing to give information vital to understanding the structure
and activities of the syndicate, they did not reveal information
that could legally be used against anyone. In some instances the
informants asked that their names be withheld from the author.
Other informants included elderly Italians, many of whom had
remained on the fringe of criminal activity and had first-hand
knowledge about "Black Hand" and other criminal activities

of the early 1900s. Others among the elderly Italians were some who were not involved in syndicate criminal activities themselves, but associated on a social level with many who were. These informants provided case histories and other information about syndicate life.

The author considers himself fortunate in having obtained information from these informants on both sides of the law. This is particularly true in view of the fact that both the police and the underworld guard and are careful not to reveal certain types of information necessary to the adequate functioning of their respective groups.

Obtaining interviews with the underworld was facilitated by three major factors: First, cooperative colleagues, friends, and students brought informants to the author's attention and kindly made the initial introduction, after having first explained the purpose of the interview as being one of sociological analysis, and not of getting data for an exposé. Second, the author's Italian background and acquaintance with several Italian communities, coupled with a knowledge of the Italian language as well as Italian customs and values was of help. Third, the author's position as a university professor was of great assistance. During the time this study was conducted the author taught a course, dealing specifically with organized crime, at Wayne State University, Detroit, Michigan. At first conceiving this position as possibly disadvantaging access to underworld sources, it soon became apparent that this was in fact an asset—most informants correctly interpreted that the author was interested only in what one informant phrased "how things are run, not who runs them." The interviews obviously consisted of open-ended questions that related specifically to organization and structure as well as the methods employed in syndicate activities.

The interviews with law enforcement personnel also consisted of open-ended questions that allowed an ample amount of freedom to discuss related topics with the focal point being the structure and function of the syndicate as they viewed it.

As the study progressed, the author realized that he was inadvertantly serving as a liaison between the underworld and the police. However, several law enforcement officials as well as some underworld sources advised the author that, since he was not discussing information that could become a matter of legal action, there was no cause for concern. As a matter of ethics, however, each interview, whether with the police or with informants, was begun with a brief explanation of the nature of the study, specifically clarifying the author's role as one of a social scientist trying to objectively analyze criminal behavior in the syndicate setting.

A product of four years of research, this book is an attempt to describe as well as analyze syndicated crime through the use of sociological frameworks and concepts. Since the subject matter is extremely complex and since the major goal is one of describing the criminal syndicate and how it functions there has been no attempt to employ any one particular model of study except that of a broadly-based structural-functional analysis. Studies conducted within the methodological contexts of a particular approach have their merits. And indeed, there are methodological implications and problems of clarification surrounding the use of concepts such as social system as well as structure and function that must be considered (cf. the works of Storer,[56] Wiseman[57] and Demerath and Peterson[58]). Because of the basic lack of literature in the field of syndicated crime, the purpose here is to describe in traditionally accepted concepts how the phenomenon of syndicated crime is structured and how the criminal enterprises relate to as well as emanate from this structure. It is hoped that by using these general concepts in place of more specific model-oriented concepts, a broader description of syndicated crime as a social system containing unique norms, values, and techniques will emerge.

We begin in Chapter 2 by raising questions about problems created by traditional definitions of organized crime, and we ultimately recommend a distinction as well as a new classification of types of organized crime. In this proposed classification, syndicated crime is given a specific meaning that is employed throughout the book.

In order to illustrate the structural-functional relationship of the syndicate criminal to American society, Chapter 3 delves into the basic role or function he performs. The theme is in opposition to the popular belief that syndicated crime was infused into the United States by foreign elements. Thus "The Mafia," "Cosa Nostra," and other mysterious secret societies have too long been offered as camouflages and scapegoats for what is a truly American phenomenon. It exists because segments of the American public have and continue to demand its services. Chapter 3 illustrates how criminal syndicates establish structures through which they offer illicit goods and services. We illustrate also the "broker" role of the syndicate criminal who provides himself with forms of legal immunity that permit him to operate within the very society that has outlawed his services. In this and subsequent chapters we show that historically in America, criminal syndicates, irrespective of whether their participants were of foreign or native birth, have always functioned within the American political and economic system. They exist because Americans want their products. They exist because the American political machines and politicians have given political protection in exchange for votes and other services provided by syndicate participants. It exists because American judges, police, and other public officials are willing to sell various forms of protection for an outright fee.

Chapter 5 traces the historical development of criminal syndicates in the United States in an effort to document our argument that these syndicates have emerged and developed in response to the varying illicit needs of the American public during different eras of its history. Specific attention is given to the various methods syndicates have employed in obtaining protection from the legal sources of American society. In Chapter 5 we develop the thesis that syndicated crime in the United States is *Developmental-Associational* in nature; that is, it has never been limited to any one specific ethnic or nationality group. Rather, as we show, its participants come from virtually every kind of ethnic background in America. It is true, as we note, that at certain times in history one or two ethnic or nationality groups may be predominant in the number of their participants in syndicated crime. This we explain as a function of the lower class status of these ethnic groups, some of whose members see syndicated crime as a rapid way to achieve higher status. We illustrate that the political machine in America, although rapidly disappearing, has nonetheless provided the lower class ethnic group with both legitimate and illegitimate avenues to success.

Recognizing the psychological conditioning of the American public toward automatically accepting the belief in a "Mafia" or "Cosa Nostra," we dedicate several chapters to an analysis of these two associations. Throughout the book we note the ridiculous and unfounded proofs that purport to prove that these two organizations exist. We purposefully, continuously cite the multitude of contradictions in these so-called proofs. In an effort to develop our thesis that syndicated crime is American and not a phenomenon infused from another country an entire chapter is dedicated to a discussion of what has continuously been offered as the genesis of syndicated crime in America—"The Sicilian Mafia."

Chapter 4 begins with an evaluation of the various popular theories of the origin of "The Mafia" in Sicily, only to show that none of these adequately support their own assumptions. We then illustrate that the confusion over "The Mafia" lies in inconsistent usage of the term in the Italian literature itself. We propose that the confusion in the use of the term "Mafia" lies in the fact that various authors have used it to refer to an organization, when in reality "Mafia" is better understood as a method employed in a specific type of criminal activity.

Employing historical sources we then describe what the phenomenon "Mafia" consists of in Sicily. We illustrate that it is a criminal phenomenon that can be understood only within the context of the historical development of Sicilian society. It functions within the context of the Sicilian social system and as such can be described and understood only within that context.

With this background, we are able to argue in Chapter 5 that no such thing as a "Sicilian Mafia" ever came to the United States. Rather we show that the writings that proposed this thesis, which we refer to as the *Evolutional-Centralization* approach, suffer from inconsistencies in defining "The Mafia" to the point that they often are nothing more than studies in semantics. In a detailed analysis of these writings we pay particular attention to indicating what these inconsistencies are. This is not done to berate or degrade the writers themselves, but rather to locate the source of those assumptions of the migration of "The Sicilian Mafia" to America that have come, in time, to be accepted as truths.

In keeping with our refutation of the *Evolutional-Centralization* approach, we turn our attention to the question of the existence of a national organization that came into public view in 1963 through the testimony of the now famous underworld informant, Joseph Valachi. Valachi called this organization "La Cosa Nostra." Chapter 6 delves into the testimony of Valachi merely to show that his description of the organization as a highly systematic, bureaucratically organized, national criminal association is not borne out by his own testimony, nor by other materials that we also examine.

After refuting the thesis of the existence of a national cartel of crime, we go on to describe in Chapter 7 the structure of criminal syndicates in the United States. We note that their structures, contrary to the *Evolutional-Centralization* conception, are not characterized by a consistent bureaucratic format composed of specific ranks. Rather we describe syndicates as systems of patron-client relationships varying from syndicate to syndicate. As such, each syndicate can be understood only within the context of its own development. So too, the types of patron-client relationships that exist within and between syndicates come in a multitude of variations.

Chapter 7 describes various types of such patron-client relationships, as well as modus operandi by which syndicates carry out their functions. We note the use of certain techniques, such as the skilled use of violence and intimidation, necessary to the functioning of syndicates. However we also illustrate that syndicates and their participants often further their interests not through the use of force but through the use of cooperation and accommodation.

In Chapter 8, using information given by informants as well as information drawn from the literature, we look at the personal life of the syndicate criminal. Here we try to break the stereotype of the syndicate criminal as a bizarre individual. We show instead that his personal life and behavior has many parallels found in general American society.

Finally, Chapter 9 takes a brief look at the past, the present, and the future of syndicated crime in America.

References

1 *The New York Times,* October 29, 1967, p. 31.

2 *Ibid.,* p. 53.

3 Andrew Varna, *World Underworld* (London: Museum Press Ltd., 1957), pp. 57–69.

4 Renée Buse, *The Deadly Silence* (New York: Doubleday and Co., Inc., 1965), p. 21.

5 Harry J. Anslinger and Will Oursler, *The Murderers* (New York: Avon Book Division, 1961), p. 73.

6 *Ibid.*

7 *Ibid.,* p. 79.

8 *Ibid.,* p. 81.

9 H. J. Anslinger and William F. Tompkins, *The Traffic In Narcotics* (New York: Funk and Wagnalls Co., Inc., 1953), p. 11.

10 Estes Kefauver, *Crime In America* (Garden City: Doubleday and Co., Inc., 1951), p. 29.

11 Daniel Bell, *The End of Ideology* (New York: Collier Books, 1962), p. 139.

12 Ed Reid, *Mafia* (New York: The New American Library of World Literature, Inc., 1964), pp. 28–34.

13 Ed Reid, *The Shame of New York* (Scranton: The Haddon Craftsmen, Inc., 1953), p. 225.

14 *Ibid.,* p. 131.

15 *Ibid.,* p. 50.

16 Edward J. Allen, *Merchants of Menace* (Springfield, Illinois: Charles C. Thomas, 1962), p. 3.

17 *Ibid.,* pp. 26–28.

18 *Ibid.,* pp. 14, 29.

19 *Ibid.,* p. 36.

20 Frederic Sondern, Jr., *Brotherhood of Evil* (New York: Bantam Book, 1960), p. 3.

21 *Ibid.*

22 Gavin Maxwell, *The Ten Pains of Death* (New York: E. P. Dutton and Co., Inc., 1960), p. 6.

23 Hank Messick, *The Silent Syndicate* (New York: The Macmillan Co., 1967), pp. 10, 161, 168.

24 Giuseppe Prezzolini, *I Trapiantati* (Milano: Longanesi and Co., 1963), pp. 169–172.

25 Alson J. Smith, *Syndicate City* (Chicago: Henry Regnery Co., 1954), pp. 86–89.

26 *Ibid.*, p. 89.

27 *Ibid.*

28 Reid, *Mafia*, p. v.

29 *Combating Organized Crime,* Report of the 1965 Oyster Bay, New York, Conference on Combating Organized Crime (Albany: Office of the Counsel to the Governor, 1965), p. 24.

30 Varna, *op. cit.*, p. 58.

31 Sondern, *op. cit.*, p. 48.

32 Craig Thompson and Allen Raymond, *Gang Rule in New York* (New York: The Dial Press, 1940), p. 4.

33 Sid Feder and Joachim Joesten, *The Luciano Story* (New York: David McKay Co., Inc., 1954), p. 48.

34 Smith, *op. cit.*, pp. 59–61.

35 Anslinger and Oursler, *op. cit.*, p. 16.

36 Burton B. Turkus and Sid Feder, *Murder, Inc.* (Garden City, N.Y.: Permabooks, 1952), pp. 87–88.

37 Giovanni Schiavo, *The Truth About the Mafia* (El Paso: The Vigo Press, 1962), pp. 133–135.

38 *Ibid.*, p. 133.

39 Fred J. Cook, *The Secret Rulers* (New York: Duell, Sloan and Pearce, 1966), pp. 12–13.

40 Fred D. Pasley, *Al Capone* (Garden City, N.Y.: Garden City Publishing Co., 1930), p. 11.

41 Walter Noble Burns, *The One-Way Ride* (Garden City, N.Y.: Doubleday, Doran and Co., Inc., 1931), p. 30.

42 Kenneth Allsop, *The Bootleggers and Their Era* (Garden City, N.Y.: Doubleday and Co., Inc., 1961), p. 295.

43 F. J. Cook, *op. cit.*, p. 354.

44 Norman Lewis, *The Honored Society* (New York: G. P. Putnam's Sons, Inc., 1964), p. 209.

45 Michele Pantaleone, *The Mafia and Politics* (London: Chatto and Windus, 1966), p. 191, footnote.

46 Courtney Ryler Cooper, *Here's to Crime* (Boston: Little, Brown and Co., 1937), p. 331.

47 Richard H. Dillon, *The Hatchet Men* (New York: Coward-McCann, Inc., 1962), p. 18.

48 Dean Jennings, *We Only Kill Each Other* (Englewood Cliffs, N.J.: Prentice-Hall, Inc., 1967), p. 17.

49 Emile Durkheim, "On the Normality of Crime," in *Theories of Society,* ed. by Talcott Parsons, Edward Shils, Kaspar D. Naegele, and Jesse R. Pitts (New York: The Free Press, 1961), pp. 872–875.

50 Robert K. Merton, *Social Theory and Social Structure* (Glencoe: The Free Press, 1957), pp. 192–194.

51 Eric R. Wolf, "Aspects of Group Relations in a Complex Society: Mexico," *American Anthropologist*, LVIII (December, 1956), p. 1072.

52 Eric R. Wolf, "Kinship, Friendship, and Patron-Client Relations in Complex Societies," in *The Social Anthropology of Complex Societies*, ed. by Michael Banton (New York: Frederick A. Praeger, Inc., 1966), p. 1.

53 Norbert F. Wiley, "The Ethnic Mobility Trap and Stratification Theory," *Social Problems*, XV (Fall, 1967), p. 157.

54 Joseph S. Hines, *The Study of Sociology* (Glenview, Ill.: Scott, Foresman and Co., 1968), p. 489.

55 Donald R. Cressey, "Methodological Problems in the Study of Organized Crime as a Social Problem," *The Annals*, CCCLXXIV (November, 1967), p. 102.

56 Norman W. Storer, *The Social System of Science* (New York: Holt, Rinehart and Winston, 1966).

57 H. V. Wiseman, *Political Systems* (New York: Frederick A. Praeger, 1967).

58 H. J. Demerath III and Richard A. Peterson, *System, Change and Conflict* (New York: The Free Press, 1967).

2

Types of Organized Crime:
A Plea For Clarification

In an investigation, completed in 1963, into organized crime in the province of Ontario, Canada, the Honorable Justice Wilfrid D. Roach called attention to a distinction vital to the understanding of organized crime—the distinction between organized crime and syndicated crime.[1] In this statement Justice Roach pointed out the error in using the terms *organized crime* and *syndicated crime* interchangeably. Organized crime, he argues, can exist in the absence of syndicated crime whereas syndicated crime cannot exist without organized crime. On the basis of this distinction, Justice Roach found the presence of organized crime in Ontario but indicated that syndicated crime, as such, had never existed in the province.[2]

Almost inevitably law enforcement officials, in interviews with the author, would ask him to clarify what he meant by organized crime. One police official in Cleveland astutely pointed out to the author, "The presence or absence of organized crime here or anywhere else depends upon how you define it." Both Justice Roach and this police official have recognized a fact that has been viewed as either irrelevant or inconsequential by many writers in the area of organized crime.

Misclassifications of Organized Crime

As a result of this attitude, many writers have approached the study of organized crime within the framework of static rather than dynamic conceptualizations. They have never given adequate attention to the fact that there are many types of organized crime and that these vary both in their structure and methods of operation. There are those who attempt to explain the existence of contemporary syndicated crime in the United States in terms of a unilateral development of groups such as "Black Hand," "Unione Siciliana," "Cosa Nostra," and "Mafia," which are in their opinion all the same organization with variations in name only. These writers are not giving adequate attention to the multitude of different types of criminal organizations or associations that have existed and do exist in the United States and in other parts of the world.

One of the basic reasons for the confusion of beliefs and theories about organized crime is that many of the current concepts themselves are confusing. When the historical literature is examined we find that there exists either an absence of analytically useful terminology or an abundance of completely erratic terminology with no consistency of meaning.

Those who maintain that "Black Hand," "Mafia," etc. are the same organization have overlooked the need to view organized crime in the United States as a dynamic interplay of structural-functional relationships between criminal associations and the general American society, throughout the country's history. Crime, like other segments of society, changes both in format and in areas of endeavor. As Gus Tyler[3] so succinctly puts it, the underworld has come to "mimic" the very society it wars against. The underworld, Tyler says, has learned to utilize the modern means of trade, commerce and business consolidation.

Herbert Bloch reinforces Tyler's view in noting that the American public erroneously viewed the 1957 Apalachin meeting in New York as a meeting of the leaders of the underworld. In reality, he argues, this was a "business meeting" of the leaders of a criminal organization that "has now become an integral part of the American social scene."[4]

If syndicated and organized crime are to be adequately understood they must be analyzed in terms of their structural-developmental, as well as historical differences.

The more scholarly attempts at definition and classification of organized crime, although worthy endeavors, have not made for a clarified and consistent formulation of contemporary concepts or frameworks of classification. These attempts have employed a variety of criteria in an effort to distinguish organized crime from other forms of crime but the end products have only engendered more confusion. A brief examination of these writings should bring into focus some of their contradictions and conceptual problems.

Among the various criteria considered in an effort to differentiate organized crime from other forms of criminal activity have been the following: the existence and degree of organization; the degree of specialization and training of the criminal participants; the ultimate goal of the criminal association as direct monetary profit orientation (versus profit in the sense of gain or retention of social or political position); whether victimization is accomplished by use of fraud versus force, intimidation, and fear; and finally the time span within which the criminal enterprise is perpetuated.

Anyone familiar with the problems of classification of any phenomena will readily perceive that an effort to distinguish and define organized crime using these criteria is destined toward frustration. These criteria in themselves are not mutually exclusive. Any effort to isolate organized crime on the basis of any one of these standards necessitates by its very nature the inclusion of a continuum of attributes both within the realm of behavior as well as that of structure.

In a sweeping approach, Mabel Elliott argues that there are many types of professional criminals ranging from "overlords" or heads of illicit enterprises to gamblers, prostitutes, swindlers, counterfeiters, kidnappers, bootleggers, and those who deal in the narcotics trade.[5] She goes on further to point out that organized crime consists basically of professional criminals who

form collusions or relationships aimed at mutual aid and increased efficiency and protection.[6] Then subsuming organized
and professional crime into one category, she lists and defines
five types of organized criminal activities: thieving, receiving
stolen goods, swindling, racketeering, and gambling.[7] Later in
her discussion she defines the "gangster" as a functionary whose
existence emanates from the services that he performs for
racketeers and other types of professional criminals, these including the use of violence when necessary.[8]

After citing the standards employed in adjudging professionalism in American society, Johnson argues that no criminal
group can be properly classified as professional. However, he
goes on, some criminal groups, because of skills and other
capabilities, are often regarded as such.[9] Johnson then moves
into a discussion of syndicated crime that both includes and
excludes some of the enterprises that Elliott encompassed under
the category of organized and professional crime. Syndicated
crime, for Johnson, is "the perversion of the organizational
scheme of legitimate business to provide illicit 'services' such as
prostitution, gambling, liquor or 'protection'."[10] He further distinguishes syndicated crime from planned burglary and robbery
by virtue of the fact that the latter are "autonomous operations"
while the former is a continuous daily profit-making enterprise.[11]

Robert Caldwell holds the view that professional criminals
specialize in a certain area of criminal endeavor and view crime
as a business based upon developing an underworld value system.[12] He then lists ten types of professional criminals, including
pickpockets, robbers, fences, burglers, sneaks, purse snatchers,
auto thieves, forgers, and others.[13] Organized crime, Caldwell
points out, differs from professional crime in that the former
involves, among other attributes, an associational nature with
centralization of authority, a fund of money, and a division of
labor with specialized functions.[14] For Caldwell there are three
types of organized crime: organized gang activity, racketeering,
and syndicated crime.[15] Without making a definite distinction
between his aforementioned professional type robbers and
thieves he subsumes under organized gang criminality such
enterprises as bank robbery, murder, hijacking, automobile

thefts, etc., that are committed by gangs "organized to engage in such activities on a large scale."[16] Organized criminal gangs use violence. When they apply this in the form of intimidation and force in an effort to extort from legitimate or illegitimate business this becomes racketeering, the added difference being that in racketeering the goods are not taken and carried away as they are in ordinary criminal gang activity.[17] Syndicated crime, for Caldwell, refers to organized criminal gang activity in which illegal goods or services are supplied to those who are willing to pay for them.[18]

Barnes and Teeters view what Caldwell calls syndicated crime not as minute and localized criminal gang activity but as an "aggregate of organized criminals, national in scope, which through strong arm methods controls any vice or business it may choose to enter."[19] Racketeering they define as extortion by violence or the threat of reprisal.[20] Placing the discussion of criminal gangs in another chapter, Barnes and Teeters, without actually defining what a criminal gang consists of, explain it in terms of its activities which include bank robbery, kidnapping, and hijacking.[21] Then the authors cite the "Black Hand or Mafia" as an example of criminal gangs.[22] It is interesting to note, however, that Barnes and Teeters sneak in "the Mafia" and "Black Hand" in their discussion of crime syndicates. They never clearly indicate whether or not they intend inclusion of these two criminal associations into their definition of a syndicate. Instead they further cloud the issue by stating that "the Mafia" is a "terroristic Italian organization"[23] that has committed "extortion, mayhem, kidnapping,"[24] all forms of criminal activity that they earlier referred to under their discussion of racketeering.[25]

Ruth Cavan loosley defines organized crime in terms of varying and increasing degrees of complexity of structure of the groups that participate in it. Its major characteristics include a continuity of purpose and organization, specialization, planning, and protection from interference by the law.[26] Cavan divides organized crime into four types—theft using firearms committed by mobile criminal gangs; criminal syndicate operations of illegal enterprises; racketeering, which incorporates the use of extortion from legal or illegal establishments; and corruption as executed by political and law-enforcement groups.[27] Cavan then further subdivides the first of these four types by comparing adolescent gangs and criminal gangs for their similarities and differences. Criminal gangs and adolescent gangs, she observes, have a close rapport between the members. Unlike the adolescent gangs, however, the criminal gang concentrates primarily upon profit-producing crime, planning such crimes with care, and each member performing a specialized role.[28] Cavan describes the mob as a professional crime unit which is small in size and whose members are skilled in certain tasks (pickpocketing, shoplifting, confidence games), however, she seems to indicate that the mob is not to be included in the category of organized crime.[29] Differing from Caldwell who classified syndicated crime in the realm of organized criminal gang activity, Cavan maintains that the organization of the criminal gang is quite different from the criminal syndicate, whose main object is to provide new or to coordinate already existing illegal enterprises without using much violence save that necessary to control competition.[30]

Whereas Cavan, Caldwell, and Barnes and Teeters view racketeering as falling within the realm of using force and intimidation, Sutherland's work, based upon information obtained from a professional thief, classifies rackets as including such activities as pickpocketing, shoplifting, blackmail and various forms of confidence games.[31] In this respect, the reader will recall that Caldwell and Cavan place these three types of activities under professional or mob criminality.

Although Thrasher's[32] conception of the adolescent gang is similar to that of Cavan, he adds that many gangs composed of older members number adolescents among their membership and that these gangs are often associated with criminal rackets where they generally perform enforcement and other types of services. In this article, Thrasher emphasizes that the gang in the American city is usually found in the immigrant or lower class area, a position with which Bloch and Niederhoffer take issue by indicating that gang characteristics and attributes can be found among middle class adolescent groups as well as in

middle class residential areas.[33] In their work, Bloch and Niederhoffer call for further clarification of existing concepts regarding
the gang and delinquency in general.

A special report on teenage gangs,[34] emphasizing the killings
of four teenagers in one week, calls attention to the fact that
juvenile gangs are a criminal force and entity in their own right.
This report indicated that memberships in some gangs numbered two to three hundred. It further noted that through the
alliances existing among these gangs, a force of one thousand
youths could be brought together for a fight.

Returning to the various general classifications of organized
crime we find that Taft and England divide this form of crime
into two general types: predatory and service-oriented.[35] In the
first category are placed such crimes as robbery, extortion, car
theft, pickpocketing, or counterfeiting, crimes which, as indicated earlier, other authors have classified under the category
of professional, criminal gang, or mob enterprises. Service-
oriented crime or racketeering, Taft and England maintain,
differs from predatory types in that, in the former, there is a
demand for illegal goods or services that this form of crime
supplies. In this respect, Taft and England—differing from
Cavan, Caldwell, and Barnes and Teeters, who view racketeering
primarily within the context of extortion enterprises—include
gambling enterprises under racketeering that the aforementioned three authors subsumed under syndicated crime.

Somewhat allied to Taft and England's conception is that of
Alfred Lindesmith, who in making a synonym of underworld and
organized crime maintains that underworld activity varies in its
degree of skill and organizational complexity. This variance
ranges from its simpler forms of thieving to a second and more
complex type involving swindling or confidence game activities
to a third and very intricate format which includes illegal enterprises and various types of racketeering.[36] This conception
obviously differs from those heretofore presented in that Lindesmith further breaks down his first category of thieving into
thefts committed by violence and those committed by stealth.[37]
This is a completely different conception from those authors
who reserve violence almost exclusively to the realm of racke-

teering or criminal gang activity. In referring to swindling or
confidence games as a form of crime distinct in its degree of
sophistication and complexity from racketeering, Lindesmith
differs from MacDonald, who equates rackets specifically with
forms of short-confidence games.[38]

Without giving specific labels to their four forms of criminal
organization, Sutherland and Cressey[39] describe organized crime
as including criminal groups whose size and structure is determined by the type of activity engaged in. All these groups,
they maintain, are similar in their acceptance of an underworld
code of mutual protection and hatred for the law. Some of these
are small in size while others constitute syndicates that control
such enterprises as gambling, prostitution, and narcotics. A cooperative relationship exists between these groups and the legal
agencies of the society.

By employing such a broad conception of organized forms of
crime, Sutherland and Cressey's description includes some and
excludes other types of organized crime that our previously
mentioned authors placed under the more specific categories of
criminal gangs, mobs, juvenile gangs, racketeers, organized predatory crime, and syndicated crime.

Employing a continuum approach to organized crime, George
Vold calls attention to the utility of organization to criminal
enterprises, indicating that organization brings about more efficiency and the extension of criminal endeavors into more complex activities.[40] Vold's conception of the criminal gang, similar
to Cavan's, is characterized by intense loyalty among the members, with a leader and structural division of labor, and specialization in the use of violence or intimidation with the ultimate goal of making a fast profit.[41] Vold includes among
professional criminals skilled thieves, shoplifters, pickpockets,
and confidence men, a classification with differences and similarities to those previously cited in this chapter.[42] Criminal
syndicates are distinguished from criminal gangs by Vold in that
the former are rather stable organizations that serve to coordinate existing criminal activity while the latter are action-oriented
and highly mobile groups. Rackets, on the other hand, refer
more specifically to the practice of extortion of business enterprises.[43]

Some Views on "Rackets"

Taken alone the term *racket* presents a vast array of conflicting usages. Coupled with the many different conceptions of this term already cited, there stand a variety of more specific as well as more confusing applications of this word.

To dispense with a contemporary belief that rackets are a product of contemporary industrial society, McConaughy begins his work by emphasizing that racketeering is an ancient institution, and cites examples of its existence in ancient Greece and Rome.[44] The word "racket" itself has a variety of origins, all of which are obscure. Gunther maintains that the term originated in Chicago during the 1920s and referred to the noise or racket made by hoodlums in the hangouts which they frequented. The term later gained common usage when these individuals came to be referred to as "racketeers" by the newspapers.[45] Courtenay Terrett offers other possibilities for the origin of the term including its derivation from a mechanism of torture—the rack—indicating a racketeer's slow and continuous method of inflicting pain without effecting the ultimate death of the victim. He also cites the possibilities of derivation stemming from the Biblical term *raca* meaning "contemptible or worthless" or from the "Levantine" alcoholic beverage *arrack*.[46]

Gurfein offers other sources of derivation, among which is the theory that the term originated in vaudeville and was used to describe a specific type of entertainment or act, the word in essence being synonymous to meaning an easy way of making a living or getting through life. Another possible source of origin, he states, is that of a statement made by a New York official who, while investigating a teamster's union, implied that what he was investigating was not just a "noise" but a "racket." Finally, he notes that the term may have originated around the 1890s in reference to "rackets," the name given to the social functions sponsored by politically affiliated social clubs in New York City. The "racket" consisted of the fact that these clubs employed neighborhood gangs to coerce merchants and businessmen into buying tickets for these functions, with the ultimate outcome being that soon tickets were being sold purely as a money-making criminal enterprise without any social affairs taking place.[47]

The term's origin is no less confusing than its use in the literature. Thus Gunther preludes the topic of the range of usages of the concept by pointing out that racket has come to refer to any plan or technique of making easy money, legally or illegally, and often is used as a coverall term for any form of organized crime.[48] O'Connor takes this very broad dimensional approach in his definition of racket, which he describes as any deal that cleverly or crudely evades the law. He goes on to describe various types of schemes that basically involve fraud.[49] Ellison and Brock, also viewing rackets in this vein, describe and use the term *racketeer* in their works as one who employs fraud rather than violence against his victim.[50]

Hostetter and Beesley, differing from this fraud-oriented conception, define rackets as parasitic activity in which the racketeer lives from the industry of the victim, the latter being kept under control by the use of terror, force, and intimidation.[51] Coinciding with this view, an article in *The New Statesman* described racketeering as a form of blackmail in which operators of various types of business enterprises including funeral homes, laundries, food markets, building trades, and musicians and others were forced to pay a certain sum of money weekly or monthly in order that their business places or their lives go unharmed—the harm obviously being in the form of bodily or property damage by those who demanded the tribute.[52] Following in the same conception, Shepherd adds that as rackets become larger they seek and obtain the cooperation and protection of public officials and the police, assuming legitimate-sounding names for their associations which soon obtain an air of respectability.[53] Gowen, somewhat contradicting this elite-like conception, makes a distinction between those racketeers who use force and those who employ stealth, referring to the former as "thugs" and to the latter as pursuants of a more gentlemanly or refined art.[54]

Constance Marshall gives a structural twist to the aforementioned typologies of racketeering when she incorporates police, bondsmen, and lawyers under the category of racketeering. She argues her position by citing scandals in New York City which exposed the practice of police, bondsmen, and lawyers who joined forces in framing women by using false charges of prostitution through which they forced the victim to pay a certain price in order to have the case fixed.[55] Landladies became victims of this form of racket which an article in *The Literary Digest* refers to as "The Landlady Racket."[56] In these cases plainclothes members of the vice squad would enter a rooming-house where an unmarried couple had been planted and, upon finding them, the vice squad men led the landlady to jail, where in cooperation with bondsmen and lawyers, her case could be "fixed" for a fee.

Along with the confusion in the use of the term "racket," those writers such as Haney who make a distinction between criminal and business enterprises are confronted with a complicated task, in view of the many varieties of business and criminal organizations cited in the literature.[57]

Gustavus Myers presents a challenge to those making a clear division between the legal and illegal conceptualization of business enterprises by citing a number of cases where the so-called giants or pioneers of American business did in fact use methods that could be classified within the aforementioned typologies of racketeering. Thus Myers refers to the incident in which Russell Sage and his business partners planned and executed a swindle of their creditors in Milwaukee with the ultimate irony being that Sage himself hoodwinked his own partners out of their profits from the swindle.[58] Closer to the traditional conception of racketeering is Myers' appraisal of Cornelius Vanderbilt's method of building his fortune which included forms of blackmail, theft, and extortion.[59] Hansl points out that during the late twenties, the Wall Street Stock Exchange, in terms of some of the unethical and devious techniques that were used, was in fact a form of racket.[60] Epstein concludes that insurance companies during the twenties that charged extravagant prices to policy-holders, practiced nepotism resulting in financial gain to the company officials, and allowed excessive numbers of policies to lapse, were definitely rackets.[61] Silas Bent offers evidence that Chicago newspapers, in themselves legitimate business, employed various newspapermen who were engaged in racketeering. He further observes that the newspaper circulation wars in Chicago at the turn of the century, during which strong-arm techniques were used, may have been a major catalytic agent responsible for the later rise of racketeering gangs in that city.[62] In support of this view one could point to the case of Dion O'Banion, one of the most prominent underworld leaders in Chicago's prohibition era, who in his early days served as a strong-arm man during these newspaper circulation wars.[63]

Finally, several writers have referred to as rackets several schemes that contemporary criminologists would most probably classify as white collar offenses in that they primarily involve violations of positions of trust. Sparkes relates several cases where large numbers of individuals were induced to join clubs, the organizers of which made fast profits from quickly collecting membership fees and then declaring bankruptcy.[64] Another such activity referred to as a racket but classifiable as white collar crime was the practice of paying prominent people for use of their names in advertising products which they themselves had never consumed and in some cases actually despised.[65]

In short, then, the efforts at producing a typology of organized crime has produced instead a confusion of terms, a lack of uniformity in classification, and in general a semantic collage. The basic reason for this confusion stems from the fact that writers have not recognized that each category of crime whether it be racketeering, professional, white collar, syndicated, predatory, or mercenary, has a continuum of types within each specific category itself. These categories in turn have elements that overlap into the other categories. The same can be said of the individuals or groups who participate in criminal actvities. A group of professional criminals could work alone or, as we shall see often happens, become a part of an ongoing syndicated enterprise. In either case the individual criminals may simply view each other as specialists working together in the sense of a mob. But how shall we classify them in the event that they develop feelings of loyalty and emotion toward one another? Should we employ Cavan's classification and categorize this group as a criminal gang? This would be difficult in that Cavan's conception maintains that the criminal gang is less specialized than the mob. What then does one call a specialized criminal gang? Also, at what point in time do they become such? What do we do if only certain members of an original mob develop these feelings of closeness toward one another? Shall we call these a semi-mob? Or can we simply place all of these into Caldwell's embracing category of organized gang criminality? Then, of course, there is the question of numbers. Sutherland and Cressey maintain that the number of individuals in a mob is generally limited to about two to five members. What then does one call the group of fifteen that Gosling and Craig[66] believe perpetrated the now famous train robbery in England in 1963? Cavan maintains that, numerically, criminal gangs may include twelve or more, which would permit us to place this group of fifteen into this category. However, we cannot do so, in view of the fact that these men had specialized roles in this robbery—a characteristic which she attributes more to the mob than to the criminal gang.

Taking the concept of *gang* alone we find that gangs are very difficult to classify both in structure and function across their large variety of mutually inclusive and exclusive characteristics.

As early as 1912, Puffer[67] noted that gangs were of a variety of types, a proposition that is just as true today as it was then. Today we have gangs ranging in type from small, predatory, profit-oriented types to the outlaw motorcycle gangs that primarily emphasize group solidarity and activity directed at maintaining their conception of masculinity and bravery through effective use of violence.[68] Yet even in the latter type there are variations. As Reynolds and McClure[69] point out, Hell's Angels are somewhat divided between the Northern and Southern chapters. The latter, they note, are more profit-oriented, being willing to make money by participating in movies and other forms of profitable enterprises. The northern chapters, on the other hand, openly reject any method of making money that sacrifices the purity of their group, which in essence lives for itself. Shall we categorize these gangs as mobs, adolescent gangs, criminal gangs, or simply subsume them under organized gang criminality?

More intricately, how shall we categorize those individuals who, as Sylvia Porter[70] states, are known to be underworld figures yet have infiltrated some of the legitimate firms selling stocks to the public? Are they racketeers? Are they white collar criminals? Or to make the issue even more complex, how shall we classify those legitimate businessmen or companies whose executives violate the Sherman Antitrust Act? When we consider, as an article in The Yale Law Journal[71] illustrates, that many antitrust suits are increasingly originating with private parties seeking redress for personal damages incurred, the problem of this classification is grossly magnified.

Dealing more specifically with a case of antitrust violation, how do we classify those forty-five leading executives from major corporations who, as Fuller[72] describes, over an extended period of time, arranged secret meetings by using blank stationery signed in coded names, used public phone booths instead of office phones to make their calls, and were careful never to be seen together in public. The goal of all this secrecy: fixing prices in the electrical industry. Does the conspiratorial nature of their method allow for their being classified as racketeers in the sense of perpetrating a fraud? On the other hand, because of their positions of trust are they more readily classifiable as white collar criminals?

It is not necessary to continue illustrating the vast number of combinations of mutually exclusive and inclusive dimensions that could be offered to question the feasibility as well as utility of existing typologies. We do not call attention to these deficiencies to criticize the individual typologies or writers. Instead we wish to emphasize the inherent rigidity of past and contemporary typologies as well as the futility of any future attempt to create a uniform satisfactory conceptualization that will not inculcate similar deficiencies. No classification could possibly take into account the vast variations that exist within each different category of crime, nor the divergencies among those who execute these crimes, particularly when neither time nor place are constants.

What Is Organized Crime?

What is essential in attempting to understand organized crime, then, is to seek those fundamental characteristics that help make a basic distinction between organized and other forms of crime along a continuum of various types of crime, while allowing for the existence of variation of types within the category of organized crime itself.

It appears that the most primary distinguishing component of organized crime is found within the term itself, mainly, *organization.* It is true that there are some types of crime which more than others lend themselves readily to organization. Thus, blackmail, extortion, hijacking, kidnapping are crimes which require several individuals working together to execute the crime; while individual crimes such as petty theft, shoplifting, and purse snatching lie more within the realm of individual execution. However, it is theoretically conceivable that almost any crime could be organized—in the sense of two or more individuals interacting in the mutual performance of the criminal act. Interaction is a key concept here: a mere aggregation of individuals performing a criminal act in the presence of one another would not, in itself, constitute an organized act.

Organization, then, is the basic distinguishing element between organized and other types of crime. Although there are many worthy theoretical and descriptive conceptions of organizational structure, as found in the writings of Presthus,[73] Thompson,[74] Greer,[75] and others, for our purpose we need concern ourselves only with those basic elements which are generally found in any organizational structure.

Here the works of Etzioni[76] and Caplow[77] are helpful, and, although some basic differences exist between their conceptions, these authors provide a range of organizational requisites from which we can extract some basic essentials necessary to an understanding and description of criminal organizational structures.

First, any organization, legal or illegal, comes into existence for the fulfillment of certain goals; these may be specific or general in nature. Thus a gang may organize for the purpose of hijacking, or as in adolescent gangs, merely for the sake of belonging to a group that promises potential excitement and adventure. Etzioni makes an observation that seems to be particularly applicable to criminally oriented groups; that is, that organizations more than other types of social units tend to have more control over the nature as well as the directionality of their goals. Second, as Etzioni emphasizes, there is a division of labor, a distribution of power, and some division of communication responsibilities which are deliberately structured and planned in accordance with achieving the intended goal. We might add an obvious point that in reference to criminal organizations, the degree of division of power, labor, and communication is dependent upon the size of the group as well as the complexity and nature of the activity. A "muggers' gang," for example, composed of two or three whose enterprises involve quickly executed robberies on the street would differ radically in each of these three characteristics by comparison to the group of eleven men who executed the now famous Brink's robbery in Boston after approximately two years of planning and preparation. Third, as Etzioni indicates, every organization must have a center or centers of power or leadership that coordinate the activities of the group, in the direction of achieving its intended goals, and that constantly evaluate the functional and dysfunctional aspects of the structure as well as the modus operandi of the group. This is true of criminal groups and it appears that the larger and more complex or bureaucratic the group the more distinguishable are these centers of control. In small groups, however, particularly in those involving two or three, leadership may not be as well defined because this may be a shared and somewhat equal function. Fourth, both Caplow and Etzioni recognize that organizations must devise some means for recruitment, removal, and transfer of personnel. Again the existence as well as the degree of refinement in methods of recruitment, transfer, and removal depends upon the permanence, goals, type of activity, and structure of the group. Thus a group of criminal specialists who are joining efforts toward the completion of one single criminal enterprise would not be concerned with future methods of recruitment or transfer of members, since they do not view themselves as an ongoing or permanent group. By contrast, however, a more complex group such as a syndicate operating a gambling enterprise would, of necessity, have to establish formal and informal means of selecting individuals who are viewed as participants in a continuous enterprise. Such a syndicate would have to devise a means of transfer whether in the sense of promotion or merely as a movement into another type of activity for which the individual is better suited. It would also have to develop some means of removing any individual who threatens the welfare of the organization.

We should note also that there are groups such as adolescent gangs where only the original members compose the group for the entirety of its existence and no attention is paid to recruiting since no new members are desired.

These four characteristics then—interaction oriented toward the attainment of specific or general goals; some form of structure entailing a division of labor, power, and communication; some form of leadership or central control, and some means, if such is an inherent goal of the group, of recruiting new personnel and providing for transfer and removal of members— for our purpose compose the essential requirements for the delineation of what constitutes organization. Hence, the basic distinction between individual and organized crime is that the latter has organization.

In a very broad sense, then, we can define organized crime as any criminal activity involving two or more individuals, specialized or nonspecialized, encompassing some form of social structure, with some form of leadership, utilizing certain modes of operation, in which the ultimate purpose of the organization is found in the enterprises of the particular group.

This definition permits us to view organized crime on a vast continuum allowing for freedom of analyzing and defining a given particular criminal group as an entity in itself possessing a variety of characteristics, as opposed to a rigid classification based upon certain specific attributes. Viewed from this wide perspective there are many forms which organized crime can take, with variations, of course, to be found within each form.

Let us examine, briefly, some of these forms. It should be understood that these are not meant as classifications but instead should be viewed as an illustration of the many varieties of organized crime. Also it shall allow us to distinguish between syndicated and other types of organized crime, which is the ultimate objective of this chapter.

Political-Social Organized Crime

In illustrating the diversification in types of organized crime one could begin by distinguishing between those whose goals include a direct financial profit motive and those whose do not. Thus there are organized groups who originate as or become criminal enterprises, whose ultimate goal is not direct financial profit, but rather is that of either changing or maintaining the existing social or political structure. These types we refer to as *Political-Social Organized Crime*. Within this type would fall organizations such as guerilla or terroristic groups attempting to overthrow existing political regimes. Also included under this heading are labor organizations that use illegal means such as sabotage or violence to bring about a change in their social conditions. So, too, would we include any specific interest group that uses violence or other illegal means of repressing the advancement of any group which threatens its social position.

In the United States, a celebrated example of a terrorist band is one that is currently praised as heroic both in deed and ideology. In 1859, however, its leader John Brown was hanged, having been found guilty of treason. As Weyl relates, Brown, in his crusade against slavery, led a small guerilla band in a series of raids in Kansas hoping to bring into open action the Northern versus Southern stand upon the question of slavery. His raid at

Harper's Ferry, although ultimately serving to bring Brown's goal to fruition, resulted in his capture and hanging as well as the dispersement of his group.[78]

It is true that in this type of crime one can, along with Sellin,[79] plead for a clear distinction between the legal and social definition of crime; however, the reality of the situation resolves itself to the fact that any act which is in violation of the criminal law is a crime. One recognizes also (see Sax[80]) the fact that violators of criminal statutes receive differential treatment in the hands of the law and that this treatment varies with time and place. Yet, the act itself, so long as it is a violation of criminal law, is by legal definition a *crime*. Organizations that may be seeking their conception of social justice but who in the process commit illegal acts, are by the legal definition *criminal*.

Currently, for example, the Black Panthers, the Negro militant organization, is viewed as a victim of injustice by segments of the white community and by a Detroit newspaper dedicated to the Negro revolutionary cause.[81] Yet this group is also shown as having the characteristics of a military organization, which includes a military-structured hierarchy of officers.[82]

The American Civil Liberties Union, on the other hand, states that in one case the police in Paterson, New Jersey used unjustified violence against Negroes and Puerto Ricans. Their behavior, which included breaking store windows and ransacking offices, constituted a police riot. Here the force used under the guise of law enforcement was not legal enforcement at all but instead a *crime*.[83] An article by Fox carries this theme further by showing that a new rightist segment in the New York City Police Department, just as militant as the left, is emerging. This is reflected by an incident in which several off-duty policemen joined private citizens in an attack on a Black Panther group in a Criminal Court in Brooklyn.[84] Certainly on a continuum of political-social organized crime, these actions by police bring into focus the fact that legally prescribed organizations can and do engage in organized criminal activity.

Another form of political-social organized crime is found in the activity of the Ku Klux Klan. Rather than consisting of one organization, Lipset shows that there have been three Klans in the United States: The first was formed in 1865 and served to intimidate the slaves who had been freed. The second, formed in 1915, after the United States' entrance into the First World War, functioned as a self-appointed patriotic protector of Americanism. As such it constantly sought to find spies and other types of subversives. Later, however, it directed its attention toward vigilance over Catholics, Jews, Negroes, orientals, and other groups, whose Americanism, in the Klan's opinion, was suspect. The third Klan, not as effective as the first two, and located primarily in the south, was formed after World War II and consisted primarily of various lower class white racist groups.[85] Lipset goes on to point out that most of the violence used by the Klan was not against minority, religious, or nationality groups, but rather against those individuals who engaged in acts of immorality—which included bootlegging, adultery, prostitution, and overindulgence in drink.[86]

Jackson, who concentrates upon the urban aspects of the Klan movements, points out that the use of terror and violence as a means of retaining white supremacy in the South were typical only of the first and the third periods of the Klan formations. The second period, around the 1920s, was characterized by an organizational structure and ideology which was "neither predominantly southern, nor rural, nor white supermacist, nor violent."[87] During this period the Klan, a chartered organization, commanded a great deal of power by virtue of its large membership, which between 1920 and 1926 was estimated at over two million.[88] Chalmers notes that during this era the Klan drew its membership from the middle class and soon took on a form "not unlike the Elks, the Masons and the Odd Fellows."[89]

These authors have rightfully drawn attention to the variation which the several Klans subsumed under the general name "Ku Klux Klan" have manifested both in time and location. Our interest in these Klans centers only around their criminal activity.

As late as 1963, a Klan rally in St. Augustine that was openly advertised through distribution of handbills resulted in the severe beating of four Negroes, three of whom were hospitalized.[90] Referring to the Klan as "The Masked Mafia," Gillette and Tillinger cite innumerable cases of criminal activity. These include the kidnapping of a three-year-old child in Beaver Falls, Pennsylvania and the kidnapping of several Catholics, Jews, and Negroes in Dayton, Ohio. In the state of Georgia alone, within a two year period, 135 Negroes were lynched.[91] Note that these crimes were not committed for direct financial profit. Rather they were viewed as violent means of ultimately achieving and retaining social and political control. However here again, as is true of other forms of organized crime, Klan criminal activity can be placed on a continuum. This is borne out by several cases of corruption and racketeering practiced within the ranks of the Klans themselves, where the motive was purely that of personal aggrandizement.[92]

Although most authors agree that the Klans have lost the power they once had, the contemporary existence of "The United Klans of America, Inc.,"[93] reveals that the needs that generated this type of organization have not disappeared.

The labor union movement in the United States offers another example of political-social organized crime if we include its use of violence, sabotage, and other forms of criminal behavior. Graham Adams[94] cites incident upon incident of violent outbreaks between unions and government forces, which in some instances consisted of full-fledged battles between workers and the National Guard. Again, this violence may have been justified from a social and ethical point of view. In keeping with our position, however, we must view this activity, which was at the time illegal, as criminal behavior. So, too, was the behavior of the governmental forces themselves when they exceeded the boundaries of the law.[95] In some cases violence was a part of the ideology and strategy of labor organizations. The Industrial Workers of the World, for example, viewed the use of assault as its only effective negotiating weapon against management.[96] Here again, we find a continuum of behavior among labor organizations. Some groups deliberately caused riots and other altercations in order to harass management. Others became involved in violent acts resulting from peaceful attempts at picketing.

A unique organization was that known as "The Molly Ma-

guires." This organization used murder, assault, and sabotage as
deliberate methods to terrorize operators of anthracite coal
mines in Pennsylvania during the 1860s and 70s. The Molly
Maguires existed both in Ireland and the United States. Whether
or not they were one and the same organization remains a
matter of dispute. The organization in Ireland dedicated its
efforts toward fighting landlords and the rent system. The one
in the United States directed its vengeance toward owners and
operators of coal mines.[97] Our discussion concerns only the
latter. Occasionally the Molly Maguires turned their hatred
toward those labor leaders and unions who advocated non-
violence.[98] For the most part, however, their targets were the
managerial class.

The Molly Maguires became so powerful that they were able
to place members of their organization in influential political
positions.[99] Their major source of power, however, generated
from the fear generated by their use of violence. Severe beatings,
sabotage of company property, and murder became a Molly
Maguire trademark. Organized as a secret society, its members
swore allegiance and secrecy. This secrecy coupled with public
fear made prosecution of their offenses difficult. Murders were
often committed in broad daylight. Townspeople often witnessed
these murders but, fearing their own safety, behaved as though
they had seen nothing.[100] When an arrest did occur, members
of the society would establish an alibi for the accused and he
would soon be released.[101] Although the Molly Maguires murdered primarily for revenge and terror, they occasionally engaged in profit-oriented crimes such as murdering for the specific
purpose of robbery.[102]

Largely through the efforts of a Pinkerton detective who infiltrated the organization, coupled with a public outcry after
the killing of a policeman, several Molly Maguires were convicted and hanged in 1876. After this, the organization lost its
power, and the society gradually disappeared.[103]

A fitting ending to our discussion of political-social organized
crime is the examination of the structure and activity of a terrorist or guerilla organization. One of the more interesting of
these arose as a result of the Enosis movement in Cyprus be-

tween 1954 and 1959. Unfortunately the scope of this work does not permit a lengthy discussion of this very intricate and fascinating movement. Here we are concerned specifically with one aspect—its terrorist organization, E.O.K.A., and its leader, George Grivas.

As an organization, E.O.K.A., as Barker states, takes its name from the Greek initials which stand for "National Organization of Cypriot Combatants."[104] It emerged as a terrorist organization which sought by the use of sabotage, killing, bombing, and other techniques to rid the island of British rule—a necessary step to the fruition of the Enosis movement's goals. In its simplest form, the Enosis movement can best be defined as a demand by the Greek population of Cyprus for union with mainland Greece.[105] Although the Turkish Cypriots and the political rulers of Cyprus, the British, resisted the movement, Enosis was not aimed directly against the Turks or the British.[106] The movement must be viewed as historically stemming from the longing for unification of the Greek Cypriots with their motherland, rather than from any hatred for either the British or the Turks. Nor was the union motivated by any anticipated material gains, because, as Hill[107] observed in 1952, Cyprus would have stood to lose economically, rather than gain from such a union. In essence, unification was both the major motivation as well as goal of the movement.

From this historical background, there emerged in 1954 the E.O.K.A., the guerilla-terrorist manifestation of Enosis which sought to rid Cyprus of British rule. It was supported by the Greek Orthodox Church, which is both a spiritual and political force in Cyprus: the Archbishop since 1949 has been elected into office by popular vote.[108] The leader and central figure of E.O.K.A. was George Grivas. A colonel and later a general in the Greek army, he had an extensive background in guerilla warfare from his underground efforts against the German occupation forces in Greece during World War II and later against the Communist underground forces in 1944. He was retired in 1945 for his extreme right wing views but returned to military activity after his association with Archbishop Makarios III of the Cypriot Orthodox Church.[109] From 1952 to 1953 Makarios

had attempted to call international attention to the Enosis
struggle by touring countries like France, Britain, and the
United States, but met with no success.[110] Preparations were
then made to use techniques involving sabotage and violence.
This culminated in the birth of the E.O.K.A. organization.
While Grivas continued to make plans involving strategy and
tactics, the Orthodox clergy added their support by recruiting
youth into the movement and preaching the cause of Enosis
from the pulpit.[111] In 1954, Grivas arrived on the island and
final preparations were made to commence the guerilla campaign. This was to include attacks upon British military personnel and installations, as well as the terrorizing and killing
of Greek Cypriots who refused to support the movement or
collaborated with the British.[112]

The E.O.K.A., as Grivas[113] himself describes it, was a highly
disciplined, bureaucratic, secret organization whose members
took an oath never to reveal any secrets even if subjected to
torture. When a British order made support of Enosis an act of
sedition in 1954, E.O.K.A. became, by legal definition, a criminal
organization. As an organization, committing some 1200 acts of
terrorism,[114] it was very effective in waging war against the
British forces and unsympathetic Cypriots. Throughout its campaign, however, it gained and maintained the support of a large
part of the Greek Cypriot populace.

Today, some writers[115] continue to view E.O.K.A. and its terroristic techniques as necessary to the completion of the cause.
Byford-Jones, on the other hand, equates E.O.K.A. and Grivas
with German Nazism.[116] Others argue that Grivas' only interest
in the movement was personal power and popularity in
Greece.[117]

In any event the E.O.K.A., along with the efforts of Archbishop Makarios III, was instrumental in ultimately bringing
about Cypriot independence from British rule in the Zürich and
London agreements of 1959. After this Grivas returned to
Greece. Following this independence, however, Enosis itself has
not been realized and internal strife between the Turkish and
Greek segments of Cyprus continues. As of 1964 this has necessi-

tated the intervention of United Nations troops.[118] Grivas again returned to Cyprus in the capacity of head of the Greek National Guard. Several Turks were killed in village raids which followed. The Greek government, fearing international consequences stemming from Turkey's threat to invade Cyprus if the raids continued, recalled Grivas to Greece, leaving Cyprus essentially under the guardianship of the United Nations Forces.[119]

These then are examples of types of political-social organized crime.

Mercenary Crime

Another type of organized crime is one that could be referred to as *Mercenary* or what some writers often refer to as predatory organized crime. Here a basic distinction from other forms of organized crime is the fact that this type is committed for the purpose of direct financial profit. As MacDougall[120] indicated a number of years ago, it is difficult to determine what crimes should and should not be subsumed under the category of mercenary crime. We find it necessary to place mercenary or predatory, like other forms of organized crime, on a continuum. These, like the others, have overlapping characteristics. On a continuum then, we may have forms of *theft-oriented* organized crime which include the use or potential use of force in executing the criminal act. Here may be included any organization committing such crimes as larceny, burglary, and robbery for the purpose of financial gain. These can range from a loosely organized small group of two to a well-organized group of burglars such as "The Break O'Days"[121] of Detroit, a band so called because they burglarized in the early hours of the morning. Here also can be included those groups which other writers refer to as mobs—criminal, juvenile, and other types of gangs, providing that the major goal of the act committed involves direct financial profit and that force or the threat of its use is present in the particular act. If these same groups, however, committed a criminal act where violence was used purely for the sake of violence, then their crimes would not be of a theft-oriented nature.

More distinct from groups that employ force or violence are those which use fraud or stealth to achieve their goal of direct financial profit. Here on our continuum we include those organizations described in the work of VanCise,[122] those which use confidence techniques instead of violence. These would include what some authors, cited earlier, called mobs or racketeers, meaning those groups which used fraud as their modus operandi. Further distinct from these forms of theft-oriented types are those groups that practice extortion—those using fear of violence or the threat of exposure to obtain money from victims. In this range would fall criminal organizations that engage in kidnapping, blackmail, white slavery, and other forms of what previously mentioned authors called racketeering, referring to groups using violence or fear as their method of operation. In the latter form of extortion, we could further distinguish between a forced-service type of extortion where the victim is literally forced to continuously pay for a service over a long period of time, as compared to those where the victim pays a certain amount of money only once.

In-Group-Oriented Organized Crime

Another form of organized crime is what we choose to call *In-Group-Oriented* organized crime. Here can be included such organizations as motorcycle gangs, adolescent gangs, and street-corner gangs whose major goal is not financial profit, but providing members with the psychological gratification of belonging to a group and engaging in adventurous activities. Within this type on the continuum of types lie a number of differentiations. As Cohen points out, some delinquent groups who appear to be theft-oriented are not in reality: they steal not for the profit involved but for the recognition and other thrills that accompany the act.[123] There are gangs, however, which, as Puffer illustrates, although organized to provide emotional response, also have as their function the commission of thefts.[124] In some in-group-oriented organizations, violence directed toward nonpeer-group members may be the sole or major source of activity. Yet as Miller, Geertz, and Cutler point out, this agression of gang members often is directed not toward outsiders but instead toward one another.[125] There is no better example of a continuum of types of gangs than that found in Thrasher's classic work, *The Gang*.[126] Here, he describes characteristics of gangs ranging from secret societies to federations.

Syndicated Crime

Finally on the continuum of types of organized crime we come to the major topic of this work—syndicated crime. Since this type will be discussed in detail throughout the following chapters, suffice it here to draw only certain basic distinctions from other forms on the continuum.

Syndicated crime in its most constricted sense differs from other types of organized crime primarily because it provides goods and/or services that are illegal, yet for which there is a demand by certain segments of society. When the nature of these goods and services is such that the demand continues over a long period of time the syndicate develops a structure which makes it possible to provide these services. The specific structure the syndicate takes, as we shall see, depends upon the activity in which the particular syndicate is engaged.

Because, however, syndicates provide goods and services on a continuous basis, their activities are more visible than other criminals' to both the public and the police. Hence, syndicate participants must provide for "protection" of their activities. That is, they must devise means by which the police and other legal agencies are "paid off" or given other forms of remuneration in return for allowing syndicate activities to continue undisturbed.

One of the reasons that the services and goods provided by

syndicates are so costly is that the syndicate participant, serving as a "broker" between the law and the consumer, must incur the risks and expenses involved in making such products available. In reality, the high prices which the consumer pays for these products is not based upon the cost of the goods themselves. Rather he is paying the syndicate criminal for the risk and operation involved in moving the goods from producer to consumer within a legal system which can and does bring legal action against violators. As we point out in the next chapter, the degree of the risk varies in time and place and is basically dependent upon the quantity and quality of corruption of members of the legal agencies. Nonetheless, the syndicate participant, even with pay-offs guarding his immunity, is always in a position of risk.

Concerning the delimitation of syndicated crime, what Frank Hartung[127] observed about the chain-like aspects of involvement in White Collar offenses in Black Market activities can also be applied to the realm of syndicated crime. As we shall show, syndicate enterprises involve the use of a variety of individuals and groups, both criminal and noncriminal.

Summary

The existing definitions and classifications of organized crime do not allow for the overlapping aspects of the many forms of this type of crime. Rather than attempting a new classification which would have manifested the same difficulties as previous typologies, we have instead tried to suggest a continuum of different types of organized crime each of which has variations within it. We presented a continuum which includes *political-social, mercenary, in-group* and *syndicated* organized crime. Each of these types, when viewed individually, can be found to have some characteristics that are common to the others. As such, these four types are not meant to represent the entire spectrum of possible types. Along with these, one could add *violence-oriented, white collar,* and many other forms. Rather these are offered merely as examples of types on a continuum. We suggest, however, the substitution of the terms *extortion-oriented* and *fraud-oriented* to differentiate between the two different forms of organized crime which have, until now, been nebulously subsumed under the wide category of racketeering.

Rather than developing more complex systems of categorization, we suggest that the description of a criminal group be based upon the nature of a specific criminal act which it has committed at any given time, not on the basis of its possession of certain traits. Criminal groups are dynamic entities, not static ones. As such, they change with the nature of the criminal acts they commit. Only when this is recognized can we begin to appreciate the basic similarities as well as differences between criminal groups.

With this introduction, let us move to a discussion of the social prerequisites of syndicated crime.

References

1 *Report of the Honourable Mr. Justice Wilfrid D. Roach* (Toronto: March 15, 1963), pp. 351–354.

2 *Ibid.*

3 Gus Tyler, "The Roots of Organized Crime," *Crime and Delinquency, VIII* (October, 1962), 333–334.

4 Herbert A. Bloch, "The Juvenile Gang: A Cultural Reflex," *The Annals,* CCCXLVII (May, 1963), 25.

5 Mabel A. Elliott, *Crime in Modern Society* (New York: Harper and Brothers, 1952), p. 133.

6 *Ibid.*, p. 136.

7 *Ibid.*, pp. 139–140.

8 *Ibid.*, p. 149.

9 Elmer Herbert Johnson, *Crime, Correction and Society* (Homewood, Ill.: The Dorsey Press, 1968), p. 243.

10 *Ibid.*, p. 248.

11 *Ibid.*

12 Robert G. Caldwell, *Criminology,* 2nd ed. (New York: The Ronald Press Co., 1965), pp. 133–134.

13 *Ibid.*, p. 134.

14 *Ibid.*, p. 150.

15 *Ibid.*, p. 151.

16 *Ibid.*, p. 152.

17 *Ibid.*, p. 155.

18 *Ibid.*, p. 158.

19 Harry Elmer Barnes and Negley K. Teeters, *New Horizons in Criminology*, 3rd ed. (Englewood Cliffs: Prentice-Hall, Inc., 1959), p. 24.

20 *Ibid.*, p. 19.

21 *Ibid.*, p. 51.

22 *Ibid.*

23 *Ibid.*, p. 28.

24 *Ibid.*

25 *Ibid.*, pp. 19–24.

26 Ruth Shonle Cavan, *Criminology*, 3rd ed. (New York: Thomas Y. Crowell Co., 1962), pp. 123–124.

27 *Ibid.*, p. 124.

28 *Ibid.*, pp. 127–129.

29 *Ibid.*, p. 123.

30 *Ibid.*, p. 123.

31 *The Professional Thief*, annotated and interpreted by Edwin E. Sutherland, Phoenix Books (Chicago: The University of Chicago Press, 1965), p. 43.

32 Frederic M. Thrasher, "Gangs," *Encyclopedia of the Social Sciences*, VI, p. 566.

33 Herbert A. Bloch and Arthur Niederhoffer, *The Gang* (New York: Philosophical Library, 1958), pp. 7–8.

34 Douglas M. Allen, "The Gangs of New York," *Newsweek*, September 14, 1959, pp. 53–55.

35 Donald R. Taft and Ralph W. England, *Criminology*, 4th ed. (New York: The Macmillan Co., 1964), pp. 184–194.

36 Alfred R. Lindesmith, "The Nature of Organized Crime," in *Criminology* ed. by Clyde B. Vedder, Samuel Koenig, and Robert E. Clark (New York: Holt, Rinehart and Winston, 1953), pp. 376–377.

37 *Ibid.*, pp. 377–378.

38 John C. R. MacDonald, *Crime Is a Business* (Stanford, California: Stanford University Press, 1939), p. 3.

39 Edwin H. Sutherland and Donald R. Cressey, *Principles of Criminology*, 7th ed. (New York: J. P. Lippincott Co., 1966), p. 277.

40 George B. Vold, *Theoretical Criminology* (New York: Oxford University Press, 1958), p. 222.

41 *Ibid.*, pp. 223–224.

42 *Ibid.*, p. 225.

43 *Ibid.*, pp. 226–230.

44 John McConaughy, *From Cain to Capone* (New York: Brentano's, 1931), p. 3. See also Chapters 2 and 3.

45 John Gunther, "The High Cost of Hoodlums," *Harper's*, October, 1929, pp. 530–531.

46 Courtenay Terrett, *Only Saps Work* (New York: The Vanguard Press, 1930), pp. 16–17.

47 Murray I. Gurfein, "Racketeering," *Encyclopedia of the Social Sciences*, XIII, p. 45.

48 Gunther, *op. cit.*, p. 530.

49 John O'Connor, *Broadway Racketeers* (New York: Horace Liveright, 1928), p. vii.

50 E. Jerome Ellison and Frank W. Brock, *The Run for Your Money* (New York: Dodge Publishing Co., 1935), p. 5.

51 Gordon L. Hostetter and Thomas Quinn Beesley, *It's A Racket!* (Chicago: Les Quin Books Inc., 1929), p. 4.

52 "The Rackets of New York," *The New Statesman*, December 6, 1930, pp. 262–264.

53 William G. Shepherd, "What's the Racket?," *Collier's*, April 11, 1931, pp. 10–11.

54 Emmett Gowen, *A True Exposé of Racketeers and Their Methods* (New York: Popular Book Corporation, 1930), p. 3.

55 Constance Marshall, "Racketeering in Vice," *The Woman's Journal*, May, 1931, pp. 18–19.

56 "The Landlady Racket," *The Literary Digest*, March 7, 1931, p. 11.

57 Lewis H. Haney, *Business Organization and Combination* (New York: The Macmillan Company, 1922), pp. 3–4.

58 Gustavus Myers, *History of the Great American Fortunes*, Vol. III (Chicago: Charles H. Herr and Company, 1910), pp. 14–18.

59 Myers, *op. cit.*, Vol. II, p. 112.

60 Proctor W. Hansl, *Years of Plunder* (New York: Harrison Smith and Robert Haas, 1935), pp. 184–197.

61 Abraham Epstein, "The Insurance Racket," *The American Mercury*, September, 1930, pp. 1–10.

62 Silas Bent, "Newspapermen–Partners in Crime?," *Scribner's*, November, 1930, pp. 520–526.

63 Edward D. Sullivan, *Rattling the Cup* (New York: The Vanguard Press, 1929), p. 6.

64 Boyden Sparkes, "The Club Racket Has You," *Nation's Business*, September, 1930, pp. 44–47.

65 "The Inside of the Testimonial Racket," *Advertising and Selling*, January 7, 1931, pp. 20–21, 56–58.

66 John Gosling and Dennis Craig, *The Great Train Robbery* (New York: The Bobbs-Merrill Company, Inc., 1965), p. 104.

67 J. Adams Puffer, *The Boy and His Gang* (Boston: Houghton Mifflin Company, 1912), pp. 8–25.

68 *Detroit's Daily Express*, January 8, 1968, p. 5.

69 Frank Reynolds and Michael McClure, *Freewheelin' Frank* (New York: Grove Press, Inc., 1967), pp. 110–111.

70 Sylvia Porter, "On Wall Street," in Gus Tyler, *Organized Crime in America* (Ann Arbor: The University of Michigan Press, 1962), pp. 298–302.

71 "Antitrust Enforcement by Private Parties: Analysis of Developments in the Treble Damage Suit," *The Yale Law Journal*, LXI (June–July, 1952), 1010–1011.

72 John G. Fuller, *The Gentlemen Conspirators* (New York: Grove Press, Inc., 1962), pp. 13–14.

73 Robert Presthus, *The Organizational Society*, Vintage Books (New York: Random House, 1962).

74 Victor A. Thompson, *Modern Organization* (New York: Alfred A. Knopf, 1961).

75 Scott A. Greer, *Social Organization* (New York: Random House, 1955).

76 Amitai Etzioni, *Modern Organizations* (Englewood Cliffs: Prentice-Hall, Inc., 1964), pp. 3–4.

77 Theodore Caplow, *Principles of Organization* (New York: Harcourt, Brace and World, Inc., 1964), pp. 1–3.

78 Nathaniel Weyl, *Treason* (Washington, D.C.: Public Affairs Press, 1950), pp. 238–239.

79 Thorsten Sellin, *Culture Conflict and Crime* (New York: Social Science Research Council, 1938).

80 Joseph L. Sax, "Civil Disobedience: The Law Is Never Blind," *Saturday Review*, September 28, 1968, pp. 22–25ff.

81 *Inner City Voice*, April, 1968, pp. 7, 10.

82 Earl Caldwell, "Angry Panthers Talk of War and Unwrap Weapons," *The New York Times*, September 10, 1969, p. 31C.

83 *Civil Liberties*, September, 1968, p. 1.

84 Sylan Fox, "Many Police in City Leaning to the Right," *The New York Times*, September 6, 1968, p. 1.

85 Seymour Martin Lipset, "An Anatomy of the Klan," *Commentary*, October, 1965, pp. 74–83.

86 *Ibid.*, p. 78.

87 Kenneth T. Jackson, *The Ku Klux Klan in the City, 1915–1930* (New York: Oxford University Press, 1967), p. xi.

88 *Ibid.*, p. xii.

89 David H. Chalmers, *Hooded Americanism* (Garden City: Doubleday and Company, Inc., 1965), p. 30.

90 Paul J. Gillette and Eugene Tillinger, *Inside the Ku Klux Klan* (New York: Pyramid Books, 1965), pp. 112–123.

91 *Ibid.*, pp. 40–52.

92 Poyntz Tyler, ed. *Immigration and the United States* (New York: The H. W. Wilson Co., 1956), p. 25.

93 Michael Maharry, "Klan Wizard Due Here for Cheers, Cash," *The Detroit News,* April 27, 1967, p. 1.

94 Graham Adams, Jr., *Age of Industrial Violence, 1910–15* (New York: Columbia University Press, 1966), pp. 156–161.

95 *Ibid.,* p. 155.

96 Marion Dutton Savage, *Industrial Unionism in America* (New York: The Ronald Press Co., 1922), p. 23.

97 Arthur H. Lewis, *Lament for the Molly Maguires* (New York: Harcourt, Brace and World, Inc., 1964), pp. 3–12.

98 Louis Adamic, *Dynamite* (New York: The Viking Press, 1934), pp. 15–16.

99 *Ibid.,* p. 18.

100 Lewis, *op. cit.,* p. 31.

101 Edward Winslow Martin, *The History of the Great Riots* (Philadelphia: The National Publishing Co., 1877), pp. 466–467.

102 F. P. Dewees, *The Molly Maguires* (New York: Burt Franklin, 1877), pp. 62–63.

103 Martin, *op. cit.,* pp. 492–516.

104 Dudley Barker, *Grivas, Portrait of a Terrorist* (New York: Harcourt, Brace and Co., 1959), p. 74.

105 Daniel S. Wosgian, "Turks and British Rule in Cyprus" (Unpublished Ph.D. dissertation, Columbia University, 1963), p. 137.

106 *Ibid.,* p. 139.

107 Sir George Hill, *A History of Cyprus,* Vol. IV, ed. by Sir Harry Luke (Cambridge: The University Press, 1952), p. 490.

108 Wosgian, *op. cit.,* p. 159.

109 Charles W. Thayer, *Guerilla* (New York: The New American Library, 1963), pp. 110–111.

110 Christos Leonidas Doumas, "The Problem of Cyprus," (Unpublished Ph.D. dissertation, University of California, Los Angeles, 1963), p. 155.

111 Thayer, *op. cit.,* pp. 111–112.

112 *Ibid.*

113 Charles Foley, ed., *The Memoirs of General Grivas* (New York: Frederick A. Praeger, Publishers, 1965), p. 25.

114 Doumas, *op. cit.,* p. 181.

115 Doros Alastos, *Cyprus Guerilla* (London: William Heineman, Ltd., 1960), p. 59.

116 W. Byford-Jones, *Grivas and the Story of EOKA* (London: Robert Hale Limited, 1959), pp. 82–83.

117 Barker, *op. cit.,* p. 202.

118 Arnold Agnew, "Cyprus—A Challenge to the Art of Keeping the Peace," *Detroit's Daily Express,* November 28, 1967, p. 5.

119 *Ibid.*

120 Ernest MacDougall, "Report of Committee on Mercenary

Crime," *Journal of Criminal Law and Criminology*, XXVI (May-June, 1932), 94–100.

121 "The Break O'Days," *Detroit Post and Tribune*, January 27, 1878, p. 4.

122 Phillip S. VanCise, *Fighting the Underworld* (Boston: Houghton Mifflin Co., 1936).

123 Albert E. Cohen, *Delinquent Boys: The Culture of the Gang* (Glencoe: The Free Press, 1955), pp. 26–28.

124 Puffer, *op. cit.*, pp. 16–17.

125 Walter B. Miller, Hildred Geertz, and Henry S. G. Cutler, "Aggression in a Boys' Street-Corner Group," *Psychiatry*, XXIV (November, 1961), 286.

126 Frederic M. Thrasher, *The Gang* (Chicago: The University of Chicago Press, 1927), pp. 58–76.

127 Frank E. Hartung, "White-Collar Offenses in the Wholesale Meat Industry in Detroit," *The American Journal of Sociology*, LVI (July, 1950), 31–32.

3

The Social Locale of Syndicated Crime

Writing to the Commission of Investigation of the State of New York, a citizen of Westchester County related the following incident:

> A child who wished to buy some candy at a local candy store complained to his mother that he was hesitant to do so because, as he put it, the "place is full of bookies." His mother replied, "Oh, go ahead, you'll probably find a policeman in there."[1]

This incident brings to light a structural reality and necessity of syndicated crime—the collusion between the criminal, the police, and the politician. London cleverly refers to this collusion as the "triple alliance."[2] However, syndicated crime, as goods- or service-oriented crime, cannot be complete without adding a fourth functionary, the individual citizen who seeks these goods or services. It is true, as we shall illustrate in a later chapter, that those who participate in syndicated crime also involve themselves in other forms of crime including burglary, larceny, fraud, and others. However, there seems to be a general agreement among students of organized crime that the major source of syndicate funds has always been society's need for illegal services and goods.

Individual burglaries, larcenies, and other crimes of stealth can be committed without police and political protection. Provision of illegal services, on the other hand, because they necessitate contact between the criminal and the client on a continuous basis, cannot be readily carried on without soon coming under police or public scrutiny. It is true that syndicates employ certain camouflage techniques; they do not flaunt their activities. Yet these are often so standardized that only the naive citizen or police officer would not be able to detect them within a short length of time. As one informant put it, "A guy has to either be blind or paid off if he doesn't start wondering how some son-of-a-bitch who has had the same set of dishes and other junk for sale for two years could stay in business." Referring to a "front" where "numbers" slips were purchased, this informant continued, "If he still ain't convinced, then he should go in and try to buy one of the dusty things and he'll hear the best sales pitch he's ever heard—that is, against buying it." These protected fronts are an accepted reality and part of most syndicate enterprises. In some enterprises these are so standardized that they are referred to by a specific name. In the numbers racket, for example, the term frequently used for these places is *the Pad*.[3]

To repeat, the *raison d'être* for crime syndicates rests with those sources in society that desire the illicit goods and services. Too often this is forgotten by those who seek to explain syndicated crime as criminal activity which is "forced" upon the public through the alliances among syndicates and public officials. Although some syndicate participants engage in protection and extortion activities that are forced upon individuals, even here the interpretation of "force" necessitates more careful evaluation. Cooper shows that many merchants who claim they were forced to place slot or vending machines in their business establishments are in reality merely hiding their selfish motives of making profits from the machines. These profits the merchants share with the syndicate, having been promised by the syndicate that they will not have any competition.[4]

The widespread acceptance of a belief in the existence of a "Mafia" or other foreign criminal group that is blamed for importing syndicated crime to the United States further serves to divert attention away from the fact that it is the American public that keeps syndicates in business.

Much more realistic however is the approach taken by Mays, who argues that a proper sociological analysis of crime necessitates a study of the entire complex of society. Only then can we understand the origin as well as the continuing existence of the criminal elements which are part of a given social structure.[5]

Illicit Goods

American criminal syndicates, then, must be evaluated in terms of the function they perform. In American society this consists of providing illicit goods and services which are in demand by certain segments of that society. By virtue of the fact that these are defined as illegal it becomes necessary that both a structure and a method be devised through which these goods may be made available.

There are those who argue that these illicit goods and services should be kept from the individual because they are harmful to him. This argument is meaningless, however: history has taught us that illegallity does not prevent people from using certain goods or pursuing activities, even when they are known to be injurious to their well-being. The paradigm is the case of Prohibition.

Injurious or beneficial, the fact remains that, in America, illicit goods have always been in demand. Were it not for this, syndicated crime could and would not exist. Along with London's "triple alliance," then, in order to complete the total conception of syndicated crime, we must consider the participating individual who requests and uses the products of syndicated criminals.

Americans have asked and continue to ask for a variety of illicit goods and services. Prohibition of alcohol in the 1920s brought forth "speak-easies" and other outlets of illegal alcoholic distribution. The extremes to which people would go to get a drink is evidenced by the fact that they were willing to risk their lives to do so. One newspaper story tells of how De-

troiters risked the possibility of falling through ice and drowning
as they drove their automobiles across the frozen Detroit River
in an attempt to smuggle alcohol from Canada.[6] Other countries
had similar public reactions to the prohibition of liquor. In
Finland, during 1919 to 1928, prohibition gave rise to smuggling, moonshining, and bootlegging.[7] Dorr further shows that,
despite the fact that alcohol was prohibited during this period,
drunkenness was quite common.[8] In Norway, prohibition resulted in the populace distilling from cereal and potatoes a
home-made liquor called "thunder." It got its name from its
so-called thunderous effects, which included possible harm to
the body when it had not been properly aged.[9] In India prohibition has produced the development of many techniques of
manufacturing and distributing illicit liquor. One interesting
and common technique currently used in India is that of transporting liquor in a rubber bladder tied around the stomach of
a woman, giving the impression that she is pregnant.[10]

Quite similar to the reactions against the prohibition of
alcohol is the current response in American society to the prohibition of narcotic drugs. Formerly considered the prerogative
of extreme deviants numbering about 45,000 to 60,000,[11] today
narcotics and hallucinogens are used at practically all levels of
society. Their use on college campuses, high schools, and other
locales has become a daily subject in newspapers across the
country. A recent article drew attention to the trend of LSD
usage among the younger age groups living in the wealthy
suburbs of Detroit.[12]

Harold Finestone and Seymour Fiddle have illustrated how
drug use can become a subcultural activity in itself.[13] It becomes an in-group phenomenon in which the participants are
expected to abide by established norms of behavior.

Gambling

One of the most profitable sources of income of syndicated crime
in the United States stems from the widespread American desire

to gamble. Many Americans do not view gambling as either a harmful or illicit activity. In fact, in many subcultures it is viewed simply as a form of recreation. Only when carried to excess does the subculture react negatively to gambling. This attitude was recently reflected in Detroit when a raid was carried out on a business establishment operated by a Greek-American. Many in the Greek community were angered by the raid, indicating that they viewed gambling, particularly card-playing, as a form of harmless fun. They saw this action by the police not only as unnecessary but as unjust.

In the black subculture, "policy" or numbers is such an integral and accepted pattern of behavior that, as Drake and Cayton state, policy stations in the community of "Bronzeville" are "almost as numerous as the churches."[14] As Carlson illustrates in his very interesting and informative doctoral dissertation, numbers gambling in the Detroit black community consists of a "culture complex" made up of norms, values, and practices that take on their significance only within this subculture context.[15]

A vivid example of how ingrained and accepted the numbers has become in the black community can be illustrated from a recent situation that occurred in a suburb of Detroit. The author was apprised of this occurrence by an informant familiar with the black community. In an effort to enforce what Lincoln[16] refers to as Muslim "social morality"—the achievement of "a rigorously high moral standard of personal and group behavior" —the Black Muslims in this suburb have employed various methods of persuasion to curb prostitution and the use of drugs and alcohol. Their efforts in this direction have been very successful; however, within the scope of this purification process, the numbers was not included as an evil from which to abstain.

Gambling, as Carlson points out, has been a universal activity of man; in past and present societies, industrial as well as primitive.[17] Several studies, however, view gambling as an individual personality need. One such study suggests that gamblers have certain personality characteristics distinguishable from nongamblers.[18] Another argues that personality problems are at the root of the gambler's need.[19] Herbert Bloch views the problem of gambling as one which is socially based. Gambling, he argues, becomes a problem "only when there is widespread resentment against it" in a given society. It is the element of chance which makes it universally appealing.[20]

Whatever the reason for its appeal, evidence is overwhelming that gambling is a desired form of activity and one that, in many cases, is publicly tolerated despite its illegality. The late Senator Robert F. Kennedy called attention to the fact that the American people spend more on gambling than on medical care or education.[21] Recognizing the need for gambling, several governments have capitalized upon it via national lotteries.[22] Recently New York established a state lottery.

The fact that gambling is a tolerated practice in America is reflected in various displays of acceptance by segments of the American public. A study of attitudes toward gambling in a middleclass industrial city found that although citizens displayed attitudes of hostility toward official corruption, there was general community approval of gambling itself.[23] Testifying before the Kefauver committee in 1950, the Attorney General of the State of Florida stated that various types of gambling violations were not prosecuted in certain Florida counties because of the tolerance for gambling inherent in the customs of the people in these counties.[24]

Other Illicit Services

Along with alcohol, narcotics, and gambling, other illicit needs of the American public have been met by syndicated criminals. Loan sharks make fast money available to those who need it and are willing to pay high rates of interest. Prostitutes are provided. Bars, clubs, and other hang-outs are made available to homosexuals so that they may engage in their behavior without the fear of arrest. In those states with high taxes on cigarettes, less expensive black market cigarettes are provided by syndicate participants.

Of these, loan-sharking, which was already prevalent in the 1930s,[25] has currently become one of the major sources of syndicate revenue. The demand for this service generally comes from individuals who cannot obtain loans through legitimate sources. We actually know very little about the type of person who turns to the loan shark for money. However, as Duffy[26] notes, much of the borrowing through this source is by gamblers who are trying to pay off gambling debts or other obligations incurred as a result of their gambling losses.

The victim, as the borrower is often referred to, is frequently portrayed in newspapers and by investigative bodies as innocent "victims of circumstance." It is true, as we shall show later, that the interest rates charged by the loan shark are exploitive, but we must also note that the person borrowing the money is not exactly the best security risk around. Rarely does anyone ask why this person finds it necessary to go to the loan shark. Certainly it would be economically more sensible for him to borrow the money from legitimate sources that charge far less interest. If a more objective portrayal of the victim or borrower in the loan-sharking enterprise were given we would most probably find, with minor exceptions, a person who is a very poor credit risk, and who must of outright necessity turn to illegitimate sources. The loan shark, who is not functioning within a legal framework, cannot take this person to court in order to collect his debt. Instead he must use illegal techniques such as harrassment and assault to accomplish this end. We might note in passing that many legitimate small loan agencies have been known to use, with the exception of outright assault, collection techniques that in many respects resemble those of the loan-shark.

In short, syndicated crime as a product-service enterprise needs individuals or segments of the public who will pay for the product-services. Without customers, economically and otherwise, there would be no reason for syndicates to exist. As Pileggi observes, the success of syndicated crime (which he subsumes under the term "Mafia") in America today "depends upon the excellence of its services; more important, it depends upon the loyalty of its millions of satisfied customers."[27]

Syndicate Structure

Since the satisfaction of the needs met by the syndicate is continuous in nature, the syndicate must create a structure which will achieve two major ends: one, arrange a means of providing the goods or services to the client and two, make certain that the law does not interfere with the enterprise. In the accomplishment of these two ends, syndicated crime must create a social system that comes to develop its own values, norms, roles, statuses, and means or techniques for accomplishing its purpose. For this reason, Donald Cressey adequately describes syndicated crime as a rational system designed for "safety and profit."[28]

The social system of syndicated crime can be described in a variety of ways depending upon what one wishes to incorporate or exclude as parts of the system. For our purposes we include within the system what this author believes compose the basic functionaries necessary to the system as it operates in the United States. These include the client, the syndicate criminal, and the corrupted public official.

We do not wish this definition of these elements of the system to be taken as an absolute definition or model for syndicated crime that transcends both time and place. Obviously the system will vary with different societies depending upon the form of government, the effectiveness of law enforcement, public attitudes of tolerance, the structure of the criminal organization, and other factors. Thus, for example, if absolute secrecy could be obtained by the syndicated criminal or if the penalty for his illegal act were not severe there obviously would be no need to pay off police or public officials.

It should be remembered that syndicated crime, like other forms of social structure varies from society to society. In Singapore, for example, the gambling syndicates "conduct their operations in great secrecy" and when apprehended "have enough money to pay the fines imposed on those who are convicted of betting offences."[29] In Japan, on the other hand, syndicated crime is carried out in an atmosphere of chivalry. Approximately 5000 different gangs, using swords, fight openly in the streets for territories.[30] In Tokyo, a leader of one of these gangs explained that the gang's territory is protected by stationing look-out men in various night clubs who, upon spotting a member of an enemy gang, alert their own members and a fight immediately follows.[31] In India, according to Balakrishna, syndicated crime is carried on primarily by secret societies which make use of corrupted policemen.[32]

Wherever syndicate criminal activities are carried out in a setting where clients demand illicit goods and the law is enforced, the protection of the police and public officials becomes a syndicate necessity. Such protection assures the syndicate criminal of a smooth, uninterrupted continuation of his enterprise. Also, in the event that he is apprehended, this assures him the most lenient penalty or no penalty at all. When this assurance cannot be obtained, syndicates, of necessity, must resort to more camouflage and secret techniques.

In brief review, the three functionaries associated with the social system of syndicated crime consist of the client who seeks the goods or service; the syndicate criminal who provides these products or services; and the corrupt public official who is remunerated for his function of protecting the enterprise.

In order to better understand the structure and system of syndicated crime it is necessary to define more specifically the functions of each of these three participants.

The Client

Although the client is not directly associated with the providing of the goods and services, he serves the role of buyer or user and thereby constitutes an important element in the total system. Although he commits crimes associated with using or partaking of the goods, these are not the same types of crime as committed by those who provide the service or products. However, as a recipient, the client comes to learn and abide by certain norms of behavior that, if accepted, will permit him to continue the satisfaction of his needs. Among these one of the most important is the willingness to keep the source of his illicit enterprises secret. This he does, if for no other reason, simply to assure himself the continuation of the syndicate's services. Coupled with this, the client must learn various techniques such as codes used to enter certain establishments, how to make new contacts if the old ones are severed rapidly, how and to whom to express any grievances, and in general to abide by the rules necessary to the specific enterprise. Other than these, the client's major function is that of user or buyer, which although not synonomous with the role of the syndicate criminal, lays the basis for the creation of this role.

The Syndicate Criminal

One of the most important, and, in terms of activity, the most important, of the three functionaries is the syndicate criminal. It is he and his associates who undertake the responsibility and the procedures of procuring as well as distributing the illicit goods. In so doing he must take the risk that goes along with engagement in any illegal activity—incurring the penalty of the law if apprehended. He is paid for the risk involved as well as his labor in procuring the illicit goods. Despite the fact that he may pay for protection, there constantly looms the possibility of his arrest and imprisonment, which to the syndicated criminal is a serious economic and social concern. It must be remembered that, despite their power and despite protection, even such prominent underworld figures as Al Capone, Charles "Lucky" Luciano, and Vito Genovese were incarcerated. Much worse, Louis "Lepke" Buchalter, New York's prominent under-world figure, went to the electric chair. In the world of syndicate crime, immunity from the law is always a matter of probability; like most aspects of life, immunity can never be absolutely guaranteed.

Economically, syndicates seek to gain a monopoly. Since they are dealing with illicit products they are not competing with legitimate business over the services and goods they offer. Rather they are competing with other illegal agents supplying the same goods or services. Schelling notes that both the formation and the continuation of an underworld monopoly is largely de-pendent upon the number and degree of illegal sources of supply. For this reason the underworld could not, for example, monopo-lize the sales of cigarettes to minors since any person of legal age could be a source of supply.[33]

In the world of syndicate economics one cannot speak of a monopoly in those cases where several syndicates located in the same geographic area are offering similar products. In these circumstances, syndicates may use coercive and forceful tech-niques of gaining control. They may attempt to destroy their competitor's business by hijacking his goods, intimidating his customers, and other such techniques. Often, however, two or more equally powerful syndicates may effect a compromise, de-lineating territories where each has control, and agreeing to "multilaterally" fight any other competitors who tamper with their enterprises. Such agreements are only as trustworthy as those who make them and are largely kept in existence by the threat of the power which each syndicate has in its ability to destroy the other.

Along with providing himself with "protection" from the legitimate world then, the syndicate criminal must continuously meet the challenge of his underworld competitors.

As an intermediary between the legitimate and the illegitimate segments of society, the syndicate criminal then in fact serves a function. From the standpoint of the total society it may be argued that his activities are "dysfunctional." As Johnson states, syndicate criminals do divert money from the legitimate sources of society into the hands of illegitimate sources.[34] However, this criminal's activities are "functional" when we consider along with Lippmann[35] the fact that he provides for the needs of those individuals who desire illegal commodities and services. Interestingly, in this respect, an informant noted to the author a facet about syndicated crime that he had not considered. This informant argued that since syndicates employ many workers in illegal enterprises, these workers are taken off the legitimate labor market. Since they are not competing for legitimate occupations, they make more jobs available to workers in legitimate society. We realize that this may not be the most ethical method of solving an unemployment problem, but when we consider, that in 1950, 10,000 were employed in the policy enterprises in Pittsburgh alone,[36] this informant's observation becomes much more meaningful.

In his role of broker between the law and the client, the syndicated criminal turns to the use of bribery in an effort to forestall police action against his enterprises.

Noting along with Pileggi[37] that "the line between lobbying and bribery grows thinner every year," one must view bribery in syndicated crime as a method of persuading or giving public officials a financial reason for permitting illicit enterprises to operate. Bribery in syndicated crime is considered one of the major operating costs of the enterprise. Too often, estimates of the huge income made by syndicated crime, which always (and probably correctly) range into billions yearly, do not take into consideration the large amounts that are paid yearly for protection. In New York during the 1920s, the graft paid to maintain speakeasies alone, which at one time numbered 32,000, amounted to sixty million dollars a year; one governmental agent was "offered a retainer of $300,000 a week."[38] In Detroit, according to Carlson, the baseball pool paid 50 to 100 thousand dollars a year for protection while other establishments had the following set amounts: "houses of prostitution $100 to $300 per month, gambling establishments and handbooks $50 to $1000 per month, and operators of gambling machines $10 per month per machine in operation."[39]

A former police official informed the author that during the course of his service he was once offered $12,500 cash and promised $1000 per week for as long as he permitted one gambling establishment to operate. Several years later he was made another offer of $50,000 cash and $5000 a week to permit the operation of two clubs. These were only two of the many bribery attempts made during the three and one-half years he was in office. Thus, syndicated criminals are willing to pay large amounts of money in order to run their enterprises.

Bribery

Corruption is a study in itself. Individuals seem to vary in their willingness to accept bribes, some capable of being bought for as little as twenty-five dollars a month while others like the police official just mentioned cannot be bought with thousands. Obviously there are certain economic and social forces that determine the amount that will be paid for a bribe. Most commonly, a person is paid in proportion to the service he can perform. Some bargaining usually takes place, and the decision regarding the amount rests primarily upon how much need exists for the individual or his service. Bribery costs will vary from time to time depending upon how much public tolerance versus public pressure exists in a given area.

Bribes are generally paid on a continuous basis, particularly in those cases where a public official agrees to permit an enterprise to operate over an extended period of time. When political pressure or public opinion becomes too vehement, however, raids are conducted to demonstrate to the public that something is being done. Often in these raids "front men" are used to take the "rap." For example, after the accused criminal's first arraignment, the syndicate sends a "stand-in," or person other than the real accused, to stand trial and, if found guilty, even to serve the sentence.[40] In return, the stand-in may receive payment in the form of cash or of favors.

Another form of bribery takes place when a special service is needed. If probation or parole is seriously desired for a syndicate member, it may be possible to financially persuade those in power in the particular probation or parole system to grant action for a price. Usually the amount paid depends upon how important the individual is to the syndicate, the degree of willingness or unwillingness of the probation or parole personnel to cooperate, and the degree of public exposure and clamor which this "fixing" might create. The author was told by an informant about an individual quite important to the syndicate who was scheduled to be paroled through bribery of a high ranking public official. So much public reaction was aroused, however, by a newspaper that had constantly served as a source of vigilance over syndicated criminal activities in this particular city, that the entire scheme had to be dropped. The amount offered to this official was allegedly in the realm of $100,000.

The Press

A few words should be said about newspapers and their role in fighting and suppressing syndicated crime. Citing a few of the positions found in the literature will illustrate the diversity of opinion on this subject.

Some take the view that newspapers are a powerful force and should serve as the vanguard in the fight against crime and municipal corruption that aid its existence.[41] Others feel that newspapers can serve a vital role merely by arousing public interest in the fight against syndicated crime.[42] The Massachusetts report on organized crime adds an interesting twist by noting that newspapers themselves may be under the influence of the syndicate criminal. Although this report found "no major newspaper in the commonwealth either owned or controlled by the racketeers" it did find that "some racketeers have more influence in newspapers than they should have."[43]

There is no doubt that newspapers play a major role in

directing attention away from or toward syndicated criminal activities. Many newspapers send reporters into syndicate establishments on a routine basis. In their stories these reporters openly expose the location of the various fronts and other syndicate enterprises. They perform the service of creating public awareness, which often forces some form of police action to be taken. One informant noted that for quite some time a local newspaper was responsible for the suppression of much syndicated criminal activity in Cleveland. Constantly exposing the names and addresses of various enterprise locations and calling attention to any lack of police action after this exposure, this newspaper made it difficult for these places to remain open. Since the editor of this paper was quite wealthy and too renowned for the syndicate to openly threaten, it was impossible for the syndicate to employ any means of persuasion to curb this action.

In evaluating the role of any newspaper in its fight against syndicated crime one should always consider the ultimate motivation for the particular stand being taken. Newspapers that are partisan in political affiliation may be more critical and vigilant during the administration of an opposing political party than they are during the administration of their own party affiliates. Their direct motivation in such cases can hardly be considered to be the elimination of syndicated crime itself.

The Bribed

One could answer this in a very general manner by stating that anyone who can perform a service or favor for the syndicate is a potential subject for bribery. Quite often, however individuals vary in what they consider a bribe. For example several police officers have told the author that a frequent concern in supervising rookie policemen is that of convincing rookies that the acceptance of a mere bottle of whiskey, a ticket to the fights, or a box of cigars from owners of certain establishments constitutes a potential bribery relationship. When these gifts are given on a regular basis, the policeman is placed in the position of feeling obligated to comply should the owner request a favor of him. It is true that a common technique employed by syndicate criminals is that of placing individuals, whenever possible, into an obligatory position. This technique is not unique to syndicated criminals: it is a behavior manifestation found frequently in legitimate society.

The recipients of continuous bribery, specifically, are those who are responsible for allowing the syndicate enterprises to operate; namely, political officials who control the legitimate sources of power. Schermerhorn describes the dimensions of power as ranging on a continuum from legitimate to illegitimate and from coercive to noncoercive.[44] Although syndicates employ a form of power which is illegitimate and coercive, by obtaining the cooperation of legitimate sources of power they can carry on their enterprises with more assurance.

Turkus and Feder[45] emphasize the fact that the practice of using political connections in the United States became more efficiently employed after the creation of a national criminal syndicate in 1934. Historically, however, we find that the use of political corruption was widely employed by the criminal gangs in California as early as the middle 1800s.[46] Subsumed under a variety of names such as the "boss system," "the political machine," and "Tammany Hall" (the notorious New York City machine), the political power of public officials has played a tremendous role in both the legitimate and illegitimate life of American society. Legitimately in an industrial and democratic society the politician, as Lowell states, serves as a broker between the voting public and the legislative body.[47] Similarly, within an illegitimate context, one could argue that some politicians serve as brokers between the law and syndicated crime.

Historically in the United States, political officials have served this broker role for a variety of individuals and groups engaging in syndicated crime. Arthur "Dutch Schultz" Flegenheimer is known to have paid Jimmy Hines, a Tammany Hall leader, a total of $5000 a week.[48] Hines was evidently paid this amount in return for the political immunity he provided Schultz's beer enterprises. More currently, Wallace Turner referred to the late Senator Pat McCarren as the "gambler's senator" indicating that "when they had trouble, they went to him and he would help if he could."[49]

Campaign Contributions

Often, political protection is given not on a direct pay-off basis, but instead in exchange for the syndicate criminal's help in advancing the politician's career. For this reason, money contributed by syndicate personnel frequently constitutes a major source of election funds for political candidates. According to Peterson, it is estimated that Al Capone contributed a total of $250,000 to the Chicago mayoralty campaign of William "Big Bill" Thompson in 1927.[50] Reid cites the political contribution that Thomas "Three-Finger Brown" Luchese made to the campaign of William O'Dwyer, New York's former Mayor, in 1949. This contribution is of particular interest in that, as Reid points out, it was made approximately two months after the election had taken place.[51] During the presidential campaign of 1968, Drew Pearson drew attention to a statement made by Mickey Cohen, whom Pearson refers to as the "former king of the Los Angeles gambling world."[52] The statement indicated that the Republican candidate Richard Nixon had accepted $26,000 in campaign funds from Cohen and his fellow gamblers. Another article published during the same time period called attention to the fact that there was a link between organized crime, police, and the Democratic ward organization in Chicago.[53]

Often, the syndicate may raise funds to be used not to support but to defeat a candidate who threatens their enterprises. Graham cites such a case in Washington, where the numbers operators raised $100,000 in an attempt to defeat two senators who had attempted to investigate gambling in their locality.[54]

Again, it should be noted that the syndicate in contributing

money to election campaigns is not participating in unique behavior. Lundberg reminds us of the powerful role which some
corporations and their executives play in this regard.[55] Lowe
tells us that the Ku Klux Klan used its power to win the election
of both the President of the State Senate and the Speaker of
the House in Oregon in 1923.[56] Obviously none of these special
interest groups are interested in the general welfare of society.
Like the syndicate criminal, each of these contributors is interested in promoting the welfare of himself or his affiliates. For
this reason, Graham suggests that campaign contributions should
be made by individual families in the community, rather than
by such interest groups.[57]

Procuring Votes

Another method by which syndicated criminals aid the political
machine or politicians is by procuring votes for the candidate.
Al Capone, for example, made a deal with the political machine
in Cicero, Illinois whereby he supplied the votes for the candidates for Mayor, Town Clerk, Town Collector, and Town Attorney, in return for which he received the full protection of the
law. Capone accomplished this simply by having his men intimidate, assault, and terrorize people into staying at home while
those voters favorable toward his candidates were permitted to
cast their ballots.[58]

Particularly functional to delivering votes is the system of
politics generally referred to as machine politics or the boss
system. As Sait observes, such terms as *boss* or *machine* which
bear negative connotations, are often used by one partisan
organization when referring to another.[59] In the literature, the
boss or machine system has been both praised and condemned;
praised for promoting citizen awareness and participation in
political activity; condemned for facilitating corruption via
patronage.

Whether called the boss system or political machine, the system refers to a political party organization, which in the United States has both a Republican and Democratic counterpart. The organization may have minor variations from locale to locale and may often be called by a specific title. Only "Tammany Hall" has the special status of serving both as a synonym for "political machine," and as the title for the executive committee organization of the Democratic party organization in Manhattan, New York.[60]

The major purpose of the boss or machine system is to obtain and control votes, especially those cast in the primary elections. In municipal governments machines function only where ward divisions and representation exist. In order to deliver votes within each ward, a structure is set up. This structure varies from organization to organization. Basically, it is composed of ward or district leaders, who in turn appoint district captains. These captains elicit the help of workers who are friendly to their party's cause and candidate. Together they work to bring out more voters. The individual power and influence of the district leader and captain lies in his or her ability to deliver votes. In order to produce these votes, however, as Banfield and Wilson state, inducements are generally given.[61] These inducements may be in the form of physical rewards such as gifts sent to helpers at Christmas and Thanksgiving.[62] On the other hand the voter may be promised a job. Often votes may be obtained in exchange for favors. A case of such would be where the district captain uses his influence with a judge who he has helped put into office, to "fix" a case for one of his district voters. For all these favors the district leader or captain expects the beneficiary to vote in the manner which he or she dictates. Obviously the voter feels obligated to do so. Coupled with this feeling of obligation is a practical aspect. The voter views his relationship with the leader as one which ultimately serves to provide him with an avenue for future favors. The district leader in turn views the relationship as one that will benefit him with future votes. In many cases this relationship, as Banfield and Wilson point out, may eventually come to be viewed by both parties as one not based upon a utilitarian need but rather one based on friendship.[63] (The machine also rounds up votes by mere canvassing and electioneering, incidentally.)

It is very easy to see how, in this setting, the syndicated criminal can influence with money and favors the votes of many. He can supply votes, in return for which he receives political favors in the form of protection for his enterprises and immunity from prosecution. Through this avenue of influence he can put into office judges, district attorneys, court clerks, and others who can grant him all the protection he needs.

McKean goes one step further in noting that in some cases the boss of the political machine is himself a member of the organized criminal world.[64] A very interesting illustration of McKean's observation is found in the relationship between ward politics and syndicated crime in Pittsburgh as noted by Ray Sprigle. In a series of newspaper articles written in 1950, Sprigle maintained that the numbers operations in Pittsburgh were primarily under the control of ward chairmen themselves.[65] He further argues that the reason no one syndicate has taken over control in the East Liberty section of Pittsburgh is because there are too many wards involved and each chairman guards his territory well.[66] Under the control of the ward chairman, the police, whom the chairman has the power to appoint and promote, are used to raid and perform "protection and enforcement" services. Thus the police themselves are used both to keep the operators of the various enterprises in line and to keep out competition.[67]

The boss system is rapidly disappearing in the United States.[68] However, as we shall show in Chapter 5, it has played a vital role in the past development of syndicated crime. Much of the contemporary relationship between syndicated crime and politics takes the form of direct contributions to election campaigns. However, in those areas where the machine continues to exist, the syndicate functionary continues to produce votes in return for protection. He no longer uses street gangs to muscle his votes as he did in former times.[69] Today his means of persuasion are those of finance rather than force. The end result, however, is still the same.

The Police

Because police forces are the agencies most likely to come into direct contact with the enterprises of syndicated crime, they become important objects of syndicate bribery. In those cases where they are directly under the control of a political official there is no absolute need to bribe police officers; however, even under this arrangement they often give some form of remuneration to avoid possible discontentment.

The type of bribery taken by police may vary. Thus, as Carlson shows, in the numbers establishments in Detroit, police would put in a numbers slip; if the number hit they would come to collect; however, if it did not hit they never bothered to pay.[70] This served as their bribe. In other cases, police may receive a stipulated amount per week or month. Where there is a connection between the syndicate and a political machine, the police may be bribed by receiving a promotion via the efforts of a ward leader. The 1966 investigation of organized crime in Rochester, New York indicated that this was a widely used technique of police bribery.[71] One can see that this technique of promotion serves to benefit the syndicate criminal in two ways. First it provides the means of bribing the police officer. But more important, it provides the syndicated criminal with a means of placing the officer into a more powerful, and therefore more useful, position.

It is true that by comparison to the number of dishonest policemen there are far more who are honest. However, so far as syndicated crime is concerned, it is neither desirable nor necessary to bribe every policeman on the force. So long as the syndicate can reach certain key positions in the hierarchy of the police force, such as those of captain or inspector, they have the medium by which they can control large segments of the force. With control of such key positions, if an officer begins reporting syndicate activities it is very easy for his superior to divert both attention and action regarding these reports. Should the officer continue to create problems in this respect, he can easily be transferred to another area of service or to another area of the city.

A very common form of bribery to police and political officials is giving gifts, particularly at holidays.[72] When collected from several sources these gifts can amount to a very lucrative payment. Christmas appears to be one of the most bribe-giving seasons of the year. Matthews, a syndicate participant in Philadelphia, refers to this season as "envelope time,"[73] noting this was the time of year when a mass of envelopes containing money were delivered to politicians. As one informant related to the author, "It was disgusting as a child to watch at Christmas time the number of policemen and other people who came to my uncle's house for their take. What really got me was the way they would smile and hold out their hand."

The extreme of the relationships between police and syndicated crime is found in the cases where the police actually participate in criminal activities. Matthews cites cases where police served as chauffeurs at gambling establishments as off-duty jobs.[74] Hughes tells of a policeman who stole liquor during raids and then resold it in his own nightclub.[75] In a Buffalo investigation, evidence showed that a policeman was a bookie and his area of operation was the Police Department Headquarters.[76]

The Courts

Along with politicians and police another area of bribery involves the court system. Bailiffs, court clerks, and other attachés of the court may become subjects of bribes when their services are needed. It goes without saying that judges are an important source of bribery. As Borkin[77] illustrates, a bribed judge will alter justice as well as the length and severity of sentences.

Juries, particularly in trials of important syndicate figures, become potential subjects of bribery. In Chicago two jurors in the trial of underworld figures Dion O'Banion and Dan McCarthy were offered $50,000.[78] Many other cases are found in the literature. Currently, in cases involving important syndicated criminals, extreme care is taken by the prosecution to prevent such bribery attempts. A juror who served recently on one such case in Boston, told the author that during this trial he and the other jurors slept in the courthouse and never left it except when they were taken out as a group for meals. (However, it should be added that sequestering jurors is also to protect the accused from being tried by juries influenced by media coverage of cases.)

Prosecutors and district attorneys by the nature of their positions also are bribery subjects and we need not elaborate as to why. Probation and parole officers can perform services for syndicated criminals that include not reporting probation or parole violations. Also they can write positive presentence reports that may help shorten prison or jail sentence or, better still, result in probation instead of imprisonment. Finally there are those constant allegations of tie-ups between legislatures and syndicated crime.[79] There are also those instances where athletes are corrupted by bribes,[80] but this type of bribery is not related to protection.

The continuum of bribery, then, spans all types of individuals including, as Chamberlain states, "politicians, bailiffs, jail guards, clerks, and other attachés of courts, sheriff's offices and others."[81]

Summary

This chapter has focused attention upon the social nature of syndicated crime, showing that its essence lies in the interaction between three functionaries; the client, the syndicate criminal, and the corrupted public official. Thus syndicated crime in the United States is a social system that, as Sellin observes, develops characteristics which are in many respects comparable to many of our legal business structures.[82] It is of little value, then, to place blame upon only one segment of the system, the criminals; rather to better understand the system, it should be viewed as an interacting functional unit. The syndicated criminal is essential to this system since his role involves the creation and performance of the necessary activities in providing the commodities and services. It is with the explanation and analysis of this functionary then—the syndicated criminal—that the remainder of this book is concerned.

Let us begin first then by asking a question most vital to the understanding of his contemporary existence in American society —where did he come from?

References

1 Temporary Commission of Investigation of the State of New York, *Summary of the Activities During* 1963, March, 1964, p. 31.

2 Geo. London, *Deux Mois avec les Bandits de Chicago* (Paris: Editions des Portiques, 1930), p. 11.

3 Ted Poston, "The Numbers Racket," in *Organized Crime in America,* ed. by Gus Tyler (Ann Arbor: The University of Michigan Press, 1962), p. 261.

4 Courteny Cooper, *Here's to Crime* (Boston: Little, Brown and Co., 1937), p. 62.

5 John Barron Mays, *Crime and the Social Structure* (London: Faber and Faber, Ltd., 1963), p. 73.

6 "Runners Haul Liquor Across Frozen River," *The Detroit News,* February 12, 1930, p. 1.

7 John H. Wuorinen, *The Prohibition Experiment in Finland* (New York: Columbia University Press, 1931), p. 124.

8 Rheta Childe Dorr, "The Other Prohibition Country," *Harper's,* September, 1929, p. 498.

9 "Prohibition Produces a New Crop of Vikings in Norway," *The Literary Digest,* September 18, 1920, p. 69.

10 Kulamarva Balakrishna, *A Portrait of Bombay's Underworld* (Bombay: P. C. Manaktala and Sons Private, Ltd., 1966), p. 49.

11 Edwin M. Schur, *Crimes Without Victims* (Englewood Cliffs: Prentice-Hall, 1965), p. 134.

12 Stephen Cain, "Youngsters Taking LSD Trips Tax Treatment Centers Here," *The Detroit News,* December 8, 1968, p. 14.

13 Schur, *op. cit.,* pp. 140–145.

14 St. Clair Drake and Horace Cayton, *Black Metropolis* (New York: Harcourt, Brace and Company, 1945), p. 470.

15 Gustav G. Carlson, "Number Gambling: A Study of a Culture Complex," (unpublished Ph.D. dissertation, University of Michigan, 1940).

16 C. Eric Lincoln, "On the Black Muslims," in *The Sociological Perspective*, ed. by Scott G. McNall (Boston: Little, Brown and Co., 1968), p. 312.

17 G. Carlson, *op. cit.*, p. 1.

18 Robert P. Morris, "An Exploratory Study of Some Personality Characteristics of Gamblers," *Journal of Clinical Psychology*, XIII (January, 1957), 191–193.

19 Edmund Bergler, *The Psychology of Gambling* (New York: Hill and Wang, 1957), Chapter 9.

20 Herbert A. Bloch, "The Sociology of Gambling," *The American Journal of Sociology*, LVII (November, 1951), 215, 216.

21 Robert F. Kennedy, "The Baleful Influence of Gambling," *The Atlantic*, April, 1962, p. 76.

22 Bloch, *op. cit.*

23 John A. Gardiner, "Public Attitudes Toward Gambling and Corruption," *The Annals*, CCCLXXIV (November, 1967), 125–127.

24 U.S. Congress, Senate, Hearings before a Special Committee to Investigate Organized Crime in Interstate Commerce, *Investigation of Organized Crime in Interstate Commerce*, S. Res. 202, Pt. 1, 81st Cong., 2d sess., 1950, p. 187.

25 Arthur M. Murphy, "Small-Loan Usury," *Crime for Profit*, ed. by Ernest D. MacDougall (Boston: The Stratford Co., 1933), p. 209.

26 William J. Duffy, "Organized Crime—Illegal Activities," in *Law Enforcement Science and Technology* (Washington, D.C.: Thompson Book Co., 1967), pp. 29–30.

27 Nicholas Pileggi, "The Mafia is Good for You," *The Saturday Evening Post*, November 30, 1968, p. 18.

28 Donald R. Cressey, "Organized Crime as a Social System," in *Law Enforcement Science and Technology*, p. 5.

29 "Gamblers Evade Ban in Singapore," *The New York Times*, January 5, 1968, p. 6C.

30 "Japan: The Way of Chivalry," *Newsweek*, September 14, 1964, p. 42.

31 Max Vanzi, "Tokyo Gangster Describes His Work, Philosophy," *Columbus Dispatch*, December 10, 1967, p. 27B.

32 Balakrishna, *op. cit.*, Chapter Two; p. 15.

33 Thomas C. Schelling, "Economics and the Underworld of Crime," in *Law Enforcement Science and Technology*, p. 38.

34 Earl Johnson, Jr., "Organized Crime: Challenge to the American Legal System," *Journal of Criminal Law, Criminology and Police Science*, LIII (December, 1962), p. 402.

35 Walter Lippmann, "The Underworld: Our Secret Servant," *Forum*, January, 1931, p. 3.

36 Ray Sprigle, "Numbers Take $50,000,000 Yearly in City," *Pittsburgh Post-Gazette*, July 10, 1950, p. 1.

37 Pileggi, *op. cit.*, p. 18.

38 David Loth, *Public Plunder* (New York: Carrick and Evans, Inc., 1938), p. 348.

39 Carlson, *op. cit.*, pp. 65–66.

40 James D. Horan, *The Mob's Man* (New York: Crown Publishers, Inc., 1959), p. 143.

41 Robert S. Allen, ed., *Our Fair City* (New York: The Vanguard Press, Inc., 1947), p. 12.

42 Morton Mockridge and Robert H. Prall, *The Big Fix* (New York: Henry Holt and Co., 1954), p. 130.

43 Commonwealth of Massachusetts, Senate, *Report of the Special Commission Revived and Continued for the Purpose of Investigating Organized Crime and Other Related Matters*, April, 1957, pp. 136–137.

44 Richard A. Schermerhorn, *Society and Power* (New York: Random House, 1961), pp. 36–39.

45 Burton B. Turkus and Sid Feder, *Murder, Inc.*, Permabooks (New York: Garden City, 1952), pp. 112–115.

46 Stanton A. Coblentz, *Villains and Vigilantes* (New York: Thomas Yoseloff, Inc., 1936), pp. 203–205.

47 A. Lawrence Lowell, *Public Opinion and Popular Government* (New York: Longman's, Green and Co., 1913), pp. 60–64.

48 Rupert Hughes, *The Story of Thomas E. Dewey* (New York: Grosset and Dunlap, 1944), p. 24.

49 Wallace Turner, *Gambler's Money*, Signet Books (New York: The New American Library, 1966), p. 14.

50 Virgil W. Peterson, *Barbarians in Our Midst* (Boston: Little, Brown and Co., 1952), p. 137.

51 Ed Reid, *The Shame of New York* (New York: Random House, 1953), p. 75.

52 Drew Pearson, "Racketeer Details His Aid to Nixon," *The Free Press* (Detroit), October 31, 1968, p. 19A.

53 Sandy Smith, "You Can't Expect Police on the Take to Take Orders," *Life*, December 6, 1968, pp. 40–42.

54 Philip L. Graham, "High Cost of Politics," *National Municipal Review*, XLIV (July, 1955), 348.

55 Ferdinand Lundberg, *The Rich and the Super-Rich* (New York: Bantam Books, Inc., 1969), p. 17.

56 David Lowe, *Ku Klux Klan: The Invisible Empire* (New York: W. W. Norton and Co., Inc., 1967), p. 65.

57 Graham, *op. cit.*, pp. 346–351.

58 Fred D. Pasley, *Al Capone* (New York: Garden City Publishing Co., 1930), pp. 37–39.

59 Edward McChesney Sait, "Machine, Political," *Encyclopedia of the Social Sciences*, IX, p. 657.

60 Justin N. Feldman, "How Tammany Holds Power," *National Municipal Review*, XXXIX (July, 1950), 330.

61 Edward C. Banfield and James Q. Wilson, *City Politics* (Cambridge: Harvard and the M.I.T. Press, 1963), p. 115.

62 *Ibid.*, p. 117.

63 *Ibid.*, p. 118.

64 Dayton D. McKean, "Who Gets the Billion Graft," *National Municipal Review*, XXXVII (December, 1949), 547.

65 Ray Sprigle, "Roll Call of Democratic Chairmen in Racket Wards Shows Good Jobs Go Hand-in-Hand with Vote Power," *Pittsburgh Post-Gazette*, August 5, 1950, p. 1.

66 Ray Sprigle, "East End 'Fix' Gives Numbers Mobs Free Rein," *Pittsburgh Post-Gazette*, July 12, 1950, p. 1.

67 Ray Sprigle, "It Isn't the Original Cost, It's the Cops' Upkeep That Keeps the Poor Racketeer 'Broke'," *Pittsburgh Post-Gazette*, August 4, 1950, p. 1.

68 Edward C. Banfield, *Urban Government* (New York: The Free Press of Glencoe, 1961), p. 132.

69 Brewster Adams, "The Street Gang as a Factor in Politics," *The Outlook*, August 22, 1903, pp. 985–988.

70 Carlson, *op. cit.*, p. 67.

71 State of New York Commission of Investigation, *Report of an Investigation of Certain Organized Crime Activities and Problems in Law Enforcement*, New York, September, 1966, pp. 52–59.

72 William Foote Whyte, *Street-Corner Society* (Chicago: The University of Chicago Press, 1965), p. 124.

73 John D. Matthews, *My Name Is Violence* (New York: Belmont Books, 1962), p. 51.

74 *Ibid.*, p. 86.

75 R. Hughes, *op. cit.*, p. 24.

76 New York State Commission of Investigation, *An Investigation of Law Enforcement in Buffalo*, New York, January, 1961, p. 85.

77 Joseph Borkin, *The Corrupt Judge* (New York: Clarkson N. Potter, Inc., 1962).

78 James O'Donnell Bennett, *Chicago Gangland* (Chicago: Tribune Publications, No. 35, 1929), p. 50.

79 Walter H. Waggoner, "Jersey Jury Inquiry Asked on Mafia-Legislator Links," *The New York Times*, December 18, 1968, p. 1.

80 John L. McClellan, *Crime Without Punishment* (New York: Popular Library, 1963), pp. 210–212.

81 Henry Barrett Chamberlain, "Some Observations Concerning Organized Crime," *Journal of Criminal Law and Criminology*, XXII (January, 1932), 654.

82 Thorsten Sellin, "Organized Crime: A Business Enterprise," *The Annals*, CCCXLVII (May, 1963), 13.

4

The Mafia and the Camorra: Prelude to the Analysis of American Syndicated Crime

One can scarcely pick up a newspaper, turn the page of a magazine, or listen to the daily news without soon coming across the word *mafia*. Despite constant exposure to the term, there are few who can give a logically consistent, reasonably lucid definition or interpretation of what the term stands for. In an effort to define it individuals often describe it simply as a group of gangsters. Others view it as an Italian organization which runs all types of rackets and practices a code of secrecy. Yet when asked the basis of their information, the bearers of these beliefs offer either "the newspaper" or what they "have heard about it" as their sources of information. Some recall the hearings they watched on television many years ago. The image here is one of sinister-looking gangsters who sat next to their lawyers and answered each question with the phrase "I refuse to answer on the grounds that it may incriminate me."

In these expressions lies the American public's conception of "Mafia." It is a credible enough conception to assure the average American of the "Mafia's" existence yet intangible enough to allow each individual his own interpretation of it. As with most phenomena which are not clearly understood, there are mixed reactions to it. We find those who view "Mafia" as a realistic terror and those who view it as a myth.

It is this very ambiguity about the meaning of "Mafia" which contributes to public apathy so frequently encountered, toward syndicated crime. This is illustrated by the variations of public response to governmental investigations, which reveal both the existence of corruption and its link with syndicate functioning. To corruption itself, the American public has frequently responded by taking some form of action. This action has frequently been either too shortlived or poorly organized to be of lasting benefit.

Corruption was revealed in the study of "Wincanton" (later identified as Reading, Pennsylvania)[1] that appeared in the 1967 *Task Force Report on Organized Crime*,[2] and the voters reacted by ousting the majority Democratic party candidates. In 1967, "Republican candidates were elected for the first time since the 1920s."[3] But Wiebe, in his study of the reactions of 260 New Yorkers to the televised Kefauver Hearings in 1951, revealed the presence of a feeling of "social impotence."[4] In this type of reaction, he notes, concern for the problem became dissipated. Much energy was exerted in talking and other forms of protest. However, none of this resulted in any responsible and effective behavior aimed directly at the solution of the problem.

If this is true of a phenomenon as real as corruption, what type of public reaction can we expect toward something as ephemeral as the "Mafia." We must admit the public's inertia is warranted by the fact that the public isn't exactly sure what "The Mafia" really is. This is no small wonder when we note what the public has been told it is. In reviewing the literature we find that "the Mafia" has been described to the American public as all of the following: an American secret criminal society composed of various ethnic and nationality backgrounds; an American secret criminal society composed exclusively of Italians, which originated in Sicily and was imported to the United States; a Sicilian secret society found only on the Island of Sicily and composed exclusively of Sicilian families who perpetuate it by intermarriage; simply another name for the

Black Hand and *Unione Siciliana*; a new, streamlined American version of the old Sicilian "Mafia," which disappeared; another term for the organization, *Cosa Nostra*; an organization different from and often confused with *Cosa Nostra*; a secret Sicilian criminal society which during the 1920s was completely exterminated by Benito Mussolini; a world-wide organization based in Sicily; and finally, just a legendary creation. On the basis of these descriptions is there any wonder why the American public is troubled yet also confused by this thing called "Mafia?"

Along with these contradictory descriptions we have the continued arguments regarding the very existence of a "Mafia." The report of the Subcommittee on Rackets in 1959 found that it definitely existed in California.[5] A special investigation requested by Governor Edmund G. Brown in 1959, however, found no such evidence.[6] The author of the report, Alvin H. Goldstein, stated that the existence of a "Mafia" was not proven by the law enforcement officials; rather it was merely assumed. These officials used "the Mafia," he argues, to excite popular opinion, receive increased funds, and gain public acceptance of extreme police techniques, which they were employing in their investigations and arrests. The Chief of Police of Los Angeles retorted that the reason Mr. Goldstein didn't find evidence of the "Mafia" was because the police had succeeded in "keeping the organization under cover."[7]

In November of 1963, the Chief of Police of Hamilton, Ontario, when asked if a "Mafia" existed in his city, replied that he saw no evidence of its contemporary existence. However, he admitted the possibility that such an organization may have been present among criminals of Italian extraction during the Prohibition era.[8]

What then is this "Mafia" that is so elusive: it exists yet at the same time does not exist; it is exterminated yet it reappears; it never was exterminated, it was merely kept under cover; it is an American branch of the Sicilian organization; it is found only in Sicily; it has branches throughout the world; its correct name is "Mafia" or is it *Cosa Nostra*; it used to be called *Mano Nera*, later *Unione Siciliana*; no, *Unione Siciliana* was created

by Lucky Luciano in the 1930s; finally, it can be called anything because it is always the same organization, only its name
changes.

The presence of such an array of contradictions, descriptions,
and conclusions results, as we shall show, from the fact that
many authors who have written on this topic have merely accepted rather than proved their own assumptions. They can do
so very easily since they rarely indicate their sources of information. In few other subjects or areas can one find a more confused and less scholarly approach to a topic. The literature in
this area has been primarily the province of journalists and free-
lance writers. Their works are loaded with undocumented statements and internal inconsistencies. Frequently, Italian or Sicilian
terms are taken out of context, in what appears to be an effort
to alter their original meanings to support a given theory.

This is not to say that all these works, particularly those by
some law enforcement officials and journalists, have not been
useful: many are worthy historical and descriptive works. Also,
in criticizing journalistic writings we do not underestimate the
role played by individual journalists in continuously exposing
syndicated criminal activities in various cities.

We should also bear in mind the findings of de Sola Pool and
Shulman concerning newsmen and their audiences; namely, that
audiences as "reference persons" have a powerful influence upon
what and how newswriters write.[9] It is safe to assume that some
journalists, aware of pockets of public belief in a clandestine,
sinister, and secret organization, "Mafia," respond to their read-
ers' beliefs by putting them into print. They lend excitement to
their writings by loading them with lively accounts of emotion-
arousing events. We are often treated to detailed accounts of
events which, by the author's own admission, have taken place
in absolute secrecy. Yet, without being there, the author is
somehow able to give a detailed account of what happened.
Often killings are described in vivid detail. These include quotations of the screaming victim, beaten to death by the hard-
jawed criminal who always has that certain smile that is the
exclusive property of a syndicate torpedo. Judging from these

descriptions one cannot help but believe that newspapermen are constantly crawling in bushes, hanging around areas where "gangland-style killings" frequently occur, or positioning themselves upon the roofs of syndicate members' cars, in anticipation of the killing or meeting which they are about to witness. The cause-effect relationships suggested by these writers are enough to turn rationalists like David Hume and John Stuart Mill in their graves.

As stated in Chapter 1, these writings serve to help rather than hinder syndicates. They allow those who are thrilled by a belief in that which is sinister and conspiratorial to reinforce their beliefs. Through these writings the general public is presented with a picture of a secretive, all-powerful criminal organization under whose influence anyone can fall if he is not constantly on his guard.

It is within the confines of such confusing, largely undocumented, and oversimplified analyses that the term "Mafia" has significance. As we shall illustrate, there is little evidence to warrant belief in the existence of a "Mafia" in the United States. Nor do we find the existence of a centralized, well-defined organization of "Mafia" even in Sicily.

Our immediate basis for taking this stand is that there is little relationship between the term "mafia" and the large variety of criminal organizations that have been given that name both in Sicily and the United States. The term "mafia," in both Italian and American historical as well as contemporary writings has been used to describe so many differently structured criminal organizations that the term is virtually meaningless. It should soon become evident that the existence of "Mafia" simply indicates whether or not the criminal group being referred to in the literature is given the title "Mafia." On the basis of such usage, then, it should not be surprising that today the concept "Mafia" means nothing more than the sum total of the confusing definitions given it by individual writers.

The term "Mafia" like the term "organized crime" suffers from inconsistencies in meaning and usage. As is true of the continuum of characteristics found in organized crime, so too those organizations which have been labeled "Mafia" display characteristics too varied to allow their inclusion under one typology.

Writers have frequently isolated certain characteristics such as secrecy or the practice of not giving information to the police. Without recognizing the practice of these by criminal groups other than "the Mafia," they have made these the basic criterion of differentiation.

In its broadest sense, the term "Mafia" has become a synonym for any secret, bureaucratically structured, criminal organization. This interpretation of "Mafia," in itself, would not be incorrect if instead of designating a secret criminal organization, the term would be used to refer to a particular modus operandi employed by various criminal groups. As we shall show in this and the following chapter, there are and have been many *Mafias* or if one uses the plural of *Mafia* in the Italian, *Mafie*. Here we are equating *Mafia* with a method of operation in which a group or organization participates in illicit activity in any society by (1) the use of force, intimidation or threats of such; (2) the structuring of a group or organization whose purpose is that of providing illicit services through the use of secrecy on the part of its associates; (3) and the assurance of the protection of the legal structure necessary to its operation.

On the basis of this conception we will argue that there are many *Mafie* in Sicily, the United States, and elsewhere; noting of course that we are here not referring to the name of a criminal organization, but rather to a method or type of operation which can be practiced by a variety of criminal groups. In this context the *Dadas* of India[10] and the Chinese "Tongs"[11] in the United States, as we shall see, are examples of *Mafias*.

Much of the confusion about "the Mafia" in Sicily has arisen from the unfounded belief that this organization consists of one centralized national organization having one supreme leader who directs its activities. This is also true of the beliefs about "Mafia" in the United States. Barring variations found in different writings, "the Mafia" here is also defined as a national organization with centralization and power in the hands of some kind of ruling "council." Both "Mafias," the Sicilian and the American, we are told, have some form of connection with one another. The degree and type of connection depends upon the particular writer's conception. Some argue that the Sicilian "Mafia" merely spawned the American one, while others contend that the American "Mafia" is a branch of the Sicilian, directed by its leader in Sicily.

Mafia in Sicily

In order to clarify this confusion, it is necessary to first examine what "Mafia" means within the context of Sicilian society itself. Only then can we evaluate the nature of its influence upon American syndicated crime.

We begin our discussion of *mafia* in Sicily by noting what will emerge as our conclusion: that *mafia* in Sicily is generic to the nature and development of Sicilian society itself. Its development, as Hobsbawm notes, can be understood only as a result of the social movements which brought it about; movements which, as he states, were more reformist in orientation than revolutionary.[12] Such a movement orientation helps place the development of *mafia* in Sicily into a proper context for our discussion in that it immediately locates the source of its origins —the social and economic conditions of the country and the historical development of the structure of Sicilian society. Because of the variation in what has been called "Mafia" in Sicily, its definition as a social movement becomes somewhat complex.

In this writer's conception, what constitutes *mafia* in Sicily did not emerge until after unification in 1860. It was, in fact, the universal suffrage instituted by this unification which allowed *mafias* to emerge, by virtue of the fact that the role of "vote-procurer" made their development possible. Prior to 1860, as will become more clear as one reads this chapter, various organizations referred to as "the Mafia" were not that at all. Their classification as such results simply from a lack of consistent usage of the term. Thus, it would be difficult to argue that these various organizations referred to as "Mafia" had what

Heberle refers to as "constitutive ideas" or the goals and strategy of a social movement.[13] Given the problems encountered in defining what constitutes a social movement, any attempt to classify *mafia* as such a movement necessitates an evaluation of what have been defined as "Mafia-like" organizations at different points in Sicilian history.

Accepting the fact that social movements include those which use both legitimate and illegitimate methods of achieving their goals, this in itself presents difficulties in categorizing as social movements the goals and activities of the many groups which have been called "Mafia" irrespective of their variation in structure, location, and time. Our objective here is not to argue whether *mafia* can or cannot be classified as a social movement. Rather, our desire is that of calling attention to the fact that any attempt at such classification must first define what groups, goals, and activities are being described as *mafia*. We hope that the distinctions we offer in the remainder of this chapter will be of some benefit in this regard.

Perhaps the proper method of beginning a discussion of what constitutes *mafia* in Sicily is to do so by first refuting those popularly held yet historically unsupportable beliefs concerning the origin of *mafia*.

One of the most popular conceptions of the Sicilian "Mafia" is that it consists of an organization that began as a beneficial organization that later turned into a criminal society that sought only to exploit the populace. It seems logical at the outset that even if this were true, the organization, when it so drastically changed, would not, in terms of its goals or activities, have been the identical organization. Without appealing to logic, however, we find that the reason for this belief in a humanitarian-oriented "Mafia" lies in the synonymous use of "Mafia" with associations called *Fratellanze* or "brotherhoods." These *Fratellanze* functioned as quasi-vigilante and quasi-criminal groups depending upon whether one wishes to employ a strictly legalistic definition or a social-normative definition of crime and criminal groups. Having introduced these we postpone a detailed description of their goals and structure until later so that we may continue our examination of the popular theories which view "Mafia" as a benevolent organization turned criminal.

Genesis of the Term "Mafia"

Many of the theories regarding the origin of "Mafia" attempt to locate the genesis in the term itself. Among these theories we note those cited by Renato Candida:[14] that the term "Mafia" may perhaps be derived from the Tuscan word *Maffia* meaning "misery"; that it may be a derivative from the French word *mauvais* meaning "bad"; that it may have come from the Arabic tribe *Ma-afir* which was located in Palermo during the time of the Arab conquest of Sicily; that the word is derived from the name of a place in the province of Trapani where the Mafiusi (those belonging to the Mafia) and Carbonari (a secret political society) held their meetings; that the term comes from the initials M.A.F.I.A. for the name of a secret society originating with Giuseppe Mazzini—these initials being derived from the motto *Mazzini Autorizza Furti Incendi Avvelenamenti* (Mazzini authorizes thefts, arsons, and poisonings).

Candida himself suggests that the word comes from the Arab word *mu'afàh*. This he states is derived from the root *mu'* which means "health," "strength," "well-being," or "sturdiness" and from the verb *afàh* which means "to guard from" or "to protect." He further suggests that the word may have been derived from the noun *mu'afàh* which means "protection," "safety," and "guardianship."[15]

Brean believes that in the ninth century a Sicilian organization came into existence whose specific purpose was that of fighting the Arab conquerors. Later this organization became known as "Mafia"; the name possibly coming from "the Arabic phrase 'Mu'afy' roughly translated as 'protect us from death in the night'."[16]

Gaetano Mosca notes that the word "Mafia" is not found in Italian writings prior to the nineteenth century. Traina's dic-

tionary, published in 1868, defines it as a "neologism denoting
any sign of bravado, a bold show"; Mortillaro's dictionary of
1876 designates it as a "word of Piedmontese origin equivalent
to gang (*camorra*)."[17] This latter term, *Camorra*, as we shall
see, refers to a Neopolitan criminal association and in common usage among Italians has become a synonym for graft, gang,
or organized criminality. One source argues that "Mafia" came
from the Arabic word *maha* meaning "stone cave."[18]

Lewis maintains that the term "Mafia" may derive from the
"identical word in Arabic," meaning " 'place of refuge'."[19] Unfortunately Lewis doesn't explain what he means by "identical
word in Arabic." Consultation with sources knowledgeable in
Middle Eastern languages failed to reveal an Arabic word spelled
"Mafia." Perhaps Lewis is referring to a colloquial usage.

There are many Arabic terms which could be offered as possible derivations, the following among several suggested by the
above-mentioned sources of consultation: *marfa'*, which translates contemporarily as "a place of refuge" or "harbor" (this
possibly may be the word Lewis is referring to, however, if
such is the case one can readily see that it is not identical to
"Mafia") ; *ma fi'at* translated liberally as "a place of shade" has
also been suggested.

Maehfal, meaning "a gathering" or "a place of gathering,"
was offered as another possible derivation by a consultant source
who is an authority in the Italian language. Finally an Italian
writer, Cesare Bruno,[20] mentions another source, the Arabic
term *mahias*, which translates into *spaccone*, an Italian word
meaning a braggart or boaster.

In deriving words from Arabic, one must bear in mind that
in this language as is true of others, the social context in which
the word is used largely influences its meaning. Thus the same
word can vary both with time and place. This makes the study
of the derivation of "Mafia" from Arabic origins extremely
difficult. Also, when we consider the fact that the Sicilian language contains many dialects that include words derived from
the languages of its past conquerors[21]—the French, Normans,
Germans, Spaniards and many others—any attempt at such
derivation appears futile.

Melville Post's theory that the name "Mafia" came from a racetrack located near Trapani[22] lacks any historical foundation and is here mentioned only as an example of the extreme in derivation attempts.

Extremely interesting are the popularized accounts of the origin of "Mafia," particularly those where legend has become accepted as fact. These are important in view of the fact that this acceptance of legend as fact has aided in perpetuating, if not creating, the contemporary confusion concerning "Mafia." This is especially true regarding the conception of "Mafia" as a benevolent organization which went astray.

Legend of the Sicilian Vespers

One of the more popular legends in this regard is that stated by Reid;[23] one generally referred to as the Legend of the Sicilian Vespers. According to Reid, who doesn't give us the source of the legend, the incident giving rise to "Mafia" occurred during the Sicilian Vespers. The latter is the name given to the revolution in which the Sicilians rose against the occupying French forces on March 30, 1282. As Reid's legend has it, a young lad and his girlfriend had gone to church alone to be married. Leaving the girl outside the church the boy went to seek the priest. Soon a drunken French officer appeared, pulled the girl to a nearby shelter and assaulted her. She tried to escape, but tripped and fell, her skull smashing against the church wall. The young boy, upon returning and seeing his sweetheart dead yelled "Morte Alla Francia" meaning "Death to all the French." The news of the event spread and thousands of Sicilians took up the boy's cry, adding to it the words "Italia Anela." Soon this cry became a slogan—"Morte Alla Francia Italia Anela," or "Death to the French is Italy's Cry." Later, when the French retaliated, Reid continues, the Sicilians formed a "secret organization to fight back and its password was 'Mafia' made up of the initial letters of words in the tragic death cry."

Reid evidently takes his legend as fact, because without offering any other source of origin, he goes on to tell us that for
many years this secret organization "aided the poor and down-
trodden stretching out its hand as a savior to practically the
whole population of Sicily." After the unification of Sicily in
1860, however, Reid finds that these very "Mafiosi turned on
their own people," committing "extortion, murder and arson
against all classes."[24] How or why this organization so abruptly
changed Reid never explains.

There are many aspects of Reid's account that should be re-
viewed critically, particularly since this is one of the accounts
that has become popularly accepted as fact rather than legend.
First, in an effort to separate fact from fiction, let us examine
various historical accounts of the Sicilian Vespers. These detailed accounts are given to show that lack of agreement exists
even within the historical accounts themselves. These narratives
will also serve as a basis of evaluating the historical validity of
this legendary development of "Mafia."

According to Crawford, the Vespers occurred as a result of a
French captain named Drouet who ordered his men to search
various Sicilians who were leisurely strolling along one of the
roads leading out of Palermo. Soon Drouet himself, in a very
vulgar manner, searched the young wife of a Sicilian. Outraged,
this husband yelled, "Now let these Frenchmen die at last!"
and the revolution began. As the bells of the churches of San
Giovanni and the Holy Ghost were ringing for evening vespers,
the Sicilians, armed with knives, sticks, and stones were un-
mercifully slaughtering the French.[25] Crawford is of the opinion
that some kind of plans and preparations for a revolt against
the French were being made prior to the occurrence of the
Vespers themselves.[26]

The account in *Chamber's Encyclopedia* parallels Crawford's,
except that this version indicates that the revolt was planned
and that the signal to begin was to be "the first stroke of the
vesper bell."[27]

In his very comprehensive and scholarly work on the Sicilian
Vespers, Runciman states that on Easter Monday, March 30,
1282, as was the custom, a festival was held at the church of

the Holy Spirit. This brought together a crowd of people who came from Palermo itself as well as from many surrounding villages. The entire holy week, although it was celebrated with the traditional dancing and singing, was characterized by an atmosphere which was "tense and explosive." As evening approached on Easter Monday, the crowd outside the church awaited the beginning of the Vesper service, passing the time away by singing and talking. Into the crowd came some French officers who, despite their receiving inhospitable reactions from the crowd, began making advances toward the young girls. Among them, a sergeant, named Drouet, "dragged a young married woman from the crowd and pestered her with his attention." Her husband, viewing this, drew his knife and stabbed Drouet to death. Drouet's comrades rushed to his defense, an action to which the Sicilians responded by attacking the French officials. As this occurred the bell of the church of the Holy Spirit and the other churches of Palermo began ringing for the Vespers. As these bells were ringing, messengers ran through Palermo's streets yelling to the men to rise up and kill the French. Soon the streets were filled with men armed and crying out " 'Death to the French'—'moranu li Franchiski' in their Sicilian dialect." A mass slaughter followed in which neither Frenchmen, Frenchwomen nor children were spared. The Sicilians went into taverns, houses and even the "Dominican and Franciscan convents" where "all the foreign friars were dragged out and told to pronounce the word 'ciciri,' whose sound the French tongue could not accurately reproduce." Those who could not pronounce this word were killed.[28]

Runciman disagrees with those who hold the viewpoint that the Vespers occurred spontaneously.[29] Instead, he concludes that, although the complete accuracy of what really occurred and why is difficult to ascertain, his historical appraisal of the evidence leads him to believe that the uprising was planned.[30] We should note also that this uprising was not confined to the city of Palermo alone, but spread to the cities of Corleone, Trapani, Caltanisetta and many others.[31]

The disagreements in these historical accounts should stress the fact that even here there is confusion as to exactly why and

how the Sicilian Vespers occurred. We bear this in mind in
continuing our evaluation of the "Sicilian Vespers" theory of
the origin of the "Mafia."

Reid's oversimplified historical account gives no attention to
the political and other struggles which followed the Sicilian
Vespers. Instead Reid leaps over this vast span of history with
the mere statement that during this time a secret organization
was formed to fight the French and its password became "Mafia."

One of the arguments we offer in refutation of this theory is
that during the period immediately following the Sicilian Vespers, there was no need to form a secret society in order to fight
the French oppressors. Any Sicilian who desired to fight the
French could do so openly without need to resort to secrecy.
King Peter of Aragon, the king of Sicily as elected by the
nobles of Palermo, had "called out every fighting man in Sicily
above fifteen and under sixty years of age"[32] to help in the
fight against King Charles. This is not to say that it is impossible that such a society would have formed. However, it seems
unfounded to argue the need for its formation at a time when
the Sicilian Vespers had been successful. The argument is further weakened when we consider the fact that the organized
resistance which followed the Vespers resulted in the virtual
extermination of the French across the island.[33]

On the basis of this, we do not understand what Reid means
when he states that after the Sicilian Vespers "retribution came
in the form of well-armed French soldiers" which he maintains
spawned the organization "Mafia."[34] In this author's opinion
Reid's statement is historically unfounded in view of the fact
that, after the Vespers, it was the French forces of King Charles
who continued to be the victims of defeat and not the Sicilians.

The continuous defeats of the French forces are noted by
Runciman. On April 8, 1282, when vice-admiral Matthew of
Salerno was ordered by King Charles to attack Palermo, two
of his four galleys were captured by Messinese ships that had
come to Palermo's defense after Messina's revolt against the
French. Later in July of 1282, King Charles himself commanded
his army into the vineyards located just to the north of Messina.
Here again after trying the techniques of compromise with the

people of Messina by promising wide reforms if they surren-
dered he finally had to resort to attacking Messina. Still later
he was forced to add a naval blockade which he hoped would
starve the Messinese out. The Messinese, blessed with a good
crop of fruit and vegetables, again held off repeated attacks. On
September 2, 1282, King Peter of Aragon, the newly elected
King of Sicily, arrived in Palermo and from that point on the
"rebellion" was "a European War." The final outcome of this
war was settled not by the Sicilians themselves but was to be
decided by a duel between King Peter and King Charles. It was
agreed that the victor in the combat would assume possession
of Sicily. Since Charles was much older than Peter it was decided not to have a single combat but instead to have Peter and
Charles each select one hundred of their best knights whose
battle would decide the victor. On June 1, 1283, the two groups
of knights and their respective kings met in Bordeaux, France,
the site selected for the battle. As Runciman notes, neither
Charles nor Peter had any intention of fighting. They merely
wanted to save face. Since no one had stipulated what hour the
battle was to commence, this was easily accomplished. Peter,
arriving first at the place of battle, announced his presence and
claimed victory since his opponent had failed to meet him.
Charles, arriving later did the same thing, each accusing the
other of having been the coward.[35]

Rather than suffering defeat and the retribution from the
French as Reid maintains, the Sicilian Vespers represented a
great victory for the Sicilians. This was followed by the successful resistance of Charles of Anjou's armies. Even when French
forces attacked again in 1298, followed by a series of other
attacks which lasted until May of 1302, each of these met with
successful resistance from the Sicilians. Finally, in August, 1302,
through the Treaty of Caltabellota, Sicily received its independence.[36] This period of independence lasted about one
hundred years. Reid's contention that the Sicilians suffered
retribution from the French after the Vespers, necessitating the
rise of "Mafia" seems to be without justifiable motivation and
without historical foundation. Also, for the sake of argument,
if an organization "Mafia" did in fact emerge after the Vespers,

we should like to know why it would not have disappeared
after 1302, when for 100 years Sicily was an independent state
and therefore had no need for a secret society to fight foreign
oppressors.

Coupled with this lack of historical support for Reid's theory,
his version of the legend does not stand the test of plausibility
within the realm of legend itself. We should expect, if this
legend were among the more commonly known, to find it in
the definitive writings of Giuseppe Pitré. His authoritative
twenty-five volume work on Sicilian legend, tradition, and folk-
lore is universally recognized as the definitive work in this area.
Its content, as Whyte illustrates, is as useful today as it was
when it was written at the turn of the century.[37] In a section
dealing with legends specifically concerning the "Sicilian Vespers," Pitré[38] cites eighteen, none of which includes the one
reported by Reid. In none of these is there mention of the use
of the phrase, "Morte Alla Francia Italia Anela" (death to
the French is Italy's cry) whose initials Reid tells us form the
password "Mafia."

The lack of inclusion of Reid's legend in Pitré's work is not a
complete argument against its acceptability, since Reid may
have obtained it from a more colloquial source. However, even
in this assumption we encounter problems in that the use of
"Italia Anela" in the cry is historically and logically inconsistent.

There appears to be no reason why the Sicilian rioters in 1282
would have employed the word *Italia* or "Italy" to refer to an
event which was specifically Sicilian. Historically there is no
evidence that Sicilians have ever viewed themselves as Italians.
In any event, they did not in 1282. As a political unit Sicily did
not officially become a part of Italy until the Unification of
Italy in 1860. Separatist movements were common in the period
prior to this unification.[39] Maxwell finds them in existence as
late as the period following the Allied occupation in 1943.[40]
The height of this sentiment was expressed by the Sicilian outlaw, Salvatore Giuliano, when he wrote to President Harry S.
Truman in 1947 requesting that Sicily be annexed as the forty-
ninth state of America.[41]

There is no reason then why the Sicilians, particularly in 1282, should or would have referred to themselves as Italians. Hence the inclusion of the words "Italia Anela" in the Sicilians' cry in Reid's legend seems totally inconsistent. As we recall in the historical accounts of the Sicilian Vespers related in the previous pages, the only cry was, as Runciman stated, *Moranu li Franchiski*—"death to the French" or as Crawford related, "now let these Frenchmen die at last." Never do we find the addition *Italia Anela*—"Italy's Cry."

Also, as an expert on the Italian language pointed out to the author, the grammatical style and structure employed in this slogan is too modern for any Italian used during the time of the Vespers, particularly in Sicily.

Finally, an addition to the above argument would be the consideration of the following question: if the Sicilians in 1282 used the phrase "Italia Anela" because they, in fact, considered themselves to be a part of Italy, why were the Vespers themselves not referred to as the "Italian Vespers" instead of the "Sicilian Vespers?"

Mazzini's Organization

A second popular account of the origin of "Mafia" traces it to a secret society created by Giuseppe Mazzini. Its original source seems to be found in the work of A. Vizzini.[42] Vizzini attributes to Mazzini the founding of an organization known as *Oblonica*. This was composed of thieves, vagabonds, and various other criminals. From the membership of this organization he later formed a more closely knit ritualistic group trained to carry out crimes beneficial to the organization. Since *Oblonica* was basically a politically oriented society these crimes generally included arson, theft, and assassination. To these select members Mazzini gave the name *Mafiusi* which he took from the initials of his motto: *Mazzini autorizza furti, incendi, avvelenamenti*,[43] which translates as "Mazzini authorizes thefts, arsons and poisonings."

This account was later included in Charles William Hecke-

thorn's work on secret societies published in 1897.[44] This work
was probably the major source of the diffusion of Vizzini's
theory into the English-speaking world. In fact, Heckethorn's
inclusion of "Mafia" into his own work seems to be synonymous
with his acquaintance with Vizzini's writing. This is attested to
by the fact that Heckethorn cites Vizzini (1880) as his major
source of reference for his discussion of "Mafia"; also, in his
earlier edition of 1875,[45] written before the publication of
Vizzini's book, there is absolutely no mention of "Mafia." We
stress the account of Vizzini and its inclusion in Heckethorn
because these seem to be the only works that attempt to argue
that "Mafia" was the creation of Giuseppe Mazzini. An examination of other sources, however, has failed to reveal any valid
evidence to support this theory.

There is no doubt that Mazzini spent a major part of his life
as a participant or organizer of secret societies. *Young Italy* was
definitely his creation and he had been a member of the famous
political secret society, the *Carbonari.* Yet in the literature
relating to Mazzini's involvement with secret societies we never
find any evidence of a secret society *Oblonica* or *Mafia* attribu-
table to him.

We do find mention of *Oblonica* in Candida's[46] work. Here,
however, it is cited merely as the name of the old "Mafia" of
Agrigento, Sicily. So too Cutrera tells us that *L'Oblonica*[47] was
the name of the "Mafia" organization located in Girgenti.

The existence of such an organization does not, in itself, however, establish the fact that it was Mazzini's creation. As we
shall soon illustrate, there were many such organizations with
colorful names, many of whose origins are buried in mixtures
of fact and legend.

An examination of Luzio's[48] work dealing with Mazzini's activities as a member of the *Carbonari* did not mention any association with *Oblonica* or *Mafia.* The rare work, *Memoirs of the
Secret Societies of the South of Italy, Particularly the Carbonari*
(London: John Murray, 1821) was also examined. The content
of this work, despite the fact that its authorship is unknown,
coincides with much of the other literature on the *Carbonari,*
and therefore appears valid. It too contained no mention of

Mazzini's relationship with an *Oblonica* or "Mafia." Such was true also of the examination of the works of Frost,[49] Johnston,[50] and Hales[51] relating to secret societies.

The literature on Mazzini's creations, *Young Italy* and *Young Europe*, serves to cast further doubt on Vizzini's theory of derivation. We recall that the term "Mafia," according to his thesis, originated with the initials of Mazzini's motto that stressed the crimes theft, arson, and poisoning. Of the many types of crime a revolutionary may be required to commit, theft, arson, and poisoning are but a few. Why Mazzini should choose these three may be questioned. It appears that Mazzini always showed preference for the use of rifle and dagger rather than poisoning or arson. This is also true of the weapons which he required for use in his secret societies. Thus when a member was to be initiated into his society, Young Italy, he had to furnish himself with "a dagger, a rifle and fifty cartridges."[52] These hardly seem to be the weapons which would be selected by one who insisted upon the use of poisoning or arson—insisting, in fact, to the point of creating a motto to emphasize his point.

When his method of achieving national unity lay in a national insurrection, Mazzini wrote a manual on guerilla warfare.[53] This was to serve as a training manual for guerrilla bands that were to participate in a national insurrection directed at bringing about national unity. In this manual Mazzini writes, "The essential weapons are a musket or rifle with a bayonet, and a dagger. Each soldier will carry his cartouche-box, a case containing bread and spirits, a thin but strong cord, a few nails, and if possible, a light axe."[54] These requirements and equipment do not strongly indicate the thinking of a leader who seriously urged the use of poisoning and arson.

One might also ask, in view of the fact that Mazzini's involvement with secret societies is well documented in the literature, why except for Vizzini's account, we find no other mention of *Oblonica* or "Mafia" in these writings. We wonder also why Mazzini, himself, who was very open about his activities in his own writings, never mentions it.

Finally, even if Vizzini's theory were in itself tenable we would be presented with the problem of explaining why the name of this one association, "Mafia," gained such a widespread usage. After all, there were many secret societies similar to that described by Vizzini. These too had specific names—the *Scaglione* of Castrogiovanni, the *Zubbio* of Villabate, the *Scattialora* of Sciacca.[55]

Why then from all of these did the name "Mafia" gain such importance? Why isn't *Zubbio* or *Scattialora* today used in the same contexts as "Mafia." There is an explanation for this which we will defer to a more appropriate point in our discussion. We turn momentarily to a discussion of the third popular belief concerning the origin of "Mafia": the stone quarry theory.

The Stone Quarry Theory

This stems from a belief that the term "Mafia" originates not with a group but with a location. This source of origin is mentioned by Loschiavo[56] who maintains that the term comes from the name of a stone quarry in the area of Trapani. This area served as a central meeting place or residence of the various rebel groups who were fighting for national unity. The quarry itself was called *mafie* from which came the term "Mafia."

The late Michael Musmanno[57] offers a variation to Loschiavo's account. He maintains that the term came from a criminal gang, the "Mafie gang," which inhabited the quarry called by that name. Soon the term "Mafia" came to be used to describe all criminal groups which used extortion and terror.

In an attempt to evaluate the possibility of this source of derivation, the author requested information from the Italian *Instituto Geografico Militare*, well known for its knowledge of the geography of both Italy and Sicily. An effort was made to learn if there were any stone quarries in the area of Trapani which are known by the name "Mafie." According to the research findings of this institute no such quarry was known in the province of Trapani. If such quarries did exist, referring to them by the name "Mafie" was probably a colloquial usage confined to a small area; if they did not exist, as evidence seems to indicate, then this derivation of "Mafia" probably falls within the realm of a localized legend.

Again, however, even if such a quarry did exist, we would have a difficult time proving how and why from among a multitude of criminal gangs and stone quarries the "Mafie" gang or quarry was selected as the name which has become the general term for organized crime in Sicily—"Mafia."

The answer to the question of the derivation of the term "Mafia" seems not to be found in sources or explanations mentioned thus far. The reason seems to lie in the fact that these accounts have attempted to derive the term from origins which were too specific and isolated to explain its widespread usage. Since the term has been applied to a variety of criminal associations and activities in Sicily, it seems more fruitful to seek its origin within a context that allowed for its general rather than specific usage.

It goes without saying that the derivation of the word "Mafia" itself presents a challenge to any linguist or etymologist. However, historically and sociologically we are attempting to understand why the word developed its use both as a term referring to specific criminal groups and as a general term synonymous to organized crime.

The most logical answer to this question seems to lie in the explanation given by Pitré. In his writings on the subject Pitré notes that Traina's dictionary in 1868 is the first to include the term "Mafia." However this does not necessarily mean that the word itself did not exist prior to this date. Sicilian dictionaries, Pitré notes, were for the most part compiled by Sicilian poets who often did not include popularly or colloquially used phrases or terms.[58] Bruno,[59] for example, cites a poem containing the term *Mafiusedda* which was found in an eighteenth century manuscript containing Sicilian and Spanish poetry. Here *Mafiusedda* is used to refer to the beauty of the girl who is the subject of the poem. Pitré himself believes the word "Mafia," prior to the early part of the 1860's was confined to the Borgo district of Palermo. Here its meaning was always one implying beauty, graciousness, perfection or excellence. A lovely girl, *Una ragazza bellina*, in the Borgo district would have been referred to as

Una ragazza mafiusa or *Una ragazza mafiusedda*. So too, a lovely house would have been referred to as *una casa mafiusedda* or *una casa ammafiata*.[60]

Along with Pitré we doubt that the later use of "Mafia" as a term relating to crime originated in the Borgo district. Rather we find that its criminal connotation does not appear nor become widespread until the period following 1860. Migliorini and Griffith find that the words "Mafia" and "Mafiosi" came into the Italian language from Sicily after 1861.[61]

Hobsbawm calls attention to the difficulty of establishing a definite date or year for the birth of this connotation of "Mafia." In some parts of Sicily, currently known as areas of heavy "Mafia" concentration, the term was unheard of prior to 1860. In others, on the other hand, by 1866 and 1870, the use of the term was commonplace. Based upon this evidence, Hobsbawm argues that some form of "Mafia" perhaps restricted to the Palermo Province must have existed prior to 1860.[62]

Although we agree with Hobsbawm that certain structures that he calls "Mafia" did exist prior to 1860,[63] the question in our mind is whether or not these can be defined specifically as "Mafia." Hobsbawm himself illustrates that "Mafia" has manifested itself in three ways—as a socially expressed attitude toward the government and its laws; as a system of patron-client relationships, and as an organization composed of secrecy-oriented and structured gangs.[64]

"I Mafiusi Di la Vicaria"

Recognizing such variation in its manifestation, it appears futile to discuss the existence of "Mafia" in a given area or at a given time unless we first define the structure and function of the particular organization or institution that we are referring to as "Mafia."

In order to decide what "Mafia" is then we must first examine the various social structures, institutions, or associations which have been called by that name. Only then can we begin to

appreciate the confusion that has resulted from the practice of
applying the same name "Mafia" to groups and structures which
were basically different from one another. Preceding this ex-
animation, however, we offer Pitré's explanation of how the
term "Mafia" acquired its widespread criminal connotation and
use. By presenting this now we can more readily illustrate how
the practice of loosely applying the term "Mafia" to a variety of
criminal organizations developed.

Pitré attributes the rapid diffusion of the term "Mafia" after
1860 to a play written by Giuseppe Rizzotto. The play was en-
titled "I Mafiusi di la Vicaria."[65] The play depicted life in a
large prison in Palermo. Various scenes dramatically described
the habits, characteristics, customs, and argot of the camorristi
of Palermo. Camorristi in Pitré's usage here refers to criminals
who make a living from economic forms of crime such as
gambling, prostitution, and confidence games.[66] The original
play consisted of two acts, but, because of its immediate success,
Rizzotto added another two acts and produced it again under
the title of I Mafiusi. This play's success, as Pitré notes, is
evidenced by the fact that it had 2000 performances in 23
years.[67]

Unfortunately Pitré doesn't tell us where Rizzotto got the term
Mafiusi in his title. Paton translates the title of the first version
I Mafiusi di la Vicaria as "The Heroes of the Penitentiary."[68]
Perhaps this translation correctly represents Rizzotto's intended
meaning. However, acknowledging the fact that playwrights can
and do often give new meanings to old terms or create new
ones, any further attempt at an explanation of Rizzotto's term
Mafiusi without substantiating evidence would be sheer conjecture.

Regardless of its intended meaning, Pitré concludes that because of the widespread production of Rizzotto's play, both the
name and activities of these Mafiusi came to be popularly
known. The word itself entered the vocabulary of journalists
and politicians. Soon it was a household term used by all levels
of society. The term "Mafia," then assumed by Pitré to be
derived from Mafiusi came to be popularly used as a synonym
for organized crime of all types.[69] Today, as Schiavo emphasizes,

"Mafia" continues to have the same general and nonspecific meaning.[70]

Realizing that it has shortcomings, Pitré's explanation of derivation seems to be the most plausible to date. It helps explain why "Mafia" was used as an expression of beauty and excellence prior to 1860, yet after the appearance of Rizzotto's play in 1863, it assumed a negative or sinister connotation. It also helps explain why in certain localities the term was not used before 1860 but suddenly came into common usage shortly thereafter.

The general usage of the term "Mafia" has resulted in many criminal associations differing in structure and goals being equated with the name. It is primarily because of this that there is so much confusion about "Mafia." We now return to the task of discussing the differences between these associations. It is hoped that by the end of our discussion a more descriptive understanding of "Mafia" in Sicily will emerge. We hope to show after our description of these various criminal associations, that *mafia* in Sicily is best described not as an organization but as a system of social relationships which is part of Sicilian society itself.

Before describing these criminal associations we should note a possible methodological problem in regard to the historical sources which will be employed. These sources vary in their degree of authenticity and reliability. As a whole, the literature is laden with major contradictions and confusion of terms. If we were attempting to build an historical analysis based upon these sources we would obviously be faced with the problem of first establishing the reliability of the sources themselves before we could lay claim to the reliability of our conclusions.

Our purpose here, however, is not to develop an historical explanation of these various associations. Instead we intend to illustrate that their historical accounts are themselves contradictory. In this respect the contradictions in the literature will not hinder our discussion but rather will serve as the basis of it.

Needless to say, those scholarly sources employed in our discussion do not fall into the above category.

Sicilian Historical Factors

An understanding of the system of relationships which we will describe as *mafia* necessitate an understanding of certain basic social patterns and social structures in Sicilian society.

One of the most important elements in the development of the Sicilian culture has been that of the continuing invasions and conquest by foreign powers. First came the Phonecians, followed by the Greeks and the Carthaginians, after which Sicily was conquered by the Romans and became part of the Roman empire. Next came the Vandals followed by a conquest of Sicily by the forces of the Byzantine empire. Then came the Arabs and the Berbers, the occupation often jointly referred to as the Saracen conquest. After this came the Normans, followed by the French Angevins during whose reign the Sicilian Vespers occurred. Next, Sicily, after about 100 years of independence, came under the rule of the Spaniards, followed by the Bourbons, who controlled the island until it was liberated by the forces of Giuseppe Garibaldi in 1860. That same year, Sicily, by popular vote, became a part of Italy. During the period of World War II, it was again occupied by the Nazis and later, the Allied Armies.

These constant changes in the history have left their imprint upon the Sicilian culture. One such imprint is the emergence of *omerta*. Often cited as a unique characteristic of "the Mafia," we find it present at all levels of Sicilian society, legitimate as well as illegitimate. *Omerta* is both a Sicilian value and behavior pattern. It emphasizes resolving one's problems without recourse to the law; in so doing one's "manliness" is confirmed. It is a social value and attitude which manifests itself in the Sicilian's ego as well as in his actions. Too often *omerta* has been described as "a code of silence" by those writers who argue the existence of a sinister secret society—"Mafia." These writers are obviously not familiar with its larger meaning in Sicilian society itself. They are also not aware of the fact that *omerta*, as such, is not unique to any one organization or society.

Omerta is a behavior and attitude which is often found among

groups and societies which have long been victims of governmental and other forms of persecution and prosecution. Often
the practice may develop when a new code of law which conflicts with an established social normative system is imposed
upon a given group. Sellin illustrates such a case when France
forced upon the Algerians its penal code which included laws
prohibiting murder. The Khabyles, whose custom necessitated
the killing of adulterous wives to save the family's honor, refused to bring charges or testify against anyone whom the
French officials might suspect of such a crime.[71]

Omerta as a form of activity and belief is not, as it has often
been erroneously described, an open defiance against all law and
government. Rather, it represents suspicion and resentment of
government and law. One can understand how such an attitude
could come about, after the repeated change of government in
the history of Sicily. Government and law came to be recognized
as mechanisms of exploitation. Even after unification with Italy,
Maxwell notes that Sicily continued to contribute far more in
taxes than it received in benefits from the Italian government.[72]

As a result of such treatment we find that Sicilians have developed not only a distrust of government but an accompanying
distrust of those individuals who lie outside the bounds of family
and kinship relationships. For this reason, as is true of many
close-knit peasant societies, it is difficult to generate any form
of community cooperation since such cooperation requires the
surrendering of the autonomy of the individual family or kinship unit.

Related to these conditions is the attitude toward life found
in Sicily. This attitude, found also in Southern Italy and other
economically depressed areas, is one which the Italian or Sicilian
captures in his expression *La Miseria*. It is a fatalistic, alienated
view of life in which a man conceives himself as having little if
any control over it. With such a view of life, Friedman observes,
a man does not desire to cooperate with his neighbors because
in so doing, he jeopardizes his position in a competitive world
where goods are scarce. Instead he must use whatever means,
fair or unfair, in order to get his share. *Omerta* is the only form
of social cooperation he engages in and this he does primarily

because it does not require the individual to surrender or sacrifice anything.[73]

Although an expression of fatalism, *La Miseria* in Sicily is unfortunately a reality. As Allen reports, the 1953 Vigorelli Report, a government survey, found 27 percent of Sicily's population in a state of complete destitution and another 20 percent in a semi-state of such. Almost half the population exists in a state of poverty.[74] Illiteracy and its accompanying social vestiges —superstition, fear of innovation, and the protection of tradition and custom have taxed the efforts of many to bring social reform.

Danilo Dolci has done much to draw attention to this poverty and frustration. His medium of expression is the impoverished Sicilian himself. In his well-known works, *Report from Palermo*, *Waste*, and *Outlaws of Partinico*, the poor tell the world how it feels to be poor. Dolci, who has been compared to Oscar Lewis,[75] has, like Lewis, allowed the voices of poverty and alienation to speak.

As a social reformer, Dolci has organized action groups and promoted his ideas through teaching. He has also used the Ghandi technique of fasting in order to call attention to certain injustices. He has attempted to alter those conditions about which he has written. Because of these activities he is said to be a threat to both the government and *mafia*. The government has reacted to his threat by using the power of arrest. As to why he has had no retaliation from *mafia* sources, Dolci himself can give the only answer—"I don't know . . . I really don't know."[76]

To poverty and persecution throughout its history the Sicilian has developed a defensive reaction—a psychological means of resisting and combatting the various governments which ruled his land. It consists of an ego-stimulated and socially reinforced conception of honor that comes from "being a man." It is another manifestation of *omerta*: to be a man one must remain silent in the face of the law and settle his own affairs without the help of the law. The real meaning of *omerta*, argues Pitré, is found in those qualities which represent manliness—seriousness, sureness, and strength.[77] It is this quality or conception of

honor and manliness that lies at the root of the meaning of
omerta. For this reason we do not find it present in those areas
where the populace has lost its sense of dignity.[78]

For the Sicilian, *omerta*, the quality of remaining silent and
of being a man with honor and dignity, is equated with life
itself. It is his means of survival in a world where one is forced
to rely only on himself in a constant struggle for scarce goods.
It is a world where all must cooperate, individually, to frustrate
the efforts of a government which seeks only to exploit, never
giving anything in return.

Along with the daily problem of survival the Sicilian faces a
social system where upward mobility is the exception rather
than the rule. On a continuum of stratification systems the
Sicilian resembles a caste rather than an open class system.
Through experience the Sicilian has learned that in order to
have any semblance of power he must develop relationships
with those who have the power. Based upon this assumption
there has developed in Sicily a system of relationships which
has come to be referred to as the "patron-client" or "patronage"
system. We do not imply that this system is unique to Sicily. It
exists in a variety of societies, as illustrated in Kenny's[79] study
of Spain and Campbell's[80] study of a Greek mountain community.

For our purposes, however, this system in Sicily is of particular importance in that it becomes the basis upon which the
system which we refer to as *mafia* developed and continues to
sustain itself. Only when we understand *mafia* as a system of
patron-client relationships within a larger social system of patronage relationships, will we understand what *mafia* actually
consists of in Sicily.

In describing a patron-client relationship, we must begin by
defining the terms *patron* and *client*. For this we turn to the
work of Jeremy Boissevain and of Eric Wolf. Boissevain defines
patron as any person who is in a position of power and influence
and thereby can help or protect others who are not in this
position. A *client*, on the other hand, is the person who seeks
and receives the assistance or protection for which he in return

offers services to the patron. *Patronage* itself, Boissevain explains, refers to the system of intricate relationships which develop between those who provide the services inherent in their position and power and those who receive and in turn reciprocate by providing whatever services they are capable of providing.[81] As Wolf illustrates, no two functionaries in the patron-client relationship are equal. This is evidenced in the fact that the patron provides assistance and protection in reference to both the legal and illegal forms of social control. The client in turn reciprocates by showing loyalty to his patron. This he does in the form of esteem, providing him with information important to his personal and social welfare, and by political support.[82]

The services provided, although the specific patronage pattern varies from society to society, always consist of expected future behavior on the part of both the client and the patron. As Boissevain notes, once a favor is performed by a patron for a client this places the client in an obligatory position to the patron; that is, the client now owes a favor to the patron.[83] The patron does not have to collect immediately but until he does the client remains in the patron's debt. Obviously, the more individuals that a patron has in his debt the more powerful he becomes since he now demands more of a variety of favors from a variety of individuals in different positions. By the same token, the more patrons a client has, the stronger he becomes since he too can request more favors. Once a client has many patrons he can further strengthen his power by serving the function of introducing new clients to his patrons.

In Sicilian society then, patronage can be viewed as a way of life, a pattern of power interaction, and a system whereby the powerless are able to feel some sense of power. The roles of patron and client often change and overlap. Thus a client of a patron may become so powerful that he in turn becomes the patron. So too, an individual at any one time or over a span of time may serve both as a patron and client.[84] This relationship, as Blok illustrates, generally terminates when either the patron or client is no longer in a position to perform his original function.[85] Patron-client relationships interweave throughout all social levels of society and form a complex system of obligations, power positions and mutually-binding responsibilities. Often the patron may serve the function of acting as a "mediator" between the community and the outside world; as such he may serve as the link between the government or urban center and the rural village.[86]

So imbued are the Sicilians with the social pattern of patronage, argues Russo, that even the Saints are viewed as mediators between God and the sinner. Such patronage is possible because a Saint, being in the good graces of God, can thereby intercede for the lowly sinner. For this reason, cults of superstition and fanaticism often accompany the worship of Saints.[87]

The structure and function of *mafia* in Sicily lie within the realm of patron-client relationships. It is not an association as such but rather a system of patron-client relationships which weaves itself through both the legitimate and illegitimate segments of Sicilian society.

A further distinction is necessary between this conception and those institutions and associations which historically have been referred to as "the Mafia."

Bandits, Brigands, and Brotherhoods

First, "The Mafia" has been employed to describe a series of protective societies which organized to fight the oppressions of the foreign governments. Among those cited by Candida[88] are the *Mano Fraterna* (The Fraternal Hand) and *Oblonica* (no English equivalent) in the province of Agrigento; the *Code Piatte* (flat tails) of Palma Montechiaro; *La Fratellanza* (the brotherhood) of Favara; the *Birritti* (berets) of Cattolica Eraclea; the *Fratuzzi* (brothers) of Bagheria; *Fontana Nuova* (the new fountain) of Misilmeri. Cutrera[89] mentions in addition to those cited by Candida *La Scattialora* (no English equivalent) of Sciacca; in Castrogiovani, the *Scaglione* or *Scagliuni* which Cutrera translates as meaning an "eye tooth"; the *Stoppaglieri* (cork stoppers) of Monreale; and the *Zubbio* (no English equivalent) of Villabate. Reid mentions among others already cited here the *Beati Paoli*,[90] which Heckethorn translates as the *Blessed Pauls*.[91]

All these associations have obscure origins, but there seems to be a general belief that they arose to fight the oppression of the Bourbons whose rule began in 1738. These associations had certain characteristics in common. They were structured as secret societies; they practiced elaborate initiation rites; they swore allegiance to a chief.

The literature dealing with these associations is scarce. However, we do have reliable and extensive accounts regarding two of these associations. These are the works of Montalbano[92] and Lestingi.[93]

Describing the *Stuppagghiari* (or *Stuppagghieri*) association, Montalbano tells us that its rules were as follows: a promise on the part of each member to vindicate any offense against another member of the group; to help defend one's comrades if they should fall into the hands of the law; to share with comrades the spoils of their crimes; to keep the oath of allegiance; and to never reveal the secrets of the association. Any violator of the latter two rules was to be killed within twenty-four hours of the commission of the violation.

The initiation rite consisted of the initiate's being taken to a room where he was made to stand before the paper image of a saint (use of a specific saint was not required). Then the initiate extended his right hand to his comrades, who, using a needle drew enough blood from his thumb to wet the image. The initiate then took his oath after which he burned the image with a candle. Now considered baptized he henceforth was referred to as *Compare* (a title used among Italians and Sicilians to designate those related through the religious sacrament of baptism). The association had a chief or leader and was broken down into groups, each of which had a division leader or underboss.

Lestingi's account of the *Fratellanza* of Girgenti begins by noting that neither the exact date nor origin of the association is known. The initiation was similar to the *Stuppagghiari* one with the difference that the initiate's forefinger was tied with a string and then punctured. Also, after the paper image was burned, the ashes were thrown to the wind. The string on the finger symbolized the unity among the members. The rules were similar to those of the *Stuppagghiari*, with one addition: the promise of providing for the family of a member in the event of his death or incarceration.

The *Fratellanza* was divided into groups of ten. Each of these had a leader—a *capo-decima*—or chief of the ten. The leaders knew one another whereas the members of each group knew only their *capo-decima*. *Capi-decime* in turn were subservient to a supreme leader—*capo-testa*—who ruled all the groups in a given area. This *capo-testa* had contacts with other criminal organizations in other localities. Upon entering this association, the initiate had to pay an initiation fee of one lira and thereafter, on a monthly basis, paid his division leader from 25 to 50 centimes. The members also had secret recognition techniques by which they could discern whether an individual from another locale was a member of the association.

Cutrera, comparing the structure and function of the *stoppaglieri* with other *frattellanze* or brotherhoods, notes that they were identical.[94] Cutrera is probably correct in stating that these associations were identical in structure and function. They all stressed secrecy and their major function was that of making profits from theft and extortion. However, historically, we find differences in how and why these brotherhoods emerged.

Bruno, for example, maintains that these brotherhoods were generated by the injustices and oppression of the Bourbon government, which led even the most honest peasant to join.[95] However, if this is correct, then we have to include brigandage or banditry into this category. Many brigands enter into a life of crime as a result of the injustices they feel they have received. These "social bandits," as Hobsbawm calls them, become symbols of social protest, protected and idolized by the poor who view them as their champions.[96] The injustices which bring bandits into being vary. Thus Salvatore Giuliano, whom we mentioned earlier in reference to the Separatist movement, became a bandit as a result of shooting a policeman: On September 2, 1943 several policemen threatened Giuliano with a beating in an effort to force him to reveal the source of contraband he was caught transporting. Soon however, he observed that the same police took a bribe from another man and allowed his blackmarket goods to pass. Outraged at this injustice and corruption, he attacked the police and in the scuffle that followed he killed one of them.[97] Sought by the law for this crime, he was forced into a life of banditry.

Unlike Giuliano, who became a bandit because of his reaction to an incident of corruption, Musolino[98] became one as a result of being accused of a crime he maintained he did not commit. He vowed vengeance for this injustice. Escaping from prison, he knifed one person, shot and killed six others, and dynamited a house. Throughout this he was protected by the people. He suffered from hallucinations which included visions of St. Joseph who promised him help. When captured Musolino argued that Jesus had appeared to him on Easter Sunday and had commanded him to escape. Musolino was tried and confined to prison for the remainder of his life.

Brigandage or banditry then, like the brotherhoods, can be viewed as being generated by reaction to oppressive government. The concept and goal of rebellion against the injustices of government is present in both. The only major difference between the two is that bandits, more so than the brotherhoods, employed kidnapping for ransom as a major source of revenue.

The literature seems to indicate that the poor have shown more veneration for the bandit than for the brotherhoods. The brotherhoods, after all were organized for the benefit of the members. Brigandage is spawned more directly by injustices with which the poor can identify. Why then are bandits and their bands not viewed, like the brotherhoods, as "Mafia." They, too, demand secrecy of their members. They demand supreme obedience to the leader. Violations of these demands are also punished by killing the violator. And although not a part of their formal structure, we find that bandits, too, engage in various forms of ritualistic behavior. Thus as a pledge of eternal fidelity, the bandit Giuliano and his cousin, a member of his band, cut their wrists and exchanged blood.[99]

The *fratellanze* or brotherhoods, despite the benevolent connotations which have been attributed them, were simply organized criminal gangs. The extent to which they differed cannot be properly evaluated because of the lack of historical documentation regarding each specific group. That variation did exist, however, seems to be indicated by the scant and confusing literature regarding one such association—*I Beati Paoli* (the Blessed Pauls). This group, whose origin, Heckethorn[100] tells us, is hidden in mystery, was a sect of religious heretics found both in Sicily and Calabria, Italy. The group supposedly began in opposition to the government. Later it began committing acts that earned it a purely criminal reputation.

To date the only historical account of this sect is that given us by Vincenzo Linares,[101] who traced its history and visited its meeting place, Villabianca. Linares' account, an English abridgement of which is found in Heckethorn's discussion mentioned above, reveals that the sect may have taken its name from one of its rogues whose name was Paul (Paolo). On the other hand, argues Linares, the name may come from the fact that this rogue imitated the life of St. Paul. During the day he could be seen praying in church, thus becoming designated by others as "Beato Paolo" (blessed Paul), while at night, much like Paul persecuting the Christians, he would lead a band of assassins. According to Linares the group existed in Sicily as early as 1185. It was then known by the name *Vendicatori* (Vindicators). Later the name was changed to *Beati Paoli*. Linares does not believe that the sect was still in existence at the time of his writing (1886); he feels it disappeared around the early 1700s. Others, however, notes Linares, believe that the sect remained in existence. Linares, who views the sect as composed of vile men, states that their leaders were heretics from the Minor Brethren of St. Francis. These believed themselves to be possessors of the power of the papacy and the priesthood. This power was believed to be received through an angelic revelation. Their crimes of villainy, argues Linares, were committed under the pretense of promoting the public welfare.

Such then is the account of a sect which is frequently referred to in the literature as a form of *Fratellanza*. Its true purpose, according to Linares, was not noble in deed. Yet this one account is an insufficient basis for making a valid appraisal. Let us briefly look at others.

Heckethorn seems to feel that the *Beati Paoli* may have been a socially beneficial group. This conclusion he bases on the fact that even at the time of his writing (1897) many a Sicilian who had just suffered an injury or loss could be heard to utter the saying—"Ah, if the *Beati Paoli* were still in being!"[102] It is obvious that such a saying could be merely a traditional one, not based upon fact, but upon legend.

To confuse the issue further, Johnston implies that *Vendicosi*, a secret society arising during the twelfth century, and the *Beati Paoli* who followed them later were two distinct associations. And, adding to the confusion, he maintains that both were direct ancestors to "Mafia."[103] Finally, Alongi states that the *Beati Paoli* were a violent expression of the same sentiment which the *carbonari* (a secret political society) expressed in nonviolent forms; as such in Messina, from 1858 to 1859 the *Beati Paoli*, through intimidation, attempted to correct the wrongs committed by the Bourbon officials.[104]

The confusion here again lies, as we have indicated earlier, in the indiscriminate use of the term "Mafia." If secrecy, obedience to a chief, mutual protection, and the committing of crimes for the sake of fighting governmental oppression are all characteristics of "Mafia" then virtually any association with these characteristics must be placed into that category. However, as we have briefly displayed above, it would be impossible and incorrect to assume that these organizations or brotherhoods were truly interested in fighting the tyrannical rulers and governments. One can, in fact, better argue that their major purpose was that of committing crimes for their own profit. This at least seems to be the purpose as depicted in the rules of the two brotherhoods described by Montalbano and Lestingi. One can question if even the names by which these brotherhoods became known were those given to the association by the members themselves, or whether they merely represent names given to them by others. As Montalbano[105] points out, *Stuppagghiari* is not the term which the group known by that name gave to itself; rather it is a derogatory name given to it by an enemy group.

Finally, as for the assumption that these brotherhoods were formed solely to fight governmental oppression, an examination of the origin of the *Fratelli Amoroso* (the Amoroso brothers) of Palermo shows the opposite to be true. This brotherhood, Cutrera[106] tells us, was created not for the purpose of fighting oppression, but as a result of a feud between two families, the Amoroso and the Badalementi. After the feud the Amoroso family and those friends who had helped them fight the Badalementis formed a criminal association whose name became *Fratelli Amoroso*. Alongi's version differs from Cutrera's. He maintains that the *Fratelli Amoroso* and the Badalementi were two well-established "Mafia" groups that came into conflict with one another only after each sought to control the extortion of landowners in the Palermo area.[107] Neither Cutrera's nor Alongi's version indicates that the *Fratelli Amoroso* was spawned by benevolent, socially minded motives.

Since these brotherhoods were not referred to as "Mafia" until after the 1860s, it seems that writers, after that date, merely assumed these to be "Mafia." They did not evaluate or consider the contradictions that we have shown exist in the historical accounts themselves. They did not consider the fact that variations existed in the goals and structure of the various groups that they simply lumped together and called "Mafia." So long as these criminal groups had the one characteristic—secrecy— that was enough for their immediate classification as "Mafia." Yet we showed that brotherhoods, irrespective of their cohesive and secretive aspects were primarily interested in theft and extortion. Thus, rather than being a form of "Mafia" they were merely gangs. If their major goal was truly and honorably that of fighting governmental oppression, why, as indicated by the literature itself, did these groups fight each other for control of certain areas? It seems that such a noble cause would have produced unity rather than dissention among the groups. The conflicts that occurred between these groups seem not to have been motivated by differing political or social ideologies; instead, their fights occurred over control of criminal enterprises.

The Camorra

Adding to the confusion existing in the use of the term "Mafia" is its equation with other associations that have always been known by entirely different names. An example of this is the *Camorra*, a Neopolitan secret society. This is mentioned here not only as an example of the above-mentioned confusion, but because we shall refer to it later in our discussion of the growth of syndicates in the United States. The date of origin of the *Camorra* (the quarrel) is not known but Heckethorn[108] places it as no earlier than 1820. Merlino emphasizes that although writers have attempted to trace it back to Spanish and Arabic origins prior to 1820, it did not exist before that date.[109]

As a secret criminal society, Littlefield attributes the origin of the *Camorra* to the oppression of the Bourbon regime. It was, at its inception in Naples in 1830, a movement directed at the protection of political criminals. Soon, the criminally oriented among them organized into gangs and preyed upon the citizens, later offering them protection for a price.[110]

David Hilton, in one of the most thorough accounts of the *Camorra*, states that the society originated in the prisons of Naples and then spread into the city itself. Its name, he holds, derives from the name of the type of short jacket or coat worn by the *Camorristi* (members of the society).[111] Using several sources describing prison practices similar to those of the *Camorra*, Hilton argues the possibility that the organization may have been taking shape as early as the middle of the sixteenth century. He qualifies this, however, by adding that the society as a specific organization did not come into being until sometime during the eighteenth century.[112]

More extensive than those of the brotherhoods, the *Camorra* had a vast array of rituals, with different ceremonies accompanying a member's movement up into different ranks of the organization. In the hierarchy, as shown by DeBlasio,[113] there were three positions, each having a specific initiation ceremony. These ranged from the lowest rank, *giovinotto onorato* (a respected youth), to *piccinoto* (lad), to the highest rank, whose title was drawn from the name of the organization itself, *camorrista*. Heckethorn notes that there were some differences in the titles applied to the three ranks and that these varied with locality.[114]

The *Camorra* engaged in a variety of enterprises. These included extortion in the form of placing levies upon various forms of gambling. Protection for a fee was forced upon prostitutes and those who sold produce and other goods in the market-place.[115]

In its structure, Heckethorn[116] informs us, the *Camorra* was composed of various centers, of which there were twelve in Naples. Each center was further divided into subcenters, *paranze*, all acting independently of one another but each subservient to a center chief (*masto*). This head of a center was elected by the members of that center and was not permitted to make any important decisions without first consulting his members. All the money from various enterprises in the center was given to this chief who, on Sunday, would distribute it among the members keeping a healthy sum for himself. The chief was permitted an accountant (*contarulo*), a cashier (*capo carusiello*) and a secretary. All the center chiefs recognized as their head the chief of the Vicaria center.

DeBlasio's description of the structure, although basically in agreement with Heckethorn's, reveals some differences. DeBlasio[117] maintains that there was a major or high and a minor or low *Camorra*. The former consisted only of the third degree members, the *camorristi*. The latter was made up of only first degree (*giovinotti onorati*) and second degree (*piccinotti*) members.

Once a year there was an election of a head chief (*capintesta*), a section or center chief (*caposocieta* or *capintrito*), and a secretary (*contajuolo*). Only the section chiefs were permitted to vote for the head chief. If there were only two candidates and the vote results were close, the one who received the highest number became the head chief and the other became the vice-head chief (*vice-capintesta*). The section chiefs were elected only by the *camorristi* of each respective section. The secretaries (*contajuoli*) were elected by a vote of all the members.

The head chief was obeyed with blind allegiance, the section chiefs being responsible to him, having to appear before him every eight days to give a report regarding their sector. The secretary reported to the section chief every night giving him the money that was collected during the day. DeBlasio adds that, technically, the secretary was supposed to be elected once a year, but since there were not too many members who could read and write, he generally held that position for a longer period.

The *Camorra*, DeBlasio continues, made provisions for a tribunal to settle questions of honor and infraction of rules. Presiding over this tribunal were the section chief, the secretary of the sector, and two *cammoristi* who served as lawyers, one for the plaintiff and one for the defense. Also present were those members who wished to offer arguments for or against the accused. The section chief (the president of the tribunal) listened to the facts and then passed sentence. The sentence could be modified by the secretary, but since the president had two votes, his was the final decision. The sentence, depending upon the severity of the crime, could range from embarrassment by receiving a slap in the face in front of the members, to expulsion from the organization. This expulsion could be temporary or permanent. In severe violations the punishment was death.

The *Camorra*, after 1860, takes on an added function whose explanation we should prefer to enter into at a more meaningful point in our discussion.

Referring back to the confusion of "Mafia" with *Camorra* in the literature, we call attention to a note concerning *Camorra* which appeared in 1883.[118] This note describes the *Camorra* in Reggio, a town in one of the southern provinces of Italy—Calabria. In noting the existence of a *Camorra* outside the city of Naples, this writing contradicts the thinking of many writers who maintain that it was confined to the city of Naples. We also learn that the organization in Reggio had various levels of functionaries (*capo, camorristi, picciotti*) similar to those mentioned by Heckethorn and DeBlasio. The enterprises described are also those associated with *Camorra*, namely: gambling, prostitution, and forms of confidence games. Yet what makes this writing interesting for our discussion is that the author, throughout his discussion, refers to this organization interchangeably as "Mafia" and "Camorra"; its participants, however, he refers to as "Mafiosi." This account truly makes one wonder what exactly is in a name.

Along with the mention of confidence games in the above account we have another incident of "Mafia" involvement in this type of criminal act. Lewis in 1964 attributes to "Mafia" the confidence game executed in a town near Foggia, Italy. Here members disguised themselves as Padre Pio, a renowned priest who possessed stigmata that caused the palms of his hands to bleed. Other "Mafia agents" waited at bus stations where they cajoled tourists, for a price, into going with them to these impersonators who heard their confession.[119] Was this, however, a "Mafia" enterprise? Luigi Barzini maintains that the "Mafia" is a Sicilian social phenomenon and today exists primarily in western Sicily.[120] What then was it doing in Foggia, Italy?

Smith,[121] although in agreement with Barzini's observation of the absence of "Mafia" in eastern Sicily, notes that the most common forms of crime there are those of confidence games. Becoming even more specific Barzini argues that the provinces of Messina, Catania, and Siracusa, all in eastern Sicily, have never been penetrated by "Mafia."[122] Franchetti, on the other hand, cautions that the nonexistence of "Mafia" in these provinces may appear such because of the absence of violence. However, a closer look might reveal its existence with the difference that here it uses more shrewd or cunning techniques of retaining control than violence.[123]

Barzini believes "Mafia" exists in western Sicily. Lewis says "Mafia" carried out a confidence game in Foggia, Italy. Smith maintains there is no "Mafia" in eastern Sicily, but the practice of confidence games is common there. Franchetti says that it just looks like there is no "Mafia" in eastern Sicily—it probably is really there. Just what and where is this thing called "Mafia?"

A State of Mind

A final conception of "Mafia" which necessitates brief mention is that which views is not as a criminal organization but rather, as "a state of mind." "Mafia," argues Monroe, is an expression of an idea rather than a definite or specific organization.[124]

This conception or definition of "Mafia," most emphatically expressed in an article by Puglia,[125] and more concisely described by King and Okey,[126] Hobsbawm,[127] and others, represents an attitude of protest against and distrust of the government. It is a belief that injustices can and should be corrected by the person or persons who have received them; recourse to the law is both the sign and the method of the weak. Only those who are strong in this sense and make themselves respected by this manifestation of strength are worthy of the name *Mafiusi*; as such they are not criminals because theirs is the fight for justice. Obviously this conception of "Mafia" does not refer to a specific organization and, as such, is an attitude not unique to Sicily.

Refuting this conception, an article by LoSchiavo[128] argues the thesis that we have no way of knowing just when, if, and why associations which fought injustice became criminal. Adding to LoSchiavo's argument we must point out that the authors who write about such associations never adequately explain the process which transforms such groups from benevolent to criminal. Here again we must present the argument of a legal versus a social definition of crime. That is, if one accepts that the legality of an act is defined by the individual or group committing it, then we are faced with a subjective form of legality. Within such a framework everyone is free to define moral and immoral government according to their subjective definitions. Crime and its definition is thereby made relative only to the individual or group's acceptance of the law.

"Mafia" viewed as a state of mind, then, originates with the assumption that the "justice" of a man who settles his own dispute is "more just" than the "justice" of the existing government. Since justice under these conditions becomes relative we can only say that "Mafia" as a state of mind must rest within the realm of an assumption and not a fact.

It is this conception of "Mafia" as a state of mind, however, that has helped spawn the definition of brotherhoods as benevolent rather than criminal organizations. It was and is assumed that these organizations fight injustices. For this reason the literature presents these brotherhoods as champions of the people. Yet the same literature has failed to show us why they deserve such definition. Their major purpose, as we have shown, was one of acquiring and sharing money and goods for their own aggrandizement. Had they perhaps even shared these with the poor one might find reason to apply social or moral justification for their crimes. Yet such does not seem to be the case. Even in those instances where we are told that the poor employed these brotherhoods to help repossess goods or property, the brotherhoods helped only for a fee. We are told that these groups never stole from the poor. The reason for this should be obvious. What do the poor have that is worth stealing?

Such then are the confusing questions, facts, concepts, opinions, writings and definitions of "Mafia." What conclusions can be drawn from this array of historical and conceptual chaos? Or, better still, what is the basic cause of this confusion? In our opinion the historical and conceptual difficulties described thus far were and are created by a simple yet overpowering error—the confusion of *mafia* as a *method* with "Mafia" as an organization.

What "Mafia" Is

Let us move on to a clarification of this point from which we feel will emerge a more realistic and consistent description of what *mafia* actually is.

First, we should indicate several points basic to our description of *mafia* in Sicily—it is not a centralized, highly complex national and international organization with a supreme head in Palermo. It does not have a rigidly defined hierarchy of positions. It does not have specific rules and rituals. In other words it has none of the characteristics generally attributed to it in popular and clandestine descriptions. In noting the absence of these characteristics the author is not alone, as evidenced by the agreement found in the works of Pitré,[129] Barzini,[130] Bruno,[131] Sladen,[132] Hood,[133] King and Okey,[134] Neville,[135] Candida,[136] Maxwell,[137] Paton,[138] Monroe,[139] and Pantaleone[140] to mention only a few.

Those who subscribe to the international-clandestine organization concept tell us that the chief of "the Mafia" is located in Palermo from where he directs his international activities. No one however has ever been able to validate the existence of such a chief. As Schiavo points out, neither of the two individuals most recently described as supreme heads of the Sicilian "Mafia" resided in Palermo. One, Calogero Vizzini, lived in Villalba, which had a population of 4,900. The other, Giuseppe Genco Russo, lived in Mussomeli.[141] Varna maintains that after Vizzini's death the chief may have been Russo or perhaps Charles "Lucky" Luciano.[142] Feder and Joesten's[143] account, on the other hand, maintains Luciano was only assumed to be the head. These conflicting statements should be enough to show that both the existence of such a leader and who he is are a matter of sheer conjecture.

The most critical argument offered to those who insist on viewing the Sicilian "Mafia" as an international, centrally organized, rigid association is that of Barzini.[144] He observes that in order for an international organization to exist, the "Mafia" in Sicily itself would first have to be centralized. Yet, he argues, it is not. If it were, he continues, the efforts to demolish it, including that of Benito Mussolini, would have been successful. The fact that it is not centralized and easily definable, he notes, is what makes it so difficult to attack. How can it control the American underworld, he concludes, when it hasn't even succeeded in crossing over into Italy; for that matter it hasn't even spread to the entirety of Sicily itself.

If "Mafia" then is not an association what is it? We argue that it is a method of executing a criminal enterprise—*syndicated crime*. As such it can exist in different places and at different times. When this conception is employed, one can readily see why the various organizations—brotherhoods, *Camorra*, brigands—and the enterprises attributed to them (extortion, confidence games, and others) become much more distinguishable over time and place. What we are saying here about *mafia* is what we said previously regarding *syndicated crime*. Like *syndicated crime*, the concept *mafia* has been used to describe virtually every form of organized crime ranging from confidence games to international criminal conspiracies.

Mafia and *syndicated crime*, as a method, must be viewed as a type on a continuum of types of organized crime. If we do not view it as a method differing in some form from others, then obviously we shall be forced to place all organized crime into the same category. This results in the confusion which has thus far composed the topic of discussion in this chapter.

As a method then, *mafia* is equated with that of *syndicated crime*. Its characteristics are identical; namely, (1) the use of force, intimidation, or threats of such, (2) the structuring of a group or organization whose purpose is that of providing illicit goods and services, and (3) providing legal and political forms of protection that assure its operation. Employing this context, then, we can argue that until such time that a system of relationships allowing for the combination of these three characteristics developed in Sicily, *mafia* did not exist.

The major point that one must remember here is that the *method* is the basis for distinction, not the organization. The individuals, groups, or organizations that carry out the functions can vary with time and place. Also, as we stated earlier, within this usage *mafia* is a synonym for *syndicated crime*.

An application of our framework to an analysis of the Sicilian *mafia* and the Neapolitan *Camorra* should help further clarify our conceptualization.

Our contention is that *mafia* in Sicily, as we define it, did not begin to emerge until after 1812. It was only then that the breakdown of feudalism allowed for the appearance of two social elements influential to its development—the *gabellotto* (tax collector or excise man) and his relationship to the growth of the large landed estate (*latifondo*). *Mafia* itself, as we shall show, did not come into existence until 1860. It was only after this date that the institution of universal suffrage allowed for the development of the third characteristic necessary for *mafia*— political protection. After that date the phenomenon *mafia* becomes an integral part of Sicilian society. To understand this we must examine the creation and rise of the *gabellotto* and the growth of the *latifondo* in Sicily.

These two phenomena, although having historical influences which date back many centuries prior to their emergence, emerged as a result of the peasant revolt and the abolition of feudalism in Sicily in 1812. Prior to that year, the barons who owned the land had protected it by hiring their own private bands of guards. After 1812, despite the legal abolishment of feudalism, the structure of Sicilian society did not in reality lose its former feudalistic structure. There now existed a similar structure with two classes—a small number of rich landowners at the top and the large mass of farmers or peasants at the bottom.[145] Along with these rich landowners, as Nicotri observes, there also emerged a new class of patrons—the banker, the politician, and the public administrator.[146]

The abolition of the feudal structure resulted in the replacement of the old serf-lord relationship with one based on a system of land tenure. The baron no longer had to continue his previous role of governing the barony. Nor did he wish to involve himself with the problems of cultivating the land. Therefore, he was very amenable to entrusting these tasks to anyone who would agree to take on these responsibilities. All he asked was payment in return for the use of his land. The functionary or middleman who adopted this new role came to be known as a *gabellotto*. The word itself probably is derived from the term *gabella* meaning tax or duty.

These *gabellotti*, charged with the responsibility of guaranteeing the nobleman a stipulated yearly rent for the use of his land, had to assure themselves a sufficient income from the land. In their effort to achieve such profits these *gabellotti* soon began exploiting their laborers. Before long the *contadino* (farmer or peasant) became the slave of the *gabellotto*.[147] Impoverished, with no means of support, the peasant was forced into the role of a client. The *gabellotto* obviously became his patron. As a client the peasant was at the mercy of his patron. To whom could the peasant turn if he was dissatisfied? To another *gabellotto*? Perhaps, if he were not in debt to his current one. But even then would the next one be any different? The system, as Paton[148] illustrates, was made even more stringent, when many *gabellotti* themselves took on the role of their landowners. They too passed on their duties and responsibilities to a *sotto-gabellotto* (a sub- or secondary *gabellotto*). This functionary now had to assure himself an income whereby he could pay the *gabellotto* and make a profit himself. In order to do this, the *sotto-gabellotto* generally divided his part of the estate into small holdings which he sublet to small farmers. Often, these small farmers would themselves have to employ laborers to help work their land.

Generally, Paton notes, the *sotto-gabellotto* was paid by the small farmer in crops. These small farmers were required to help pay (in crops) for the cost of hiring guards to protect the land. Also, they generally contributed crops that constituted the gift given by the *sotto-gabellotto* to the priest who blessed the field.

One can readily perceive the futile as well as feudal aspects of this system. Unless one were fortunate enough to successfully and continuously produce profits, this system by its very nature functions to enrich those at the top and impoverish those at the bottom. Several years of bad crops could put both the *sotto-gabellotto* and the small farmer in debt for the rest of their lives.

The *gabellotto* and his landowner had to provide protection for the estate. Because of inadequate means of communication and insufficient roads, the government could not assure adequate protection. Therefore these landowners and their *gabellotti*, like their predecessors, the feudal Barons, turned to the use of private guards. These groups of guards came to be generally referred to as *bande* (bands), *squadre* (squads), or more specifically as *campieri* (armed guards). Since their major purpose, that of protection, necessitated men acquainted and accustomed to the use of violence, such guards were generally recruited from the ranks of criminals.

At first these bands were employed to protect the estates, but soon they were given other tasks. The *gabellotto* saw the opportunity by which these private guards could be used to further his ends in a twofold fashion; as a means of controlling, whenever necessary, his subordinates in the tenant system, and as a means of acquiring more land from other landowners. As Pantaleone[149] observes, the *gabellotto* by the threat and use of violence was able to extort the most profitable tenant arrangements from his subordinates and pay the lowest possible wages to those who worked his land. Soon, Pantaleone continues, the *gabellotto* began using these bands to intimidate his own landlord. The landlord would receive threatening letters. Often he would be shot at in an attempt to frighten him further. The landlord of course, not suspecting that it was his own *gabellotto* who was promoting these activities, would seek protection from him. The *gabellotto* in turn would assure him that everything possible was being done to catch these evil-doers. In payment for this service, however, the landowner had to cancel part of the *gabellotto's* payment for the use of the land. Naturally the threats and intimidation continued. Some landlords, no longer able to withstand the anxiety, would put this land up for auction. At this point the *gabellotto*, whose power no one wished to challenge, was the sole bidder. The land became his.

By the middle of the nineteenth century then, there had arisen in the Sicilian social structure a new powerful functionary, the *gabellotto* and his new source of power, the *latifondo* (large estate). There had risen also the *squadre* or *bande* of private guards who had established themselves as efficient perpetrators of violence. Together with their *gabellotti* they constituted what D'Alessandro interestingly refers to as "*l'industria della violenza*"[150] (the industry of violence). With this violence at his disposal the *gabellotto* could now force small landowners in his locale, but not under his tenancy, to pay for protection of their land. Protection from whom? Protection from the *gabellotto* and his band. Those who refused such protection had their crops destroyed and their livestock stolen or poisoned. Frequently the tenant or members of his family were assaulted or killed.

Wherever the opportunity presented itself the *gabellotto* was prone to take over the land of a weaker *gabellotto*. This he did by means of destruction of crops and stealing, which eventually forced the subdued *gabellotto* to sell his land. Viewed within the context of a struggle to maintain one's land, protection by the bands became both a necessity and a plague for landowners, both large and small.

Throughout these struggles the bands enriched themselves by engaging in two activities—theft of livestock and extortion. The *gabellotto* did not necessarily receive a large percentage of the profits of these enterprises. Instead he viewed this as a profit incentive for his bands, whose "force and violence" he needed in order to keep his land, obtain more land, and keep his tenants under submission.

Perhaps it is here that the *fratellanze* or brotherhoods discussed earlier could have played a role. As the reader may recall, Alongi's version of the war between the Amoroso and the Badalementi groups began over control of the extortion of property owners on the outskirts of Palermo. Unfortunately, as we stated earlier, the contradictory historical accounts of these prohibits any definite conclusions. Pantaleone mentions a source that noted the existence of types of brotherhoods which, for a price, would mediate to regain stolen property.[151] Rather than being affiliated with a *gabellotto*, however, it appears that these were criminal gangs which were established for the specific purpose of conducting their own criminal enterprise.

By the first quarter of the nineteenth century many *gabellotti* had begun to assume the powerful roles of landowner and patron. In a less powerful but nonetheless influential role, many functioned as clients to their landlords by providing them with protection. Serving in both capacities, the *gabellotto* gradually gained a foothold into both the legitimate and illegitimate segments of Sicilian society.

At this point mention of Sylos-Labini's[152] hypothesis about the absence of *mafia* in the eastern provinces of Sicily seems appropriate. He attributes this absence to the fact that in eastern Sicily, the landlords, as contrasted to those in the west, used tenure contracts. These allowed for the use of the land on a long term basis which resulted in the eventual emergence of an agricultural bourgeoisie. These new landlords, unlike those in the western provinces, were not interested in exploiting the land. Instead they saw their interests best served by reinvesting part of their profits back into the land. They had no need to exploit either the land or the tenant farmer. This hypothesis, which Sylos-Labini himself states needs further investigation, seems nonetheless to offer a possible basis of explanation for the existing economic and social differences between eastern and western Sicily.

The *gabellotto's* power prior to 1860 was primarily that associated with his being a landlord and a patron to his subservient tenants. The institution of universal suffrage after that date, however, created conditions which were to allow him to assume another role—that of broker or intermediary between the peasant and the government. This was the first step necessary to the emergence of *mafia*. The two functionaries necessary to the development of *mafia*—the *gabellotto* and his armed guards —were already in existence prior to 1860. The only characteristic lacking for its final emergence as *mafia* was the protection of the law. We must remember that although the *gabellotto's* bands extorted and stole either to further their own or the *gabellotto's* interests, they did so without the protection of the law.

It is true, as Pantaleone[153] states, that there were bands prior to 1812 that served the Barons with the assurance of receiving legal protection for any crimes which they committed. Under the feudal system, which by definition means the absence of central authority, the Barons were in fact the law in their area of jurisdiction. Hence their bands, whether they committed criminal or legal acts, nonetheless represented the law. They were a form of police force. One might equate this situation to that of the Paris police force during the eighteenth century. As Radzinowicz[154] describes it, this force had spies, was allowed to intercept and read letters, and was empowered to maintain unlimited custody of any person accused of a crime. These powers, which one could argue are in themselves criminal in nature, were nonetheless upheld by the law because they were in fact incorporated within the law.

After 1812, however, with the legal abolition of feudalism, neither the new *gabellotti* nor their landlords had the authority of the law. Their armed guards or bands were by legal definition simply private guards. After 1860, however, this changed. The *gabellotto*, a patron to tenants and small farmers, with his band of men prepared to enforce his will, was now himself in a position to become a client for the government. He could now provide votes for governmental officials. In this position, he could become a powerful patron for any candidate. His control of votes would assure the election of the candidate. Once elected this official would become the patron of the *gabellotto*, providing him with any legal services he may need. Note, however, that the roles of patron and client in this type of relationship were not distinct from each other. Obviously they merge into one another at different points in time. Since the elected official wishes the *gabellotto's* help in future elections and the latter desires continued legal protection, their relationship would be one characterized by continuous compromise. To assure the continuation of the *gabellotto's* power, the governmental official must provide him the "legal protection" necessary to his functioning as a vote mediator. This includes allowing the *gabellotto* the freedom to use violence and other illegal means of keeping control over his tenants and small farmers. In order to have the agents of this violence at his disposal the *gabellotto* in turn must allow his bands the freedom to make profits from their criminal enterprises—cattle rustling and extortion.

Historically the groundwork for the *gabellotto's* assuming the role of vote mediator was laid in the peasant revolts and the continuing threat of them after 1812. A peasant revolt in 1812 was followed by one in 1820 and 1848. Between 1820 and 1848 parts of Sicily were plagued with revolutions and counterrevolutions. These manifested the struggle between the rich and the poor or, as Romano puts it, the class struggle between the landed bourgeoisie and the agricultural proletariat.[155] In these struggles many peasant squads were organized to fight against the rich.[156]

The most severe of these in terms of governmental reaction was the peasant revolt or general insurrection of 1848. On a national scale, the government again found it necessary to institute *La Guardia Nazionale*, (the National Guard). It was again used as it had been in 1820, as a measure of combatting and suppressing the peasant squads. As Romano observes, this National Guard represented only the interests of the wealthy. Its program consisted of a forceful method of further subjugating the poor.[157]

On a local scale, many governments responded by reestablishing in 1848 the *compagnie d'armi* (armed companies), which had been abolished by royal decree in 1837.[158]

These governmental reactions are cited to emphasize the anxiety and fear which accompanied the 1848 as well as previous revolts. Both the aristocratic classes and the Bourbon government were interested not only in suppressing contemporary revolts but in finding a means of curbing their future occurrence. Yet revolts continued even after Unification. In 1866 the peasants revolted in Palermo.

The anxiety experienced by the landowner, coupled with the continuous peasant uprisings, slowly allowed the *gabellotti*, both immediately before and definitely after Unification, to assume the role of helping suppress these peasant disturbances. The *gabellotto* took on another role of brokerage between the peasant and government. Both in those cases where the *gabellotto* had managed to become the landowner himself and, more frequently, where the *gabellotto* served as a protection-broker for his landowner, these functionaries were in a position to impose their will upon the peasant. By using violence, by subjugating the tenant into accepting impossible leases, by extorting the small farmer with threats of attacks upon person and property, the *gabellotto* entrenched himself in a patronage system which continues today. As a client to his landowner in return for certain favors he promised the continued suppression of the peasant. As a patron to the peasant he promised work and the continuation of tenant contracts. These he promised and gave only if the tenant abided by the patron's wishes. Being poor, the tenant had little choice but to do so. The government, continuously interested in finding a means of controlling peasant outbursts, recognized the benefit and efficiency of this local control over the peasant. It was therefore quick to condone any actions, legal or illegal, just or unjust, which the *gabellotti* or their landlords found necessary to use against the peasant. This obviously served to help the *gabellotto* further subjugate his tenant farmers. With such power over them, by 1860 the *gabellotto* was able to demand one more thing from all his tenants—their vote.

By 1860, then, because of these intermediary functions, the *gabellotto* had at his disposal (1) the use or threat of use of violence, (2) an organization (his private bands) to carry out this violence, and (3) the assurance of governmental protection through his new role as vote procurer. After 1860, with the presence of the three elements stipulated in our conception of *mafia*, we have in Sicily the existence of *mafia* as method and the *mafioso* as functionary.

As time went on, the *mafioso* slowly entered all areas and classes within Sicilian society. Those *gabellotti* who seized property by the methods formerly described became landed *mafiosi*. As such, because of their association with other members of the aristocratic and professional classes, they were now in positions to give patronage to a new variety of clients. Also they themselves could now serve as clients to various agencies of government and public administration.

The *gabellotto* or *mafioso* who served his landlord by offering protection was, by virtue of the patronage owed him for this service, in a position to ask favors of the landlord. These favors often constituted the avenue by which this *mafioso* sent his sons to the university, helped his daughter marry into a better class, and in general climbed the path of upward mobility.

Of extreme importance, however, is the fact that the *mafioso* was and remains distinguished from other forms of patrons and clients by virtue of his monopoly or specialization in the efficient use of violence. It is here where *omerta, the patronage pattern,* and *mafia* come to compose a system of relationships.

Tradition in Sicily makes *omerta* a value; it demands that certain serious wrongs be settled only through the use of the vendetta or by violence. Yet in many cases, because of the person's professional position or because of his weak position, he himself cannot or is unwilling to consummate this task. He then must turn to those who can—the *mafiosi*. After all, these men have at their disposal clients who are adept in the use of violence. Coupled with this the *mafioso* is in a position to offer political protection for the killer. As a broker of votes he can demand protection for his client. This protection may come from the police official who was appointed by the political candidate whom the *mafioso* helped elect. If the police official finds evidence that he cannot hide without eliciting unfavorable public reaction, there is always a judge who will conveniently find loopholes in the law or other means of helping the accused escape justice. Witnesses and members of the jury, already predisposed to silence because of their value system, may be given an added incentive—the *mafioso's* statement that he would consider it a personal favor if they would be lenient to his dear friend, the accused. The incentive here lies in the fact that a favor done for a *mafioso* means a favor returned.

In this system the Sicilian is a victim of his own social structure and history. He is socialized to remain silent and settle his disputes without recourse to law. He cannot retain his or his family's honor unless he revenges his injuries. He lives in the world of *La Miseria* where individuality coupled with distrust of one's neighbor are his accepted means of gaining access to scarce goods. Finally the historical development of his island allowed for the growth of an intermediary who managed to exploit the rich through favors and the poor through fear. In these aspects of Sicilian life and history are found both the creation and the perpetuation of *mafia*.

Mafia then is not an organization. It is a system of patron-client relationships that interweaves legitimate and illegitimate segments of Sicilian society. *Mafioso* is not a rank or position within a secret organization. Rather it represents a type of position within the patron-client relationship of Sicilian society itself. It refers specifically to one who can and does use violence to enforce his will. It refers also to one who is assured the protection of the law. However the occupation or social status of the individual who serves this function varies from place to place. So, too, the nature of his patron-client relationship will vary. His strength, however, depends upon the extent and kinds of patrons and clients that he has at his disposal. Thus when an individual comes to be recognized as a *mafia* head or leader in a given area, this does not mean that he was elected to the post. It simply means that there is a public awareness of the power he can command through effective patrons and clients. The extent of a *mafioso's* power can be evaluated by observing what he has been able to accomplish in the way of effecting certain types of action. In any one locale then, differing levels of power are manifested by *mafioso* based upon the number and types of relationships they have managed to develop.

Relationships between *mafiosi* located in different areas are also structured on a patron-client basis. Thus at one time a *mafioso* from one area may serve as a patron to another. This occurs when one needs the services of the other. In stealing cattle for example, it may be necessary for one *mafioso* to route his cattle through the land of another. He may also have to hide his cattle or let them graze in an area sufficiently distant from their original place of theft. This necessitates using another *mafioso's* land. Usually in such cases, one *mafioso* helps another since each knows that someday he may need the services of the other.

In some locales certain enterprises may be controlled by a particular group of mafiosi. Thus if water is a scarce commodity in a certain area, it may be under the control of the *mafiosi* of that area. Hence private citizens and *mafiosi* from other areas are dependent upon these for the use of this commodity. In Palermo, which is a large trade center, we find many *mafiosi* each operating a specific enterprise. One may specialize in collecting extortion for the protection of market-produce enterprises. Another may specialize in serving as the agent by which stolen cattle are butchered and put up for sale in the marketplace. During the 1963 Mediterranean Fair in Palermo, for example, diseased livestock were sold by *mafia* functionaries.

This involved a system of contacts which included butchers who slaughtered the meat, and owners of restaurants and meat markets who helped sell the stolen meat.[159]

Two major enterprises of past and present *mafiosi* are those of extortion and theft of livestock. Originally, we recall, the *gabellotto* used these as means of enriching himself, providing profitable enterprises for his private guards and injuring his competitors. When the *gabellotto* took on the role of *mafioso*, in some cases he continued to make this a major source of income for himself. Others, on the other hand, continued to permit their guards this form of payment in return for the services they performed for him. Today the livestock-stealing that continues in Sicily is conducted on a similar basis. Thus the *mafioso* in a given area may have his subordinate gangs steal the livestock as a direct means of making a profit for himself. Or he may allow these gangs to steal for their own profit, offering them also the contacts necessary to market the livestock. In return these gangs must be ready to offer him services when needed. The same arrangements are found in the enterprises involving extortion.

Thus the powerful *mafioso*, having many contacts, patrons, clients, and ample land can afford to allow his subordinate functionaries to make profits from a variety of enterprises. In so doing he has at his disposal an ample supply of men ready to commit acts of violence when he so commands.

According to Pesce[160] the major reason for the past and present flourishing of livestock stealing is simply the lack of sufficient roads. This, he argues, makes it difficult for police to adequately patrol the areas where these thefts are common. Lack of sufficient roads also hampers the pursuit of the thieves. The far-reaching aspects of patron-client relationships are also reflected in Pesce's statements implying the possibility of political and other forms of collusion that may have impeded road-building programs.

Today it appears that *mafiosi* are increasingly engaging in commercial business. This seems to be true more of *mafiosi* located in the industrial areas, like Palermo. Such infiltration into business enterprises as well as the medical profession itself is suggested by a case occurring during the 1968 earthquake in the Palermo-Trapani area.[161] The scarcity of bulldozers during this emergency was attributed to the fact that the equipment was in the hands of *mafiosi* who wished to avoid public scrutiny of their activities.

The *mafioso* then can be found in a variety of occupations. His influence reaches into every level of the Sicilian social structure. His major characteristic lies in his ability to carry out acts of violence. It should be understood that in many cases violence is not necessary to accomplish his purpose. Fear of his threats is often sufficient. Boissevain cites a case where a professor had been insulted by a colleague. Disturbed by this insult, this professor went to see a *mafioso* who was obligated to him. It seems that the professor's father had helped keep this *mafioso's* father from going to prison several years earlier. The *mafioso* visited the colleague who immediately sent an apology.[162]

Often because a *mafioso* has many informants in the form of clients, he learns many secrets. He may later use them as blackmail to elicit services from those who do not have a patron-client relationship with him.

In short, then, the *mafioso* is a functionary who transcends both the legitimate and illegitimate worlds of Sicilian society. As a mediator of violence he performs a service for a society in which vendetta is the only accepted form of justice. In performing this service he is aided by segments of all social classes. To those above him in status and power he becomes a client, to those below him he becomes a patron. Functioning between these two worlds, the legitimate and the illegitimate, it is difficult to clearly define him as a criminal. The *mafioso* himself may never commit an act of violence, yet he may serve as the broker for many such acts. However, in a sense, he may serve to avert potential violence by the fear he instills. Such is true in those cases where an apology which he negotiates may be all that is demanded by the offended party. *Mafia*, then, is a method which can be understood only in the complex patron-client relationships which center around its major functionary, the *mafioso*.

Although the power of the *mafioso* may be found in various occupations, the major source of *mafia* control is currently found in its original source—the *latifondo*. In most cases, today as earlier, the large estates are in the hands of a small minority. In Licata, for example, the land is broken down into small landholdings, all of which are in the hands of only five families.[163]

Under such a system, land becomes a major source of power. *Mafia* functionaries have long guarded this source. The frustration with which various land-reform programs in Sicily have met attest to the dedication with which *mafiosi* have confronted this challenge. Again, however, the *mafioso* has been aided in this cause by many factors in the Sicilian social structure itself, including the negative reaction of the peasant toward the government. As Anton Blok[164] illustrates, an attempt at land reform initiated by the Sicilian government during the 1950s was frustrated by the very farmers whom it sought to help. The program was rendered ineffective because these small farmers divided their land holdings among their future heirs and reduced them to a size that would not be affected by the reform. Many sold sections of their holdings to *gabellotti* and other agriculturalists. In general these farmers simply refused to cooperate with the government. They outrightly rejected those changes necessary to make this reform measure effective. The most general and damaging attitude was the farmer's suspicion that this reform was just a new form of governmental corruption.

The struggle for land is evidenced further when we note the victims of recent *mafia* murders are labor union organizers and those who attempted agricultural reform. A monument dedicated recently to one such victim in Tusa reads "martyr in the struggle for agrarian reform."[165] Between 1947 and 1955 approximately fifty trade unionists have been assassinated by *mafia* forces.[166]

Labor unions, it must be remembered, represent an organized attempt at action which, like the peasant movements of old, presents a threat to the landowner. These unions, as a power block, can make demands. They therefore represent the first step in breaking the bonds of servitude that keeps the laborer in the position of client. A labor union which has the power to call strikes and demand higher wages could obviously force the *mafioso* into an arbitrating position. Also, powerful labor organizations would serve to eliminate the *mafioso's* mediator position of vote broker; a position which he needs in order to ultimately continue his service as a violence broker.

The *mafia*, then, is a method, not an organization. Its roots and its survival lie within the very social structure of Sicilian society. Until these are changed *mafia* will remain since the *mafioso* has a function or service to perform. It is therefore unrealistic to assume that *mafia* can be destroyed by eliminating a certain number of *mafiosi* through legal convictions. It is the system that survives and its functionary positions can be and are filled by others on various levels of the *mafioso* patron-client ladder.

We are told by some writers that Mussolini demolished "the Mafia" through the efforts of his subordinate, Cesare Mori, who at that time was the Prefect of Palermo. Mori[167] himself tells of many encounters with various elements of *mafia*. DiGregorio,[168] on the other hand, finds many of Mori's and Mussolini's claims to success unfounded. He maintains that the prosecution of many so-called *mafiosi* was in reality a persecution of political opponents to the Fascist cause. There is no doubt that Mussolini had no desire to allow a form of control such as that exercised by the Sicilian *mafiosi* to subsist along with his totalitarian system. However, we also doubt that he could have destroyed a system imbedded in Sicilian society itself by merely incarcerating a number of known *mafiosi*. According to one account, Cesare Mori, when asked if he had in fact destroyed "the Mafia" replied "how can you stamp out what is in a people's blood?"[169] Although there is evidence that some landed *mafiosi* joined the Fascist regime, the majority, according to DiGregorio,[170] did not. In either case there is no evidence that they lost their major source of power—the large estate. One study definitely shows that they did not. Using data regarding landed property from the period 1929 to 1947, Blok found that in Contessa, the *latifondi* throughout that time had remained intact.[171] Hence, at most, during Mussolini's reign the power of the *mafioso* was temporarily interrupted. In any event it returned to its previous role after the Allied invasion.

There are allegations in the literature indicating that Charles "Lucky" Luciano helped the Allies make contact with a *mafioso* leader in Villalba. Later we are told this leader, with the aid of other *mafiosi*, helped direct the Allies to victory. This story is often given support in the literature by the fact that Luciano was later paroled from prison by former Governor Thomas E. Dewey. This parole, according to several writers, was given as a reward in return for Luciano's help. In these accounts the impression is given that Governor Dewey pardoned Luciano. In reality, however, as Feder and Joesten[172] emphasize, Dewey merely signed a parole order based on the deportation action which followed. Feder and Joesten contend that there was nothing unusual about Luciano's parole. The New York State parole system, they argue, often employed parole on the grounds of deportation as a method of ridding the country of undesirable aliens.[173]

Throughout this controversy, one fact does remain—the Allies did allow a *mafioso*, Don Calogero Vizzini, to become mayor of Villalba. In contrast, however, to the explanation implicating Luciano's involvement, Romano[174] offers a different one. He maintains that the Allies were cognizant of the fact that Vizzini had two brothers who were priests and two uncles who were Bishops. They also knew that Vizzini was a powerful *mafioso*. Therefore in supporting him for mayor they were merely attempting to use both forces—the church and the *mafia*—to help establish and maintain order on the island.

Although there is no doubt that the Allied Armies did allow for various *mafia* functionaries to emerge after the occupation, it would be difficult to argue, as some writers do, that the Allies brought "the Mafia" back to Sicily. This again assumes that *mafia* is an organization. Rather, the revival of various *mafiosi* after the occupation can best be attributed to another factor— the resumption of functions which the *mafiosi* had performed prior to Mussolini's reign. These were, as before, those of mediator of violence, vote broker, and suppressor of possible peasant unrest. After the war the need for the Sicilian to settle his disputes via the vendetta had not changed; hence this role was again assumed by the *mafioso*. Votes were necessary to the election of candidates; again the *mafioso* became a mediator between peasant and government. Finally, as Gaja[175] notes, the aristocracy in 1943 had come to believe that a social revolution after the war was inevitable; the old fears of the aristocracy again welcomed the role of *mafioso* as subjugator of the poor.

The survival or revival of the *mafioso's* role then cannot be attributed to the Allies whatever their motives in supporting various sources of *mafia* may have been. Rather the basis of this continuation must be again found in the nature of the Sicilian social structure.

Mafia as Method: The Camorra

As a note of comparison and a further illustration of our use of *mafia* as method, a return to our discussion of Camorra is here appropriate. Until 1860, the Neopolitan criminal association, *Camorra*, had developed the structure and function of a criminal organization. Beginning around 1830, however, as Hilton[176] indicates, the *Camorra* slowly became, in a sense, an arm of the government. The government at this time was primarily interested in political crimes and devoted most of its attention to this area. In so doing it allowed the *Camorra* to virtually gain control over all crime in the lower class areas. Hilton argues that the poor came to view the *Camorra* as their form of protection agency. Although the *Camorra* continued its extortion and other practices, those who paid for the protection were never molested by other criminals. Merchants, therefore, who wished to run their businesses without criminal and other interferences, would hire *camorristi* to supervise the transportation of their goods.[177] *Camorristi* were also used to guard railway stations, hotels, and many other forms of business enterprises. Along with these services, the *Camorra* continued to make available to the public such enterprises as gambling and prostitution.

Comparing it to the Sicilian form of *mafia*, the *Camorra*, too, offered services; namely, those of protection, gambling, and prostitution. However, although it made several attempts to organize and manifest itself as a political society after 1848, the *Camorra* never succeeded. Unlike the Sicilian *mafioso*, the *camorrista* never had a means of economic and political entrenchment in the social structure. As Schneider[178] points out, the *gabellotto* in the neopolitan provinces did not have similar opportunities or resources to become a vote broker. He controlled only small portions of estates. This did not give him the economic or political power that accompanied the *gabellotto's* control of the *latifondo* in Sicily.

The *Camorra*, nonetheless, represents a form of *mafia*. Its methods included the use of violence and the provision of services, the establishment of a secret organization to carry out these threats and services, and protection from the police. In its early history police protection was offered to the *Camorra* in return for the role it played in controlling crime in the lower class areas. However, with the termination of this role, probably after 1848 and definitely after 1860, the *Camorra* had to procure police protection through direct payment. Thus, as Merlino notes, one third of the gross income from *Camorra* enterprises was routinely set aside for bribes to police officers.[179]

In conclusion, then *mafia* manifested in its Sicilian form of patron-client relationships or in its Neopolitan form of a secret criminal society, *Camorra*, performs services. In both forms it represents a method. Any structure or organization, then, that uses this method, regardless of its location in time or place, we refer to as *mafia*.

In Sicily, the relationships through which *mafia* manifests itself cannot be eliminated until the very structure and value system of Sicilian society itself are altered. In 1967, Franco Ferrarotti, an Italian sociologist, speaking before the Parliamentary Anti-Crime Commission (established in 1963) emphasized this point. He called attention to the fact that in Sicily the level of aspiration among the poor is very low. This, he notes, may be a function of the educational system itself. In those areas of heavy *mafia* concentration, the school as an agent of personality formation helps condition pupils to accept and expect a patron-client system of social organization. Such a conception of society, he notes, reinforces the belief that those who are at the bottom must be subservient to those at the top. Any aspirations are viewed within a context where one hopes to achieve success only by attaching oneself and being subservient to a patron.[180]

In a sociological study employing 1000 questionnaires distributed to residents in the province of Palermo, Ferrarotti documents the observations made in his address. In this area of high *mafia* concentration, he found that respondents expressed feelings of alienation, frustration, and a continued distrust and lack of faith in the government as a source of economic or social betterment.[181]

In a study of student attitudes, however, Corrado Antiochia notes that there are signs of change. Among the young and the educated, he concludes, there lies a potential force, an attitude which may ultimately sever the social breeding grounds of *mafia*.[182]

In concordance with this view of the relationship of *mafia* to Sicilian social structure, Pecorini adds that the church, too, must change its directions. Future priests must instigate social action by coming out of the pulpit into the streets. In order to gain the respect of the people and serve as a potential agent of reform, the church itself must break its ties with *mafia* functionaries. How can the church justify, he asks, its practice of excommunicating communists but not *mafiosi*?[183]

Mafia as method then can and does manifest itself in a variety of forms. In this chapter we have attempted to define, show the various dimensions, and give descriptions of two forms—the Sicilian and the Neopolitan.

In Sicily, *mafiosi* originated and maintained their structure and function through the society itself. Through its history, *mafia* functionaries have affiliated themselves with various political parties in an open manifestation of political assimilation. Obviously the *mafiosi* have not infiltrated all areas of Sicilian power centers, otherwise they would be the government itself. The *mafiosi* have, instead, had to continually combat opposing forces. During the 1950s, for example, they struggled to maintain control of the Christian Democratic party of Agrigento.[184] *Mafiosi* have continuously fought other *mafiosi* in an attempt to gain or retain control of areas and enterprises. The history of *mafia* in Sicily can be best sociologically described as a continuing system of conflict, cooperation, and accommodation.

Having thus laid conceptual foundations that, we hope, clarify the meaning and use of the term *mafia*, let us now confront another area of interest and confusion—the origin and development of syndicated crime in the United States.

References

1 Gene Friedman, "Crime Fighters Zero In On Us," *Reading Times*, May 15, 1967, p. 1.

2 John A. Gardiner, "Wincanton: The Politics of Corruption," *Task Force Report: Organized Crime* (Washington, D.C.: Government Printing Office, 1967), pp. 61–79.

3 John A. Gardiner, "Public Attitudes Toward Gambling and Corruption," *The Annals*, CCCLXXIV (November, 1967), 132.

4 G. D. Wiebe, "Responses to the Televised Kefauver Hearings: Some Social Psychological Implications," *Public Opinion Quarterly*, XVI (Summer, 1952), 195–199.

5 *Organized Crime in California*, Report of the Subcommittee on Rackets of the Assembly Interim Committee on Judiciary (Sacramento: Assembly of the State of California, 1959), p. 24. Other references to Mafia are found throughout the report.

6 *The New York Times*, May 3, 1959, p. 46.

7 *Ibid.*

8 Ontario Police Commission, *Report to the Attorney General for Ontario on Organized Crime* (Toronto, 1964), pp. 60–61.

9 Ithiel de Sola Pool and Irwin Shulman, "Newsmen's Fantasies, Audiences and Newswriting," *Public Opinion Quarterly*, XXIII (Summer, 1959–60), 145.

10 Kulamarva Balakrishna, *A Portrait of Bombay's Underworld* (Bombay: Manaktala and Sons Private, Ltd., 1966), pp. 22–24.

11 Eng Ying Gong and Bruce Grant, *Tong War* (New York: Nicholas L. Brown, 1930).

12 E. J. Hobsbawm, *Primitive Rebels* (Manchester, England: University of Manchester Press, 1959), p. 5.

13 Rudolf Heberle, *Social Movements* (New York: Appleton-Century-Crofts, Inc., 1951), p. 24.

14 Renato Candida, *Questa Mafia*, 3rd ed. (Roma: Salvatore Sciascia Editore, 1964), pp. 54–55. Translation mine.

15 *Ibid.,* p. 54.

16 Herbert Brean, "Men of Mafia's Infamous Web," *Life,* February 1, 1960, p. 59.

17 Gaetano Mosca, "Mafia," *Encyclopedia of the Social Sciences,* Vol. X, p. 36.

18 "The Mafia" A Criminal Phenomenon," *International Criminal Police Review,* XXI (1966), 94.

19 Norman Lewis, *The Honored Society* (New York: G. P. Putnam's Sons, 1964), p. 19.

20 Cesare Bruno, *La Sicilia e La Mafia* (Roma: Ermanno Loescher e Co., 1900), p. 132.

21 Gavin Maxwell, *The Ten Pains of Death* (New York: E. P. Dutton & Co., 1960), p. 5.

22 Donal E. J. MacNamara, "Criminal Societies," *Encyclopedia Americana,* XIII (New York: Americana Corporation, 1963), p. 200b.

23 Ed Reid, *Mafia* (New York: The New American Library of World Literature, Inc., 1964), p. 25.

24 *Ibid.,* pp. 25–26.

25 Francis Marion Crawford, *Southern Italy and Sicily and the Rulers of the South,* Vol. 2 (New York: The Macmillan Co., 1907), pp. 320–321.

26 *Ibid.,* pp. 316–318.

27 "Sicilian Vespers," *Chamber's Encyclopaedia,* IX (New Edition; London: W. & R. Chambers Limited, 1927), p. 368.

28 Steven Runciman, *The Sicilian Vespers* (Cambridge, England: The University Press, 1958), pp. 214–215.

29 *Ibid.,* p. 288.

30 *Ibid.,* p. 293.

31 *Ibid.,* pp. 216–219.

32 Crawford, *op. cit.,* p. 324.

33 John S. C. Abbott, *Italy and the War for Italian Independence* (New York: Dodd, Mead and Co., 1882), p. 456.

34 Reid, *op. cit.,* p. 25.

35 Runciman, *op. cit.,* pp. 220–241.

36 *Ibid.,* pp. 272–275.

37 William Foote Whyte, "Sicilian Peasant Society," *American Anthropologist,* XLVI (1944), 65.

38 Giuseppe Pitré, *Biblioteca della Tradizioni Populari Siciliane,* Vol. XXII: *Studi di Leggende (Popolari) in Sicilia* (Torino: Carlo Clausen, 1904), pp. 198–223.

39 Jane Catherine Thompson Schneider, "Patrons and Clients in the Italian Political System" (Unpublished Ph.D. dissertation, the University of Michigan, 1965), p. 137.

40 Gavin Maxwell, *Bandit* (New York: Harper and Brothers, 1956), p. 60.

41 *Ibid.*, p. 3.

42 A. Vizzini, *La Mafia* (Roma: Tipografia Artero e Comp., 1880).

43 *Ibid.*, pp. 67-72.

44 Charles William Heckethorn, *The Secret Societies of All Ages and Countries*, I (New York: University Books, 1965), p. 279.

45 Charles William Heckethorn, *The Secret Societies of All Ages and Countries*, 2 Vols. (London: Richard Bentley and Son, 1875).

46 Candida, *op. cit.*, p. 12.

47 Antonino Cutrera, *La Mafia e I Mafiosi* (Palermo: Alberto Reber, 1900), p. 121.

48 Alessandro Luzio, *Giuseppe Mazzini, Carbonaro* (Torino: Fratelli Bocca, Editori, 1920).

49 Thomas Frost, *The Secret Societies of the European Revolutions, 1776-1876*, 2 vols. (London: Tinsley Brothers, 1876).

50 R. M. Johnston, *The Napoleonic Empire in Southern Italy and the Rise of the Secret Societies* (London: Macmillan and Co., Ltd., 1904).

51 E. E. Y. Hales, *Mazzini and the Secret Societies* (London: Eyre and Spottiswoode, 1956).

52 *Ibid.*, p. 61.

53 *Life and Writings of Joseph Mazzini* (London: Smith, Elder and Co., 1890), pp. 369-378.

54 *Ibid.*, p. 373.

55 Cutrera, *op. cit.*, p. 121.

56 Giuseppe Guido Loschiavo, *Piccola Pretura* (Roma: Colombo, 1948), p. 6.

57 Michael A. Musmanno, *The Story of the Italians in America* (Garden City: Doubleday and Co., Inc., 1965), p. 195.

58 Giuseppe Pitré, *Biblioteca della Tradizioni Popolari Siciliane*, Vol. XV: *Usi e Costumi, Credenze e Pregiudizi* (Palermo: Libreria L. Pedone Lauriel di Carlo Clausen, 1889), p. 19.

59 Bruno, *op. cit.*, p. 132.

60 Pitré, *op. cit.*, Vol. XV, pp. 289-290.

61 Bruno Migliorini and T. Gwynfor Griffith, *The Italian Language* (London: Faber and Faber, 1966), p. 439.

62 Hobsbawm, *op. cit.*, pp. 36-37.

63 *Ibid.*, p. 37.

64 *Ibid.*, pp. 32-33.

65 Pitré, *op. cit.*, Vol. XV, p. 290.

66 *Ibid.*

67 *Ibid.*, p. 291.

68 William Agnew Paton, *Picturesque Sicily* (New York: Harper and Brothers, 1900), p. 360.

69 Pitré, *op. cit.*, Vol. XV, pp. 291 and 293.

70 Giovanni Schiavo, *The Truth About the Mafia* (New York: The Vigo Press, 1962), p. 75.

71 Thorsten Sellin, *Culture Conflict and Crime* (New York: Social Science Research Council, 1938), pp. 64–65.

72 Maxwell, *Bandit*, pp. 28–29.

73 F. G. Friendman, "The World of 'La Miseria'," *Partisan Review*, XX (March-April, 1953), pp. 224–225.

74 Edward J. Allen, *Merchants of Menace* (Springfield, Ill.: Charles C. Thomas, 1962), p. 11.

75 Robert Coles, "Danilo Dolci: The Politics of Grace," *The New Republic*, August 19, 1967, p. 23.

76 James McNeish, *Fire Under the Ashes* (London: Hodder and Stoughton, 1965), p. xvi.

77 Pitré, *op. cit.*, Vol. XV, p. 294.

78 F. G. Friedman, *op. cit.*, p. 225.

79 Michael Kenny, *A Spanish Tapestry* (London: Cohen and West, 1961).

80 J. K. Campbell, *Honour, Family and Patronage: A Study of Institutions and Moral Values in a Greek Mountain Community* (Oxford: Clarendon Press, 1964).

81 Jeremy Boissevain, "Patronage in Sicily," *Man*, I (March, 1966), 18.

82 Eric R. Wolf, "Kinship, Friendship and Patron-Client Relations in Complex Societies," in *The Social Anthropology of Complex Societies*, ed. by Michael Banton (New York: Frederick A. Praeger, Publishers, 1966), pp. 16–17.

83 Boissevain, *op. cit.*, p. 22.

84 *Ibid.*, p. 24.

85 Anton Blok, "Peasants, Patrons and Brokers in Western Sicily," *Anthropological Quarterly*, LXIII (July, 1969) 159–170. Permission for citation through the courtesy of Eric R. Wolf and William D. Schorger, eds.

86 Sydel F. Silverman, "Patronage and Community-Nation Relationships in Central Italy," *Ethnology*, IV (April, 1965), 178.

87 Giovanni Russo, "Piety and Poverty in Sicily," *Atlas*, X (August, 1965), 93.

88 Candida, *op. cit.*, pp. 12–13.

89 Cutrera, *op. cit.*, pp. 118–121.

90 Reid, *op. cit.*, p. 27.

91 Heckethorn, *op. cit.*, (1965), Vol. I, p. 171.

92 Giuseppe Montalbano, "La Mafia," *Nuovi Argomenti*, V (Nov.-Dec., 1953), pp. 168–182.

93 F. Lestingi, "L'Associazione della Fratellanze nella provincia di Girgenti," *Archivio di Psichiatria, Scienze Penali ed Antropologia Criminale*, IV (1884), 452–463.

94 Cutrera, *op. cit.*, p. 120.

95 Bruno, *op. cit.*, pp. 16, 149–150.

96 Hobsbawm, op. cit., p. 13.

97 Maxwell, Bandit, pp. 52–53.

98 H. D. Sedgwick, Jr., "Musolino the Bandit," The Outlook, LXXI (August, 1902), 1057–1060.

99 Maxwell, Bandit, p. 80.

100 Heckethorn, op. cit., (1965), Vol. I, p. 169.

101 Vincenzo Linares, Racconti Popolari (Palermo: Luigi Pedone Lauriel, Editore, 1886), pp. 2–33.

102 Heckethorn, op. cit., (1965), Vol. I, p. 171.

103 Johnston, op. cit., p. 23.

104 G. Alongi, La Mafia (Milano: Remo Sandron, 1904), pp. 268–269.

105 Montalbano, op. cit., p. 169.

106 Cutrera, op. cit., p. 152.

107 Alongi, op. cit., p. 272.

108 Heckethorn, op. cit., (1965), Vol. I, p. 264.

109 S. Merlino, "Camorra, Maffia and Brigandage," Political Science Quarterly, IX (September, 1894), 466.

110 Walter Littlefield, "Camorra," Encyclopedia of the Social Sciences, Vol. III, p. 161.

111 David Hilton, Brigandage in South Italy (London: Sampson Low, Son, and Marston, 864), pp. 290–291.

112 Ibid., pp. 293–296.

113 A. DeBlasio, Usi e Costumi dei Camorristi (Napoli: Luigi Pierro: Editore, 1897), pp. 6–17.

114 Heckethorn, op. cit., (1965), Vol. I, p. 265.

115 Merlino, op. cit., p. 473.

116 Heckethorn, op. cit., (1965), Vol. I, pp. 266–267.

117 DeBlasio, op. cit., pp. 3–5, 39–41.

118 L. B. "Camorra in Calabria," Archivio di Psichiatria, Scienze Penali ed Antropologia Criminale, IV (Roma: Fratelli Bocca, 1883), p. 295.

119 N. Lewis, op. cit., p. 37.

120 Luigi Barzini, The Italians (New York: Bantam Books, Inc., 1965), Chapter 14.

121 Dennis Mack Smith, "The Mafia in Sicily," Atlas, III (June, 1962), 438.

122 Luigi Barzini, Jr., "The Real Mafia," Harper's Magazine, June, 1954), p. 46.

123 Leopoldo Franchetti and Sidney Sonnino, La Sicilia Nel 1876, Vol. I (Firenze: Vallecchi Editore, 1925), p. 68.

124 Will S. Monroe, Sicily (Boston: L. C. Page and Co., 1909), p. 141.

125 G. M. Puglia, "Il 'Mafioso' non e Associate per Delinquere," Antologia della Mafia (Palermo: Il Punto, edizioni, 1964), pp. 603–613.

126 Bolton King and Thomas Okey, *Italy To-Day* (London: James Nisbet and Co., Ltd., 1901), p. 120.

127 Hobsbawm, *op. cit.*, pp. 32–33.

128 G. LoSchiavo, "La Mafia e il Reato di Associazione per Delinquere," *Antologia della Mafia*, pp. 615–642.

129 Pitré, *op. cit.*, Vol. XV, p. 292.

130 Barzini, *op. cit.*, p. 264.

131 Bruno, *op. cit.*, p. 138.

132 Douglas Sladen, *Sicily* (New York: E. P. Dutton and Co., 1907), p. 23.

133 Alexander Nelson Hood, *Sicilian Studies* (New York: Dodd, Mead and Co., 1916), p. 74.

134 King and Okey, *op. cit.*, p. 120.

135 Robert Neville, "The Mafia Is Deadlier," *The New York Times Magazine*, January 12, 1964.

136 Candida, *op. cit.*, pp. 10–11.

137 Maxwell, *Bandit*, p. 141.

138 Paton, *op. cit.*, p. 361.

139 Monroe, *op. cit.*, pp. 142–143.

140 Michele Pantaleone, *The Mafia and Politics* (New York: Coward-McCann, Inc., 1966), p. 34.

141 Schiavo, *op. cit.*, pp. 52–53.

142 Andrew Varna, *World Underworld* (London: Museum Press, Ltd.), pp. 68–69.

143 Sid Feder and Joachim Joesten, *The Luciano Story* (New York: David McKay Co., Inc.), pp. 8–9.

144 Barzini, "The Real Mafia," p. 41, 46.

145 Enzo D'Alessandro, *Brigantaggio e Mafia in Sicilia* (Firenze: Casa Editrice G. D'Anna, 1959), p. 150.

146 Gaspare Nicotri, *Rivoluzioni e Rivolte in Sicilia* (Palermo: Alberto Reber, Editore, 1909), pp. 90–91.

147 Bruno, *op. cit.*, p. 61.

148 Paton, *op. cit.*, pp. 381–382.

149 Pantaleone, *op. cit.*, pp. 26–29.

150 D'Alessandro, *op. cit.*, p. 133.

151 Pantaleone, *op. cit.*, pp. 27–28.

152 Paolo Sylos-Labini, "Problems of Sicilian Economic Development Changes in Rural-Urban Relations in Eastern Sicily," *Mediterranean Social Sciences Research Council*, General Assembly, Catania, October 30–November 4, 1961, pp. 94–95.

153 Pantaleone, *op. cit.*, p. 28.

154 Leon Radzinowicz, *Ideology and Crime* (New York: Columbia University Press, 1966), pp. 2–3.

155 Salvatore Francesco Romano, *Momenti del Risorgimento in Sicilia* (Firenze: Casa Editrice G. D'Anna, 1952), pp. 291–292.

156 Schneider, *op. cit.*, pp. 145–146.

157 Romano, *op. cit.*, p. 285.

158 Pantaleone, *op. cit.*, p. 28.

159 "Bovini infetti nella Fiera di Palermo," *L'Unita*, June 2, 1963, p. 6.

160 Livio Pesce, "I segreti della Mafia," part 2, *Epoca*, December 10, 1967, p. 127.

161 Herbert Mitgang, "The Black Hand of Disaster in Sicily," *The New York Times*, January 21, 1968, p. 4E.

162 Boissevain, *op. cit.*, pp. 27–28.

163 Candida, *op. cit.*, p. 157.

164 Anton Blok, "Land Reform in a West Sicilian Latifondo Village: The Persistance of a Feudal Structure," *Anthropological Quarterly*, XXXIX (January, 1966), pp. 9–14.

165 Pesce, *op. cit.*, p. 127.

166 D. Smith, *op. cit.*, p. 440.

167 Cesare Mori, *The Last Struggle with the Mafia* (London: Putnam, 1933).

168 John DiGregorio, "Mussolini and the Mafia," *The Nation*, March 7, 1928, p. 263.

169 Leonardo Sciascia, *Mafia Vendetta* (New York: Alfred A. Knopf, 1964), p. 6.

170 DiGregorio, *op. cit.*, p. 264.

171 Anton Blok, "Peasants, Patrons and Brokers in Western Sicily." *Anthropological Quarterly* XLIII, July, 1969, p. 167.

172 Feder and Joesten, *op. cit.*, p. 171.

173 *Ibid.*

174 Salvatore Fancesco Romano, *Storia della Mafia* (Milano: Sugar Editore, 1963), p. 229.

175 Fillippo Gaja, *L'esercito della Lupare* (Milano: Area Editore, 1962), p. 210.

176 Hilton, *op. cit.*, pp. 297–299.

177 Heckethorn, *op. cit.*, (1965), Vol. I, p. 270.

178 Jane Catherine Schneider, *op. cit.*, p. 168.

179 Merlino, *op. cit.*, p. 473.

180 "Testimonianza resa alla Commissione parlamentare d'inchiesta sul fenomeno della mafia in Sicilia nella seduta 22 Febbraio 1967 (trascrizione verbatim)," *La Critica Sociologica* (Summer, 1967), pp. 12–16.

181 Franco Ferrarrotti, "La Mafia di Sicilia come problema dello sviluppo nazionale," *La Critica Sociologica* (Winter, 1967), pp. 134–135.

182 Corrado Antiochia, "Gli studenti di Alcamo fra mafia e autonomia," *La Critica Sociologica* (Winter, 1967), p. 141, 146.

183 Giorgio Pecorini, "Chiesa e mafia in Sicilia," *Communita*, January-April, 1967, pp. 51, 54, 60.

184 D. Smith, *op. cit.*, p. 441.

5

The Genesis and Development of Criminal Syndicates in the United States

Like the writings concerning the Sicilian "Mafia," there is confusion in the literature of syndicated crime in the United States. Here again the literature reveals a lack of distinction between syndicated crime as a method and as an organization.

Syndicated crime is a method. The association or group that engages in it is a syndicate. Syndicated crime as a method is the same as *mafia*—that is, if the term *mafia* is used to refer only to the method. Although syndicated crime and *mafia* as method are identical, the structure of the groups or associations who use it vary.

Syndicated crime in the United States has been carried on by a variety of groups among which may be found elements from all levels of society, legitimate and illegitimate. Among these we find criminal gangs; police; political officials; and a structure composed of individuals who, as patrons, bring into syndicate relationships a variety of legitimate and illegitimate clients. Never rigidly structured as an organization, it nonetheless operates as an efficient system of carrying out syndicate functions.

Although *mafia* and syndicated crime are identical as method, for the sake of consistency and because *mafia* has clandestine connotations, we prefer the use of the term *syndicated crime*. Using this latter term and avoiding the former will facilitate our attempt to show that syndicated crime in the United States has developed from within the American social structure. Contrary to the thesis that syndicated crime was imported into the United States, we shall show that, although foreign elements entered into American syndicated crime, their structure and function was one of adaptation to the American model. We shall contrast this view with the widely held misconception that the innocent, unguarded American public is a victim of foreign evildoers who secretly rob it of its moral virginity.

It should be obvious from our discussion of *mafia* in Sicily and *Camorra* in Italy that syndicated crime may function in differing manners depending upon the variations in historical, political, and economic aspects of any given society.

In the United States, as we shall illustrate, syndicates have existed only as a means of providing illicit goods and services to those segments of the American public who desire them. Syndicated criminals, unless they held governmental or police positions, never had an opportunity historically to entrench themselves in the legitimate structure. This is not to say that syndicated criminals have not been politically influential. However, this form of influence has come from their ability to pay for protection or to offer their services to political candidates.

With the exception of isolated cases of complete political control, such as that described earlier in Al Capone's municipal government in Cicero, syndicate criminals in America have functioned primarily within one segment of the American political structure—the political machine. In this form of political attachment, however, the syndicate criminal has not been able to entrench himself in the social and political structure of America as was true of the *mafioso* in Sicily.

Because they never became powerful political brokers in the United States, syndicate functionaries have had primarily to use direct pay-offs as their method of obtaining political protection for their enterprises.

Regardless of the cultural and other differences of participants in American syndicate crime, the basic structure of syndicates has always been the same, since this structure is determined not by the participants but rather by the nature of the criminal activity itself. The syndicate criminal in the United States serves as a broker between those who want illicit goods and a government that defines them as illegal.

The structure of syndicates, then, is largely determined by the social nature of the participants' role. Although there are variations between syndicates, their basic structure is always the same. Since their activities are illegal, syndicates must of necessity structure their groups and conduct their activities with secrecy a norm of behavior for participants and a vital part of the modus operandi. Also, since they have no recourse to the law, syndicates must employ violence to operate enterprises and keep control over participants. Furthermore, participants must be recruited from the ranks of individuals who display characteristics in keeping with these structural-functional needs. As we shall show, these characteristics have not been the prerogative of any one specific ethnic group or of any one criminal association in the United States.

In this chapter, we wish to compare and evaluate two conceptions of the growth of syndicated crime in the United States; one we call the *Evolutional-Centralization* approach, the other the *Developmental-Associational.*

The *Evolutional-Centralization* approach assumes and concludes that the criminal syndicates in the United States represent the evolution of an organization that had its roots in Sicily, where it was called "the Mafia." After or during its development, this "Mafia" was transported into the United States where it changed its name to *Mano Nera, L'Unione Siciliana, Cosa Nostra,* or retained its original name, "Mafia." Once established in the United States it evolved into a national association with a centralized structure. This structure consists of a ruling body or council which directs the activities of the various subdivisions sometimes referred to as "families," each of which have leaders who are ultimately responsible to the central national council.

The *Developmental-Associational* approach, on the other hand, views the origin and development of syndicated crime in the

United States as one emerging from social conditions and factors within American society itself. This development was not uniform. Rather, it varied both in time and place so that each syndicate must be studied individually. This approach views the contemporary structure of syndicated crime as including not one national-centrally organized syndicate but many syndicates which may or may not cooperate with one another.

Our conception of syndicated crime in the United States is *Developmental-Associational*. However, in order to fully explain and support this position, we first discuss and evaluate both the assumptions and the conclusions of the *Evolutional-Centralization* approach. This in turn necessitates a discussion and appraisal of the literature concerning *L'Unione Siciliana, Mano Nera, Cosa Nostra* and "Mafia" in the United States. As we shall illustrate, the major confusion here lies in the indiscriminate application of these names to various dissimilar associations or groups.

"The Mafia" Transplanted from Sicily?

In beginning our evaluation and comparison of the *Evolutional-Centralization* and *Developmental-Associational* approaches we must ask a basic question of those who uphold the former conceptualization. What exactly is meant by the general statement expressed by writers expounding this viewpoint—that "the Mafia" came to the United States? What in this case do these writers mean by "the Mafia?" We have shown that *mafia* as method can be found to exist in different places at different times. Since they are using "Mafia" in the context of an organization these writers are referring to an organization—the Sicilian "Mafia." This they define in general terms as a tightly knit, centralized organization that came to the United States where it spawned its evil influences. We are told that the heaviest migration of "the Mafia" to the United States took place during Mussolini's purge in the 1920s. Again, however, what do these writers mean by "the Mafia?" Was it a secret society? We have already dispelled this conception of *mafia* in the previous chapter. Was it individuals who had occupied the role of a *mafioso* in Sicily?

As we also formerly explained, the role of *mafioso* in Sicily has meaning only within the context of the Sicilian patron-client system of relationships. Even if this functionary, as such, came to the United States, what would his role have been within the context of the American social structure? One may argue that he may have continued such a role among the Sicilian immigrant neighborhoods in the United States. This would be plausible only if the American social structure had allowed for the Sicilian role of *mafioso*. In Sicily, we must remember, the *mafioso* gained and maintained his power because of his entrenchment in a caste-like system where he assumed positions of wealth and power through which he could serve as a patron to those in the lower client positions. The American social structure, as we have noted, has not produced such a functionary.

There is cause to question the meaning of those writers who maintain that the *mafia* either came or was brought to the United States from Sicily. The issue is further confused by inconsistencies in the use of the term itself. An excellent example of this is Brennan's[1] account of the origins of "Mafia" in the United States. He maintains that it was a form of criminal gang that existed in New York during the early 1900s. Then it was known not as "Mafia" but as "Unione Siciliane." It had control of various areas of New York City. Ignazio Saietta, for example, who emmigrated from Sicily in 1899, was supposedly in control of the Brooklyn and downtown area, while Ciro Terranova bossed the Harlem and Bronx area. This criminal gang, Brennan tells us, was a secret society that employed "blood-rite initiation" ceremonies in which "wrists were slashed, wounds were laid upon the other, and members became blood brothers as their scarlet fluid flowed together."

In the above account, Brennan describes those characteristics often attributed to the "Sicilian Mafia." The existence of these such characteristics, however, as we illustrated in Chapter 4, cannot be documented even in those organizations described as such in Sicily. How then can we trace their movement to America. Also, the initiation ritual which Brennan describes resembles that practiced by the *fratellanze* or brotherhoods in Sicily. These, we recall, were not forms of *mafia*.

Further confusion is added by contradictory explanations such as that appearing in *Life* magazine[2] in 1959. This described syndicated crime in the United States as an ongoing national organization that began with "the Mafia," of which Ignazio Saietta was the boss during the 1920s. This account tells us that Saietta perfected and structured the practice of sending "Black Hand extortion letters to Italian immigrants." Later, around 1931, the article continues, Lucky Luciano purged "the Old Mafia" by killing several of its old members. Without clarifying how or why it happened, this version maintains that syndicated crime after that time fell into the hands of some type of national organization. This consisted of a mixture of youthful-thinking members of "the Mafia," but also included Al Capone —who was independent of the "Mafia"—and various other ethnic and native-born groups all working together.

Feder and Joesten add further confusion by speaking of an "American branch of Mafia."[3] Later we are told that this branch of "the secret Sicilian Society" was brought to New York through the efforts of Ignazio Saietta. The American branch, however, was later "purged and succeeded by Unione Siciliano" which, under the leadership of Lucky Luciano, "came to dominate organized crime."[4]

We note the confusion between Brennan's and Feder and Joesten's accounts. Brennan maintains that "Unione Siciliane," synonymous to "the Mafia," was a secret society that took the form of a criminal gang in New York from 1900 to 1920. Feder and Joesten, however, argue that "Unione Siciliano" was an organization that came into existence with Lucky Luciano after his purge of "the old Mafia" around 1931.

The contradictions in these writings are indicative of much of the literature on *mafia* in the United States. It is a literature in which authors use terms without accurate definition, and draw conclusions for which they offer no source or documentation. In the three writings mentioned above, Ignazio Saietta is referred to as boss of the entire "Mafia," as boss of a division of the New York "Mafia" or *Unione Siciliana,* and as the transporter of the Sicilian "Mafia" to America's shores. Yet why? Who was Ignazio Saietta? We are told by various sources that he was a criminal who had escaped from justice in Sicily where he had been charged with homicide. All this tells us, if the accounts are correct, is that he was a Sicilian fugitive from justice. What makes him a *mafioso*? His engaging in extortion, killing, and other crimes in New York during the early 1900s are certainly not behaviors unique to Saietta. As for sending extortion letters, as we shall soon note, this was a practice of a multitude of Black Hand gangs operating in many towns and cities during that period of time. Saietta's position as head of the Sicilian "Mafia" is simply a creation without any basis in fact. Yet one finds its constant mention in the literature as though it were indisputable.

Unfortunately, as we shall see, an examination of more reliable accounts, investigations, and scholarly sources only further serves to confuse the issues. However, in the interest of clarification we should here like to give attention to such sources.

The Hennessy Case

Probably the only historical incident in the United States directly attributed to a Sicilian *mafia*-related group is the killing of the New Orleans Superintendent of Police, David C. Hennessy. On the evening of October 15, 1890 as Hennessy was walking home he was assaulted and killed by five armed assailants. What preceded and followed the shooting is confused and rests largely within the realm of conjecture.

One account states that "four blunderbusses, or sawed-off folding shotguns, and one double-barreled shotgun were found within a block or two of the scene of the murder."[5] Another account refers to one such shotgun found near the Hennessy home as "a typical Mafia weapon."[6] The latter conclusion, since there has never been a typical "Mafia" weapon, seems to be characteristic of the type of evidence and reasoning by which Hennessy's murder was attributed to "the Mafia."

Both Coxe's and Asbury's accounts note that Hennessy, before dying, stated that "Dagoes" had killed him; however, according to Asbury's rendition, he had not been able to recognize who they were.

In order to evaluate what is meant by those writers who attribute this incident to the influence of a Sicilian "Mafia," it is necessary to examine the basis upon which this conclusion was drawn.

Asbury[7] indicates that around 1869, a society that was a branch of the Sicilian "Mafia" was organized in New Orleans by four criminals who had been ousted from Palermo by governmental authorities. The name of this organization was the "*Stoppagherra* society."

The reader will note that *stoppagherra*, despite its variation in spelling, appears to be a name similar to that of the *fratellanza* or brotherhood (*Stoppaglieri* or *Stuppagghiari*) which we described in the previous chapter. Whether it was or not Asbury doesn't explain. He merely describes it as "a branch of the Mafia." In our opinion there is no relationship between the two since the men who started the "*stoppagherra*" came from Palermo while the *Stoppaglieri* brotherhood was located in Monreale.

Around 1869, Asbury continues, New Orleans became the "headquarters" for "Mafia" in the United States, which by that time had branches in various other cities including New York, Chicago, and San Francisco.[8] It is rather odd that in Asbury's work dealing specifically with the underworld of San Francisco,[9] there is absolutely no mention of this "Mafia."

Asbury's account has other discrepancies. He states, for example, that during the period of "Mafia" development in New Orleans, the "chieftain of the society in Sicily was the celebrated Leoni" who Asbury goes on to describe as a leader of a band of brigands.[10] As we noted in Chapter 4 there are distinctions between brigands, *frattellanze* and *mafia*. Yet Asbury simultaneously refers to a brigand, Leoni, as the chieftain of the "Mafia" in Sicily whose branch in New Orleans was called the *"Stop-pagherra* Society." We wonder why the New Orleans branch simply didn't continue to call itself "Mafia?" Irrespective of this, we have already sufficiently argued the improbability of the existence of a chieftain of "Mafia" in Sicily. In any event, its chief would certainly not be a brigand. When we consider the patron-client power position necessary to a *mafioso*, a brigand being outrightly sought by the law would be the least probable individual to maintain such a position.

At the time of Hennessy's assassination, Asbury[11] notes, without giving any reasons, that the New Orleans "Mafia" had come under the control of the Matranga brothers, Tony and Charles. They sought to take over the business of unloading ships, which was then in the hands of the Provenzano brothers. Forced out of this and another business venture by the repeated assaults of Matranga henchmen, the Provenzanos began a vendetta. At this time David Hennessy was superintendent of police. He was also a friend of the Provenzano brothers. Therefore, when two of the Provenzano brothers—Joe and Pete—were arrested as a result of an assault involving the Matrangas, Hennessy tried to help them. He did this by offering to testify against the Matrangas at the trial of the Provenzanos. According to Asbury, Hennessy also promised during his testimony to reveal evidence against the New Orleans "Mafia" and the Matrangas' involvement in it. To keep him from testifying, Asbury seems to argue, Hennessy was murdered.

Again, however, Asbury's contention that Hennessy had evidence about the "Mafia" seems to be merely a supposition. We find no evidence that the Matranga activities were anything more than those of a criminal gang. Also, the vendetta between the Matrangas and Provenzanos was not specifically a "Mafia" mode of behavior, but rather one common to Sicilian kinship groups. If Hennessy had information, it probably was evidence he could offer against the Matrangas themselves rather than against a "Mafia" as such.

In our conception, the Matranga family in their use of violence and extortion did not constitute a form of *mafia*, but rather a form of extortion-oriented organized crime. Asbury's contention of "Mafia" being present in New Orleans seems to lie, as it does with other writers, in his confusion of "Mafia" as an association with *mafia* as a method. Other accounts such as the following commit the same error.

Coxe's[12] account, like Asbury's, states that the Provenzanos and Matrangas had been opponents in the shipping business. Coxe, however, unlike Asbury, does not mention that the Matrangas had used extortion or violent techniques. Instead he simply states that they had been "successful in securing the business formerly enjoyed by the Provenzano crowd." Because of this, however, he maintains, six associates of the Provenzano group attempted to murder seven of the Matranga group on May 6, 1890. A trial was held and the Provenzanos were found guilty.

During this trial, several policemen had testified in behalf of the Provenzanos. This, coupled with the fact that the Provenzanos were granted a new trial that was to take place on October 22, 1890, led the Matrangas to view Hennessy as prejudiced against their faction. Charges of bias were brought against Hennessy and the other policemen testifying in the trial but a grand jury found no proof. It was learned, however, that Hennessy had evidently attempted to bring about a settlement of the dispute between the two groups. This attempt, Coxe notes, brought resentment toward Hennessy on the part of the Matrangas. Coxe maintains that on October 19, two days after Hennessy's killing, the Provenzanos gave a letter to the *Times-Democrat,* a New Orleans newspaper. The Provenzanos offered this as proof that the Matrangas were "members of a branch of the Mafia, known as the Stoppaghiera." The letter began with the sentence, "You had better wake up and think of your outrage against justice if you don't want to be done up by the Mafia." Coxe himself states that it was never proven that the Matrangas had in fact written this letter. However, he argues that "the significance of the letter lay in the fact that it revealed the presence of the Mafia in New Orleans and demonstrated some of the methods of this oath-bound organization."[13]

Again as with Asbury, we must question what Coxe means by "Mafia." Certainly the use of the term "Mafia" in the letter presents some problems. Even in Sicily, those who participate in *mafia* enterprises never refer to themselves as members of the "Mafia" or, for that matter, as *mafiosi*. We also wonder that if the Matrangas were members of the "Stoppaghiera" society, why did they not refer to themselves as "Stoppaghieri" rather than as "Mafia?"

It seems to be obvious that Coxe, like Asbury, failed to adequately understand what *mafia* entails. His derivation of the existence of "Mafia" from a letter whose authorship he himself states was never proven, seems to be a matter of circular reasoning. However, even if the authorship of the letter had been shown to be that of the Matrangas, this in itself would not establish the Matrangas as a *mafia* group. It was not a unique form of letter. Like other types of threatening letters this one threatened death if the Provenzanos did not change their testimony in the retrial that was about to take place. Certainly, sending threatening letters is not unique to the "Mafia."

The so-called Mafia Incident in New Orleans, then, seems to have been, in reality, a vendetta between two factions vying for control over a business enterprise. Hennessy's death most probably was related to the fact that he took the side of the Provenzanos in this dispute. This by definition made him, in the eyes of the opposing faction, a collaborator with the enemy.

Another reason for attributing the Hennessy killing to "the Mafia" stems from testimony during the trial itself. Asbury,[14] basing his evidence on a newspaper account, states that during this trial one of those indicted, a man named Politz, confessed that he had been present at the society's meeting where Hennessy's death had been planned. Politz included in his testimony a list of some of the members of the society and even revealed some of its "signs and signals." Coxe notes that Politz, soon after the taking of testimony began in the trial, "became insanely frantic" and stated that he desired to confess. He made his confession, with the aid of an interpreter, to the state's attorneys; however, the district attorney did not accept the confession. Nor was any official declaration of the confession ever released to the public. Yet, according to Coxe, newspaper stories told of how a meeting had been held at a particular house on the night prior to the killing. At this meeting "lots were drawn" to decide who would actually participate in the killing and then large sums of money were paid to the killers by the leaders.[15]

Needless to say, the accuracy of these newspaper accounts is questionable. Even if they were not, the description of what took place at this alleged meeting does not appear consistent with what would occur at a "Mafia" conclave. Certainly, as "Mafia" is usually described, members swear allegiance to a leader, the leader would not be paying them for a service that he could easily command them to carry out.

Thus the existence of "Mafia" in New Orleans during the Hennessy incident has not been established. The mere attribution of what are assumed to be "Mafia"-associated characteristics to individuals and groups in the Hennessy incident does not establish the presence of "the Mafia." Rather, it merely serves to further display the confusion about "Mafia" that emerges from writings in which terms are merely assigned rather than defined.

If one examines other writings concerning the incident, one finds more material that serves only to add further to the confusion. Horan states that in a report issued by Hennessy himself, Hennessy "described the Mafia in New Orleans as a tightly knit band of Sicilian immigrants who employed stabbings, shootings and bombings to control the dock areas." In this report Hennessy added that the New Orleans "Mafia" was "not 'supported' by the parent organization in Italy."[16]

Interestingly, Horan also tells us that a Pinkerton detective, Frank Dimaio, had been planted among those prisoners accused of Hennessy's murder. This detective succeeded in frightening Emanuel Politz (the witness mentioned earlier who gave testimony during the trial) into believing that the other prisoners were attempting to kill Politz for fear that he might turn informant.

Horan describes how Dimaio convinced Politz that the cheese covering a plate of spaghetti he was about to eat had been poisoned with arsenic and later that wine sent to Politz's cell also was poisoned.[17] Although none of this was true, Politz became very disturbed that his friends wanted to kill him. This may help explain why Politz became, as Coxe described earlier, "insanely frantic" after the taking of testimony began during the trial. Horan adds that, after the incident of the supposed poisoned wine, Politz broke down and told Dimaio about how Hennessy's murder had been planned and that he thought the other prisoners were trying to kill him because they thought he would "betray the society." Later, Dimaio testified to a grand jury about the information Politz revealed about Hennessy's murder, including the fact that the "Mafia" had funds with which they could bribe any jury.

As a result of Dimaio's testimony, Horan tells us, the District Attorney subpoenaed "numerous witnesses to events leading up to and including the murder itself."[18] Interestingly, however, we are not told anything about the so-called Mafia or society Politz had revealed.

It seems obvious that what Dimaio gave as testimony based upon Politz's information consisted, at most, of knowledge about the individuals involved in Hennessy's murder and not about an organization—"Mafia." In Horan's discussion the concept *mafia* is employed in such a variety of contexts that as a descriptive term it becomes absolutely meaningless. We also wonder why the testimony of Dimaio, based upon Politz's confession, was accepted by the Grand Jury, yet later during the trial itself, Politz's own confession to the state's attorneys was not.

Similar to the above accounts in its use of the term "Mafia" is that of Kendall.[19] Like Coxe, he tells us that Giuseppe Esposito, who was present in New Orleans around 1881, was formerly a "lieutenant" in a band of Italian bandits headed by a leader named Leone. Later Kendall implies that this band was a manifestation of "Mafia." However, further on in his writing, he implies that the "Mafia" was a "society." As though not presenting enough confusion in his nebulous usage of the term, he later states that "The Mafia, the Camorra, and in the United States, the Black Hand" stood for or, "some twenty or thirty years ago," used to stand for "practically the same thing." That is, these names represented "Italian secret criminal organizations which, long active in Southern Italy and Sicily, were imported into this country by the malefactors who, between 1860 and 1890, were driven from their native land and found refuge in America." Later we learn that the "Mafia" was introduced into the United States by the bandit, Esposito. We are told that Esposito, along with "two other of Leone's lieutenants" who had escaped from the clutches of the Italian government's campaign against "the Camorra and Mafia" had, along with other escaped criminals in New Orleans, "formed a little group of plotting scoundrels who were the nucleus of the Mafia."

We need not go any further to illustrate that Kendall, like the other writers mentioned above, employs "Mafia" without any definite meaning. According to him it was originally composed of bandits who brought it to the United States where it was a society. Yet he tells us, without clearly specifying when or where, that "the Mafia was distinct from other secret societies" in that "it had no passwords, no meetings, no initiations, no elections, no promotions." Instead, he goes on, it was founded on a system in which its services were performed for those who had come in conflict with the law. In turn the recipient of these services would be in debt to the "Mafia," which could later call upon him for some service. "If he refused, he was punished."

In this latter statement, one has the feeling that Kendall is attempting to explain "Mafia" in terms of a patron-client relationship; however, he does not develop this conception further. Later he states that "In 1890 the Mafia was fully organized and flourishing in New Orleans." He offers evidence from the Hennessy trial to show that "Mafia" was a secret society that had "officers" and "members." Still later he states that whether the "Mafia" that existed in New Orleans in 1890 had any connection to the "Mafia" created by Esposito around 1878 is a question that has never been definitely answered.

At this point in Kendall's account one is at a complete loss as to what "Mafia" is. Is it a band of criminals organized in New Orleans by Esposito, a former bandit; is it a secret society different from Esposito's original form of *mafia* with a hierarchy of officers and rules; is it the Black Hand; is it the *Camorra*; is it merely a system of protective, loosely knit relationships structured among certain Sicilian criminals?

Needless to say, Kendall's discussion makes no distinction between *mafia* as method and as association. His inconsistent usage of the term indicates that Kendall never adequately defined *mafia*. Yet, he tells us that its existence in New Orleans in 1890 is a "fact."

In short then, the existence of "Mafia" in the Hennessy incident was never proven; rather, at most, it was merely assumed. One cannot examine the writings of the various authors mentioned above without concluding that they had no clear conception of what *mafia* was.

As a final note of interest, the acquittal of some of those accused of the Hennessy killing brought about the formation of a lynch mob in New Orleans that hanged two and shot nine of those who the mob believed were directly responsible for Hennessy's death. Of the original nineteen indicted for the crime and incarcerated in the prison when it was stormed by the lynching mob, Coxe informs us that eight escaped and were later permitted to go free by the Prosecution; of those eleven that were killed, five had not yet been tried, three had been acquitted, and three, although tried, had received no verdict because the jury could not reach an agreement on their cases.[20]

The incident created a temporary but serious diplomatic problem between the United States and the Italian government. In the United States, President Benjamin Harrison called the incident "deplorable and discreditable."[21] In Rome, feelings were running high, but became less tense when it was learned that only three of the eleven victims of the lynching mob were Italian subjects. The issue was finally settled when, as an act of friendship, the United States paid twenty-five thousand dollars in restitution to the Italian government.[22]

Immigration Data

Another source of evidence offered by those who subscribe to the *Evolutional-Centralization* conceptualization of syndicated crime in the United States is immigration data, through which they argue that the *mafia* was brought to this country. Again we ask the same question: what is meant by *mafia*? There is no doubt that many criminals from a variety of countries entered the United States through illegal means. The difficulty comes in making an accurate estimate of how many did enter.

The 1911 report of the Immigration Commission attempted to give an estimate of the number of Italian criminals (those who had been convicted of a crime in Italy) in New York who had entered illegally. According to this report "More than 500 cases were investigated in New York, some 70 penal certificates were secured from Italy, and as a result of information furnished by the Commission a number of Italian criminals were deported."[23] The actual number deported is never mentioned. Five cases in which deportation resulted are discussed, but we cannot be certain that these represent the total number. The report also notes the legal problems that made deportation difficult. It indicates that according to Italian law, Italians and Sicilians accused of crimes in their homeland could be tried in absentia. Since many of these had entered the United States prior to their conviction, they were not, at the time of their entry, adjudged criminals. Therefore, since they were not convicted criminals at the time of their entry, they could not be accused of violating the immigration law and thus could not be deported.[24]

Another report of the same commission indicated that the Italian government was aiding the curbing of criminal migration to the United States by refusing to issue passports to anyone with a criminal record. This effort, the commission reports, was not very effective since criminals who were not issued passports to the United States in Italy simply embarked from ports in other countries. Since passports were not demanded at U.S. ports, entry under this procedure was easy.[25] Also, some came into the country as seamen on foreign vessels while others embarked from Canadian ports and later made their way into the U.S. at various places along the Canadian border.[26]

There is no doubt that criminals from various foreign countries entered the United States illegally. Among these were criminals from Italy and Sicily. The question, for our purpose, is can it be demonstrated, as many writers maintain, that the

"Mafia" came into this country with these immigrants? Those writers who subscribe to this hypothesis do so by merely making the statement. They never explain upon what evidence such a thesis is based.

It is difficult to estimate the number of Italians and Sicilians who entered the United States illegally. It is even more problematic to determine how many of these had engaged in *mafia* activity in Sicily or were members of the *Camorra* or other organized criminal groups in Sicily and Italy. First, as we have emphasized before, we must remember that *mafia* in Sicily is not a rigidly defined or structured organization. Hence we may argue that some individuals who participated in *mafia* activities on various levels of the patron-client structure in Sicily came to the United States. Also we may assume that some members of the *Camorra* in Naples came to the United States. But then so did other criminals—bandits, common thieves, murderers—and other types not only from Sicily and Italy, but other countries as well. Again we fail to understand what these writers mean when they state that the "Mafia" came to the United States.

Although one of the immigration reports mentioned earlier cites penal certificates referring to certain Sicilian-Italian criminals as being members of the "Mafia" and the *Camorra*, the terms again reflect the same unclear usage we find in the literature. One certificate, for example, dealing with an Italian who had not been convicted of any crime includes the following statement of the Italian courts: "although the records do not show any conviction, he is held and looked upon by all in his village as a mafioso." In another case the certificate bore the comment that the man being discussed, although not convicted of any crime, was nonetheless "looked upon by all in his village as a mafioso" and was a man "of evil reputation."[27] In a footnote, however, it is mentioned that the term "mafioso" employed in the above quotations is used to designate "a 'tough'—one having an habitual disregard for the law."[28]

In another case, the penal certificate and record included a letter from a police official of Palermo stating that the man in question, a former resident of Palermo, although never convicted was "a most suspicious character, and one capable of organizing and directing any criminal enterprise, having been affiliated here with the Mafia, not only of this district and province, but elsewhere."[29]

Here we are faced with the problem of determining the meaning of the statement "affiliated with" the "Mafia." Does this mean affiliation as a member of an organization or is it in terms of a patron-client relationshp? Since the letter is a translated version of the original, the exact original meaning becomes even more difficult to determine. We note that in this latter case, "Mafia" is employed within a context of some form of organizational structure as compared to the two previously cited cases where reference to being a "mafioso" was used in the context of someone who uses violence or has an attitude of defiance of the law. An agent of the Immigration Commission adds further confusion when in his testimony concerning an Italian criminal residing in New York, commented "Here he belongs to the Mafia and Camorra."[30]

What can we conclude about "Mafia" from these reports? Practically nothing. We have only the opinions of those officials or agencies submitting the testimony or items of evidence. Even in their opinions there is insufficient consistency to provide any basis of agreement. The literature seeking to relate the existence of *mafia* in the United States to sources of Italian and Sicilian immigration shows, at most, the degree of confusion that exists in the literature itself.

As observed in aforementioned accounts and reports, the nebulousness of terms is found not only in regard to *mafia* but to *Camorra* as well. A specific example of this is the work of Arthur Train, a former Assistant District Attorney in New York. His writing is concerned primarily with the *Camorra* in America, which he implies was "imported."[31] Since this article is basically a condensation of Chapter 9 of his book, *Courts, Criminals and the Camorra*[32] we will here treat these two sources as one and the same.

Although Train speaks of immigration and its relationship to the existence of *Camorra* and "Mafia" in the United States, it is never made clear what this relationship is. First, we are told that "The Mafia, a purely Sicilian product, exerts a much more obvious influence in America than the Camorra, since the Mafia is powerful all over Sicily, while the Camorra is practically confined to the city of Naples and its environs." On the basis that there were more Sicilians in America than Neopolitans, Train concludes that in New York City "for every one Camorrist you will find seven or eight Mafiusi." One cannot help getting the feeling from Train's conclusion that a proportional quota of "Mafia" and *Camorra* must have come along with each group of immigrants that entered the United States.

Later Train varies his conception of "Mafia" and *Camorra*, both of which he refers to as "great secret societies of southern Italy." He indicates that these two societies are basically similar and that "the artificial distinction between them in Italy disappears entirely in America." After having indicated that *Mafiusi* outnumbered *camorristi* by almost eight to one in New York, he then tells us that the "organization of the Camorra has never been transferred to this country." Yet later he tells of a case in New York where an Italian importer employed a "Camorrist" to collect an unpaid debt for him.[33]

Train seems to finally conclude that crime in the Italian immigrant areas of the United States can best be subsumed under the term *Mala Vita*.[34] This is a general term commonly used among Italians referring to organized criminals or organized criminal activity. Several Italian informants, however, indicated to the author that certain specific groups or bands in the area of Calabria, Italy were referred to this way around the turn of the century. When the author questioned these informants further, he found that these groups, as they were described, had structures and activities similar to those of bandits and robber gangs. Hence it appears that the use of the term *Mala Vita*, according to these informants, was more one of a colloquial usage for organized bands of criminals rather than one referring to a specific criminal organization. We should point out here, however, that Heckethorn mentions *Mala Vita* as a form of secret society. He notes that it was first publicly revealed in Bari, Italy in 1891 and was believed to be, because of similarities to it, a derivative of the Neopolitan *Camorra*.[35]

Returning to Train's discussion of *Mala Vita* in the United States, he tells us that "The majority of the followers of the Mala Vita—the Black Handers—are not actually of Italian birth, but belong to the second generation."[36] Yet speaking of "Black Hand" gangs in New York he states that these are sometimes composed of Italians in combination with members of other nationality groups. He notes later, however, that "the genuine Black Hander (the real Camorrist or 'Mafiuoso') works alone or with two or three of his fellow-countrymen."[37]

It is obvious that Train's usage of terms is so vague and inconsistent that it is virtually impossible to draw any valid conclusions regarding exactly what, if any, form of Italian or Sicilian criminal patterns or organizations were transferred into the United States.

It appears that sources arguing that "Mafia" and *Camorra* were imported to the United States do not successfully demonstrate their thesis. Statements are made but no valid evidence is offered to support these statements. Rather it appears that these sourcs assume that since "Mafia" and *Camorra* existed in Sicily and Italy, since Italians and Sicilians immigrated to the United States, since among these immigrants were criminals, that obviously the "Mafia" and *Camorra* must have been transplanted with them.

Thus Anderson tells us that "Mafias were first established in America in the latter part of the nineteenth century." Without giving us any reason or evidence for making this statement, he goes on to tell us that "During the prohibition era they proliferated and prospered" and that "Throughout this period these groups continued to function essentially like the small traditional Mafia of western Sicily."[38]

Since Anderson seems to equate "Mafia" in Sicily with *frattellanze* the criticisms against his conception are the same as those we have already discussed in the previous chapter; namely, that he is not distinguishing between *mafia* as a group and method. Defining "Mafia" as an association then, Anderson does not present evidence to show that any such association was, in fact, established in the United States. He merely makes the statement that it happened.

Other writers who do not argue direct infusion of *mafia* argue instead that contemporary syndicated crime is an adaptation of the early "Mafia" or *Camorra* to American society. This argument is very difficult to evaluate since, as we have noted, we do not have evidence to verify that *mafia* or *Camorra*, in their European forms, ever were present in the United States. We cannot argue that something whose existence has never been demonstrated adapted to anything.

The basic criticism of the writers who seek to relate contemporary American syndicates to Italian-Sicilian cultural sources lies in the failure of these writers to demonstrate what, in fact, was infused into American syndicated crime from Italy or Sicily. These writers seem to assume that syndicated crime, as a method, never existed in the United States prior to the mass immigration of Italians and Sicilians. Also, they fail to note the fact that many of the early participants in syndicated crime in America were not Italian or Sicilian. And although the contemporary syndicates in the United States contain a preponderance of Italians and Sicilians, there is no evidence that those among them who immigrated to the United States or their parents were connected with or associated with the "Mafia" or *Camorra*. If they became involved in syndicated crime, we must seek the reasons for this involvement from within the context of the American social system itself. It was, after all, this same system that gave rise to George "Bugs" Moran, Arnold Rothstein, Owen Madden, as well as to the Italians and Sicilians—Capone, Torrio, and Luciano.

The roots of American syndicated crime, as we stressed earlier, are found in the need for illicit services by segments of the American public. These needs have varied with time and place. Although syndicates must maintain the basic characteristics necessary to their functioning, each syndicate structure has a variation based upon the nature of the service or product it is supplying. Hence we find variations in syndicates both historically and in contemporary society.

Technological advancements have also served to produce changes in syndicated crime. Thus, as the Minneapolis Vice

Commission noted in 1911, the telephone was largely responsible for changes in prostitution: it moved from the organized structure of the "house" in "Red Light" districts to the practice of one or two prostitutes operating from a private place of residence.[39] The telephone also, along with faster means of transportation, allowed for an increase in interstate commerce.

It should be emphasized here that we are not suggesting that there is a direct relationship between the structure of American society and that of syndicated crime at any given time historically. Instead, we are stating that the structure of syndicated crime in both time and place is related to the nature of the activity in which it is involved. Technological advancements, in themselves, may help or hinder these enterprises. Thus the telephone helped syndicates enlarge their ecological area of distribution of illicit alcohol during prohibition. However, it was also the telephone which allowed prostitutes to operate more independently. This made it more difficult for syndicates to control them and eventually to control the enterprise of prostitution itself.

Returning to our discussion of "Mafia" and *Camorra* in the United States, we note again that their so-called infusion from Italy and Sicily has never been satisfactorily demonstrated. Of the two one could argue that *Camorra* had more likelihood of being transplanted. Since it was a criminal organization with an established hierarchy of positions and rules, we would find its movement from one society to another much more feasible than that of the Sicilian *mafia*, which is loosely structured on a patron-client system of relationships. One could also state— merely for the sake of argument—that many aspects of the so-called Cosa Nostra in the United States resemble more those of the *Camorra* than the "Mafia." Thus the structures of this "Cosa Nostra" with its boss, underboss, lieutenant, and soldiers coupled with a commission that serves as an overall governing board, is more similar to *Camorra* than the more loosely defined and changing patron-client structure of Sicilian *mafia*.

The above statements are not meant to imply that the *Camorra* was transplanted to the United States or that "Cosa Nostra" has any relationship to *Camorra*. We merely wonder why those writers who argue infusion did not select *Camorra* instead of "Mafia" as their basis of argument. The answer seems that these writers did not seriously study either of these two phenomena. Rather it appears that they merely used newspapers and other popular accounts as their source data. It can be argued that much of the confusion surrounding the concept *mafia* in the United States, is due to the indiscriminate and confusing use of the term by the press itself.

Rudolph Vecoli notes that the press in Chicago was influential in giving the impression that "Mafia" existed there. One newspaper, for example, offered the simple argument that "wherever there are Sicilians there also is the Mafia." Another argued that the Hennessy affair in New Orleans showed that there was no "doubt that the Mafia had been transplanted from the slums of Italy to American soil."[40] These are not very valid proofs. Nonetheless, Vecoli notes, through such unfounded statements the press served to create a public conception of both the origin and existence of "Mafia" in Chicago.

The influence of the press can be witnessed again when we note one of the reasons Italians were selected from among various nationality groups for the Immigration Commission's investigation of the extent of illegal entry of criminals into the United States: ". . . because of the popular opinion, voiced in the press, that large numbers of Italians having criminal records in Italy come to the United States, and that Italian crimes of violence in this country are in large measure due to them."[41]

Syndicated crime in the United States, when viewed from its early developmental forms, is an American product. It is interesting to note that many writers who uphold the infusion or *Evolutional-Centralization* theory begin their analysis of syndicated crime, historically, with a description of Italian and Sicilian involvement. It seems that these writers merely assume that no form of syndicated crime existed in the United States prior to the coming of the Italians and Sicilians.

Anderson, for example, merely describes the evolution and increased bureaucratization of the "Mafia" in the United States; he does not consider the development of other non-"Mafia" sources of American syndicated crime. He concludes that the

"Cosa Nostra is a lineal descendant of the Mafia, but it is a different kind of organization."[42] One must assume from reading Anderson that either there were no important American sources of syndicated crime in the United States or that they were not significant in its development.

Cressey does not take any stand on whether *mafia* was or was not infused from Sicily, but rather merely states that "Whatever was imported has been modified to fit the conditions of American life."[43] Yet in his historical development of syndicated crime, which he prefers to call "Cosa Nostra," we find he begins with the year 1931 when he states "The basic structure of the nationwide cartel and confederation which today operates the principal illicit businesses in America and which is now striking at the foundations of legitimate business and government as well, came into being."[44]

Such an historically fragmented approach to the analysis of syndicated crime in the United States can produce no more than a fragmented explanation and description. Also if syndicated crime is viewed as a method rather than as an association, an historical evaluation of its development in the United States reveals that the method of syndicated crime has remained basically the same irrespective of what nationality or other group participated in it.

As we have noted extensively before, syndicated crime in the United States, because of its function of supplying illicit goods, must conduct its activities and create its structure within a limited set of conditions or restrictions. Whatever the variations, the basic format must be the same. For this reason, we argue that, even if it were possible to prove that individuals participating in Sicilian "Mafia" or in the Neapolitan *Camorra* immigrated to the United States, it would make little difference. Once they arrived they would have to operate within the context of American syndicated crime. They would have to use violence to enforce conformity among their ranks. They would have to operate in secrecy. Finally, they would have to pay for protection either by extending favors to police or politicians or by direct monetary bribery. What difference then does it make whether those involved are Italian, Yankee American, Greek, Russian, Polish or any combination of these or other groups? There are perhaps different socialization processes and values among various nationality groups, which may affect the ease or efficiency with which the individual syndicate member functions within the structure of the syndicate. However, notice here we are arguing adjustment to required syndicated behaviors. We are not arguing that nationality group characteristics have any relationship or affect upon the basic structure of American syndicated crime.

Those who argue that syndicated crime in the United States resulted from infusion of "Mafia" or *Camorra* assume that something "new" was introduced into American syndicated crime with the immigration of Italians and Sicilians.

Syndicates: The Nineteenth Century

We hope to refute this assumption and to demonstrate that syndicated crime in the United States is based upon a restricted form of structure imposed upon it by its relationship to American society. In order to do this we shall examine syndicated crime in a broader historical and social context—primarily as method rather than as association.

Unfortunately, adequate and coherent histories of syndicated crime in the United States are rare. If we had complete histories for every city as we have for Chicago in Virgil Peterson's *Barbarians in Our Midst* our task would be made much easier. Instead we must use historical sources that are only partially concerned with this subject. These, although useful, do not make for a chronological description of the development of syndicates in various cities or other ecological areas. Only in the case of New York and Chicago do we find sufficient writings that lend themselves to such historical analysis. Therefore, we shall use New York and Chicago primarily as models for our historical analysis. This does not mean that all syndicates have developed in a manner identical to those in Chicago and New York. We wish to stress instead that any syndicate, in order to be adequately understood, must be studied as a unit in itself.

It should be understood at the outset that our purpose here is not to develop a history of syndicates in the United States or specifically, those of Chicago and New York. Rather we wish to present historical arguments that help demonstrate that syndicates are an American phenomenon.

When we examine the beginnings of syndicated crime in Chicago we find that organized underworld elements were present as early as the 1830s.[45] During this era, according to Asbury, burglars, pickpockets, gamblers, prostitutes, counterfeiters, gunmen, and other criminals entered the city in large numbers. In our definition of syndicated crime—which includes the providing of illicit services by an organization which generally employs violence as a method of control and which has some form of protection from the law—a syndicate, as such, did not exist in Chicago at this time. One reason for this was the simple fact that until 1835, Chicago had no police force. By 1854, the force consisted of about nine men responsible for policing a population of about 80,000.[46] Under such conditions there would be no need for organized criminals to seek protection from the law, as adequate enforcement would have been virtually impossible.

In 1855, however, a police department of about eighty men was formed and with this we begin to witness the development of syndicates in Chicago. One of these early enterprises was the resort operated by Roger Plant, an Englishman from Yorkshire. Consisting of several shacks and houses in a one-block area in 1865, Plant's resort provided prostitution, room rental for those interested in practicing homosexuality and other forms of deviation, and other illicit services.[47] Plant also provided a warning and escape system that protected soldiers from nearby camps who frequented his establishment from being apprehended by military patrols.[48] Himself quite adept at the use of violence, Plant employed others who helped him in operating and protecting his establishment. Also, he paid protection to the police on a regular basis.[49]

During the period of the Civil War, Peterson notes, gamblers were operating gaming establishments in Chicago without serious interference from the law. Through the cooperation of their mistresses who often served as madames, these same gamblers provided funds for establishing houses of prostitution.[50] They also provided the network by which "bounty-jumpers" (those who were paid a fee by draftees to serve in their place as soldiers but instead took the money and fled to a different territory, state, or country) could be smuggled from one place to another. As Cook indicates, this network often included collusion with an army recruiting officer while many of the bounty-jumpers came from the underworld. The network was such that it extended into Canada.[51]

During the era of the 1860s then, syndicates, as we have defined them, had made their appearance on the American scene. As Peterson states, in Chicago during this time period, George Trussell, a gambler, was capable of exerting political influence in the form of having competing gambling establishments raided and closed by the police. As yet, Peterson points out, these gamblers had not become a part of the political machine as was to occur later; instead the gamblers exerted their influence over politicians through financial and other forms of services.[52]

Those writers who maintain that such criminal patterns as extortion of business enterprises, demanding protection money from shopkeepers, and defiance and disrespect for the law were techniques imported into America by the "Mafia" or *Camorra* should take a brief look at the activities of some of the American-bred gangs during the middle 1800s.

The Hell's Kitchen Gang (the name deriving from a section of the west side of New York commonly referred to as Hell's Kitchen) organized sometime around 1868 and led by Dutch Heinrich, was known for such use of terror and extortion. This gang, O'Connor tells us, "made shopkeepers and manufacturers pay protection money, and systematically victimized the Hudson River Railroad."[53]

In San Francisco in the late 1840s another gang known as The Hounds "systematically extorted gold and jewelry" from the Chilean residents of that city. Setting themselves up as self-declared public protectors they demanded payment for their services from the people of San Francisco. Around 1849, The Hounds began referring to themselves as Regulators and set out on their self-designated task of protecting the city of San Francisco from what they had defined as the menace of the Spanish-Americans.[54] Asbury points out they made a practice of entering places of business and helping themselves to what they wanted without paying for it. If the merchant complained he met with a severe beating. Along with this they made a practice of eating or drinking to their hearts' content at various saloons or taverns, telling the proprietor to charge the bill to the city. If the proprietor presented any difficulty, his establishment was either ransacked or burned.

In contradiction to the thesis of writers who maintain that the protection racket was a criminal pattern transported to the United States by the Sicilian "Mafia," we note that The Hounds offered such protection on a fee basis to the merchants of San Francisco.[55] This payment was supposedly made to protect the businessmen from foreign elements. In reality it was made to protect the merchants from The Hounds themselves who routinely destroyed the property of those who did not buy such protection.

Regarding disrespect for the law being a characteristic imported by the Sicilian "Mafia" we find by 1860 that such an attitude virtually constituted a way of life in the Hell's Kitchen area of New York. Whereas in Sicily police were rarely physically attacked by participants in *mafia* activity, in this area attacking police became a sport.

O'Connor tells us that One Lung Curran, a well-known street fighter, was so aggressive toward police that they always took care to walk "wide circles around him." One Lung was also responsible for starting a fad among his street-fighting peers— robbing a policeman of his overcoat for their girlfriends.[56] Cracking a policeman across the head with a blackjack, One Lung took his overcoat for his girlfriend who had earlier indicated that she had no winter coat. His girlfriend had the coat altered and began wearing it. Soon the girlfriends of the other street-fighters were demanding that they duplicate One Lung's heroic deed for them. For several weeks a number of policemen returned to headquarters without their coats. Only after massive reprisal attacks by specially organized police squads in the Hell's Kitchen area did this practice stop.[57] In this area, O'Connor states, street fights between gangs and police were commonplace, some remembered for the severity of their violence that often included broken skulls, cracked ribs, and gouged eyes.[58]

Around the middle of the 1800s we note the beginnings of coalitions between gangs and political machines, particularly in New York and Chicago. By 1842, "Ward Heelers" had begun to use gangs to ensure winning elections by the use of violence and other forms of coercion. Armed with such a gang, a ward heeler could virtually ensure his own nomination or that of any politician he was supporting by merely filling an Assembly Hall with "shouters and fighters" who quite effectively influenced those around them to vote in a prescribed manner.[59]

Slowly, as Myers notes, these ward heelers became leaders of entire wards and their services were sought by aspiring politicians.[60] Their services included the use of gangs to smash ballot boxes, intimidate citizens so that they would not cast their vote, and other functions necessary to ensure the winning of an election.

Through this process it became possible for criminals affiliated with these gangs to move into political positions via the structure of the political machine. Isaiah Rynders, for example, the leader of one of New York's powerful political organizations —the Empire Club—was formerly a New Orleans gambler who was well known for his agility in gun and knife fights.[61] Richard Croker, who became a Tammany boss, was formerly a member of the Fourth Avenue Tunnel Gang in the Hell's Kitchen area.[62]

By the 1850s the criminal underworld in New York had become a vital power in politics. Through their gangs, ward leaders themselves became heads of criminal syndicates. Asbury notes that as early as 1834, ward bosses and district leaders in New York were operating saloons, gambling houses, and houses of prostitution.[63] It should be obvious that these ward leaders, by virtue of their patron-client relationships with political leaders whom they helped to elect would in turn receive political

protection. The gangs, on the other hand, provided the violence
necessary to keep the ward leader's criminal enterprises running
smoothly. These gangs also became the bargaining force by
which the ward boss could serve as a client to the political
candidate. Writers who argue that the Sicilian "Mafia" introduced the technique of corrupting public officials into the
United States would do well to study the development of this
American institution. Toward the middle of the nineteenth century, we find that syndicates, some operating through the protection of the political machine, others functioning by direct
payment to police, were in existence in various parts of the
country.

In 1851, New York antigambling legislation closed many
gambling houses and policy shops. Yet within months after the
passage of this legislation, the enterprises were flourishing again.
Why?—simply because the police were not enforcing the laws.[64]
Long before the passage of this legislation, both police and politicians in New York City were being paid off on a regular basis
by the operators of the various gambling establishments. In fact,
as Asbury states, "many policemen were employed by gamblers
as steerers and guides."[65] By 1857, police corruption in the city
had become so widespread that legislative action was necessary
to completely change the organization and structure not only of
the police department but also of the Police Board itself.[66]
Because the Police Board was formerly part of the municipal
government, and therefore was subject to the same control and
corruption that it was supposed to fight, this legislation in effect
sought to remove power from the hands of the municipal authorities and place it in the hands of the state government.

Many of the lush and successful gambling establishments operating in New York City during the early 1850s were in the
hands of a few gamblers among whom the most influential,
according to Asbury, were "Reuben Parsons, Pat Herne, Joe
Hall, Sam Suydam, Henry Cotton, Orland Moore and Sherlock
Hillman."[67] Although each of these gamblers had control over
several establishments in the city, they remained independent
of one another. We cannot speak of any of them as the gambling
boss of New York City. Nor do we find the existence of a city-

wide gambling syndicate. Rather, we find several of the major gambling establishments and enterprises under the control of a handful of gamblers, each of whom operated independently. Less prestigious establishments, also, primarily were run as independent enterprises.

This was the case in many other cities such as Cincinnati, St. Louis, Kansas City, Milwaukee, and New Orleans, during the 1860s and '70s. There were variations in the kinds of business relationships existing among the gambling heads in each city and in the extent and type of influence that they were able to exert.

In Cincinnati, for example, gambling enterprises were primarily under the control of approximately ten gamblers who paid the police about $50,000 to $60,000 a year for protection. In this case protection included the right of the ruling gamblers to curb competition from other gamblers. They did this by controlling the number of gambling establishments that could open in a given area. They also reserved for themselves the right to run out of town any freelancer who tried to open an establishment against their wishes.[68]

In St. Louis, on the other hand, similar to Chicago and New York during the 1860s and '70s, individual gamblers paid for police protection. By paying off politicians, in addition to police, they were somewhat influential in both the municipal and state governments. Toward the late 1870s, Asbury notes, these gamblers tried to use political influence to pass legislation legalizing gambling. Instead, however, primarily because of the efforts of a newly elected assemblyman—Charles P. Johnson —more effective antigambling statutes were passed and ultimately the gamblers were forced to leave the city.[69]

In most cities, then, major gambling enterprises or syndicated gambling during the 1860s and '70s was primarily in the hands of a few gambler-heads or bosses, each controlling his area of enterprises and establishments. With Mike McDonald in Chicago, however, we witness the emergence of a city-wide gambling syndicate under the control of one boss.

Mike McDonald came to Chicago in 1854 and by 1872 had become not only the gambling boss of Chicago but the political

boss as well. He was able to create a city-wide gambling syndicate almost entirely through the avenue of the political machine. Equipped with the skills of a professional gambler
during the Civil War he slowly advanced in status among the
gamblers of Chicago. McDonald slowly entered into partnership with other gamblers and was soon part-owner of several
gambling houses in Chicago. His fame and power came with
the establishment of his lavish gambling resort known as "The
Store," located at Clark and Monroe Streets. To "The Store"
came the ward leaders and other politicians, city officials, professional gamblers, and wealthy members of high society seeking the excitement of wagering their fortunes on the various
games of chance.

For others "The Store" was a source of excitement and
entertainment; for Mike McDonald it became his bargaining
source with the political powers of the machine politics in
Chicago. Soon, McDonald was shaping the political futures of
legislators, city officials, and ward leaders as well as the destiny
of gambling and other criminal enterprises in Chicago. As
Peterson indicates, McDonald, using the profits he made from
his gambling establishment, contributed lavishly to the political
campaigns of those he supported and further helped their
cause through his newspaper, the *Chicago Globe*.[70]

With the cooperation of other functionaries of the Chicago
underworld, McDonald slowly gained control of the gambling
enterprises in Chicago. By 1887, the extent of his control not
only over illegitimate enterprises but over public officials as
well, merited him the title of "Boss of Chicago," a title he
retained until his death in 1907. Those seeking favors from
City Hall usually found it necessary to visit the office on the
second floor of McDonald's gambling establishment.[71]

With the help of Harry Varnell and the Hankin brothers
McDonald, during the 1880s, created a bookmaking syndicate
that covered not only the city of Chicago but racetracks in
Northern Illinois and Indiana as well. By accomplishing this,
as Dedmon notes, McDonald "headed Chicago's first gambling
syndicate."[72] During McDonald's reign, Asbury points out, the
only independent bookmakers who were permitted to function

outside the realm of this syndicate were those who had been long-standing friends of McDonald. Other gamblers who prospered during this time did so only with McDonald's consent, which included periodic payment into a bribery fund McDonald collected and distributed whenever the need arose.[73]

In 1879, McDonald was instrumental in electing Carter H. Harrison as Mayor of Chicago. By 1887, Harrison had served four consecutive terms as Mayor during which time McDonald and his enterprises enjoyed the full protection of the law while the police were used by McDonald as a convenient mechanism for eliminating unwanted competition.

McDonald primarily controlled gambling while other forms of organized vice were allowed to operate as long as they did not interfere with his enterprises. Coupled with his gambling syndicate, McDonald engaged in some fraud-oriented crimes. Using money he collected through his bribery fund, he bribed the Board of County Commissioners and the Board of Aldermen to issue a contract to the American Stone and Brick Company, which an investigation later showed belonged to McDonald. Under the pretense that his company had developed a technique of preserving stone and brick, it received a contract calling for the painting of the Cook County Court House with a secret preservative fluid. The cost for this job was $128,250. In a scandal that followed it was shown that the secret fluid was simply chalk and water.[74] Several involved in the scandal were convicted but not McDonald.

With all his power, however, there were mitigating circumstances—an observation we made earlier about the nature of syndicate crime in the United States: Although the syndicated criminal can exert power and influence over the politician, once in office, the politician has the power of the law and therefore can seriously influence the continuation and welfare of the syndicated criminal who put him into power. Thus in one instance when McDonald went against Mayor Harrison, the Mayor had all the gambling houses in Chicago—including McDonald's—raided and closed. McDonald's place was reopened a few hours after it had been raided, but only after he had settled his differences with Harrison.[75] For this reason the terms *gambling boss* and *political boss* often used to refer to McDonald's power and influence in Chicago, although real-istic, must be tempered by the realization that he was in fact a boss subservient to the very political officials whom he helped elect.

The significance of Mike McDonald's gambling syndicate in our discussion of the development of syndicated crime in the United States, lies primarily in that it illustrates another form of structure syndicates have taken. That is one in which a criminal activity within a given ecological area, in McDonald's case, gambling in Chicago, is controlled primarily by one indi-vidual. McDonald was able to accomplish this through the structure of the political machine by serving as a patron to political candidates who in turn offered protection. Through this control McDonald also was able to serve as a patron to other gamblers who were allowed to operate only so long as they cooperated with McDonald and contributed to his bribery fund. This bribery fund was used primarily to bribe witnesses, fix juries, pay off attorneys, and pay for other services neces-sary to help those under McDonald's protection.

This bribery fund represented a payment which insured the gambling establishment owner against interference from police. Thus with McDonald serving as their patron, these gamblers, by contributing to his fund, were assured protection both in the form of uninterrupted continuance of their criminal es-tablishments, and legal resources against conviction if extenuat-ing circumstances resulted in their arrest.

In these aspects, then, as we shall soon observe, there is no basic difference—except for the wider field of operation and the number of participants involved—between McDonald's syndicate of the 1880s and the contemporary syndicates operat-ing in the United States today.

Another format under which syndicate criminal activity in the United States has functioned is one in which the syndicate leader is himself in a position of public office. Such was the case with John Morrissey in New York. As Chafetz points out, never before or after Morrissey has there been such a close alliance "between the gambling fraternity and the political machine."[76]

Morrissey came to Troy, New York from Ireland when he was only three. By adolescence, however, he was already a leader of a neighborhood gang known as the Downtowns, whose major enterprise was to fight another neighborhood gang, the Uptowns. As an adult, Morrissey was putting his training as a gang leader to profitable use. Having made himself a reputation for his ability to use violence to influence the outcome of elections, Tammany Hall took him under its wing.

By 1855, Morrissey owned and shared a partnership in several gambling establishments in New York City. In these establishments bouncers and sluggers were employed to use violence whenever necessary. Like Mike McDonald's "Store" in Chicago, Morrissey's gambling resort on Barclay Street soon came to be the haven of both politicians and those seeking to increase their fortunes through the games of chance. By 1876, Morrissey was one of the leading owners of gambling establishments in New York. Coupled with this he had become a powerful patron of the political machine. Morrissey had a large following among the Irish in New York since he had often helped Irish immigrants to find jobs and a place to live when they first arrived in the city. Through his connections with Tammany Hall he helped them to obtain licenses when needed as well as to obtain citizenship papers. In addition, fellow Irishmen across the entire United States held him in high esteem because of his success as a prizefighter.[77]

Because of this esteem and because of the many favors which he had done for his fellow Irishmen, Morrissey became a powerful patron for his people and an even more powerful client for Tammany Hall. The income from his gambling establishments, which over a five year period alone had netted him $1,000,000, helped further his power.[78] As a patron-client between the Irish community and Tammany Hall, Morrissey could deliver the Irish vote in virtually every election.

By 1866, Morrissey had become so powerful a force in the political machine and such a favorite among the Irish that he

was elected a representative to the U.S. Congress. The power
he personally commanded is illustrated by his reelection in
1868 to a second term, despite the fact that he no longer was
in the good graces of Tammany Hall's Boss Tweed.[79] This
falling out with Tweed, however, became serious in 1870 after
Morrissey had returned to New York and formed his own anti-
Tammany organization—the Young Democracy.[80] Morrissey
was expelled from Tammany Hall during that year. Reinstated
again a few years later by Honest John Kelly, he was again
expelled in 1875 when Kelly became concerned and threatened
by Morrissey's power. Morrissey then set out to oppose Tammany with every available means. His power again manifested
itself when he opposed Tammany Hall candidates and won a
seat in the New York Senate both in 1875 and 1877. He never
completed his second term, however, because he contracted
pneumonia and died on May 1, 1878.[81]

As a political figure Morrissey could offer both police and
political immunity to the gambling establishments under his
protection. Before his election to Congress this protection came
from the services he performed for Tammany Hall. With his
election he himself became a powerful force in the dispensing
of protection. This protection came primarily from the Police
Commissioners themselves who were put into office by the
political machine.[82] As a powerful force in the machine, Morrissey controlled which establishments would remain open and
which would close. In return for this protection, before every
election those gamblers who were protected made campaign
contributions to Morrissey, who retained some of the money
for his own personal use and distributed the rest to help meet
the needs of the political machine.[83] While a representative
in Congress, Morrissey continued to protect his gambling establishments as well as those of other gamblers in New York.
Thus when the antigambling society began to have some gambling places raided in 1867, Morrissey immediately raised
money from the gamblers and paid off those police and other
sources who had come under the influence of the reformers.[84]
While serving as a state senator in 1875 a law was passed by the
New York legislature forbidding auction pools. Yet John Mor-

rissey as a senator continued to accept auction-pool bets. Several New York newspapers called attention to the irony of a member of the legislature openly defying the very law which it had passed.[85] In 1869, during his second term as a U.S. representative, he opened one of the most beautiful gambling Casinos in Saratoga, New York. It was "a social as well as financial triumph."[86]

John Morrissey's gambling syndicate serves as an example of one whose development and continued protection was accomplished through the medium of the political machine with the added advantage that while in political office, Morrissey directly served as his own protector.

We have given examples, then, of the three basic formats under which syndicated crime functions within the American social structure—by direct payment to police and political officials as was the case with Roger Plant in Chicago; by providing services and financial support for the political machine as did Mike McDonald; and by its leader himself occupying a public office as was the case with Morrissey during his terms of office.

We should also note that the complexity or extent of the activity engaged in does not determine whether or not a syndicate exists; rather, it is the method employed that makes the activity syndicated. Thus Roger Plant's operation, which consisted of only one establishment, and those of Mike McDonald and John Morrissey, which consisted of a large number of establishments, all provided an illicit service, used violence to promote and protect their enterprises and secured, through different methods, the protection of the law.

Syndicates: The Turn of the Century

These three formats are found in the development of syndicates in the United States from the beginning of this century to the present time. There is no doubt in this author's mind that barring radical change in the American social-legal structure, syndicates in the future will continue to function in the same manner.

At the turn of the century there existed various types of syndicates in the United States. Primarily in San Francisco and to some extent in other cities there existed the Chinese *Tongs,* the term being roughly translated as "society," "lodge," or "association." The Tongs are often confused with other Chinese organizations such as the Six Companies, which were established primarily for commercial purposes. The latter also served benevolent functions such as helping newly arrived Chinese immigrants and ministering to a variety of their needs in the Chinese community.

The press, as Dillon points out, treated The Six Companies as though they were extremely mysterious, resulting in their confusion with the Tongs.[87] If many of the syndicate members today were of Chinese instead of Italian extraction, writers would no doubt attribute their origin to the "mysterious" Tongs.

The Tongs were organizations that participated in criminal activities in the Chinese-American community. They were located primarily in San Francisco and other cities on the West Coast. However, according to Gong and Grant, two groups existed in New York and one, The Hip Sing Tong, had members in every city that had a large Chinese population.[88] An Industrial Commission report notes that in 1901 fifteen such Tongs existed in San Francisco alone.[89]

The Tongs in our conception represent forms of syndicates. They employed violence through the use of "Highbinders"—individuals who specialized in fighting. They provided illicit services for the Chinese that included primarily prostitution, opium, and gambling.[90] And they functioned under the protection of the law by direct pay-offs to police and politicians.[91] Each establishment took care of its own payoff. These ranged anywhere from five dollars a week to thirteen dollars a month per establishment.[92]

The Tongs confined their syndicate activities to the Chinese community. They were at their peak of power around the turn of the century and gradually began disappearing in the early 1920s. After 1922, Dillon notes, there were no more Tong killings in San Francisco.[93] By the late 1920s, according to Gong and

Grant, the Tongs in New York had lost their criminal orientations and were moving toward benevolent ones.[94] By the beginning of the thirties they had completely disappeared. Yet Dillon notes that as late as 1961 the newspapers continued to headline any violent killing among Chinese as "Tong Killing."[95]

During the early 1900s there emerged in the United States a number of Black Hand gangs that were not syndicates, yet are often defined as such. "Black Hand," as shown earlier, has been used interchangeably with "Mafia." We need not dwell on the confused use of the term in the literature. Suffice it here to say that writers have equated "Mafia" with "Black Hand" with no evidence to support the equation.

First, there was no such thing as "The Black Hand" in the sense of a nationally organized group. Instead there were Black Hand gangs. This observation is confirmed by the report of the White Hand Society, a society that was established by Italians to fight the Black Hand. This report is, to date, the most comprehensive one on the subject. Like many of the gangs in the early 1900s, Black Hand gangs were small in membership and were generally under the direction of one leader. Cooperation among some of these gangs occurred primarily because of friendships between certain members of these gangs, not because of their being affiliated in a national society.[96] The major distinguishing feature of Black Hand gangs was their method. They extorted money by sending letters threatening the victim with harm or death if the money requested wasn't paid. Basically, then, as Landesco argues, "Black Hand" was a method more than it was an organization.[97]

Thre is no doubt that Black Hand gangs took advantage of the solidarity and frugality of the Italian family. The gangs knew that many Italians had managed to accumulate comfortable sums in savings accounts. Letters threatening the safety of an entire family were common. Sometimes a member of the family, usually a child, was kidnapped and a letter written demanding ransom money. Some writers maintain that this practice of extortion by letter was a unique Sicilian "Mafia" technique brought to the United States under the name of "The Black

Hand." Franchetti and Sonnino, on the other hand, demonstrate that the writing of extortion letters for the purpose of obtaining money was a common practice among *bandits* in Sicily.[98]

There is no doubt that Black Hand gangs operating in most cities and towns with large Italian and Sicilian populations were responsible for much violence and killing. Like other forms of extortion, the method is only as good as its enforcement. Thus we find cases of house bombings in Detroit[99] and of numerous killings and bombings in Chicago.[100] Virtually every major city had its share of such cases.

We were fortunate enough to interview several informants from the Italian community who had knowledge of Black Hand gangs that used to operate in several towns in the environs of Pittsburgh. One of the informants had been asked to become a member but refused. Nonetheless he continued to associate with several of the Black Handers on a friendly basis. According to his description of the various gangs with which he had acquaintance, they generally consisted of six to ten members. There were no limits to how large or small each gang should be. The size was determined primarily by how many members were needed to carry on the extortion activities in a particular area.

Membership was limited to Italians and Sicilians. However, as this informant indicated, membership in the gangs he was familiar with was not representative of any specific ecological area of Sicily or Italy. The literature, however, indicates that some gangs were composed exclusively of individuals from a particular provincial area. In Chicago, for example, the literature seems to indicate that Black Hand gang members were almost entirely Sicilian.

As part of the modus operandi, members would frequent public places such as barber shops, taverns and other hang-outs where the Italians congregated. Here they were most apt to learn of newly acquired wealth such as inheritance money, wedding gifts, and profits from an immigrant's sale of his property in Italy. With this information the group would decide the amount they would demand and a letter would be written threatening the victim or a member of his family if the money were not delivered at the prescribed day and hour. Not always, but in many cases, a symbol would be drawn on the letter, usually a black hand, a dagger, a heart with a dagger through it, a skull, or a combination of these. Although crudely drawn, these symbols evidently did add to the psychological effect of the letter. If the victim refused to pay the gang decided whether to carry out the threat immediately or to frighten the victim further. This was done either by sending another letter making more specific threats, damaging the victim's property, or other fear-inducing methods. If the victim continued to refuse then generally he would be killed or injured. Usually the killer was selected by drawing lots. Although most victims responded to the requests of the first letter, informants told the author of three cases where the victims not only refused to pay but themselves threatened the Black Hand gang.

It is interesting to note here that, despite their alleged secrecy, Black Hand gang members, at least those in these small towns, were known. When asked how, our informants simply laughed and said "If you see a bunch of no-goods hanging around together never doing a day's work but living in high style, aren't you going to suspect something?" This observation is borne out by the fact that the victims in the following cases knew whom to contact and threaten.

One such case was that told the author by an informant whose husband had received a letter demanding a large sum of money. This man, who was known throughout the Italian community as a robust, strong, and fearless man, immediately purchased a gun, which he began carrying at all times. He then let it be known to several sources who he knew had Black Hand associations that if any attempts were made on his life or that of his family, they would have to answer to him. That was the first and last letter he received.

Another informant told the author that he learned that his younger brother was being cajoled into becoming a Black Hand member. Being protective of his younger brother and realizing that because of his youth the gang may have influenced or perhaps even blackmailed him into becoming a participant in their activities, this man immediately contacted one of the members. He indicated to this member that he was well aware of who belonged to the gang and that if they did not leave his brother alone he would expose the entire group. This man is known in the community as one who always keeps his word. Evidently the gang members knew this because they purposefully avoided his brother.

In still another case, a man who owned a business establishment received a Black Hand letter demanding money. His brother was known for his unusual strength. One of his favorite forms of jest was that of picking up a young man by his shirt or jacket collar and carrying him at arm's length for several blocks. The more his victim protested the further he was carried. Yet as jovial as he was in jest, he was equally emotional in anger, particularly when threatened or insulted. Upon learning that his brother had received a Black Hand letter, he armed himself with several weapons and stood guard inside the business establishment. After waiting for several days without any action he chanced to meet one of the gang. Seizing him by the collar, he began shaking him, asking why he and the gang had not carried out their threat, stating that he was tired of waiting around and losing sleep. After finally putting the gang member back down on his feet he told him to give the Black Handers a message for him: He warned them that if his brother or his brother's business place was ever molested he would personally settle the score with each one individually. The brother and his place of business remained unmolested and no more letters were received.

It seems then that Black Hand gangs when presented with tactics similar to their own did not always carry out their threats. At least this was true of the gangs encountered in these three incidents.

Black Hand gangs were *not* forms of syndicates; rather, they were simply extortion-oriented gangs. They did not provide illicit services and one of the major reasons for their secrecy was that they did not have police protection. Although in a few instances they raised funds to bribe someone in order to help one of their members, this did not constitute a continuous type of protection. Their existence and survival sprung primarily from the fear they were able to generate in most of their victims.

Because Black Hand gangs did not have the protection of the police, we wonder why writers, except those who equate *fratellanze* or brotherhoods with "Mafia," would equate Black Hand and "Mafia."

One of the sources of evidence offered by such writers revolves around the killing in Palermo of Lt. Joseph Petrosino of the New York Police Department on March 12, 1909. The incident occurred while Petrosino was on a mission to review police records in Italy and Sicily, hoping to collect names of criminals who had entered the United States illegally and were currently residing in New York City. Again, we find nothing but contradictions in the literature concerning this event. Ed Reid[101] attributes the killing to a plot by Paul DiChristina, who was, according to Reid, the "top mafioso" of New Orleans around 1909. Norman Lewis[102] maintains that a "Capo-Mafia" in Sicily, Don Vito Cascio Ferro, admitted that he killed Petrosino. Lewis offers as proof of this the fact that on the evening Petrosino was murdered, Don Vito, dining at the house of a member of Parliament, excused himself from the table. Then, borrowing his host's carriage went to an area near the port where Petrosino had embarked earlier. About the time Don Vito arrived, Petrosino had left his hotel to attend a secret rendezvous. The lights of Palermo went out, at which point Don Vito, firing only one shot, killed Petrosino. He then got back into the carriage and returned to his host's house to finish his meal. How or where Lewis got all this information he never states.

Instead of leaving the hotel for a secret rendezvous as Lewis maintains, Cook[103] tells us that Petrosino had just eaten and was leisurely walking back to the hotel. Instead of one shot and one man firing it as Lewis describes, Cook states that two men fired "four bullets into his back and head." Howe maintains that when Petrosino arrested and deported Erricone, chief of the New York Camorra, "From that day every Cammorista in the world knew that the Camorra had condemned Petrosino to death."[104]

The only writer who cites his source of information is Michael Fiaschetti,[105] a New York Policeman who had served under Petrosino. Fiaschetti, who swore to get Petrosino's murderer,

later posed as a criminal and infiltrated the underworld of
Naples. Through contacts he made there, he learned of a man
in Palermo who had witnessed the Petrosino murder. By taking
this man into his confidence, Fiaschetti learned from him that
the killing had been committed by a man who Fiaschetti simply
refers to as "the *Schiffizano*," a term meaning one who sells the
blood of animals after their slaughter—which in fact was the
assassin's trade. Fiaschetti seems to believe that the murder was
planned by the "Mafia" and that the *Schiffizano* had been chosen
to commit it because among the records Petrosino was to investigate were those of two of the assassin's brothers, who were then
residing in America. Back in Naples Fiaschetti learned from
underworld sources that several years after the Petrosino killing,
the *Schiffizano* had immigrated to America. Before he could
learn where in the United States the assassin was residing, the
underworld discovered and was searching out a New York policeman who had infiltrated its ranks. Fiaschetti and his superiors,
recognizing the danger of his being discovered, advised him to
return to New York, which he did without ever learning the
whereabouts of Petrosino's murderer.

Obviously the accuracy and validity of Fiaschetti's account of
Petrosino's murder is dependent upon the validity of his informant's account. This is the evidence upon which we must let
the accuracy of Fiaschetti's account rest.

It is obvious from the above literature that it is not known
for certain who killed Lt. Petrosino. All we can say is that
Petrosino went to Italy and Sicily on the police mission described above. Because the activities of Black Hand gangs in
New York and other cities were capturing the attention of the
public and press at the time Petrosino made his journey, it was
probably assumed that he went to Sicily and Italy to uncover
"the Black Hand." Since "The Black Hand," *Camorra*, and
"Mafia" are viewed as one and the same organization it is not
surprising that Petrosino's death was linked with all of these.

To return to our discussion of syndicates during the early
1900s we find that in New York, Arnold Rothstein was beginning
to establish himself as a syndicate leader. By 1920 he had

become just that. He owned an elaborate night club that he ran with protection and through the use of "enforcers."[106]

In Chicago, Mont Tennes was becoming a powerful syndicate figure. By 1909 he was in control of the handbook gambling enterprises. Gaining a monopoly over the race results that were telegraphed to Chicago from the Payne Racing Service of Cincinnati, he established some thirty poolrooms to serve as locations for his handbooks. Any gambler desiring to make book had to become a member of Tennes's gambling ring. Applicants were carefully screened, and upon acceptance they had to pay Tennes for the use of his wire service.[107] By 1911 Tennes had a wire service that extended across the United States and Canada.[108] Using bombings and other forms of violence coupled with the paid protection of police—who were often also used to raid competitor's establishments—Tennes ruled his empire well into 1929.

Sharing the underworld activity of Chicago with Tennes were other syndicate figures. In the First Ward, Aldermen Michael "Hinky Dink" Kenna and John J. "Bathhouse John" Coughlin not only provided political protection for syndicate bosses but it was suspected that they themselves had others fronting (posing as owners) for their saloons and dance halls.[109] Their power was widespread. One gambler testified that he had to pay Kenna for permission to operate a gambling boat.[110] Peterson maintains that they controlled the major gambling enterprises in the Loop area.[111] As political patrons, their major client was James "Big Jim" Colosimo, who by 1914 was operating several saloons and houses of prostitution. At first, Colosimo served as a precinct captain to Kenna and Coughlin, but his skills as a vote bargainer eventually made him a ward boss.[112] Before his murder, whose perpetrators still remain a matter of conjecture, he brought to Chicago John Torrio, who in turn brought Alphonse Capone. These two men took over Colosimo's enterprises and Capone eventually became the leader of one of the largest syndicates in the United States.

Along with Tennes in 1909, another Alderman, Johnnie Rogers, was controlling gambling on the West Side while Jim

O'Leary was the gambling boss of the stockyards areas of the South Side.[113]

In New York during this period headlines were being made by a Lieutenant on the New York police force, Charles Becker. Defying the political machine's hold on syndicated criminal activities, by 1911 Becker had created his own unique form of syndicate.[114] Employing his own vice squad after being placed at its head by an unsuspecting police commissioner, Becker raided and smashed up gambling establishments whose owners refused to pay for his protection. He controlled competitive gangs by simply applying the Sullivan Act to those members who presented threats. This act forbade the carrying of concealed weapons. Hence Becker could apply this law to arrest anyone who got in his way. In those cases where he did not find a gun on his enemy, Becker would simply offer as evidence one of several guns he kept around specifically for that purpose. Protected by his Tammany patron, Timothy "Big Tim" Sullivan, the man who originated the Sullivan Act, Becker came to control a number of gambling establishments and brothels. While his vice squad served as his enforcers, members of underworld gangs were employed by Becker to serve as his collectors. Men like Jacob Zelig, a renown gang leader, and Harry "Gyp the Blood" Horowitz, who often broke men's spines over his knee to win bets from those who dared him, were offering their services. Along with these functionaries Becker employed a newspaper columnist, who also was a bookie, to give him a favorable public image in the press.

Becker's empire ran smoothly until he came in conflict with a well-known gambler, Herman Rosenthal. There are variations in the stories about the origin of this conflict, but its outcome was that Rosenthal openly admitted to the District Attorney that he had been "double-crossed"[115] by the police. What he meant was that his gambling establishment had been raided by Becker. After this admission, Rosenthal was murdered. Becker was indicted for his part in this crime and found guilty in a trial that brought out many details of the relationship of police, the political machine, and the underworld. The killers who claimed that Becker forced them to do it—Jacob "Whitey" Seidensher,

Harry "Gyp the Blood" Horowitz, Louis "Lefty Louie" Rosenberg, and Frank "Dago Frank" Cirofici—were all convicted and electrocuted. On July 30, 1915, Charles Becker, claiming his innocence, also died in the electric chair.

During the early 1900s, vice in Pittsburgh, Steffens noted, was directly in the hands of the ward political machines. Houses of prostitution, unlicensed saloons, and slot machines were controlled by "ward syndicates."[116] Saloons had to procure their liquor only from liquor distributors who overcharged but were approved by the syndicate. Madames had to rent their houses from syndicate-approved real estate agents who charged exorbitant rents. The prostitutes themselves were required to purchase any clothes, shoes, jewelry, or other commodities only from approved syndicate merchants. These activities as Steffens explains were carried on as legitimate functions by the ward representatives of the political machine. Along with the above-mentioned forms of payment, saloons and brothels also had to pay "blackmail" money to police and other city officials.[117]

Similar to this system was that of Albert "Doc" Ames, M.D., who when he took office as Mayor of Minneapolis in 1901, organized his own form of syndicate. As a medical practitioner Doctor Ames had done many favors that later became the basis of his political strength. Upon election as Mayor, Ames selected as his chief of police his brother, Fred Ames. As chief of detectives he chose a former gambler, Norman King. In turn, King invited to Minneapolis a variety of criminals including robbers, pickpockets, and gamblers, some of whom were obtained by releasing them from the local Minneapolis jail.[118] Soon 107 policemen out of 225 were discharged because they were not the type to cooperate in their new criminally oriented duties. Those officers who remained and those hired afterwards had to pay a certain amount for permission to be on the force. With this structure Ames received profits from gambling, prostitution, and other vices that were operated by the criminal elements under the protection of his police force. This continued until reform measures brought an end to Ames' power and regime.

In San Francisco during this era, as Asbury[119] points out, Jere McClane, more commonly known as Jerome Bassity, owned the majority of brothels, a saloon, and had interests in a number of dance halls. He attained his power and position through his relationship to the political machine of Abe Ruef. Later, in 1909, when P. H. McCarthy was elected mayor, McCarthy, Bassity, and the Police Commissioner, who also owned a bar, became the ruling forces of San Francisco.

Syndicates: The Prohibition Years

On January 16, 1920, the Volstead Act went into effect and with it followed a rise in the number of syndicates that sought to provide Americans with alcoholic beverages, which had now become illegal except for medicinal purposes. During this era many physicians in cooperation with pharmacies that sold bootleg liquor were to find, at the request of many of their clients and without a physical examination, that the only cure for many illnesses was a good dose of whiskey.

It is obvious from what we have discussed thus far that syndicates existed long before Prohibition. Because of the extensive demand for liquor, however, their number increased during the Prohibition years. Advancements in communication and transportation, coupled with the necessity for interstate transportation of alcohol and other illicit goods, stimulated an increase in cooperation between syndicates located in various parts of the country.

Much of bootleg liquor came, as Farjeon states, from British vessels docked outside the legal twelve mile area from which smugglers' motorboats transported it to various points along the east coast of the United States.[120] Of bonded quality, this liquor, like that obtained from Canada, commanded a high price and thus was desired by syndicates across the country, who sold it straight or cut (watered). This necessitated functionaries, often gangs, who would transport the liquor from the east to the midwest, south, and other locales. Many syndicate leaders came to cooperate with one another, often exchanging services that they were in a position to offer through them by control of certain ecological territories or enterprises. Often several syndicates found it more practical and efficient to combine their manpower and facilities. Such was the case with the "Big Seven," which Cook refers to as the "first organization of bootleggers."[121] It consisted of seven east coast syndicates including such underworld notables as Waxey Gordon, Charles "Lucky" Luciano, Louis "Lepke" Buchalter, Gurrah Shapiro, Frank Costello, Dandy Phil Kastel, Longy Zwillman, Benjamin "Bugsy" Siegel, Owney Madden, and William "Big Bill" Dwyer. During this era many gangs engaged not only in transporting liquor, but in hijacking that of competitors.

During Prohibition, many gangs, through their control by syndicate leaders, continued to provide services for the political machine. In contrast to the gangs of the late 1800s, these gangs had become more specialized. Instead of fighting and killing for the status inherent in showing one's strength and boldness, the new gangs engaged by the syndicates committed these acts for payment rather than glory. As one writer in 1923 colorfully put it, "three-quarters of a century have seen the New York gangs' activities develop from the gusto of a shilelah shindig to calculation and efficiency of an industrial tool."[122]

Syndicate leaders continued their role of serving as clients to the political machines. Whereas up to this time the Irish had dominated this function, now the Italians, Poles, and other nationality groups had begun to make their influence felt. In Chicago during the 1920s, as Bright tells us, Joe Saltis fulfilled this role for the Poles, Al Capone for the Italians and Sicilians, and George "Bugs" Moran and Dion O'Banion functioned in this capacity for the Irish.[123]

During the Prohibition era, some gangs themselves evolved into syndicates. In Illinois, for example, the Shelton Gang, which at its inception consisted primarily of three brothers—Carl, Earl, and Bernie Shelton—opened a saloon in East St. Louis in 1920.[124] In 1924, adding members, it successfully fought off and subjugated the Ku Klux Klan, which was competing for political power in southern Illinois.[125] Its size through the years varied, but never exceeded thirty members. Slowly the Sheltons, headed by Carl, started bribing public officials. With sufficient muscle—

the toughest was Bernie—and with paid protection, the Sheltons by 1928 had control of bootlegging and organized gambling in Illinois with the exception of Cook County. Estimates at this time placed their profits at $2,000,000 from slot machines, $1,500,000 from handbooks, and $1,000,000 from other forms of gambling.[126] In 1940 the Shelton gang still had control of gambling, but toward the end of the '40s the gang and its power and influence slowly diminished. By 1950 the Sheltons and their feats were becoming part of southern Illinois legend.

Another gang of interest in this respect was Detroit's Purple Gang. Like the Sheltons, little has been written about this gang. The author was very fortunate in obtaining an interview with a former Detroit police source who as a police officer was well versed with this gang's history and activities. This and other sources from the literature will be employed to give a brief history of this gang, which is typical of many gangs that evolved into syndicates during the prohibition era.

The gang had its beginning in the Jewish sector of Detroit, then located in the Hastings Street area. As adolescents several of the gang's members, who were schoolmates at Bishop School, began associating together. After school they began engaging in petty crimes that often included stealing fruit, candy, and other small items from Jewish merchants. Later they graduated to "rolling" drunks and more serious crimes such as shaking down merchants for money.[127] This was around 1920. Around 1922 and 1923 prohibition was in full swing and these boys had passed from adolescence into adulthood. They now began selling unrefined sugar to bootleggers. Their base of operation, the Oakland Sugar House, located then on Oakland Street, gave them the name "The Oakland Sugar House Gang." Soon the gang added a twist to this enterprise; that is, they made a double profit from it. After selling the sugar to the bootleggers, the gang would follow their trucks, learn the location of their still, and later return to demand payment for protection under the threat that they would expose the location of the still to legal authorities. In many cases they simply returned to the still and hijacked the moonshine itself.

Around 1923 or 1924 membership in the gang was enlarged

and included some recent arrivals from New York. It is around this time that the gang became known as "The Purple Gang." It seems that one of these new members from New York, a man by the name of Eddie Fletcher, was a boxer. He began working out at the Hannah Schloss Building, a recreation center for young Jewish men. It seems that when he worked out in the gym there, he wore a purple jersey. Soon those that worked out with him and hung around with him also began wearing purple jerseys. Hence they came to be referred to as "the purples" and later "The Purple Gang."

Although there are several versions of how the gang received its name the above seems to be the most plausible—the police official serving as our informant indicated that he himself had obtained this from a source who was intimately acquainted with the Purple Gang.

Known by this name the gang made headlines in 1926 in what came to be known as the "Milaflores Apartment Massacre." This took place when three St. Louis torpedoes (syndicate men who specialize in killing), attempting to move in on the Purple Gang's territory, were riddled with bullets in an apartment that had been rented by two members of the gang. Again in 1931, resulting from another attempt to cut into the Purple Gang's enterprises, another three men were shot down. Thinking that they were to meet with some Purple Gang members at the Collingwood Manor Apartments, they met only their death as victims of a trap. This killing came to be remembered as the "Collingwood Manor Massacre."

Although the Purple Gang engaged in a variety of extortion-oriented crimes involving blind pigs (speakeasies), cleaning and dyeing establishments, and other enterprises, in our conception they became a syndicate primarily because of their involvement in the sale of illicit alcohol and because they provided themselves with political and police protection.

The gang operated stills in both the United States and Canada.[128] They reached their peak of activity around 1932. After 1935, however, the gang slowly diminished both in membership and power. Some were convicted, others killed by rival gangs, and some simply retired. By 1938, the gang as such no longer existed. Throughout its existence, with the exception of one or two members, the gang consisted entirely of men of Jewish extraction, some of the more prominent ones being the Bernstein brothers, Irving Milberg, Abe Axler, Eddie Fletcher, Harry Millman, Harry Keywell, "Honey Boy" Miller, and Harry Fleisher.[129]

Today one often hears of the Purple Gang or Purple Mob having existed in various parts of Ohio, particularly in Toledo. Also, some confusion has arisen about who the Purple Gang in Detroit really were. Thus, former Governor Michael V. DiSalle speaks of a Purple Gang in Detroit of which an Italian, Pete Licavoli, was the boss.[130] Probably, this confusion emerges from the fact that a group in Toledo, which DiSalle himself calls the "Licavoli Gang"[131] led by Thomas Licavoli, who engaged in illicit distribution and sale of alcohol simultaneously with the Purple Gang's operation in Detroit. No doubt because of the proximity of Detroit and Toledo there was some cooperation between the Purple Gang and the Licavoli Gang in these activities. Hence as the Purple Gang in Detroit disappeared, their name may have been gradually applied to the Licavoli Gang. The author's informant, when asked about this confusion, definitely stated that the Purple Gang was a Detroit outfit composed of men of Jewish backgrounds. Thus if other gangs called by this name existed in Cleveland, Toledo, and Detroit itself, they should not be confused with this specific Detroit gang.

The Prohibition era, then, allowed for large sums of money to come into the hands of those who engaged in syndicated activities. This capital offered opportunities for many participants in syndicated crime to invest in further illicit enterprises when Prohibition came to an end.

This era witnessed the rise of many syndicates. In Chicago, Al Capone showed his organizational abilities in establishing one of the most powerful ever to have existed. He kept his power by doing favors for both criminal and noncriminal elements in society. He obtained protection through his relationship to the political machine. In his early career Capone depended upon the political protection of "Bathhouse John" Coughlin and

"Hinky Dink" Kenna. After his ascension to power, however, these two aldermen came to be subservient to Capone.[132]

Capone's major power seems to have come from his ability and willingness to pay large sums for immunity from the law. At the height of his career it is estimated that he was paying for protection at the rate of $25,000,000 a year.[133] In Cicero in 1924, by using violence and pay-offs to win the election for the machine-selected candidates for Mayor, Town Clerk, Town Collector, and Town Attorney, Al Capone virtually assured himself of total protection there.[134]

There were other prominent syndicate figures in Chicago. One of these was Johnny Torrio, who gave Capone his start. Their continued cooperation led to the development of the "Torrio-Capone syndicate" during the period 1920–1926. After an attempt was made on his life in 1926, however, Torrio left Chicago and his enterprises came under Capone's control.

From 1918 to 1924 Dion O'Bannion led Chicago's North Side syndicate, which at first cooperated with and later battled with Capone. After O'Banion's murder, from 1924 to about 1926, this syndicate came under the control of Hymie Wajciechowski, more commonly known by his alias "Hymie Weiss."[135] Vincent "Schemer" Drucci and George "Bugs" Moran took over the North Side Syndicate from about 1926 to 1928 and with the death of Drucci, Moran held its leadership until about 1930. Around 1932, the syndicate came under the control of Ted Newberry, who maintained control until his death in 1933.[136]

Along with these syndicates were those of the Beer Dukes, Terry Druggan and Frankie Lake, who took over the leadership of the Valley Gang and, turning to bootlegging enterprises, remained in prominence from 1920 to 1924.[137] During this era the political machine itself gave birth to Alderman Titus A. Haffa of the Forty-Third Ward, who ran a syndicate that netted approximately $5,000,000 per year.[138]

In New York City the Prohibition era produced such syndicates as that of Giuseppe Masseria, which throughout the twenties controlled vice in the downtown Brooklyn and Manhattan areas.[139] In other sections, underworld figures like Owen Mad-

den, George Jean "Big Frenchy" deMange, Arthur "Dutch
Schultz" Flegenheimer, Waxey Gordon, Frank Costello, William
"Big Bill" Dwyer, "Lucky" Luciano, and others had assumed
leadership of syndicates.

Before leaving our discussion of the Prohibition era we would
clarify the meaning of the so-called *Unione Siciliana*, which
comes into the literature around this era. Even more confusing
than the indiscriminate usage of the word *mafia* in the literature
is that of *Unione Siciliana*. Lynch states that "Unione Siciliana"
was a Sicilian fraternal organization located in various parts
of the east and midwest. He tells us that the criminal underworld recruited many of its members from this organization.[140]
Pasley, on the other hand, states that "Unione Siciliana" was
"the Mafia of Italy transplanted to the United States." Earlier,
however, he refers to Mike Merlo in Chicago as the "founder
and president of the Unione Sicilione."[141] As we indicated earlier
this term has been applied to the organization that supposedly
came into existence after the purge of the "Mafia" in the United
States around 1931. Thompson and Raymond maintain on the
other hand that "Unione Siciliane" came to the United States
around the 1900s. They alternately describe it as a criminal
gang on the lower east side of New York, a secret society derived
from the "Mafia" but sometimes including non-Italians, and an
organization that at one time "was not restricted to gangsters"
but included some respectable citizens.[142]

It is obvious in the literature that, as with the terms *mafia*,
Black Hand and *Camorra*, writers have employed the term
Unione Siciliana so loosely that it becomes meaningless. The
confusion over this term no doubt comes from the fact that
there existed in many eastern and midwestern cities during the
early 1900s a legitimate fraternal organization chartered under
the name *L'Unione Siciliana*. It was only one of hundreds of
mutual aid and fraternal organizations established by Sicilian
and Italian immigrants in the United States. In Chicago, Schiavo
tells us, this organization was founded in 1895. Prior to 1900 its
membership was primarily Sicilian but slowly Italians from

various parts of Italy began joining so that by 1925 its name was changed to The Italo-American National Union.[143]

There is no doubt that since this society had a large Italian and Sicilian membership during the early 1900s, many writers simply assumed that the society was composed of certain "Mafia" elements. Yet they never give any valid evidence that this in fact was the case. Instead they merely state that *Unione Siciliana* was another name for the "Mafia." Oddly, however, we find that in these descriptions "Mafia" now has a president rather than a chief. This again indicates the desire of these writers to force their argument that this fraternal organization, which had a president, vice-president, and other positions, was the same as "Mafia."

Rather than looking for its relationship to "Mafia" it is more realistic to view the *Unione* in terms of its role within the context of the political machine. As Landesco notes, in Chicago around 1916 Italians emerged as a new voting force in wards formerly under Irish domination.[144] The Italian vote now represented a vital base of bargaining power in machine politics. Since *L'Unione Siciliana* represented one of the largest Italian organizations, the electoral support of this society came to be desired by Italian candidates. It offered these candidates a basis of bargaining power within the political machine itself. The presidency of this organization was a highly prized position, since as president one could exert a great deal of political influence. This was revealed in a case where Carmen Vacco, a city sealer in Chicago admitted during an investigation that he owed his position to Mike Merlo, a president of *L'Unione*.[145] It was because of this power that Al Capone continuously sought to gain the cooperation of those who served as president of this organization.

In one case during the early 1920s, Anthony D'Andrea was both the president of *L'Unione* and a candidate for Alderman from the Nineteenth Ward. He was thus in a unique position as a vote broker for the political machine. During the early 1920s, D'Andrea and other *Unione* presidents, such as Mike Merlo and Antonio Lombardo, had ties with criminal elements in illicit liquor and other enterprises. This relationship naturally allowed these presidents to serve both as patrons to the underworld and clients to the political machine.

Rather than viewing *L'Unione Siciliana* as a sinister, secretive, transplanted "Mafia," then, we find that this fraternal organization during the early 1920s served both as a mutual-benefit immigrant organization and as a base of voting power for Italian candidates within the patron-client format of the political machine.

For those, however, who insist on equating the "Mafia" and the Black Hand with *L'Unione* we note one more point. According to Vecoli, *L'Unione Siciliana* was one of the few Italian organizations that contributed to the financial support of the White Hand, the society whose sole purpose was to destroy the Black Hand.[146]

Syndicates: Post-Prohibition

The 1930s saw the continuation of many existing syndicates as well as the emergence of a variety of new ones across the country. The Shelton gang of Illinois carried on its syndicate activities well into the late 1940s. In Chicago, during the late thirties several of Al Capone's original criminal enterprises had come under the direction of Edward J. O'Hare. His murder in 1939 touched off an investigation that revealed collusion between syndicated crime and the Kelly-Nash political machine.[147] From 1940 to 1950, syndicated gambling was under the control of many functionaries dating back to the Capone era. Among these the prominent names were those of Frank Nitti, Louis Campagnia, Phil D'Andrea, Charles Gioe, Paul deLucia, and Frank Maretote.[148] Sharing in the control of various gambling enterprises during this era was a syndicate headed by William R. Skidmore and William R. Johnson. One interesting feature of this syndicate was their use of a junkyard to collect payments from gamblers that were in turn used to pay off police and politicians.[149]

In New York, the 1930s revealed syndicates including those of Louis "Lepke" Buchalter, Arthur "Dutch Schultz" Flegenheimer, Charles "Lucky" Luciano, Frank Costello, and "Dandy" Phil Kastel to mention only a few. Buchalter, who sometimes dealt in the sale of narcotics, was known more for his extortion of laborers in the garment industry. For some time Buchalter and his partner, Jacob "Gurrah" Shapiro, had served as strike breakers for a variety of companies, but soon saw that they could offer their services to unions as well.[150] Violence became an illicit service during the labor-management wars. Soon after Lepke and Gurrah had successfully infiltrated the unions with their musclemen, however, they began using violence not as a service to the unions in their battle against management but rather as a threatening device to extort the laborers themselves. Many of the labor extortion enterprises in other cities during this time period began in exactly this manner.

Dutch Schultz, who had engaged in illicit liquor and narcotics enterprises during the Prohibition era, at the time of his death in 1935 was known as one of the top rulers in the policy or numbers enterprise.[151] It was estimated that Schultz was paying $100 a week to Tammany leader James J. Hines for political protection.[152] Also during the early 1930s Henry Miro and Wilfred Brender, along with an estimated ten to fifteen other important syndicate figures, controlled the numbers operations in the Harlem district of New York.[153]

"Lucky" Luciano during this period was heading syndicates dealing with policy, illicit sale of narcotics, and prostitution. In 1937, Thomas E. Dewey revealed the political tie-up between Luciano and Albert Marinelli, county clerk and influential figure in the political machine.[154]

As in Chicago, the Prohibition era in New York saw the rise of Italians as a powerful voting force in the political machine. In 1935 Peel noted that this power had already formed in the Italian Political Clubs of New York.[155] Hence by 1937, as in the Luciano-Marinelli case, it was not surprising to find criminal elements under the protection of Italian political figures in the political machine. In 1945, Mockridge and Prall indicate that there was a close and friendly relationship between underworld figures like Frank Costello, Albert Anastasia, Joe Adonis, and many of the political figures in Tammany Hall.[156]

From 1928 to 1934 in New York, Frank Costello, in partnership with Dandy Phil Kastel, was running the slot machine enterprises. When Mayor Fiorello LaGuardia began a campaign against slot machines in 1934, Costello and Kastel moved them to Louisiana where they continued to be a lucrative enterprise well into the 1950s.[157] The 1940s also revealed the scandal surrounding the New York gambling syndicate of Harry Gross, who had operated his bookmaking enterprises for years by direct pay-offs to police.[158]

In 1950 the Kefauver Senate Hearings on Interstate Commerce in Organized Crime revealed the presence and interrelationships of syndicates in virtually every major city and state in the union. Senator Estes Kefauver and his special committee must be lauded for this vast effort. Although various state and municipal investigations prior to Kefauver's had revealed the presence of specific syndicates and leaders, it was the hearings of this special committee that offered data concerning the interstate cooperation and relationships between various syndicates.

Although Kefauver states that he found the existence of "the Mafia" in the United States, in reality he merely assumed its existence. He did not prove it. One need only read his statements regarding the origin of "the Mafia" as stated in his book to learn that Kefauver's understanding and definition of *mafia* was cramped by the usual assumptions and inconsistencies regarding the term. He tells us that "the Mafia" in Sicily was originally "a protective organization of the peasant classes formed to resist oppression by the great barons but it quickly got out of hand."[159] He then tells us about "the Mafia's" secret code—*Omerta*—which tells us that Kefauver had little understanding of what *mafia* in Sicily really consisted of. His use of "Mafia" to refer to American syndicates also suffers from similar inconsistencies.

Along with revealing the existence of syndicates across the country, the Kefauver report was a study in the corruption that existed in the relationships between criminal syndicates, police, and politicians. The nation was astounded by the findings, but their reaction was a result of a lack of public awareness rather than the revelation of anything new. As we have indicated, corruption of public officials by syndicated criminals and the use of syndicated criminals by the political machine has been an existing social pattern in the United States since the middle 1800s.

In Chicago the Kefauver committee found syndicated crime in the hands of men like "Greasy Thumb" Guzik, Murray Humphreys, Tony Accardo, Rocco Fischetti, and Anthony Capezio.[160] In New York, the committee found that Frank Costello, Joe Adonis, and Albert Anastasia had continued their well-established syndicate leadership. Along with them other syndicates were under the auspices of men like Frank Erickson and Meyer Lansky.[161] The highlight of the investigation was the testimony that revealed the relationship between Frank Costello and several Tammany Hall politicians, including the former Mayor of New York, William O'Dwyer, who during the time of the investigation was the U.S. Ambassador to Mexico.[162]

In 1963 the Senate Investigating Committee chaired by Senator John L. McClellan revealed a variety of syndicates involved in illicit narcotics traffic as well as other enterprises. A detailed account of this committee follows in Chapter 6.

In conclusion, we have attempted to show that criminal syndicates in the United States have emerged and developed from within the social structure of American society itself. We have also illustrated that attributing the Hennessy affair in New Orleans to the Sicilian "Mafia," and the equating of *L'Unione Siciliana* and Black Hand with "Mafia" resulted from the use of inconsistently and nebulously defined terms. Those writers interested in supporting the *Evolutional-Centralization Theory* of American syndicate development merely called completely different organizations by the same name in an effort to try to force an historical or structural relationship where one did not in fact exist.

As we have illustrated syndicated crime in the United States has and continues to function either through direct pay-off or through a patron-client relationship with the political machine. It is of little consequence whether Italians, Irish, Chinese, or any other ethnic group is, was, or will be involved in it. Ethnic variation does not alter the structure under which syndicated crime functions in the United States.

The *Evolutional-Centralization* theorists fail to note that many of the Italian and Sicilian immigrants who entered syndicated crime did not come to this country as established, convicted criminals. Rather many of these came as children who grew up within the same American social milieu that gave rise to many native-born syndicate criminals. Such was the case with James "Big Jim" Colosimo. He came to the United States when he was ten, but grew up in a state of poverty, moving up from a shoe-shine boy to a street sweeper.[163] As a street sweeper, Colosimo organized other street sweepers in the First Ward into a voting bloc. Soon the potential of this group and its leader was recognized by the political machine.[164] Also recognized by the machine was his ability to use violence to keep his ward constituency in line.[165] As we noted earlier, it was through the added patronage of Aldermen Michael "Hinky Dink" Kenna and "Bathhouse John" Coughlin that Colosimo became a powerful figure in Chicago syndicated crime and in the political machine itself.

For those who argue that "Mafia" was transplanted from Sicily we should add, in refutation, that Colosimo did not come from Sicily. Although there is some confusion as to whether he was born in the Abruzzi[166] region or in Calabria,[167] these are both on the mainland of Italy and not in Sicily. The same is true of Al Capone. Confusion again abounds as several writers give Capone's birthplace as Brooklyn, New York, while Allsop maintains that he was born in Castel Amara in the vicinity of Rome.[168] In any event, Capone was not Sicilian. Neither was John Torrio, who various sources agree was born in Naples, Italy. He too came to the United States as a young boy and grew up as an important member of the Five Points Gang in New York.

In contrast to the *Evolutional-Centralization Theory* then we have tried to show that historically, syndicated crime in the

United States is a product of the American social system. It was this system that produced Roger Plant, Mike McDonald, Louis "Lepke" Buchalter and Al Capone regardless of their differences in ethnic background. They obtained their protection either by direct pay-off to police and politicians or by becoming patrons and clients of the political machine. Ethnicity as an historical factor in syndicated crime in the United States should be viewed in terms of the development of ethnic constituents and their power relationship to machine politics. It is the process of change in the power relationship of ethnic groups to the political machine that Daniel Bell so aptly designates as "ethnic succession."[169]

Except for historical differences brought about by changes in technology, the syndicate of Mike McDonald in Chicago during the late 1800s is basically the same as many gambling syndicates in existence today. They both use violence in certain aspects of their enterprises, they both employ elements of secrecy and they both provide themselves with some form of protection. In view of this, we cannot understand why writers desperately and unsuccessfully try to prove that "the Sicilian Mafia" was infused to the United States. First, as we explained, *mafia* within the Sicilian social structure is tightly bound to that structure and was not and cannot be transported anywhere. However, for the sake of argument, let us assume an organization "Mafia" did exist in Sicily and was transported to the United States. How, except for the fact that it was composed of Sicilians, would it differ from other syndicates functioning in America in the past and contemporarily? Perhaps we can put it another way: Let us hypothetically assume that we removed all Sicilians and Italians from syndicated crime and established a method of keeping future individuals from these ethnic groups from entering into syndicated crime. Would this bring an end to syndicated crime in America? Would the structure of syndicates or their modus operandi be radically different?

If the American public could realistically accept the fact that syndicated crime is a product of American society and exists because segments of the American public want its goods and services, then perhaps we could either learn to accept syndicated crime as a functional part of our society or take measures to abolish it completely. As it stands now American society is doing neither while those who draw attention to the transplanting of a "Sicilian Mafia" and other unfounded theories are, at most, providing rationalizations for a society that as yet has not matured sufficiently to accept itself as it really is.

References

1 Bill Brennan, *The Frank Costello Story* (Derby, Connecticut: Monarch Books, Inc., 1962), p. 34.

2 "Old-Style Mafia and Its Heirs, The Calculators," *Life*, February 23, 1959, pp. 19–26.

3 Sid Feder and Joachim Joesten, *The Luciano Story* (New York: David McKay Company, Inc., 1954), p. 16.

4 *Ibid.,* pp. 47–48.

5 John E. Coxe, "The New Orleans Mafia Incident," *The Louisiana Historical Quarterly,* XX (January–October, 1937), p. 1068.

6 Herbert Asbury, *The French Quarter* (New York: Garden City Publishing Co., Inc., 1938), pp. 411–412.

7 *Ibid.,* p. 406.

8 *Ibid.,* pp. 406–407.

9 Herbert Asbury, *The Barbary Coast* (New York: Garden City Publishing Co., Inc., 1933).

10 Asbury, *The French Quarter,* pp. 407–408.

11 *Ibid.,* pp. 409–411.

12 Coxe, *op. cit.,* pp. 1070–1073.

13 *Ibid.,* p. 1072–1073.

14 Asbury, *The French Quarter,* p. 415.

15 Coxe, *op. cit.,* pp. 1082–1083.

16 James D. Horan, *The Pinkertons: The Detective Dynasty That Made History* (New York: Crown Publishers, Inc., 1967), p. 420.

17 *Ibid.,* pp. 432–433, 434.

18 *Ibid.,* pp. 434–437.

19 John S. Kendall, "Who Killa De Chief?" *The Louisiana Historical Quarterly,* XXII (January–October, 1939), pp. 492–530.

20 Coxe, *op. cit.,* p. 1088.

21 *Ibid.,* pp. 1096–1101.

22 H. Stuart Hughes, *The United States and Italy* (Cambridge: Harvard University Press, 1965), p. 6.

23 U.S. Congress, Senate, *Reports of the Immigration Commission,* S. Doc. 750, 61st Congress, 3rd Session, 1911, p. 277.

24 *Ibid.,* p. 283.

25 U.S. Congress, Senate, *Reports of the Immigration Commission,* S. Doc. 747, 61st Congress, 3rd Session, 1911, p. 28.

26 U.S. Congress, Senate, S. Doc. 750, p. 285.

27 *Ibid.,* p. 282.

28 *Ibid.,* p. 282, footnote 2.

29 *Ibid.,* p. 283.

30 *Ibid.,* p. 279.

31 Arthur Train, "Imported Crime: The Story of the Camorra In America," *McClure's Magazine,* May, 1912, pp. 83–94.

32 Arthur Train, *Courts, Criminals and the Camorra* (New York: Charles Scribner's Sons, 1912).

33 *Ibid.,* pp. 227–236.

34 *Ibid.,* p. 232.

35 Charles William Heckethorn, *The Secret Societies,* I (New York: University Books, 1965), p. 275.

36 Train, *op. cit.,* p. 232.

37 *Ibid.,* p. 231.

38 Robert T. Anderson, "From Mafia to Cosa Nostra," *The American Journal of Sociology,* LXXI (November, 1965), p. 308.

39 *Report of the Vice Commission of Minneapolis,* Minneapolis, Minnesota, 1911, p. 74.

40 Rudolph J. Vecoli, "Chicago's Italians Prior to World War I: A Study of Their Social and Economic Adjustment." (Unpublished Ph.D. dissertation, University of Wisconsin, 1962), pp. 443–444.

41 U.S. Congress, Senate, S. Doc. 750, *op. cit.,* p. 277.

42 Anderson, *op. cit.,* p. 310.

43 Donald R. Cressey, *Theft of the Nation* (New York: Harper and Row, Publishers, 1969), p. 25.

44 *Ibid.,* p. 35.

45 Herbert Asbury, *Gem of the Prairie* (Garden City: Garden City Publishing Co., Inc., 1942), p. 37.

46 *Ibid.,* p. 42.

47 *Ibid.,* pp. 63–64.

48 Frederick Francis Cook, *Bygone Days in Chicago* (Chicago: A. C. McClurg and Co., 1910), p. 159.

49 *Ibid.*

50 Virgil W. Peterson, *Barbarians In Our Midst* (Boston: Little, Brown and Co., 1952), pp. 31–33.

51 Frederick Francis Cook, *op. cit.,* p. 136.

52 Peterson, *op. cit.,* pp. 32–33.

53 Richard O'Connor, *Hell's Kitchen* (New York: J. B. Lippincott Co., 1958), p. 57.

54 Asbury, *The Barbary Coast,* pp. 40–42.

55 Curt Gentry, *The Madams of San Francisco* (New York: The New American Library of World Literature, Inc., 1964), p. 36.

56 O'Connor, *op. cit.,* p. 61.

57 *Ibid.*, p. 62.

58 *Ibid.*, p. 59.

59 Gustavus Myers, *The History of Tammany Hall* (New York: Published by the author, 1901), p. 154.

60 *Ibid.*, p. 155.

61 *Ibid.*, p. 161.

62 O'Connor, *op. cit.*, p. 56.

63 Herbert Asbury, *The Gangs of New York* (New York: Garden City Publishing Co., Inc., 1927), p. 37.

64 Herbert Asbury, *Sucker's Progress* (New York: Dodd, Mead and Co., 1938), pp. 195–196.

65 *Ibid.*, p. 162.

66 Asbury, *The Gangs of New York*, p. 107.

67 Asbury, *Sucker's Progress*, p. 165.

68 *Ibid.*, p. 277.

69 *Ibid.*, p. 285.

70 Peterson, *op. cit.*, p. 46.

71 Emmet Dedmon, *Fabulous Chicago* (New York: Random House, 1953), p. 140.

72 *Ibid.*

73 Asbury, *Sucker's Progress*, p. 299.

74 Asbury, *Gem of the Prairie*, p. 148.

75 *Ibid.*, p. 149.

76 Henry Chafetz, *Play the Devil* (New York: Clarkson N. Potter, Inc., 1960), p. 271.

77 *Ibid.*, p. 277.

78 Asbury, *Sucker's Progress*, p. 373.

79 *Ibid.*, p. 386.

80 *Ibid.*

81 *Ibid.*, p. 387.

82 Chafetz, *op. cit.*, p. 293.

83 *Ibid.*, p. 291.

84 *Ibid.*

85 *Ibid.*, p. 285.

86 George Waller, *Saratoga, Saga of An Impious Era* (Englewood Cliffs: Prentice-Hall, Inc., 1966), p. 132.

87 Richard H. Dillon, *The Hatchet Men* (New York: Coward-McCann, Inc., 1962), p. 75.

88 Eng Ying Gong and Bruce Grant, *Tong War* (New York: Nicholas L. Brown, 1930), pp. 29–30.

89 U.S. Congress, House, *Reports of the Industrial Commission on Immigration*, H. Doc 184, 57th Congress, 1st sess., 1901, p. 762.

90 National Commission on Law Observance and Enforcement, *Report on Crime and the Foreign Born*, 1931, pp. 371–372.

91 Gong and Grant, *op. cit.*, pp. 57–58.

92 Dillon, *op. cit.*, p. 136.

93 *Ibid.*, p. 363.

94 Gong and Grant, *op. cit.*, p. 287.

95 Dillon, *op. cit.*, pp. 363–364.

96 *The Italian "White Hand" Society in Chicago, Illinois; Studies, Actions and Results* (Chicago, 1908), pp. 3–4.

97 John Landesco, *Organized Crime in Chicago* (Chicago: Illinois Association for Criminal Justice, 1929), pp. 936–937.

98 Leopoldo Franchetti e Sidney Sonnino, *La Sicilia Nel 1876*, Vol. I (Firenze: Vallecchi Editore, 1925), p. 29.

99 *The Detroit Journal*, November 11, 1908, p. 1.

100 Landesco, *op. cit.*, pp. 939–941.

101 Ed Reid, *Mafia* (New York: New American Library of World Literature, Inc., 1951), p. 131.

102 Norman Lewis, *The Honored Society* (New York: G. P. Putnam's Sons, Inc., 1964), pp. 57–58.

103 Fred J. Cook, *The Secret Rulers* (New York: Duell, Sloan and Pearce, 1966), p. 67.

104 Mand Howe, *Sicily in Shadow and Sun* (Boston: Little, Brown and Co., 1910), p. 417.

105 Michael Fiaschetti, *You Gotta Be Rough* (New York: Doubleday, Doran and Co., Inc., 1930), pp. 282–284.

106 Waller, *op. cit.*, p. 304.

107 Landesco, *op. cit.*, pp. 875–876.

108 *Ibid.*, p. 881.

109 *Ibid.*, p. 849.

110 Lloyd Wendt and Herman Kogan, *Lords of the Levee* (Garden City: Garden City Publishing Co., Inc., 1944), p. 295.

111 Peterson, *op. cit.*, p. 84.

112 Fred D. Pasley, *Al Capone* (New York: Garden City Publishing Co., 1930), pp. 13–14.

113 Peterson, *op. cit.*, p. 84.

114 Jonathan Root, *One Night in July* (New York: Coward-McCann, Inc., 1961), pp. 44–46.

115 Frederick A. Mackenzie, "Killing by Proxy: 1912" in *Sins of New York*, ed. by Milton Crane (New York: Grosset and Dunlap, Publishers, 1947), p. 124.

116 Lincoln Steffens, *The Shame of the Cities* (New York: Peter Smith, 1948), pp. 165–166.

117 *Ibid.*, pp. 166–167.

118 *Ibid.*, pp. 69–74.

119 Asbury, *The Barbary Coast*, pp. 236–237.

120 Jefferson Farjeon, *The Compleat Smuggler* (New York: The Bobbs-Merril Co., 1938), pp. 315–316.

121 Fred J. Cook, *op. cit.*, p. 75.

122 "New Gang Methods Replace Those of Eastman's Days," *The New York Times*, September 9, 1923, Section XX, p. 3.

123 John Bright, *Hizzoner Big Bill Thompson* (New York: Jonathan Cape and Harrison Smith, 1930), p. 286.

124 John Bartlow Martin, *Butcher's Dozen and Other Murders* (New York: Harper and Brothers, 1950), p. 107.

125 U.S. Congress, Senate, *Investigation of Organized Crime In Interstate Commerce*, S. Res. 202, 81st Cong., 2d sess., 1951, p. 812.

126 *Ibid.*

127 John McManis, "Murder Tieup Recalls Purple Rule of Terror," *The Detroit News*, January 14, 1945, p. 2.

128 Ontario Police Commission, *Report to the Attorney General for Ontario on Organized Crime* (Toronto, 1964), p. 16.

129 McManis, *op. cit.*, p. 2.

130 Michael V. DiSalle, *The Power of Life or Death* (New York: Random House, 1965), p. 121.

131 *Ibid.*, p. 122.

132 Wendt and Kogan, *op. cit.*, pp. 344–345.

133 Oscar Fraley, *Four Against the Mob* (New York: Popular Library, 1961), p. 16.

134 Pasley, *op. cit.*, pp. 37–39.

135 Dedmon, *op. cit.*, p. 294.

136 Peterson, *op. cit.*, pp. 160–161.

137 Asbury, *Gem of the Prairie*, p. 221.

138 Pasley, *op. cit.*, p. 206.

139 Charles Garrett, *The LaGuardia Years* (New Brunswick: Rutgers University Press, 1961), p. 153.

140 Denis Tilden Lynch, *Criminals and Politicians* (New York: The Macmillan Co., 1932), pp. 11–12.

141 Pasley, *op. cit.*, pp. 54, 59.

142 Thompson and Raymond, *op. cit.*, pp. 3–4.

143 Giovanni E. Schiavo, *The Italians in Chicago* (Chicago: Italian American Publishing Co., 1928), pp. 57–58.

144 Landesco, *op. cit.*, p. 948.

145 Pasley, *op. cit.*, p. 228.

146 Vecoli, *op. cit.*, p. 452.

147 Peterson, *op. cit.*, p. 188.

148 *Ibid.*, pp. 204–205.

149 *Ibid.*, pp. 189–190.

150 Burton B. Turkus and Sid Feder, *Murder, Inc.* (Garden City: Permabooks, 1952), pp. 348–349.

151 Lewis J. Valentine, *Night Stick* (New York: The Dial Press, 1947), p. 136.

152 Rupert Hughes, *The Story of Thomas E. Dewey* (New York: Grosset and Dunlap, 1944), p. 24.

153 *Ibid.*, p. 24.

154 *Ibid.*, p. 171.

155 Roy V. Peel, *The Political Clubs of New York City* (New York: G. P. Putnam's Sons, 1935), pp. 253–256.

156 Norton Mockridge and Robert H. Prall, *The Big Fix* (New York: Henry Holt and Company, 1954), pp. 50, 78 and 84.

157 *Time*, November 28, 1949, pp. 16–17.

158 Walter Arm, *Pay-Off* (New York: Appleton-Century-Crofts, Inc., 1951), Chapter Nine.

159 Estes Kefauver, *Crime in America* (Garden City: Doubleday and Company, Inc., 1951), pp. 20–23.

160 *Ibid.*, p. 54.

161 *Ibid.*, p. 265.

162 *Ibid.*, pp. 284–286.

163 Walter Noble Burns, *The One-Way Ride* (Garden City: Doubleday, Doran and Co., Inc., 1931), pp. 4–5.

164 Humbert S. Nelli, "Italians and Crime in Chicago: The Formative Years: 1890–1920," *The American Journal of Sociology*, LXIV (January, 1969), p. 385.

165 Burns, *op. cit.*, p. 5.

166 *Ibid.*, p. 4.

167 Nelli, *op. cit.*, p. 386.

168 Kenneth Allsop, *The Bootleggers and Their Era* (Garden City: Doubleday and Co., Inc., 1961), p. 295.

169 Daniel Bell, *The End of Ideology* (New York: Collier Books, 1962), p. 141.

6

La Cosa Nostra: The Question of the Existence of a National Criminal Organization

The proponents of the *Evolutional-Centralization Theory* view syndicate structure in the United States in terms of a highly organized, bureaucratized, and centrally directed organization. Most writers who express this view attempt to argue the existence of a national syndicate. By so doing they do not have to account for the differences that exist between syndicates. By assuming that "the Sicilian Mafia" was transported to the United States, those who expound this view find it satisfactory to prove their thesis by merely striking comparisons between the two. Thus *Don*, a title applied to men of respect in Italy and Sicily, suddenly becomes the title given to important syndicate leaders in the United States. This is done without regard for the fact that in Sicily those who perform the role of *mafioso* are given that title because of the power and prestige they hold as patrons capable of exerting their influence in legitimate areas of society.

The mere fact that contemporary syndicates in the United States have a large number of Sicilian and Italian names among their participants is sufficient evidence for these thinkers to equate an American with a Sicilian "Mafia." The fact that before the 1920s when the Italians became a force in the American political machine, syndicates in the United States were represented predominantly by Irish names is not even considered a topic worthy of attention.

Rather than viewing syndicated crime in the United States in its historical perspective and development, these writers, without any evidence to support their claim, begin their discussion with the coming of the so-called Mafia. Then realizing that non-Italians have been involved in syndicated activities, they attempt to keep their original assumptions by offering ridiculous arguments such as those that "The Mafia" in America opened its doors to non-Italians or that "the Mafia" will only allow non-Italians to serve in secondary positions in the hierarchy. They avoid explaining the difference between such groups as Black Hand gangs, *L'Unione Siciliana*, and *Camorra*, by unequivocally stating that they are all the same thing—"The Mafia."

We need not go further in illustrating that those who argue the existence of an American "Mafia" are forced by their basic unfounded assumptions to view all aspects of American syndicated crime in terms of the existence of a rigid, highly centralized, national criminal organization. Rather than viewing each syndicate as an entity in itself and having its own historical development that differs from other syndicates', these writers merely select certain characteristics common to all syndicates and on the basis of this commonality, argue the existence of a national syndicate. Yet even here, as we shall illustrate, these writers are inconsistent and self-contradictory.

Biased by a preconceived and unfounded notion that a national syndicate exists, these writers are content to offer oversimplified arguments to support their thesis. In so doing they have completely distorted what syndicated crime is in the United States. As we noted in Chapter 4, those writers who saw "Mafia" in Sicily as a secret national organization completely distorted the reality of *mafia* as part of the Sicilian social structure itself. So too those writers who describe American syndicated crime as consisting of a national secret organization serve to draw attention away from the functional relationship of syndicates to American society.

We have in the United States several syndicates, each with

its own area of operations and territory. In many cases and where it is profitable and expedient these syndicates cooperate with one another. However, syndicates are continuously characterized by conflicts both within and without. Also, syndicate leaders and members often are forced, desire, or find it expedient to settle issues by compromise in which each party gains and gives up certain important assets. Contrary to the conception of a rigidly organized national syndicate that is a smoothly running operation, we find instead that syndicates and their participants continuously come into conflict with one another in an attempt to keep control over or to gain access to various enterprises.

Rather than being a rigidly bureaucratized national organization, syndicates in the United States are more adequately understood in terms of patron-client relationships within and between syndicates. These relationships are constantly changing and are related to the amount and types of power the individual syndicated criminal can amass and command at any given time.

Those who abide by the *Evolutional-Centralization* conception then have attempted to view syndicated crime as originating outside the American social system rather than from within. As such they have had to describe syndicated crime as a large, national, centrally governed organization. Also they have always had to give the organization a name such as those we have discussed. Since 1963, however, another name took its place along with the others. This was *La Cosa Nostra*. Like the others it has only served to present the same confusions inherent not in the name itself, but emanating from the attempt to view syndicated crime in terms of a centralized national organization.

This new name came out of hearings of the Senate Subcommittee on Organized Crime and Illicit Traffic in Narcotics in 1963, which has come to be commonly referred to as the McClellan Hearings, after its chairman, Senator John McClellan. The highlight of these hearings was the testimony of underworld figure Joseph Valachi who applied the term *Cosa Nostra* to the criminal organization he was describing. It is sad that those who are not familiar with the Italian language failed to understand and continue to misconstrue the meaning of this term. *Cosa*

Nostra is a phrase commonly used in the Italian language to mean "our affair," "our concern," "our situation," or something relating to what a group may consider its particular province of concern at any given time. Thus if one Italian businessman were to extend an offer to help another group of Italian businessmen in financial straits, he may receive the courteous reply, "*Grazie, ma questa è cosa nostra,*" or "Thank you but this is our problem." In an Italian household a person wishing to enter a room where relatives or friends were discussing something of a serious nature would generally ask permission before he enters. He may be politely refused on the basis that what was being discussed was *cosa nostra*, meaning that it was of a private nature of concern only to those discussing it. In each of these contexts, *cosa nostra* is a general phrase employed by Italians to refer to a particular concern which a group of individuals may have at a particular time.

The term is never used in the context of referring to an organization. To do so would be to apply its usage completely out of context. To use *cosa nostra* as a term meaning organization would be as ridiculous as it would have been if the businessman in the above cited example had referred to those businessmen who refused his help as belonging to "the cosa nostra." Or better still, let us use the other example of the person who sought admission to the room where friends and relatives were discussing something in private. It would be rather absurd if, after being politely told not to enter the room because what was being discussed was "our concern," this individual would go to his neighbors and tell them to be careful of those congregated in the room because they belonged to "our concern."

There is much discussion among law enforcement officials about whether Valachi really said "*cosa nostra,*" "*causa nostra*" (our cause) or "*casa nostra,*" the latter term being literally translated as "our home" but often used in Italian to refer to "our group" or "our family." Despite the validity of these arguments the fact remains that during the hearings, when Senator McClellan asked Valachi to give the name of the secret criminal organization to which he belonged, Valachi answered "Cosa

Nostra" and translated the phrase as meaning " 'Our Thing' and 'Our Family'."[1]

Despite Valachi's reply, we feel that he was using the phrase in its Italian context to refer to the criminal activity of the group he was associated with rather than in the sense of a definite name by which the group was called. Were this not so, as we have indicated, the use of *Cosa Nostra* as a name in Italian simply makes no sense.

With the introduction of this term, however, after 1963 "Cosa Nostra" was picked up by the *Evolutional-Centralization* thinkers as the final proof of the existence of the national criminal organization. Basing their arguments upon what Valachi said and in many cases upon what he merely implied and in other cases on what he never said at all, there grew a new literature even more confusing than what had appeared in regard to "The Mafia," "The Black Hand" and the other so-called national criminal organizations that had preceded it. Immediately some writers began stating that "Cosa Nostra" was just another name for "The Mafia";[2] they were one and the same thing. Others said that "Cosa Nostra" was a "super-secret underworld syndicate popularly but erroneously dubbed the Mafia."[3] Still others, as we shall soon show, maintain that "Cosa Nostra" is the organization that was created after "The Mafia" in the United States was purged.

Obviously the same kind of unfounded assumptions and confusion of terms formerly used to argue the presence of "The Mafia" and "The Black Hand" is found in the writings of those who have since 1963 attempted to prove the existence of "Cosa Nostra."

Since the emergence of "Cosa Nostra" rests with the testimony of Joseph Valachi we should offer some observations regarding this testimony. Contrary to popular opinion, Valachi was not the first underworld figure to serve as an informant. As Harney and Cross note, in the late 1930s, a Sicilian informant, out of retaliation for the death of a relative, had made his services available to the Bureau of Narcotics.[4] Needless to say, every effective law enforcement official dealing with syndicated crime has made use

of informants. Virtually every law enforcement official interviewed by the author in the course of this study indicated that
much of his information had been obtained through his informants. As indicated earlier, this author has also made use of
informants for gaining access to data in reference to this study.
We wonder then why Valachi has been viewed as such an out-
standing or unique informant.

It is certainly not because he gave vital information that
resulted in developing legal cases against underworld figures.
Because of his imprisonment, as Harney and Cross point out,
Valachi had been away from underworld activities too long to
offer any significant help in this respect.[5] Another informant,
Nelson Silva Cantellops, helped by the agile work of agents of
the Federal Bureau of Narcotics, performed this role to a far
greater extent than did Valachi.[6]

Valachi's importance seems to rest in the fact that he was the
first informant who, testifying before the McClellan Hearings,
which were televised, appeared before the public. He came to
be regarded as the revealer of the secrets of the so-called Cosa
Nostra. Those believers in the *Evolutional-Centralization* thesis
immediately saw Valachi as their oracle of truth. Here at last
was someone who was going to give the nation a look into the
great secret criminal society. As Georg Simmel noted many years
ago, there is something exciting and fascinating about that which
is secretive.[7] It was within this context that Valachi took on his
importance. The book cover of his life story, *The Valachi Papers*,
bore the statement "The first inside account of life in the Cosa
Nostra."

There is no doubt that Valachi, like other informants, offered
information of value in helping to understand aspects of syndicated crime in the United States. But the fact remains that what
he offered was merely one man's view of syndicated crime. Every
informant has his own interpretation or manner of describing
how the syndicate is structured and how it functions. The author
noted this in his experiences with informants. And virtually
every police official he interviewed noted similar experiences
with their respective informants. What Valachi offered was his
own version or description of the organization and operations

of the criminal syndicate with which he was affiliated. Yet this one individual's interpretation was taken as an absolute, unquestionable, and accurate description of the format of syndicated crime in the United States. Convinced that there was some national organization of crime, the *Evolutional-Centralization* theorists were quick to interpret everything that Valachi said not only as truth from within a secret society, but to apply what he said specifically only about certain New York syndicates to all syndicates in the United States. Obsessed with the presence of a nationally organized "Mafia," "Black Hand" or whatever it was called, these thinkers were seeking some descriptive terms or some explanation of the structure that they were convinced existed. From Valachi's testimony they could and did extract such a description.

Valachi himself admitted that he had been a low status functionary in the very organization he described. He also stated that he had completed only a seventh grade education. His testimony, as we shall see, is replete with contradictions. Yet from his testimony there has emerged a description that has come to be the definitive one for many governmental agencies dealing with crime. This is evidenced by the fact that the structure presented by the Task Force Report of the President's Commission on Law Enforcement in 1967 is identical to that presented by Valachi.[8]

What in reality did Valachi reveal about this structure? He stated that each syndicate group consists of a "family." In every family there exist bureaucratically structured relationships, each designated by a title denoting the duties and power of the position. Valachi did not give a precise, rigid meaning to any of the terms which he used to describe this structure. The term *family*, for example, he used in several contexts. It was a term he applied to describe each specific group engaged in organized crime that was under the leadership of one boss. Yet he also used *Our Family* to refer to the total organization.[9]

When asked to describe the various positions in the organization, Valachi replied "Well, we have what we call *griemeson*, that is sort of like in English, would express it as a commission."[10] Later on when asked about the composition of this "commission" Valachi stated that it was "a *concerti*," a *consigia*," and still later "a *consegio*." Most probably the word Valachi was referring to was *consiglio* meaning "counsel" or "advice" and used it in the sense that the commission was a form of "Council." This commission was set up, Valachi indicated, by Charles "Lucky" Luciano to protect the soldiers or Button-men (the lowest echelon) from the next highest rank, the "lieutenant" or "*caporegime*." When asked if this commission was "kind of a kangaroo court?" Valachi answered, "You could call it a kangaroo court."[11]

In further describing the various ranks in the organization, Valachi said that each family had a hierarchy consisting of a boss at the top with an underboss or *sottocapo* under him, with a lieutenant or *caporegime* or several of these under the underboss' command. Subservient to the lieutenant and occupying the lowest echelon were the soldiers or button-men.[12]

When Senator Mundt asked whether this "army of crime" had "sergeants and captains," Valachi responded simply by saying "Well, we had, for instance we will say about 20 to 25 *caporegimes*."[13]

"What are they?" asked Senator Mundt.

Mr. Valachi answered "We call this like—I don't know how you call it in English—a regime, like you say, for instance, I will talk about my *cogini*. We had about 30 under one lieutenant—."[14]

Notice here that Valachi refers to the associates under his lieutenant as his "*cogini*," which is the Italian word for "cousins." Later when Senator Mundt asked "Within this little army, it is broken up into companies and brigades, or something?" Valachi answered, "That is right."

It is obvious from the above questions and answers that neither the questions nor the answers were precise or specific in meaning. Valachi was merely trying to explain his conception of the system of syndicated crime and used Italian terms or attempted to find English equivalents. If one examines Valachi's testimony one certainly does not come away with the conclusion that Valachi definitely set down a precise, rigid description of the organization to which he belonged.

Hence, in the above cited testimony we note some interesting inconsistencies. Although the lower echelon ranks of his organization—lieutenant and soldier—are military titles, the upper echelon positions—boss and underboss—are not. Rather than boss and underboss why aren't these titles those of "general," "major," "captain," or some other military title more consistent with "an army of crime?" Incidentally the formal term for "lieutenant" in Italian is not *caporegime* as Valachi indicated, but *tenente* or *luogotente*.

Why does he refer to his associates under the direction of his lieutenants as cousins rather than by terms more in keeping with a highly bureaucratized military structure? We are not necessarily arguing that his terms should have been consistent with those used in a military structure; rather we merely wish to emphasize the fact that Valachi did not use formal descriptive terms. Instead he was applying a mixture of English and Italian terms that at most should be taken only as attempts to outline a system of relationships rather than an exact description of a formal bureaucracy.

This is further illustrated in his use of the term *caporegime.* In Italian this means "head of a regime." Valachi explained to Senator Mundt that there were several regimes in his organization, each having a leader. Earlier in the testimony when Valachi was asked to give the Italian word for "lieutenant," he replied "*caporegime.*" The use of "lieutenant" here by Valachi is consistent with common usage of the term both in police and underworld circles to describe a person occupying a position subservient to that of the top man in an organization. The use of the term in this context is found frequently in the literature of syndicated crime. However, it is employed merely to indicate a subordinate power position, not a specific rank or office. No doubt this is what Valachi meant to imply as evidenced by the fluctuation in his use of the terms "*caporegime*" and "lieutenant."

As we examine Valachi's testimony we find further evidence to indicate that what he was describing was a loose system of power relationships in contrast to a rigidly organized secret criminal society. Thus the position of boss of a family, we find, does not in reality consist of a stipulated position of power guided by specific duties and privileges as one would assume exists in a highly bureaucratically structured organization. Valachi tells us that his boss, Vito Genovese, was not only the boss of his family but also controlled "the power in the Gambino family and the Lucchese family," however, he could not control the family of Joseph Profaci in Brooklyn.[15]

Does this indicate that the power relationship among and between the bosses is one of rigidly prescribed rules and structure or does it appear that Valachi was merely describing a structure in which power was dependent upon one's ability to secure and hold his position within a competitive system? Obviously if it were a rigidly organized society, there should be no question as to who was boss of a certain family and what powers and restrictions the office of boss entailed. Yet Valachi's testimony is filled with a multitude of statements that seem to demonstrate that his so-called organization was nothing more than a loosely structured system of power relationships. An examination of a few more of Valachi's statements should strengthen our point.

At the opening of Valachi's testimony, Senator McClellan asked him if the criminal organization to which he belonged required "absolute obedience and conformity to its policy handed down by those in authority?"

"Yes, sir" answered Valachi.

Without realizing the inherent contradiction he was presenting, Valachi later gave an example that illustrated that the exact opposite was true. In 1948, the boss of Valachi's family, who was then Frank Costello, gave an order so impressive that Valachi referred to it as "a law."[16] This law stated that no one was to deal in narcotics. Later, in 1957, states Valachi, bosses of other families laid down the same rule—no dealing in narcotics. Said Valachi of the "Cosa Nostra" member who would dare violate this rule—"You are in serious trouble."[17] The rule was so terrifying and the threat so great that everybody, soldiers and bosses included, violated it. To quote directly from the testimony:

Mr. Alderman: What was the reason why the members, the soldiers and so forth, and even some of the bosses, disregarded the rule?

Mr. Valachi: Because of the moneymaking, the profit in it.

Mr. Alderman: And there was a conflict between the desire to make money and the desire to obey the rules; is that right?

Mr. Valachi: Well, they just defied the rules.[18]

Does this sound like an organization whose rules and regulations must be obeyed? Is it one which demands "absolute obedience and conformity to its policy handed down by those in authority"? In light of such glaring contradictions, we simply can't understand how anyone can continue to believe that Valachi was describing a rigid, formally structured organization. Yet, the *1967 President's Commission Task Force Report on Organized Crime* reiterated a structure of syndicated crime that, excluding the consultants' papers in the Appendix, was nothing more than a restatement of Valachi's basic description.

As was true of the 1963 hearings, this Task Force Report tells us that the family structure consists of a boss at the top with a *"consigliere"* (counselor) who is on the same level as underboss, but serves rather as a consultant. Below the underboss there are the *caporegimes* who serve both as operating chiefs of units and as "buffers" between the upper echelons and the lowest echelon —the soldiers. Because of the similarity of the Task Force Report and the McClellan Hearings' description of the structure of syndicated crime we shall evaluate both of these simultaneously.

Our first consideration is the bureaucratic structure Valachi described. We fail to understand why it has been given so much importance. It was certainly a confused and unclear description. It certainly did not reveal anything of a complex nature. In fact, in view of the simplicity of the structure, it is an insult to police and other law enforcement agencies to maintain that they had to wait for Valachi to reveal this structure to them—a structure consisting of a boss, a *consigliere*, an underboss, "a *caporegime*, and soldiers. Even the Boy Scouts of America have a structure that is far more complex than this. Perhaps the need to see a conspiracy, a centrally organized secret society, has simultaneously resulted in the need to view Valachi's description as a complex and earthshaking revelation.

Rather than interpreting Valachi's terminology as illustrative of various levels of power in a system of relationships, his description of the hierarchy was taken literally. Although Valachi referred to families only in the New York area, "Cosa Nostra" families were soon found by law enforcement officials and journalists in major cities across the United States. Police officials testifying before the McClellan Committee displayed charts, some of which conformed identically to the structure as described by Valachi, while others revealed deviations from it.

Chicago officials, for example, displayed two charts, one showing the structure of the "Chicago-Italian Organization" and another consisting of "Non-member associates of Chicago-Italian Organization."[19] In his testimony, police official William J. Duffy explained that the "crime syndicate" he was describing was known in Chicago "as 'the outfit,' 'the mob,' the 'Mafia,' and, most recently, 'Cosa Nostra'."[20] Describing the two Chicago charts, Mr. Duffy explained that the "Chicago-Italian Organization" was a "mafia-type group" while the "Non-member associates" chart represented "those people who we believe did not belong to the Mafia-type group, but nevertheless did belong to the crime syndicate."[21]

Mr. Duffy's description is somewhat confusing. First he stated that the "crime syndicate" in Chicago is known as "the outfit," "the Mob," "the Mafia" and "Cosa Nostra." Then he tells us that the "Non-member associates" are not "mafia-type" but did belong to the "crime syndicate." What then is the "crime syndicate?" We note also that the chart for the "Chicago-Italian Organization" depicts only two positions in Valachi's description of the hierarchy—those of bosses and lieutenants.

In all fairness to those police officials like Mr. Duffy who testified before the McClellan committee, we should note an appreciation for the contradictory positions into which they were placed. They were confronted with a new name "Cosa Nostra" and new titles describing its hierarchy. In view of this, there is no doubt that these police officials felt the need to present an interpretation of the structure of syndicates in their city consistent with this new description. In doing so they were faced with the problem of trying to fit syndicated criminals known to them into the positions described by Valachi.

We are certain that many police departments had to quickly prepare information, much of which necessitated historical research. For the most part, police departments do not have sufficient manpower to dedicate the vast amount of time necessary to research and thoroughly prepare this type of report. As one police official expressed it to this author "I have a hard enough time keeping up with who they're fleecing without trying to go around studying them." Despite these hardships, however, we must compliment the various police representatives for the valuable information which they did make available regarding syndicate enterprises in various states and cities.

The various charts of syndicates presented in these hearings vary in terms of the structures they depict. The charts of the New York families of Vito Genovese, Gaetano Lucchese, Carlo Gambino, Giuseppe Magliocco, and Joseph Bonanno, are constructed according to the hierarchical format Valachi described because they were—as indicated by Inspector John F. Shanley[22]—based upon informffiation given by Valachi prior to the hearings. The Joseph Bonanno family chart, however, offers a minor but interesting difference in that the underboss, *consigliere*, and *caporegime* are all at the same organizational level with the boss above them and the "soldiers-buttons" beneath them.[23]

The Detroit area chart of the "Mafia Organization" is structured on a radically different organizational format. Here we have a Ruling Council whose members are referred to as "The Dons." Underneath them there are "The Big Men" who are over the "chiefs . . . of operating units," below which are the "lieutenants," with the lowest echelon composed of "section leaders."[24]

Quite different also is the chart of the "Mafia Organization" in the Tampa, Florida area, which Tampa Chief of Police, Neil Brown, noted "cannot be considered as a definitive 'table of organization' of the Tampa Mafia . . ." This chart simply lists a "top man" with two others alongside indicating high status ranking. Beneath the top man is an array of organizational lines

with no specific titles but assumed to be in a middle position
with "non-member associates and employees associates" constituting the lowest level.[25]

Here it is interesting to note for later reference Mr. Brown's
statements in regard to the organizational chart he described:

The Chairman: I notice you designate or refer to this group as the
              Mafia. Would you say that it is the same group
              that has been referred to by the famous witness,
              Joe Valachi?
Mr. Brown: Yes, sir; it is.
The Chairman: Whether he calls it Cosa Nostra or Mafia makes no
              difference. This is the organized crime group to
              which you referred?
Mr. Brown: That is correct, Senator; this is the group.[26]

The Rhode Island and Boston, Massachusetts Organization is
depicted as having one boss. Connected to this position are the
charts of a group designated as "Rhode Island" and another as
"Boston, Mass." We assume, from the testimony regarding this
chart, that the individuals in these two groups occupy only the
position of lieutenant.[27]

The Buffalo, New York Organization is depicted as having a
"Boss of the Entire Western N.Y. area as well as Ohio Valley
Area." Under this boss is an underboss, who is over several
lieutenants, who are in turn in charge of section leaders.[28]

Our reason for citing the differences in these charts is to
emphasize that each department employed its own terminology
to describe the hierarchy of syndicates in the cities it represented. Representatives of the New York Police Department,
since they based their structural chart on information they
received prior to the hearings, obviously represented the structure using the titles given by Valachi. Others offered their own
versions, some of which were similar, others completely different
from Valachi's conception. Our point is that syndicates as systems of power relationships can be and are described by a
variety of terms indicating power positions. Thus in the police
charts described above we note the use of such titles as top man,
the boss, the big man, the section leaders, the chiefs of operating
units, the soldiers, lieutenants, and others.

This is not surprising. Throughout his interviews the author encountered a variety of terms used by both police and underworld sources. These terms were applied, however, as means of defining power positions rather than specific ranks in an organization. Terms like "big gun," "captain," "the head man," "an important man at the lower levels of the organization," and others were used to describe these positions. Reference to "syndicate" itself was often made under such terms as "the boys," "the mob," "the troops," "Mafia," "Cosa Nostra," "the Group" or "the hoods." The author noted that "lieutenant" in the sense of describing a person occupying a middle position in a hierarchy was the most commonly and consistently used term.

Valachi, like other informants, gave his version of syndicate structure in the terms he had come to use. Like other informants he used titles to define power relationships. Naturally, after first defining what these were to himself, he could then give the names of those whom he thought occupied these positions. What we are saying is that Valachi, like other informants gave his description of syndicate structure, but instead of being interpreted as only one informant's version, Valachi's description was taken in its literal and formal sense. As a result, since Valachi's testimony, many law enforcement officials have found the need to fit syndicated criminals into one of the positions in the hierarchy described by Valachi. Thus occasionally one hears a law enforcement official stating "We know he's a big man in the syndicate, but we don't know whether he's a *caporegime* or an underboss."

What Valachi's testimony produced is a rigid, very formal interpretation of the structure of criminal syndicates. One assumes that in a highly complex and disciplined organization, members have well-defined roles in a formally structured system of interrelationships. Yet the structure Valachi described is quite the opposite. When asked, for example, about his relationship to the "Cosa Nostra," Valachi replied in a variety of contexts that certainly indicate a loosely formed system of relationships rather than a tightly knit secret society. When asked how much he earned as a member of "Cosa Nostra" Valachi replied:

You don't get any salary, Senator.

Senator Mundt: Well, you get a cut, then.

Mr. Valachi: You get nothing, only what you earn yourself.[29]

Later, Valachi indicated that the only thing he got as a member of Vito Genovese's family and in return for carrying out Genovese's assignments was protection.[30]

This type of relationship is not indicative of a formal structure. Nor does it represent a mode of behavior different from that generally found in American syndicates. The above description given by Valachi is basically no different from that which would have been given by any lower echelon participant in the syndicates of Mike McDonald, Monte Tennes, and John Morrissey. Like Valachi, during the late 1800s, lower level participants in syndicated crime also carried on their own enterprises for which, if they returned favors to more influential syndicated criminals who had political connections, they in turn would receive protection.

Going further in his testimony, we find that not only is there no formal structure for making money in his organization, but there is no definite delineation of the so-called organization he is describing. This can be noted from the following excerpt where Senator Muskie is inquiring about the nature of interactions within families:

Senator Muskie: Do these families meet, as such, or do these 450 members, for example, of 1 family, ever meet for the purpose of doing family business?

Mr. Valachi: Well, my family, I am there 30 years and they never met, not as a whole. But we have, every Christmas a table, like a dinner, and my regime consists of 30, I was telling you about, and the rest of the families here and there, some did and some didn't, but my family, the one I belonged to for 30 years never met as a whole.

Senator Muskie: So they did not even know each other?

Mr. Valachi: Well, as I said, they will get to know each other as they went along, and you know, meet, and you meet quite a bit in life, as you go along. And you may be some place, and you know a member, and

> he is with some member you don't know, and he
> will introduce him to you.[31]

Does this sound like a rigid, formally organized secret society?
We are told that this society recognizes its members by a secret
code. The following excerpt tells us just how secret it is:

Senator Muskie: This is a secret organization and how do you get
to know that someone is a member of the same
family?

Mr. Valachi: He will introduce him to you, for instance, as "a
friend of ours." That means a member. Now, if
he happens to be with someone that isn't a friend
of ours, he will just simply say, "Meet a friend of
mine," which means nothing, that is the code
between us.

Senator Muskie: So there was a code that enabled you to identify
other members of the family?

Mr. Valachi: Yes, sir.[32]

In all seriousness, we can hardly call this a code. At most it
can be categorized as part of the lingo of the syndicate criminal.
Every criminal subculture develops phrases that come to be
accepted methods of communicating among those who participate in its activities. Drug users, pick-pockets and others have
specific lingos. Are these to be classified as codes? Being introduced as a "friend of ours" obviously would imply that the
individual being introduced is part of some group involvement
whereas an introduction as a "friend of mine" would not imply
such. What is so secretive about this that it should be called a
code. In fact one could argue that the phrase "friend of ours" is
a commonly used one in American society by individuals wishing
to distinguish between individuals sympathetic to their group's
cause from those who are not. It is true then that the use of
"friend of ours" by a syndicate criminal in introducing a participant is a way of letting the other party know that he can speak
more freely regarding certain matters of mutual concern. However, this usage should not be elevated to the status of a secret
code.

"Cosa Nostra," we are told, has a structure which provides

consigliere, or counselors. This is indeed a very confusing segment of the structure, not that the rest are exactly clear. First, we are told that "Lucky" Luciano put the practice of using *consigliere* into effect in order to protect the soldiers from any injustices perpetuated by their lieutenants.[33] In his life story as told to Peter Maas, Valachi indicates that the *consiglieri* consisted of one man from each of the New York families and one representing the Newark area.[34] "The function of the councilors was to shield individual soldiers from the personal vengeance of various lieutenants who might have been their targets during the Castellammarese War."[35] It appears that this was a structure common only to the New York area families. Also, it appears that this was a creation in response to the Castellammarese war, which too was restricted to the New York families. This is evidenced by the fact that all the five charts of the New York families presented during the Hearings have a *consigliere* position in their hierarchy. Yet in the Task Force Report organization chart, this position is represented in all 24 families, 19 of which are not in the New York area and had no part in the Castellammarese War. The report simply describes the *consigliere* as an individual who gives advice or counsel and operates "in a staff capacity."[36]

Cressey, a consultant to the Task Force, states that he suspects that the " 'consigliere of six' continues to operate in the New York area and that similar local boards operate in Chicago and Detroit."[37] Yet Maas, who obtained his information from Valachi himself, tells us that even among the New York families "the councilors were as often as not ignored." At most their main function served to give "an aura of stability" which Luciano was intent on achieving after the Castellammarese War.[38] Thus a structure that was not even considered important or powerful in the New York families themselves is made to appear as a vital part of the contemporary structure of the 24 families.

Here we should note also that Valachi's testimony was primarily restricted to the New York families and even in that area he was most knowledgeable about the Vito Genovese family —the one with which he had the most acquaintance. Yet, as we

noted previously, after Valachi's testimony "Cosa Nostra" families were found across the country. Was this based on Valachi's
testimony? If it was, the facts were certainly based on weak and
contradictory testimony. Thus during the hearings Mr. Alderman asked Valachi about the location and number of "Cosa
Nostra" families outside of New York:

> Mr. Valachi: I will start with Philadelphia. In Philadelphia I would
> say about a hundred. Boston, when I left the streets,
> was about 20, 18 or 20. Chicago, about 150. Cleveland,
> about 40 or 50. Los Angeles, about 40. Tampa, about
> 10. Newark, about a hundred. Detroit, I am not
> familiar at all with Detroit.[39]

Interestingly, the above testimony contradicts what Valachi said
at an earlier point in the hearings. We can evaluate the accuracy
of Valachi's observations in this regard. When asked if he had
ever traveled outside of New York State, Valachi answered:

Well I visited Buffalo, and I visited Utica, N.Y.
Senator Curtis: You haven't gone to the Middle West?
Mr. Valachi: I went to Arkansas years back.
The Chairman: I didn't understand what you said.
Mr. Valachi: I was trying to tell him I went to the baths in
                Arkansas.
The Chairman: Did you get cleaned up down there?
Mr. Valachi: You know, the 21-day baths.
Senator Curtis: Have you ever been in Chicago and made any con-
                tracts with the Cosa Nostra?
Mr. Valachi: No; I stopped in Chicago on the way to Arkansas.
Senator Curtis: Did you make any contacts with any of the criminal
                elements there?
Mr. Valachi: In Utica; yes.
Senator Curtis: I mean in Chicago.
Mr. Valachi: No, no contacts.
Senator Curtis: Have you ever been in Kansas City?
Mr. Valachi: No, not that I recall; no.
Senator Curtis: Have you ever been in Omaha?
Mr. Valachi: No, sir.
Senator Curtis: That is in Nebraska.
Mr. Valachi: No, sir.

Senator Curtis: Do you know whether or not there are members of the Cosa Nostra operating in Omaha?

Mr. Valachi: Senator, I never heard of Omaha, and I never heard anything about Omaha.

Senator Curtis: Here is what I want to know: Are there assigned areas, or do you have regional offices? For instance, does the family or families in Chicago, do they have certain states under this jurisdiction?

Mr. Valachi: All I know, Senator, is in Chicago there was one family. Now, where they extend, I wouldn't know.

Senator Curtis: You do not know how the territory was handled outside of New York State?

Mr. Valachi: That is right.[40]

As is obvious from the above testimony, Mr. Valachi didn't have much, if any knowledge of the families outside of New York State. He certainly doesn't appear to have gained his knowledge from extensive traveling. Yet it is interesting that he was able to give the number of "Cosa Nostra" members in Boston, Chicago, Los Angeles, San Francisco, New Orleans, Tampa, Philadelphia, Cleveland, and Detroit.[41]

Of the number of members in New Orleans, all that Valachi said was, "Very few in New Orleans."[42] Of Detroit, he said: "Detroit, I am not familiar at all." Yet when asked by Mr. Alderman whether or not any families existed in Detroit, Valachi replied:

Yes, they exist.

Mr. Alderman: But do you know the number they have there?

Mr. Valachi: I have no idea of Detroit.[43]

Valachi by his own admission was not familiar with Detroit, but yet he knew that families existed there.

Other discrepancies in Valachi's testimony were noted also by Canadian authorities when they interviewed him. In the hearings Valachi made the following statements in regard to Vito Agueci, whom he described as a "member from Canada."

The Chairman: From Canada?

Mr. Valachi: Yes.

The Chairman: He is a member of another family though?

Mr. Valachi:	In Canada.
The Chairman:	The Buffalo family?
Mr. Valachi:	Buffalo and Canada is all one. When I say Canada, I mean Toronto.[44]

Later, however when Canadian police Commission authorities interviewed him, "Valachi denied vehemently that he had said that Buffalo and Toronto are in the same Cosa Nostra family," and that "If he did say it, it was a slip of the tongue" and what he really meant "to refer to was the hook up between Buffalo and Rochester."[45] One must admit that connecting Buffalo with Toronto when one means to connect Buffalo with Rochester is quite a slip of the tongue. Valachi completely contradicted his testimony on Canada during the hearings when he said that "he did not think the Cosa Nostra operated in Canada."[46]

Despite these contradictions, Valachi's testimony continues to serve as a basis for describing the nature and organization of syndicated crime in the United States. In 1965 a summary report of the McClellan Hearings extracted parts of Valachi's testimony to describe syndicated crime. This only added to the confusion already inherent in the hearings themselves. This report interchangeably uses the terms "Cosa Nostra" and "the Mafia" as though they were one and the same.[47] In the hearings, when asked if his organization was ever called "Mafia," Valachi replied: "Senator, as long as I belong to this Cosa Nostra, all I can tell you is that they never express it as Mafia."[48] Attorney General Robert F. Kennedy when questioned about using the terms "Mafia" and "Cosa Nostra" interchangeably answered "I think it is almost a matter of semantics, Senator" and added "It is an organization. It is Mafia. It is the Cosa Nostra. There are other names for it, but it all refers to the same operation."[49]

As we indicated earlier, the Tampa Chief of Police concurred with this mutual usage of the two terms. Interestingly, however, the police commissioner of the City of New York, Michael J. Murphy, when asked: "Have you been familiar with the name of Cosa Nostra very long as the name of that organization?" replied "No, sir." When questioned further as to whether or not "Cosa Nostra" was a new name for the organization, he replied, "It is a name I am not familiar with."[50] We also note again that

William J. Duffy of the Chicago Police Department characterized the crime syndicate in Chicago as composed of a "Mafia-type group" and a group composed of "Non-member associates of the Chicago-Italian Organization." He did not refer to either group as "Cosa Nostra."

If anything, in this author's opinion, the structure of "Cosa Nostra" seems more to resemble that of The *Camorra* of Naples rather than that described as "Mafia." As discussed in Chapter 4, The *Camorra* was a formally structured criminal organization, divided into groups or sections, each of which had its *Caposocieta*, while the entire society was under the leadership of a *Capintesta*. Also, trials were held to pass judgment over the conduct of its members and mete out justice. In view of this, it is rather odd that this organization rather than "The Mafia" has not been seized upon by those bent on arguing the foreign origin of American syndicated crime.

It is obvious that those who found it easy to call "Mafia" and "Cosa Nostra" the same thing were merely applying names indiscriminately. Their statements do not mean or explain anything. They first assume that an organization exists. Then without proving its existence they give it a name and add "it really doesn't make any difference what you call it—it is the same organization." What organization?

If it is "the Mafia" then why do we not find the structure of Boss, underboss, lieutenant, and soldiers described in any of the writings on "the Mafia" in Sicily prior to Valachi's testimony. Cressey cites "a book published in 1900" as showing that "one Mafia group, at least, had a structure almost identical to the structure of American 'families'."[51] No doubt the group to which Cressey is referring is the *Stuppagghiari*, a Sicilian brotherhood described in Chapter 4. Since Cressey does not seem to recognize the distinction between brotherhoods and the phenomenon *mafia* in Sicily, we can understand why he would see a possible similarity between the structure of this group and the American "Cosa Nostra" family. However, the only similarity between the "Cosa Nostra" family structure and that of the Sicilian group that Cressey says is "almost identical" is that they both have a *capo* and a *sottocapo*. It is interesting that Cressey does not add the dissimilarities between the groups—the fact that the Sicilian group did not have a *caporegime* and *soldati*. Also, by stating that this one "Mafia" group had a similar structure, Cressey is implying that other "Mafia" groups may not have had such a structure. If this is the case, then it seems useless to even discuss the possibility of any connection between this one Sicilian group and the American "Cosa Nostra." Finally, if "The Mafia" was a closed Sicilian secret society that came to the United States, why was Valachi himself, who was of Neopolitan, not Sicilian, ancestry, a member of the organization?

This question takes on further complications when we note in the 1965 Senate report the conclusion that "Cosa Nostra" was a "New Organization" that "had its genesis in the gangland war of 1930."[52] This so-called new organization was largely created by the initiative of "Lucky" Luciano who we are told closed "the books of Cosa Nostra" from 1931 to 1954, meaning that membership in the organization was restricted at first to Sicilians and later to "full Italians."[53] A "full Italian" we are informed is one whose parents are both Italian.

An examination of syndicated crime in the United States during this time, as we illustrated in the previous chapter, shows that Italian syndicated criminals, including Luciano himself, had many close non-Italian associates in their enterprises. Also the "closed books" thesis is rather absurd in view of the fact that if the organization was "The Mafia" then by definition it was a closed secret Sicilian society. Why then the need to close the books?

We are told further that the New York gangland war of 1930 "eventually involved mobs of Italian extraction throughout the United States and it led directly to the evolution of syndicated crime."[54] What this national evolution is we never learn. We are supposed to assume that it resulted in "Cosa Nostra" branches springing up everywhere across the nation. Yet, no factual evidence is offered. We are led to believe that Luciano in some manner was responsible for creating the organization across the country. Yet there is no real evidence that Luciano had any such power. He seems to have served as an arbitrator among the warring families of New York in the early thirties. Yet what power did he exert over other syndicates or families in other cities? If his organization was "new" with a "new" structure then obviously he was not functioning as an authoritative figure under the prescribed rules of any previous structure. Who then was Luciano that he could enforce his will upon other powerful syndicates across the nation. And incidently, what did he enforce? As we indicated before, the so-called *consiglieri* system that he created among the New York families was not ever effective among these families, let alone ever having been established in syndicates outside the New York area. Luciano, it seems, has been offered as an explanation of the creation of an assumed national criminal organization.

In contrast to those who explain Luciano's organization as a new one are those who speak of a purge of the old one. We are told that Luciano on "purge day," which was supposedly September 11, 1931, was responsible for executing a number of old style top leaders of the "old Mafia" across the United States. Turkus and Feder set the number at 30 to 40 within a forty-eight hour period beginning on September 11 and state that this purge created the national crime syndicate—the "ugly, savage Unione Siciliano."[55] Thompson and Raymond, on the other hand, state that this purge was of the already existing "Unione Siciliane" which was "a sort of Italo-American version of the Mafia from which it stemmed."[56] This purge, according to these authors did not place Luciano at the head of a national syndicate, as maintained by Turkus and Feder, but rather put him "in command of the Unione in New York."[57]

J. Richard "Dixie" Davis on the other hand states that "Luciano set out to change the Unione from a loose federation of Italians into a close-knit national organization, affiliated with the mobs of other national origins."[58] Incidently, according to this account, the purge was responsible for the execution of 90 underworld figures in contrast to Turkus and Feder's 30 to 40 victims.[59]

Needless to say, although we could cite other writings regarding this purge, they would surely serve to add further confusion considering that this so-called purge has never been demonstrated in fact. We keep hearing of the number of victims rang ing from 30 to 90, yet we were unable to find any source that gave the names of these so-called victims. If mere underworld killings are going to be referred to as purges then the whole history of syndicated crime could be viewed as one purge after another with the Prohibition era and its multitude of gang wars constituting a decade of purges. It appears that the purge thesis is simply another attempt to reinforce the conception of Luciano's power on a national scale.

Luciano became a powerful figure in New York syndicated crime. But even in New York there is no evidence that he was ever the top syndicate figure. As for the existence of a national supreme figure of syndicated crime, the Oyster Bay Conference concluded "there has probably never been such an individual."[60] This was the opinion of virtually all the police officials whom we interviewed. We fail to understand then why Luciano has been credited with power enough to virtually alter the structure of syndicates across the country.

Rather than viewing the 1930 gangland wars among New York syndicates simply as struggles common to other syndicates throughout the history of syndicated crime in the United States, Valachi's testimony elevated these wars to a special status. As though compromises and arbitration were something new in underworld settlement of disputes, we are told that a new structure emerged and that an arbitrator, "Lucky" Luciano, created this organization across the United States. The reason for the acceptance of this structure, we are informed, was that it brought peace among the warring factions. It is interesting to note, however, that struggles between syndicates have continued to take place even after the so-called establishment of this new organization. They are evidenced by "the Bananas war."[61] This struggle between Joseph Bonanno, alias "Joe Bananas," head of the New York "Bonanno Cosa Nostra" family and the other New York families has resulted in seven underworld executions since 1966. Another source reports that the recent gang warfare and kidnappings in New York are a result not only of the Bonanno struggle but "gang feuds among other Mafia families"[62] as well.

Similar to the special historical status given to the 1930 New York gangland war is the attention given to the now famous

"Apalachin Meeting" in Apalachin, New York in 1957. After the McClellan Hearings and Valachi's testimony, this meeting became a form of living proof of the existence of "Cosa Nostra." The allegations—contradictory, of course—existing in the literature about the purpose of this meeting are so unfounded that they are not worthy of mention.

As a meeting it was basically not very different from the multitude of meetings of underworld figures prior to and following it. But suddenly after it happened it became a phenomenon of national importance, mentioned continuously in the literature since its occurrence in 1957. Its most sensational aspect lies in the belief that it was a meeting of the Grand Council of the "Mafia" or the Commission of the "Cosa Nostra." The Commission as noted in the McClellan hearings was described as "the council of the bosses" of the various "Cosa Nostra" families across the United States.[63] What exactly this consists of was never made clear and was further complicated by the 1965 *Report of the Committee on Government Operations* and the 1967 *Task Force Report*. In the former report we note that the "commission or council was instituted by Charles 'Lucky' Luciano."[64] Yet on the same page we are told that "much of Joseph Valachi's testimony was devoted to tracing for the subcommittee the hierarchy of the American Mafia." Still earlier on the same page we are told that the characteristics of "the Sicilian Mafia" are "also common to the Mafia in the United States in the 1960s, having been brought here and maintained by Sicilian immigrants at the turn of the century." Yet, this same report later refers to the organization attributed to Luciano's creation as "The New Organization."[65]

The lack of consistent and precise definition in this type of description can hardly give us a good basis for any trustworthy or clear understanding of just what this so-called Commission that Luciano instituted really was, if in fact it ever existed at all. Assuming that Valachi's conception of the Commission as a council composed of the bosses of various "Cosa Nostra" families is correct, then we find it difficult to understand why in the *Task Force Report* there are 24 families but only nine members on the current Commission.[66] We are told that the size of the

Commission varies from nine to twelve and that "It is composed of the bosses of the nation's most powerful families." We wonder what determines the criterion for considering a family sufficiently powerful to have a member on the Commission. Also, since its composition varies from nine to twelve, are we to assume that there will never be more than twelve powerful families? If this is true then is this report really describing— as it seems to indicate—a rigid, planned, or instituted formal structure or one that simply changes with new conditions of power? It is apparent that there is no real evidence for the existence of a Commission. If merely being the head of a powerful syndicate group is the criterion for being a Commission member then there have been a multitude of Commission members throughout the history of syndicated crime in the United States.

To say that the Apalachin meeting was a meeting of the Grand Council of "the Mafia" or the Commission of the "Cosa Nostra" is at most merely an exercise in applying titles to an undefined phenomenon. We cannot even find agreement about how many were present at this meeting. Attorney General Kennedy stated to the McClellan Committee that "more than a hundred top racketeers" were present.[67] The *Task Force Report* states that there were 75.[68] If we cannot find agreement among governmental sources on the number of individuals present at this meeting, how can we trust any other conclusions about the purpose of the meeting or characteristics of those who attended it.

Contrary to those who believe that the Apalachin meeting was the first meeting of syndicate leaders on a national scale is the fact that such a meeting had taken place at Atlantic City in 1928. But, like Apalachin, writers cannot be satisfied to view this as a meeting of various syndicate leaders across the country who most probably were attempting to settle disputes through arbitration. This attempt obviously failed. Although gangland wars decreased after prohibition due largely to the fact that many small-time operators who had participated primarily in illicit alcohol enterprises dropped from the scene, they continued after this meeting. Nonetheless, Cook views this 1929 meeting as a meeting of "the American Mafia."[69] He tells us that head "Mafiosi" came from all areas of the country. Judging from some of the names on the list of those in attendance presented by Brennan[70]— Frank Erickson, Larry Fay, Maxie Hoff, Owney Madden, George Remus, Solly Weissman, and other non–Italian-Sicilian participants—we wonder exactly what Cook means when he calls this a meeting of "the American Mafia."

Suffice it to say that meetings have always been a necessity for syndicated criminals. Their frequency, their purpose, and number of attendants has varied with the nature of the enterprise. Obviously if several members of various syndicates located in different sections of the country are engaged in a mutual enterprise they may find it necessary to meet at given times to discuss certain problems. Does this mean that they all have to belong to the same organization? When several executives from different corporations meet to discuss mutual problems or mutual concerns does this mean that they constitute an organization? Why is it, then, that when syndicated criminals from various syndicates in the country hold a meeting that almost without question, they are viewed as belonging to some form of secret national crime organization? It should stand to reason that with the increase in means of transportation and communication, syndicates, like legitimate businesses, have found the opportunities to expand the ecological areas of their enterprises. As is also true of legitimate business, many syndicate criminals may find it necessary to meet with other syndicate criminals engaged in a mutual enterprise but each located in various parts of the country. If they meet does it follow that they represent an organization, or should it simply be understood as a meeting of certain syndicate criminals who at a particular point in time are engaged in a mutual enterprise.

An examination of those who attended the Apalachin meeting hardly seems to indicate a meeting of a national organization. Rather it appears to have been a meeting of syndicate criminals who had mutual or related enterprises. A very helpful listing was compiled by Arthur L. Reuter, a former Investigations Commissioner of New York State, and is cited by Frasca.[71] Out of 56 names of Apalachin attendants, Reuter was able to list, by using police histories, the major criminal enterprises or interests of 46. Of these we count 2 whose interests are in the realm of narcotics, 16 whose major enterprise is gambling, 2 who have interests in gambling and narcotics, 12 who are involved in gambling and labor racketeering, 4 in labor racketeering, 7 in narcotics and labor racketeering, and 3 whose interests lie in narcotics, gambling, and labor racketeering.

This listing seems to reveal an interest primarily in the areas of gambling, narcotics, and labor racketeering. We do not wish to imply that the purpose of the meeting was specifically that of discussing problems in these areas of interest. We are merely noting that the attendance at this meeting is more representative of interests in criminal enterprises than of ecological family areas. If it was a national meeting of the "Cosa Nostra" we would assume representation on a national basis. Yet another examination of Reuter's list, which also gives the place of residence at the time of the meeting for all 56 names for whom he collected data, shows that the representation was not as national as we have often been led to believe. Of the 56, 31 were from the New York state area, 8 from the New Jersey area, 6 from Pennsylvania, 1 from Texas, 1 from Colorado, 1 from Massachusetts, 2 from Ohio, 2 from California, 1 from Florida, 1 from Arizona, 1 from Illinois, and 1 from Cuba. Cressey, who along with the *Task Force Report*, maintains that about 75 attended the meeting states that about 23 came from the New York City or New Jersey area, 19 from upstate New York, 8 from the midwest area, 2 from the south, 3 from the west, 2 from Cuba, and 1 from Italy.[72] Using either Reuter's or Cressey's material we find the bulk of those attending coming from the New York–New Jersey area rather than being a representative national group.

Those who argue that the regions represented were in fact national in scope in that they represent the major "Cosa Nostra" families should answer why Detroit (whose family we are told has a member on the Commission) was not represented. Maas' argument that the Detroit family was represented by the Brooklyn boss Joseph Profaci because his two daughters were married to high ranking Detroit "Cosa Nostra" members[73] is, in our opinion, a very weak explanation if one can call it an explanation at all.

Since the *Task Force Report* does not specify just what the so-called 24 "Cosa Nostra" families are or where they are located, it is difficult to further evaluate the family representation at Apalachin. Using Valachi's testimony, we note that in New Orleans he claims there were "very few" members. There is no source that indicates that New Orleans was represented at this meeting. The family in Tampa, Florida, which, we can only assume, was represented by the one or two delegates from Florida, Valachi states had "about 10" members.[74] If 10 is sufficient for representation in the Tampa family, then we wonder what is meant by "very few" in the New Orleans family. We further wonder when a family is of sufficient size to merit a representative at such meetings. Boston, which was represented, had as Valachi stated "18 or 20."[75]

For those searching for a sinister, secret criminal society, Apalachin, like other underworld meetings, has to be viewed in terms of a meeting of an organization. In 1963, Apalachin was said to have been a meeting of "Cosa Nostra." Prior to Valachi's use of the term in 1963, this meeting was said to have been a meeting of "the Mafia." Yet the national meeting held in Atlantic City in 1929, despite the fact that it was attended by non-Sicilian and Italian delegates, was also referred to as a meeting of "the Mafia." For those who do not have a need to find secret criminal societies, Apalachin, like a multitude of other meetings that have been a continuing occurrence in the underworld, was an assembly of individuals who were interested in perpetuating their mutual criminal business enterprises.

In short then, neither Valachi's testimony nor any other evidence since that time has been sufficient to prove the existence of "Cosa Nostra" or a national, centrally directed criminal organization. The description of this organization in the 1967 *Task Force Report*, as we indicated before, is so filled with inconsistencies carried over from the McClellan Hearings that it offers no valid evidence whatsoever. Cressey's argument concerning "facts"[76] regarding "Cosa Nostra" taken from a wiretap published in *The Providence Journal* of May 20, 1967, should not so readily be elevated to the status of "fact." The results of this wiretap as stated in *The Providence Journal* were not the actual statements of the underworld figures themselves. Rather let us quote directly from the newspaper article as to how the results of this wiretap were recorded:

> The agent operating the tape recorder at Providence kept "logs" in which he made note of individuals speaking and the subject matter discussed.
>
> The tapes and logs were delivered daily to Mr. Kehoe (who was a special agent in the Boston office of the FBI). Listening to the tapes and checking what he heard with what the logs said, he made memorandum notes. From the memorandums he later dictated "airtels," the FBI term for air mail messages sent through FBI channels, which went to Washington FBI headquarters and other FBI offices as such subject matter indicated.[77]

We note then that it was these "airtels," not the original tapes that were reported in *The Providence Journal* and that serve as the basis of the information Cressey calls "facts." Since, as the *Journal's* article indicates, the original tapes were later "erased and used over and over" during the process of wiretapping at Providence, what we have then are the "memorandum notes" of the special agent of the FBI at Boston from which "he later dictated" the "airtels" to the FBI. With all due respect to this special agent and his integrity, we must note that all we have in these "airtels" are his interpretation of what was said. Thus, when Cressey states that in the "airtels" of October 20, 1964 and October 26, 1964 it was shown that "the organization is headed by a 'commission',"[78] are we certain that the term "commission" was actually used in the wiretap or perhaps merely the names of powerful underworld figures who have been assumed to belong to such a commission?

Cressey states that all one needs in order to understand the meaning and importance of what is contained in these airtels is "merely an elementary knowledge of Cosa Nostra's authority structure, from Commission to soldier."[79] This is precisely our point of criticism. Once an individual has been given such a listing of hierarchical positions as *"capo," "sottocapo," "capo-regime,"* and "soldiers" it is quite easy to fit names into these

positions. When this occurs it becomes nothing more than circular reasoning. For example, if an underworld figure has been
given the title of *"caporegime"* and this title is known to the
individual who is interpreting a wiretap, it stands to reason that
when the name of this individual appears in the wiretap, he will
be referred to as "a *caporegime*." So too, with "boss," "underboss" and other titles.

Mr. Cressey, without realizing it, presents us with a question
in his own writing which further reinforces our point. On page
121 he states that the airtels showed that "There is an organization called 'Cosa Nostra'," yet we are somewhat confused in view
of earlier statements in Cressey's book as to what exactly this
is supposed to prove. In one section of the book, Cressey cites
a wiretap conversation where two so-called members used the
term "Cosa Nostra" to refer to their organization.[80] However,
Cressey notes that in Chicago "the members sometimes refer to
themselves as" the "syndicate," the "organization," or the "outfit," and points out that the use of "Cosa Nostra" in the sense
of an organization is common to "Italian criminals in the eastern
part of the United States" who "have corrupted the Italian
probably because they mix it with English."[81] We wonder, however, why the Chicago syndicate doesn't use the term at all?
Even in New York where Cressey tells us the term "Cosa Nostra"
is "used extensively," he notes that "the term is often used only
in a rather indirect sense."[82]

If Cressey himself notes the different usages as well as lack
of use of the term "Cosa Nostra," we fail to understand why he
should consider the conclusion from the airtel that "There is
an organization called 'Cosa Nostra'" a startling one. If anything, all we can conclude from this airtel is that the term "Cosa
Nostra" was used by certain underworld figures in their conversation. The mere use of the word does not in itself constitute
proof of the existence of such an organization. Furthermore,
why would a nationwide unified criminal organization need to
call itself by different names. The argument that this is done
to keep the name of the organization confused so no one can
really learn what it is cannot be accepted since, if this were the

real purpose, then wouldn't it be more feasible simply not give
it a name at all?

So too with Cressey's "fact" taken from the airtels showing
that "families" are staffed by "underbosses, caporegime, and
soldiers."[83] In an earlier discussion, Cressey presents only confusion for his own argument. In discussing various terms that
are used to refer to the hierarchy he states that the *caporegime*
is often also referred to as "lieutenant, captain, head, capo-
decima, (or) capo."[84] In Chicago, however, Cressey goes on "the
terms 'soldier' and 'button' are not frequently used." Instead we
find "a 'street man' or 'operator' reports to a 'district man' (who
is either a button or a lieutenant), who reports to an 'area man
(probably a lieutenant but possibly boss or underboss), who
reports to the Chicago Council, whose chairman reports to the
Commission."[85] To confuse us further, Cressey in discussing the
general "Cosa Nostra" structure, tells us that "the lieutenant
and the men reporting to him are sometimes called a 'clique',
'circle' or 'nostra brigata', but each of these terms also is sometimes used as a synonym for 'family'."[86]

It is obvious from Cressey's statements that his acceptance of
the large variety of terms "clique," "circle," "area man," "operator," "captain," "lieutenant,'" "capo," "head" as "Cosa
Nostra" terms is grossly misleading. It seems that he first assumes the existence of "Cosa Nostra" in a particular area. Then
if the terms happen to be similar to other areas where he has
also assumed its existence he cites this similarity as a form of
proof. On the other hand, if the terms employed in a given locale
are different, Cressey simply accounts for this by indicating that
in such an area "Cosa Nostra" members simply use different
terms. Thus if in a wiretap the term "Cosa Nostra" is used this
is offered as proof of its existence. If in another wiretap "Cosa
Nostra" is not used then we are told that in that area "Cosa
Nostra" is called by a different name. Using this form of logic
one can come to no conclusion other than that "Cosa Nostra"
exists.

All Cressey is really doing is citing various terms used by the
so-called Cosa Nostra members is merely stating terms used in

underworld lingo. There is no doubt that since many Italian-Sicilian criminals participate in such activities that some of the terms will be of Italian-Sicilian derivation. If on the other hand, as Cressey seems to want to convince us, these terms are in fact rigid, consistent ones used to indicate definite positions or parts of the "Cosa Nostra" organization structure, then the least we could expect is consistency of usage from family to family, or from one locale to another. There is no doubt in this author's mind that if taperecordings and airtels could have been made of conversations between non–Italian-Sicilian underworld figures in New York and Chicago during the 1870s we would have found the use of such terms as "boss," "head," "lieutenant," "Clique," "operator," "captain," and probably many more that have since gone out of usage in underworld lingo. In this airtel, then, all Cressey has shown is the terms used by the underworld figures in the wiretap to define certain participants in criminal activities. He did not offer evidence that these were in fact definite staff positions.

As with the other so-called facts that Cressey derives from the airtels we should note that one must be very cautious in "interpreting" the contents of wiretaps, particularly when one is previously convinced of the existence of that which he seeks to find. In discussing the above-mentioned wiretap with a police official knowledgeable in the area of syndicated crime the author was cautioned against ready acceptance of "interpretations" of wiretaps since, as he put it "it is so easy to take things out of context or, better yet, it's so easy to put them into a context where they do not belong."

In short then, all the so-called evidence for "Cosa Nostra," "The American Mafia" or any other form of national, formally structured criminal organization lies only in the massive confused and contradictory assumptions of those who purport to have demonstrated its existence.

We are told that a secret society with oaths, duties, and a hierarchy of positions whose orders are passed from top to bottom and must be obeyed exists. Yet the very source of information who made these claims, Valachi himself, offered illustrations that showed that the opposite was true.

After telling us that anyone who disobeyed orders from the boss would be "in serious trouble," he went on to show that virtually everyone outrightly disobeyed Frank Costello's rule outlawing participation in narcotics. Without defining exactly what they were, he told of a group of six men or *consiglieri*, who among the New York families supposedly protected the soldiers against the *caporegime*. In Valachi's memoirs, however, Peter Maas stresses that this group wasn't even effective among these families. Cressey merely "suspects" that this group continues to exist in the New York area and that something similar to it operates in Detroit and Chicago. Yet the 1967 *Task Force Report* doesn't even mention the group. Rather, it mentions only the position *consigliere*, who we are told is an individual who acts as an advisor to the boss and underboss.

With such confusion then, we can hardly argue for the existence of *consigliere* as a real part of the so-called formal structure of "Cosa Nostra." The same is true regarding the existence of the so-called Commission. We are told of its existence. We are also told that "Family members look to the commission as the ultimate authority on organizational and jurisdictional disputes."[87] If this is true, it is rather odd that the Commission has not been effective in settling the current "Bonanno" and other recent wars. Nor was it effective in the famous Gallo-Profaci war in New York during the early 1960s. According to Martin, the Commission, which he defines as "the highest body of the Mafia," kept a "hands off" policy regarding this war.[88] The fact that this war continued is evidence in itself that it certainly was not settled by any Commission.

Other descriptions of this Commission leave us with the impression that even if it does exist, it is not a part of a formal structure. If it were we would find that it had a consistent structure and a consistent method by which membership to it was selected. Instead we find that the size of its membership varies and that the members "do not regard each other as equals."[89] We are never told how the Commission members are selected. Rather we are told only that "The commission is not a representative legislative assembly or an elected judicial body."[90] First, in discussing the recent death of a Commission member, Sandy Smith stated that the vacancy had not been filled and "is still up for grabs."[91] One must agree that such descriptions of the Commission by the *Task Force Report* and other sources hardly appear to be a part of a formally structured secret society.

Valachi's description of his relationship with his secret society in itself certainly didn't appear to be a relationship with a society at all. He told us that all he got from "Cosa Nostra" was protection, that he never attended the initiation ceremonies of any other member, and that he met other members as he went along in life. His own initiation ceremony and oath, since it took place at the time of the "Castellammarese war" sounds more like an affirmation of affiliation to one segment of a warring group rather than it does allegiance to a secret criminal society. Unfortunately, here again Valachi wasn't very explicit in his statements about the purpose of "Cosa Nostra." His statement describing the aims of the organization was simply—"They lived by the gun and by the knife and you die by the gun and by the knife."[92] When asked specifically what the purpose of the organization was, Valachi replied, "Well, I guess the purpose, that is what the rules were of Cosa Nostra."[93] We wonder also how well Valachi understood what was said during his initiation. He himself stated that he didn't understand the words because they were in Sicilian. He states that he merely repeated the words. Their meaning was explained to him later:

> The Chairman: And you repeated them, but you didn't understand what they meant.
> Mr. Valachi: That is right; and they then explained it to me.[94]

In any event, even if the oath Valachi took was for the purpose of entering a secret criminal society, he is the best example of the fact that the oath isn't very effective. He broke it. Regardless of the existence of an oath, the fact remains that informants both before and after Valachi have offered information against the underworld. Most recently, Joseph "Barboza" Baron in

Boston[95] and Peter Lazaros in Detroit[96] have given such information. Like Valachi these two informed in retaliation for having received what they considered unjust treatment from their syndicate affiliates.

In conclusion, the evidence for the existence of a national, centrally operated, highly structured criminal organization rests upon contradictory and unclear evidence as well as the resulting interpretations of this evidence. The fruitless attempt to find such an organization results from the fact that it is assumed to exist with no major evidence upon which such an assumption can be made.

Evolutional-Centralization thinkers, because they have searched and continue to search for a secret, formally structured society have failed to view syndicated crime as it realistically functions—not as a formal organization but as a system of power relationships among participants of syndicated crime who vary with time and place. What believers in the existence of "Cosa Nostra" fail to understand is that the functioning and structure of "Cosa Nostra" is no different from the functioning and structure of other syndicates in the history of the United States. What, basically, is the difference between the control of a "Cosa Nostra" boss over gambling in a given area and the control that Mike McDonald, John Morrissey, and other syndicate leaders had during the late 1800s? Certainly their enterprises necessitated criminals inferior to them in status and power to operate them. Shall we call them "underbosses" and those even lower in power "lieutenants" and the lowest "soldiers." What difference does it make what we call them? The important factor is not to give them a title or name but rather to recognize the individuals in terms of their fluctuating positions of power and importance in an overall system of informal, not formal, power positions.

To give titles as the *Evolutional-Centralization* thinkers have done is merely to force a structure or a name onto a system that does not have a formal nature. Because syndicated crime in the United States does not function within the norms of a legal system but rather, outside or in violation of it, syndicated crime in the United States has always been a system depicted by power struggles and fluctuating power positions, not a readily structured organization into which recruits are ceremoniously initiated.

The syndicate leader, or more precisely, that syndicate criminal who at any one time can exert the most influence on the legal agencies for protection and the most influence on other syndicated crime participants by offering them protection and more lucrative opportunities to make money, is in fact in a powerful position. Whether we call him a "boss," "*Il Capo,*" or whatever doesn't change the basic fact that his power comes from his relationship to the legal sources in society and to the criminal sources who view his power as an advantage to them. Nor does the fact that we call one who virtually has no power "a soldier" or "a street man" change the fact that in the system of power relationships in an illegitimately functioning social system, he is in an unimportant and weak position.

Rather than being formally structured organizations, then, syndicates in the United States are informally structured systems of patron-client relationships. The patron is the individual who has achieved a power position where he can grant favors to those beneath him in the underworld. He also serves as a client to those legal power sources who can offer him protection in return for his pay-off or services. This system of patron-client relationships—a system which, by its very nature is one constantly emersed in conflict, cooperation, and accommodation—is, in our view, the nature of the structure and functioning of syndicated crime in the United States.

References

1 U.S. Congress, Senate, Committee on Government Operations, *Organized Crime and Illicit Traffic in Narcotics, Hearings,* before the permanent Subcommittee on Investigations, United States Senate, 88th Cong., 1st sess., 1963, pt. 1, p. 80.

2 Malachi L. Harney and John C. Cross, *The Informer in Law Enforcement,* 2nd ed. (Springfield, Ill.: Charles C Thomas, 1968), p. 107.

3 *Newsweek*, August 19, 1963, p. 27.

4 Harney and Cross, *op. cit.*, pp. 107–108.

5 *Ibid.*, p. 124.

6 Renée Buse, *The Deadly Silence* (Garden City: Doubleday and Company, Inc., 1965), Chapter 2.

7 Kurt H. Wolff, ed., *The Sociology of Georg Simmel* (New York: The Free Press, 1964), pp. 332–333.

8 The President's Commission on Law Enforcement and Administration of Justice, *Task Force Report: Organized Crime* (Washington, D.C.: U.S. Government Printing Office, 1967), p. 9.

9 *Organized Crime and Illicit Traffic in Narcotics*, pt. 1, p. 80.

10 *Ibid.*

11 *Ibid.*, p. 81.

12 *Ibid.*, pp. 80–81.

13 *Ibid.*, p. 81.

14 *Ibid.*, p. 82.

15 *Ibid.*, p. 88.

16 *Ibid.*, p. 90.

17 *Ibid.*, p. 319.

18 *Ibid.*, p. 320.

19 *Ibid.*, pt. 2, Exhibits 39 and 40.

20 *Ibid.*, p. 506.

21 *Ibid.*, pp. 508–509.

22 *Ibid.*, pt. 1, p. 262.

23 *Ibid.*, pt. 3, Exhibit E.

24 *Ibid.*, pt. 2, Exhibit 18.

25 *Ibid.*, Exhibit 45.

26 *Ibid.*, p. 523.

27 *Ibid.*, Exhibit 53.

28 *Ibid.*, Exhibit 64.

29 *Ibid.*, pt. 1, p. 109.

30 *Ibid.*

31 *Ibid.*, p. 82.

32 *Ibid.*, p. 83.

33 *Ibid.*, p. 81.

34 Peter Maas, *The Valachi Papers* (New York: G. P. Putnam's Sons, 1968), p. 117.

35 *Ibid.*

36 *Task Force Report*, 1967, p. 7.

37 Donald R. Cressey, *Theft of the Nation* (New York: Harper and Row, Publishers, 1969), p. 45.

38 Maas, *op. cit.*, pp. 117–118.

39 *Organized Crime and Illicit Traffic in Narcotics*, pt. 1, p. 386.

40 *Ibid.*, p. 205.

41 *Ibid.*, pp. 386–387.

42 *Ibid.*

43 *Ibid.*, p. 387.

44 *Ibid.*, p. 91.

45 Ontario Police Commission, *Report to the Attorney General for Ontario on Organized Crime* (Toronto: 1964), p. 36.

46 *Ibid.*

47 U.S. Congress, Senate, Report of the Committee on Government Operations, *Organized Crime and Illicit Traffic in Narcotics*, Senate Report No. 72, 89th Cong., 1st sess., 1965, pp. 11–12.

48 *Organized Crime and Illicit Traffic in Narcotics*, pt. 1, p. 121.

49 *Ibid.*, p. 21.

50 *Ibid.*, p. 63.

51 Cressey, *op. cit.*, p. 142.

52 *Report of the Committee on Government Operations*, 1965, p. 12.

53 *Ibid.*, p. 13.

54 *Ibid.*, p. 12.

55 Burton B. Turkus and Sid Feder, *Murder, Inc.* (Garden City, New York: Permabooks, 1952), pp. 86, 99–100.

56 Craig Thompson and Allen Raymond, *Gang Rule in New York* (New York: The Dial Press, 1940), pp. 4, 375–376.

57 *Ibid.*, p. 375.

58 J. Richard (Dixie) Davis, "Things I Couldn't Tell Till Now," *Collier's*, August 5, 1939, p. 44.

59 *Ibid.*

60 *Combating Organized Crime*, Report of the 1965 Oyster Bay, New York Conferences on Combating Organized Crime (Albany: Office of the Counsel to the Governor, 1965), p. 28.

61 *Time*, October 18, 1968, p. 26.

62 Charles Gruntzner, "Mafia Violence Brings Fear of Open Gang Warfare," *The New York Times*, April 28, 1968, p. 75.

63 *Organized Crime and Illicit Traffic in Narcotics*, pt. 1, p. 237.

64 *Report of the Committee on Government Operations*, 1965, p. 5.

65 *Ibid.*, p. 13.

66 *Task Force Report*, 1967, p. 8.

67 *Organized Crime and Illicit Traffic in Narcotics*, pt. 1, p. 6.

68 *Task Force Report*, 1967, p. 11.

69 Fred J. Cook, *The Secret Rulers* (New York: Duell, Sloan and Pearce, 1966), p. 77.

70 Bill Brennan, *The Frank Costello Story* (Derby, Conn.: Monarch Books, Inc., 1962), p. 84.

71 Dom Frasca, *Vito Genovese: King of Crime* (New York: Avon Books, 1963), pp. 130–140.

72 Cressey, *op. cit.*, p. 57.

73 Maas, *op. cit.*, p. 249.

74 *Organized Crime and Illicit Traffic in Narcotics*, pt. 1, p. 386.

75 *Ibid.*

76 Cressey, *op. cit.,* p. 121.

77 *The Providence Journal,* May 20, 1967, p. 41. Parentheses mine.

78 Cressey, *op. cit.,* p. 121.

79 *Ibid.*

80 *Ibid.,* p. 19.

81 *Ibid.,* p. 18.

82 *Ibid.,* p. 17.

83 *Ibid.,* p. 122.

84 *Ibid.,* p. 114.

85 *Ibid.,* p. 115.

86 *Ibid.*

87 *Task Force Report,* 1967, p. 8.

88 Raymond V. Martin, *Revolt in the Mafia* (New York: Popular Library, 1964), pp. 96–97, 157.

89 *Task Force Report,* 1967, p. 8.

90 *Ibid.*

91 Sandy Smith, "The Mob," *Life,* September 1, 1967, p. 18.

92 *Organized Crime and Illicit Traffic in Narcotics,* pt. 1, p. 182.

93 *Ibid.*

94 *Ibid.*

95 *The Boston Globe,* July 9, 1968, p. 6.

96 *The Free Press,* November 27, 1968, p. 1.

7

Syndicated Crime: Its Structure, Function, and Modus Operandi

Rather than consisting of a rigid, formally structured organization with specific rules and regulations, syndicated crime in the United States is best described in terms of a system of power relationships among its participants. Like other relationships they range from those which are very business-like to those in which friendship, family ties, and other forms of emotional attachment or rejection play a role.

It is this informal nature of syndicated crime that makes *Evolutional-Centralization* explanations in terms of a formal, consistent, bureaucratic structure futile. The inconsistencies and contradictions noted in the previous chapter were shown to exist because the differences between syndicates and the variations that exist in syndicated criminal activities and behavior are not taken into consideration by those who attempt a uniform, stereotyped and homogeneous conception. Once they construct their model then they merely try to explain away exceptions by ridiculous arguments which only create further exceptions to their original thesis.

The Network of Relationships

Our approach here is to describe the structure and function of
syndicates as systems of power and therefore as patron-client
relationships both between syndicate functionaries and legitimate society and among syndicate participants themselves. We
shall show that syndicate criminals vary in the kinds of relationships they establish among themselves and between themselves and those who provide them with protection. We shall
show that syndicated crime has no rigid formal structure; rather
that the structural boundaries of syndicated crime are never
explicitly defined since it makes use of whatever resources or
persons necessary to carrying out its functions. We shall not use
titles to describe positions because in a system of patron-client
relationships titles are meaningless. What is important is the
individual's power position at any given time with the constant
reality that this may and does change. We shall show that what
Valachi and others have misleadingly explained in terms of a
formal structure can be better described and understood once
we loosen the yoke imposed by the need to find a national
criminal secret society. We shall show that titles such as "underboss," "lieutenant" and others are not useful since, contrary to
the assumption of those who argue a formal structure, not all
bosses, underbosses, lieutenants, or soldiers are equal in power
or status. These are assumed to be equal positions because the
"Cosa Nostra" theorists must view them as equal in order to
support their thesis of the existence of a national secret society.
In order to argue such a thesis they must purport the nature of
rigidly defined positions which are consistent among the national
units, be they "families," "cliques" or what have you.

Viewed as patrons and clients, however, we find that those
individuals who are powerful in syndicate crime do not in fact
hold equal power. This phenomenon is probably what Cressey
and the *Task Force Report* are really describing when they argue
the existence of a Commission whose members do not recognize
themselves as equals. What is being called a commission is in

reality syndicate criminals who have managed to assume strong positions of power, not in a formal structure, but because they are in positions to serve as patrons to a syndicate criminal clientele. We are certain that there are far more than nine or twelve such individuals. In fact to stipulate any specific number is to make the structure a very inflexible phenomenon.

Every syndicate has several powerful individuals. Because they are able to wield certain kinds of force and to deliver favors these individuals may attempt or may be called upon to settle disputes between two individuals working under their patronage. They may also be asked to intervene in a dispute outside their area because they may be a friend of one of the disputing parties. Again their influence carries only as far as their patron position allows them to grant favors or impose realistic threats at any given time. Thus a powerful syndicate leader in the west at a particular time may be influential in his area because he has excellent protection in his city and because he provides funds for a multitude of new criminal enterprises, giving other syndicated criminals continued sources of revenue. Yet he may have no power whatsoever over other syndicated criminals in other parts of the country.

On the other hand, powerful syndicate figures who serve as patrons to their functionaries may also serve as clients to others more powerful than they. Others may serve on an equal basis in that although they are both patrons having a large number of clients, they may exchange mutual services.

So it is with the other functionaries in syndicated crime. The entire system involves various levels of patron-client relationships. Thus one unimportant and weak syndicate figure may have done several favors for an equally unimportant functionary. Later, however, the latter is put into a position where he becomes a patron for an intermediately powerful person. He now becomes a patron for the former and is in a position to return favors for those that were extended to him.

Similarly, an intermediately powerful syndicate figure as a patron may develop such a large number of clients that he may become a patron equal in power to the patron for whom he had originally served as a client. It is this form of power which is evidenced when a New York Commission Report, discussing the rise of a syndicate figure, stated that this individual had "the higher syndicate connections and the henchmen to achieve such organization and control."[1] Yet, the need to find a fixed structure is evidenced when later in the report this individual is placed on an organizational chart directly under the "Don" of the "Western New York criminal syndicate."[2]

As a system of patron-client relationships, syndicate structure is never formally or rigidly bureaucratized. The variations in patron-client relationships that emerge are numerous and complex.

Add to this patron-client system, those relationships based upon family ties, friendships, and contract and the syndicate system becomes even more complex. It is not uncommon in syndicate behavior that an individual may be permitted certain behaviors that would not be tolerated in a patron-client relationship simply because the delinquent party is a relative of an important functionary. So too friendship plays an important role. Thus a friend of a powerful patron may receive added favors or be excused for behavior which would otherwise not be tolerated. Contractual relationships are exactly that. They are carried out within the context of a business relationship with no obligations other than that of the fulfillment of the terms stipulated in the contract.

It is obvious that patron-client relationships are not unique to the underworld as many relationships in legitimate society are structured in the same manner. In the underworld the only difference is that these relationships are the basis for functioning within the illicit system of syndicated crime.

In our conception then, syndicated crime is structured as a continuous system of patron-client relationships among those participating in it. The most powerful figures in this array of relationships have developed the monetary and other means to secure legal protection and the cooperation of clients who find it advantageous to continue under their patronage.

It is obvious that the number and types of formats that patron-client, contractual, friendship, and other relationships take is

endless. In offering illustrations of such in this chapter we do not
mean these to be the only possible forms that these interrelationships can take. Rather we offer these examples only to
further show the vastness of possible relationships that exist in
syndicate behavior. It is a lack of appreciation for this vastness
of differing networks of relationships that prohibits an adequate
explanation of syndicated crime by those who propose a rigid,
categorically defined, bureaucratized conception.

Characteristics, Norms, and Techniques

Yet within this system of relationships, irrespective of the power
position of the functionaries, there are certain characteristics
of the overall system itself that are an integral part of it by
virtue of the relationship of syndicated criminal activity to
legitimate society in the United States.

These characteristics, which have become the norms, values,
and roles expected of syndicate criminals, are the requirements
for participation within it, regardless of one's power position in
its array of patron-client relationships.

Among these requirements is the ability to be secretive about
one's criminal activities. Although *Evolutional-Centralization*
advocates have tried to attribute this to Italian-Sicilian secret
societies, referring to it as the "code of *omerta*," the value of
silence is a basic requirement of all syndicate participants. It
is a norm expected of those who engage in syndicated criminal
activities and the individual who violates it may suffer various
repercussions. Depending upon what has been revealed, the
violator may receive varying degrees of punishment. He may
merely receive a reprimand followed by various forms of ostra-
cism until he has proven himself again. If his violation is more
serious, he may be warned by his patron that if this occurs
again, he will be "out on the street," meaning that he will no
longer receive the patron's support or protection. Or if the
knowledge revealed might be legally devastating to important
syndicate participants, he probably will be killed. The latter is

almost always the case when an informant gives evidence resulting in the indictment or conviction of an important syndicate functionary. We say almost always because in some cases, social conditions may warrant against it. Thus if an informant is given heavy coverage in the press, the syndicate participants may feel that killing him could bring about public reaction. Public uproar will force their political protectors to permit legal action to be taken against the syndicate participants, in order to save their own necks. Although this may not have been as true during the Prohibition era, with its vast networks of corruption and the high degree of public tolerance of gang warfare, today it seems that syndicate participants find it more expedient to keep the public eye off themselves.

In such cases their logic is that the damage of the informant's evidence has already been done. To kill him would serve no purpose other than showing other syndicate participants that this is what happens to those who talk. Yet this end is accomplished even without killing the violator, since both he and others know that the possibility that he may be killed after "everything quiets down" always exists. The psychological tensions that go along with this type of situation are in themselves a form of constant punishment for the violators.

The killing, if it is done, may be accomplished in a variety of ways. The syndicate participant or participants victimized by the informer's evidence may themselves "contract" to have the individual killed. That is, they pay a certain individual or individuals a specified amount of money for the killing. This often happens when the individual to be killed is "hard to get to," meaning he is cautious and, because he knows most of the syndicate participants in his area, is able to elude them. Or it may mean that he has excellent police protection. In any event, the "contract" is given to someone from another area who is a specialist in these types of killings.

Or the killing may be "set up" by a close friend or relative of the one to be killed. Although the potential victim may be cautious of his associates, there may be one or two friends or relatives whom he trusts and who may then be put into a position where they can kill him. This is not a simple task; it is not easy to ask one to kill his close friend or relative. Here, however, we enter the realm of patron-client relationships. Regardless of friendship or kinship if a client owes a patron a "big favor" he may be placed into an obligatory position where he simply cannot refuse his patron's request. It goes without saying that the patron asking for such a favor would not do so unless he earlier performed a very important service for the client.

Or the killing may be carried out purely as a favor by a client who wants to ingratiate himself to a patron whose services he needs to further his own ends.

Secrecy then is a valued norm among syndicate functionaries. It is not the sole property of the so-called Mafia or Cosa Nostra but rather a basic requirement for the existence of syndicated crime. Thus we noted earlier its practice among the Chinese Tongs and other syndicated criminal groups in the United States, as well as other parts of the world. Siragusa notes the importance of secrecy among Corsican underworld groups participating in the smuggling of narcotics.[3]

Another basic characteristic of syndicated crime is the use of violence or the threat of it in accomplishing its task. Violence in syndicated crime is used both as a method of keeping control over the functionaries in various enterprises, to eliminate competition, and to gain control over a competitor's enterprises.

We should note that because of the relationship that exists between the subservient client and the patron or patrons above him, much control is exerted by nonviolent means. Thus a disobedient individual may lose the patron relationship necessary for him to continue his own enterprise. If his particular activity involves using the patron's place of business, his established contacts or other elements, denial of these to him by the patron may literally terminate his activity. In other cases, a seriously or continually disobedient functionary may be purposefully placed into such a position that he is literally forced into debt. Thus several informants told the author of cases where a policy or numbers operator who had attempted to cheat those above him was "disciplined" by a simple, nonviolent process. They would wait for a day or several days when a given number was played by a great many individuals placing bets with this operator. On these days, the highly played number would hit and the operator would have to pay large sums to winners, often leaving him virtually bankrupt. This technique is commonly referred to in police and underworld lingo as "changing numbers" on someone.

The manipulation of the number in policy operations is accomplished by a simple process. Recognizing the differing and sometimes synonymous usage of the terms "policy" and "numbers" in the literature, we make a distinction. In policy, the number is selected either by a "drawing" of some kind, spinning a wheel, or some other form of "random" selecting process. It is quite simple to fix the drawing or the spinning so that the selected number will appear. This is generally done if the selection is made in the presence of witnesses as is true, for the most part, in various forms of policy enterprises. Since the mid-1950s, because of its more practical aspects, policy has given way to numbers operations.

In numbers enterprises, a more sophisticated method of assuring more wins than losses is used. Although various methods of selecting the number have been used, including the use of the daily totals of the New York stock exchange, most numbers houses since the mid-1930s take their number from the results of a particular set of horse races at a specified track. Since the number here is based on the results of a stipulated number of races at a given race track, it cannot, unless outrightly changed, be manipulated. Here is where the "wire service" is important. The "wire service" is a service, provided for a fee, which gives the latest results of the races at specified racetracks across the country. With such information, the numbers house operator is in a position to protect himself against possible large losses. Since the number is generally three digits, based on the results of three races, by knowing the winners of the first two races, the operators by checking their "betting slips" can foretell how many potential winners they have. They do this by simply checking the first two numbers of each bet slip. If they find that they have a large number of slips that have the first two winning digits, they can then "lay off" a portion of these bets with other gamblers. The "lay-off" here simply refers to the process whereby the operator "bets" with a larger gambling concern a portion of the customers' "bets" having the first two winning digits. By doing this, should the last digit create a large number of winning tickets, the operator can collect from the lay-off source and hence balance his own losses.

The lay-off does not have to be used frequently; chance itself may cause the numbers "bet" to be sufficiently different, thereby creating no cluster of potential winning numbers. By having the "line" information on the results of the first two races, however, the house operator can simply calculate how many potential winners he may have and further insure himself against the possibility of heavy losses. Although an operator could function without a wire or lay-off, one can readily see that his operation would face financial risk.

We mentioned earlier that the actual number in a numbers operation cannot be manipulated. This is true only if the house or source providing the number actually uses the results at the racetrack. However, as both underworld and police sources indicate, on many occasions the number selected is not the same as the one that comes from the race results. It is changed. No elaborate techniques, as is often believed, are used. The number is simply changed. Here similar to the purposeful selection of a number in policy, the number is fixed.

Thus when we speak of a fixed number in policy or numbers we simply mean that the number that has the lowest amount of bets on it is purposefully selected as the winning number, thus assuring profit for the house. It is a known fact among both informants and police that the numbers of many policy and numbers houses are fixed. The reader may wonder whether or not those who place policy or numbers bets at certain houses know that these are fixed. According to both police and underworld sources, it seems that whether they know or not is irrelevant since those who are bent on playing, play in either case. Referring to those who play while knowing that the numbers are fixed one informant said "fixed or not, they all feel that

some day their number is going to hit and they'll be on gravy
street."

Because numbers can be fixed, untrustworthy participating
operators can be disciplined or removed from syndicate enterprises by the simple nonviolent technique of changing numbers.

As a technique for taking over a competitor's enterprises, violence is often used in the world of syndicated crime. In many
cases the violence amounts to destroying the competitor's property or theatening or buying out his functionaries to the point
where it is no longer feasible for the competitor to remain in
business. In some cases the competitor's customers are threatened. Thus one syndicate group succeeded in destroying a
gambling competitor's enterprise by continuously threatening
and in some cases mugging the customers as they came to and
from the establishment.

In other cases, fights for control of enterprises take the form
of outright warfare. In Boston, a *Life* magazine article in 1967
states, a battle for the control of loan sharking enterprises
resulted in a death toll of 43 underworld figures.[4] Various
sources in Boston interviewed by the author indicated that many
of these killings, in their opinion, involved personal vendettas
emerging from lifelong gang loyalties rather than killings attri-
butable strictly to control of illicit enterprises.

In Youngstown, Ohio between 1951 and 1963, a total of 75
bombings and 7 fatal shootings have evidenced the struggles for
control of criminal enterprises.[5] Five brutal murders in Buffalo
occurring from 1958 to 1961 were attributed to "gang conflicts
over gambling and vice rackets in the Buffalo area."[6] The entire
history of syndicated crime is itself a chronicle of syndicated
criminals struggling to keep as well as gain control over their
criminal business concerns.

Violence as a method in syndicated crime must be understood
as a necessary and functioning part of it. Violence without reason or purpose has no function within the context of organized
crime. However, as Mary Lorenz Dietz has shown in her study,
violence can be of a "controlled" nature.[7] As such it becomes a
vital weapon. Contrasted to other forms of violence, that of

syndicated crime, Geis notes, is "neither so fiery nor so inarticulately vicious as much explosive murder in families" and "is usually inexorable, spare and businesslike."[8]

Although the need for violence is found throughout syndicate enterprises, specialists in violence are generally associated with enterprises that require its use on a continual basis such as "enforcers" working for a loan sharking concern, specialists who serve as bodyguards for important syndicate criminals, or bouncers who keep order on the premises of the business establishments. Quite often one individual may serve in several capacities. Thus an enforcer for a loan shark outfit may also serve as the bodyguard of the top man or organizer of the enterprise. In some cases one enforcer may work solely in that capacity for several patrons. In other cases an enforcer may operate one or several gambling or nightclub establishments of his own while continuing to provide services involving violence for more powerful functionaries.

Occasionally enforcers themselves hire out jobs to others. Thus, John "Chesty" Matthews, an enforcer, notes that occasionally he hired out minor jobs like "an arm or a nose busted" to drug addicts whom he would pay not with money, but with a small amount of drugs.[9] Matthews's reason for doing this—"it saved a little dough for the racket" and "why waste good men on cheap stuff?"[10]

The use of violence in many syndicate activities is necessitated by the fact that syndicated crime functions outside the legal system, hence it cannot use legal means of enforcement. In legitimate society one party can file suit against another for payment of a debt. The underworld, on the other hand, cannot use legal means to collect a loan whose basis is illegal. The syndicate criminal can scarcely bring charges against an individual for failure to pay a gambling debt where gambling is defined as an illegal act. One can hardly imagine a syndicated criminal taking an individual to court because he failed to pay his weekly "extortion rate."

Financial agreements in the underworld, then, must be made with the understanding that failure to pay may result in injury or death to the debtor. One may say that the debtor's body is his only collateral. It is true that occasionally a naive individual may fall prey to a loan shark. However, as most informants indicated, the individual who borrows from a loan-shark usually "knows what he's getting into." As one informant put it:

> A lot of those bastards who come for bread are the scum of the earth. They never pay their bills, but they're always bitching that they're the ones that are getting screwed. Put the bastards out on the street and their own mother wouldn't lend them a dime. Then when they get the shit kicked out of them, they go crying to the Fuzz yelling about how they're the pillars of the community and how those dirty gangsters took them for a ride. If the Fuzz took a good look at them they would find that they've been a pain in the ass to every bank and collection agency in town.

Fear is a more valuable tool for collecting debts than killing or maiming the debtor. Neither a corpse nor a cripple are the best procurers of money. Hence the injuries inflicted by a loan shark enforcer must be painful but not incapacitating. Often the visible bruises and cuts on a victim remind other debtors what may happen to them if they do not pay. Here is where the skill of a specialist in violence is important. He knows where and how to hit so that the victim experiences severe pain, receives bruises and cuts, but is not permanently injured.

In many cases the victim is not harmed. Instead, techniques of inducing fear are employed to motivate a debtor toward payment of his loan. In one case, a man was hanged by his feet out of a window fifteen stories high. Within an hour he found the money with which to pay his loan.[11]

In still other cases both physical pain and intimidation are used. Thus one loan shark victim testified that he was held captive until his wife raised the necessary money.[12] This same victim maintains that in another instance he was handcuffed to an overhead beam in a basement where after being punched and kicked he was shown a wire clipper and told that his ears would be cut off if he didn't come up with the money. He was released, he stated, after "he arranged to get $200 from his mother."[13]

The extent and type of violence and intimidation used varies from loan shark to loan shark and from place to place. Thus a New York police official observed that loan sharks in New York were not as prone to use assault as much as those in Chicago.[14] Generally speaking the debtor in loan sharking enterprises is killed only when he has some means of paying, but outrightly refuses to do so. Then as one observer stated "it pays to make an example of him."[15]

Although violence is an important means of control in syndicated crime it is not the only method employed. Wherever it is more expedient or necessary, various nonviolent techniques are used. In many instances in loan sharking, rather than intimidating or physically injuring the debtor an agreement is made with him. In some cases a debtor is put to work at an establishment designated by his loan shark and payment of his loan is taken from his paycheck on a regular basis until the loan is paid off. This technique of paying off loans is referred to as working in a "Boiler Room."[16]

Another agreement generally made between syndicate criminals and their debtors is that of accepting or demanding an interest in the debtor's business establishment. Thus if a bookie is in debt he may agree to give, on a regular basis, part of his "take" or profit from his gambling enterprise in payment, or he may agree to make his creditor a partner in his enterprise.

Owners of legitimate businesses may agree to pay off their loans by giving their syndicate creditor a percentage of their business profits. This is often the means through which the syndicate criminal gains control of legitimate businesses. Once he has gained access to such a business, if the original owner becomes deeper in debt, the syndicate creditor may agree to accept further payment in the form of an increase in the percentage of ownership of the business. Employing this arrangement, the syndicate criminal may slowly become the sole owner of the business. As partial or sole owner, the syndicate criminal can use this legitimate business to further his criminal interests. As partial owner, the syndicate criminal may demand that the original owner hire as a worker one of the criminal's loan shark debtors for whom this job serves as a "Boiler Room" arrangement.

As complete owner of the legitimate business, the syndicate criminal can use it as a "front" for illicit enterprises. Thus a luncheonette in Long Island procured by syndicate criminals through a loan shark debt soon became "a headquarters for bookmaking and loan sharking."[17] Such legitimate businesses can also serve as a basis for claiming losses for income tax purposes. They often also provide syndicate criminals with a legitimate occupation that serves as a cover for their reporting of income to the Internal Revenue Service.

It should be pointed out here that not only legitimate enterprises obtained through loan shark debts but other forms of arrangements with legitimate sources are used as covers for income tax evasion. Thus, as Peterson notes, Tony Accardo, an important underworld figure in Chicago, arranged in 1956 to be placed on the payroll of a beer sales company, where as a "beer salesman" he made a yearly salary of $65,000.[18] The federal government later showed that Accardo had not performed any such function for the company.[19]

Legitimate businesses often serve as covers for low status criminal functionaries who participate in the criminal enterprises of important syndicate figures. Hence many individuals who serve as "pick-up" men in a policy or numbers enterprise list as their legal occupation their "position" in the legitimate company. This is also true of enforcers and other functionaries. Often the legitimate enterprises allow their syndicate operators to serve as "sponsors" for "parolees" whose services they can use or toward whom they feel an obligation because of favors owed them. This often happens in cases where a low status functionary has been arrested while participating in a criminal operation of an important and influential patron who has the political and other contacts necessary to make arrangements for the prisoner's parole. Whether such arrangements are made is largely determined by the nature of the personal relationship between the two individuals and by the value of the prisoner's skills to the syndicate operator. Also, such arrangements may be made as a favor to the wife, relative, or friend of the prisoner who offers to testify for or not to testify against an important syndicate figure during his trial.

It is commonly believed that all syndicate participants have this and other forms of syndicate protection in the event that arrests take place. The assurance and the extent of such protection is not automatic in syndicate activity. Like other aspects of patron-client relationships in syndicated crime, protection is based upon such factors as friendship, obligation, agreement, extending a favor, or the desire to create a new patron-client relationship.

A syndicate operator may offer legal and other help to someone whose services he needs. In some cases he may make an arrangement with certain of his functionaries to provide legal aid if they are arrested and imprisoned. Generally this is done where the individual's skills are of a specialized nature. Such an agreement may include the promise of providing for the individual's wife and family in the event of imprisonment and the promise of efforts at effecting an early parole if legal resources during and after the trial fail. These agreements vary but it is important to note that they are agreements and not automatic fringe benefits derived from participation in syndicate activities.

Often a low status functionary is given legal help or his family given financial help because of a display of exceptional loyalty to the syndicate operator. Such aid might be extended, for example, when an individual goes to prison rather than reveal the names of important and influential syndicate patrons who actually perpetrated the crime for which he is convicted.

Frequently a low status syndicate functionary, in an effort to persuade others to participate in a criminal enterprise that serves only to benefit him, will tell these individuals that they have the syndicate's protection. Much to their dismay when arrested these individuals find no help coming. Later they learn that the individual who promised the syndicate's protection had no such protection to offer. The syndicate participant who makes such promises may jeopardize himself. If he continues this technique, he may soon become known as untrustworthy and lose his potential clients. Also, this individual's actions may be viewed by important syndicate figures as creating unfavorable relations between syndicate patrons and potential clients. If such is the case this individual, unless he has the protection of a powerful patron, may be forced to discontinue this practice.

Whenever expedient or necessary syndicates may use nonviolent methods to take over the illicit enterprises of their competitors. This generally occurs when one syndicate is in a position to ensure itself better protection than its competitor or where one syndicate has more financial and patron-client resources.

An interesting example of such a nonviolent usurpation of a competitor's enterprises is found in the change in the control of the major numbers enterprises in Detroit during the middle of the 1940s. In keeping with the view of Carlson, who maintains that numbers games developed in the United States during the middle of the 1920s,[20] police and underworld sources in Detroit indicate that the numbers enterprise was brought to Detroit around 1922. From this time to the late 1930s, the numbers houses in Detroit were owned and operated almost exclusively by Black syndicate functionaries. Around the beginning of the 1940s, however, the ownership of various large numbers enterprises slowly began to come under the control of non-Black syndicate functionaries. Police information indicates that many of the new owners were of Italian-Sicilian backgrounds; however, many of the important functionaries in the houses were of non-Italian–Sicilian extraction. Also a number of the houses remained under the control of their original Black owners.

What interests us here primarily is the method employed in this takeover. There are many reasons offered by both police and underworld sources why nonviolent techniques were used instead of outright force. A source familiar with the underworld in the Black community maintains that a peaceful takeover was mandatory because of a particular police official who was virtually incorruptable. The syndicate leaders seeking control reasoned that any outright gang war would have been met by police interference not only in an effort to stop the war itself, but directed ultimately toward the elimination of the criminal enterprises and the functionaries themselves.

Another possible explanation may be that the non-Black syndicate participants seeking the takeover may have been leery of the degree of organization that existed among Black numbers operators at that time. As Carlson points out a group of Jewish syndicated criminals from Cleveland in 1928 had attempted to break the Black-controlled monopoly on numbers.[21] The Blacks, who, as Carlson notes, up to this time had been divided by minor differences met this situation by uniting and driving their competitors out. It was this attempted takeover that resulted in the formation of the "Associated Numbers Bankers," whose chief purpose was that of insuring "negro control of the racket against outside aggression."[22] According to this author's source of information, various informants in the Black underworld who were participants in the numbers operations at that time did not recall any organization known as the "Associated Numbers Bankers." However, the general consensus of opinion among these informants was that the Black operators were in a position of strength capable of meeting with any forceful attempt to seize control of their enterprises.

Another explanation for the peaceful takeover offered by a Detroit police official lies in an understanding of the relationship of the Black numbers operators and the Black community. In Detroit, the principle customers of the numbers operations were Blacks. As such, the customers trusted their own operators. Since the entire numbers operation is built on trust, primarily trust that the bettor will be paid if he wins, the relationship between the bettor and the operator had to be one based upon faith. Blacks trusted their Black operators. Not only did they trust them, they regarded them as highly respectable and prestigious men who were interested in the welfare of the Black community. The non-Black syndicate operators were obviously aware of the fact that an open, aggressive attack on these respected men would only serve to sever relationships with bettors in the black community.

Any takeover would have to be accomplished in such a manner that the upper echelon Black operators would abandon their establishments for reasons of a financial nature rather than by any "gangland style" slaying or intimidation. Thus it would be more tolerable to the Black community to have white owners take over a numbers establishment because the previous owners were bankrupted by a series of large "hits" or winnings, that "broke the bank," or caused the owners to go out of business. In this type of situation, the only change would occur at the upper or ownership level while the bettors would continue to interact with and place their bets with their former Black "writers" or "runners," as those who accept the actual money and bet slips are called.

Whether for these or other reasons, the fact remains that the gradual takeover of the Black-owned numbers houses in Detroit by white syndicates around the mid-1940s was intentionally accomplished via nonviolent means.

Before describing the techniques used to accomplish the change we must point out that until around 1946 or 1947 the wire service in Detroit was controlled by two prominent and powerful Black functionaries in syndicated crime. They were providing the number for both Black and non-Black controlled houses in Detroit. Between 1946 and 1947 they both were charged and tried and later imprisoned. After their imprisonment a group of whites of Italian extraction, often referred to as "The Outfit" or "the Dagoes," took over this service. Now in a position to provide both the wire service and the number, this group began a gradual usurption of the various major houses. It appears that the targets of this takeover were primarily the large Black-controlled numbers operations; many smaller Black-operated houses remained in business.

The more common techniques employed to seize control of the large houses were twofold. One simple method was to bribe a source in the house who would inform the white wire service operators of the highest played number in that house. Since the wire service decided the number, they would simply change numbers so that the house would incur a severe loss. Often the operator of the house would have to borrow money from these white syndicate functionaries in order to pay off his bettors. Once this occurred, the Black operator became a client of his white patrons and often was simply allowed to remain as a hired employee of the house. This served both to place this operator under the new owner's control and to allow for a continuation of the liaison between the Black operator and his previous bettors from the Black community.

Another technique was to hire a gang of men to rob the "office," or the place where the money and slips were being counted. According to police and underworld sources one criminal from the Black community was hired for this purpose by the white operators and was personally responsible for several of the robberies. He soon became feared by numbers operators, which gave him the basis for using a very clever method that helped further enrich himself and allowed the white operators to take over several more houses: He would simply ask a numbers operator for employment, a request with which the operator would quickly comply under the assumption that this man obviously wouldn't rob the house for which he worked. Once in the employ of the house, he would devise a method of placing a slip with the winning number into the betting slips and thus win large sums of money. Several such hits would either force the operator out of business or cause him to go to the white operators for a loan. This method, which has come to be known as "dropping a bad package," was employed by a number of "bad package experts" during this takeover.

Another less significant technique was to use bribes in the form of bonuses or higher percentages to the writers or runners of the Black operated houses in order to induce them to give their business to white controlled houses.

Employing these techniques, then, by 1954 the majority of the large, Black-owned houses had been taken over. Again we should repeat that this takeover did not turn the formerly Black-operated establishments into completely white-staffed operations. Instead, many of the Black staff, "writers," "checkers," and others, continued to work. The basic difference occurred only at the operator or owner level; instead of the Black "owner" receiving the profits of the entire house, these now went to the white operators.

As interesting as the peaceful takeover in Detroit was the peaceful method by which Black operators came to again have control of their numbers enterprises. One of the important factors leading up to this was the avid enforcement of a 1951 federal law, which among other things required gamblers to pay a ten percent excise tax on their annual gross bets. In 1968, this act was declared unconstitutional by the U.S. Supreme Court on the basis that it was a violation of the Fifth Amendment. Nonetheless its enforcement in Detroit through the cooperation of the Intelligence division of the Detroit Police Department and the Internal Revenue Service began manifesting its effects upon the numbers operations during the middle and late 1950s.

When a numbers writer was seized with betting slips in his possession, the amount of money bet on each slip was totaled. This total was then used by the Internal Revenue Service to calculate the runner's average daily gross amount of business. Since numbers is a six-day-a-week enterprise, this amount was multiplied by six. Since there are 52 weeks in a year this weekly amount was multiplied by 52. This final calculation represented the writer's gross annual numbers collection. No deductions were made for his operating expenses or for the amount of loss he incurred from his bettors' winnings. His ten percent excise tax would then be based on this total annual rate. Needless to say, this was too expensive a proposition for most writers. Being arrested with a large number of betting slips for most writers, as stated by one police official was "almost like giving them a life sentence." This police official stated that it was not uncommon for writers, when they were caught, to immediately begin begging the police officer to take the money and keep it for himself. They would virtually offer the officer anything in order to keep from being "hit by the IRS."

This method of enforcement obviously caused many writers to get out of the business. The loss of writers was followed by a loss in the amount of play for the houses. This amount of loss among the houses was further enhanced in the early 1960s by the increased use of wiretapping of the telephones of suspected numbers operators. From information gained through this source further surveillance of locations suspected to be part of a numbers operation allowed police to effect raids at a time and place where an entire numbers operation could be completely destroyed.

Another contributing factor that presented problems to the

white syndicate operators was that a radio station CKLW in Windsor, Ontario, located across the river from Detroit, began broadcasting the race results of major tracks in the United States every half hour.[23] This did not diminish the value of the wire service that gave the race results immediately as compared to the half-hour reports of CKLW. However, this half-hour reporting, as Inspector John J. O'Neill pointed out, did create "considerable consternation to the syndicate because many people that formerly were not actively engaged in this illegal enterprise eventually set up the handbook business themselves. All they require is a radio that gives results and a clock to accept the bets, to time the bets, so that they are not postdated."[24]

Coupled with these problems were the difficulties and apprehensions which top syndicate functionaries were beginning to sense regarding the possible effect of wiretapping upon their insulation. It goes without saying that because of the many risks involved, the pay-off to police and other protection sources during this period constituted a serious economic liability to the owners. Because of these problems confronting numbers operations during the mid-1950s and early 1960s, the white syndicate operators made an agreement to return the houses and operations back to Black functionaries.

According to a reliable police source this took place at a meeting between the white syndicate numbers owners and several important Black numbers operators. At this meeting, which is said to have taken place in October of 1963 at a restaurant in Detroit, it was agreed that the Blacks would take over the ownership and operation of the previously white-owned houses. The only stipulation was that these houses would continue to take their numbers from the white syndicate members. This peaceful relationship between these syndicates, according to both police and underworld sources, has continued since that time.

Syndicate Structure

As we have shown thus far it is futile to describe a syndicate as a highly bureaucratically organized group whose membership, positions, and roles are clearly defined. It should be obvious that, contrary to what the *Evolutional-Centralization* advocates maintain, a rigidly structured organization would only serve as a detriment to efficient syndicate activity. Syndicate enterprises, as we have illustrated and will further illustrate in our discussion, consist of very fluid and changing operations whose participants vary in the types of functions they perform. Syndicate patrons may find it necessary to give up certain enterprises as seen in the case of the numbers operations in Detroit. If they were part of a rigidly structured "Cosa Nostra" with underbosses, lieutenants, and soldiers, one can visualize how hampering this would be to those directing the operations.

After all, if such a highly structured organization with oaths, secret codes, and other features exists the least it can and must do is provide work for its members. Imagine how cumbersome it would be to move an entire organization from one enterprise into another. In the Detroit numbers takeover that was accomplished by white syndicate members who have been variously called "the Mafia" and "the Detroit Cosa Nostra family," white syndicate functionaries were not moved in to replace black functionaries. Only in a few cases, as indicated by informants, have white writers or runners worked in the Black neighborhoods. In these cases the individuals had been raised in these neighborhoods and had come to be trusted by the Blacks.

We assume that if "Cosa Nostra" families or "Mafia groups" work as a unit, as we are led to believe, then certainly the white Italian-Sicilian lieutenants and soldiers should have moved in to take over various house operators and runners and writers positions. Some may reply to this position by saying that the family knew the Black community would not accept this. And this is exactly the point we wish to emphasize. When confronted with such a situation, a large, rigidly organized group would serve as a detriment rather than an asset. Instead, in the Detroit operations, the white operators simply by nonviolent means placed themselves in positions as patrons over the Black operators while allowing the houses to continue to function as before. After the houses were back in the hands of the Black owners, these owners merely assumed the role of patrons to their lower echelon functionaries and the system continued to function without interruption or vast change.

What we are saying, then, is that if a highly organized group did exist in terms of the amount of cooperation, adaptation, and accommodation necessary to syndicate enterprises, such an organization would only serve to hamper rather than aid syndicate efficiency.

There is no doubt that police probably wish that such a rigidly structured organization did exist, since it would be easier to destroy. If it were truly centrally organized, then all that would be necessary to destroy it would be to remove its top echelon. This has been shown to be true of most organizations that were structured as secret societies in the past. The power of syndicates in the United States rests in the fact that they are not structured in this fashion. If a powerful syndicate figure is incarcerated all that has really been severed is his position as a patron to his clients. If it so happens that another individual is in a position to assume this role the clients may continue in this enterprise. If not, they simply must develop their own enterprises or find new patrons to whose enterprises they can attach themselves. Because of their variety of contacts syndicate participants can generally find new patrons and enterprises without much difficulty.

A criminal syndicate then can best be described as a system of loosely structured patron-client relationships in which the roles, expectations, and benefits of participants are based upon agreement or obligation and whose size and function is basically determined by the activity in which it is involved. It is a system where participants become more important as they initiate or are afforded the means of developing more patrons and clients. One's power and importance within the system is primarily gauged by the extent and types of patrons and clients one develops. As a patron, one is in a position to offer participation in one's enterprises. Also as a patron one can provide protection for one's clients. This no doubt is the system that Valachi was attempting to describe when he stated that all the "Cosa Nostra" ever gave him was protection. This was also the system he was no doubt describing when he stated "You get nothing, only what you earn yourself." Rather than positions in a bureaucratic hierarchy, what Valachi was referring to under the titles "underboss," "lieutenant," and others were levels of power based upon relationships of power. His contradictions emerged from the fact that he tried to describe a formal organizational system while in reality what he was really presenting was a loosely structured one based on patron-client relationships. When he said that you get "only what you earn yourself" but you get protection he was referring to the fact that a low status individual makes income from participating in enterprises for which he needs the protection of a patron and for whom he in turn provides services or favors.

As systems of patron-client relationships these syndicates have no definite limits on the number of criminal enterprises participants may be engaged in at any one time. Nor are there any stipulated limits to the number of participants in any one enterprise. Hence it is somewhat awkward to speak of these participants as "members" since this gives the impression that an organization with continuous membership, a roster of names, prescribed methods of recruitment, promotions, and other characteristics exists. This latter approach assumes by its very definition that there are definite limits to organizational structure and membership. Thus, from this viewpoint individuals either are or are not members of the organization.

As we have shown, this is not true of syndicate structure. An individual operating his own gambling establishment may hire individuals in it to serve as enforcers, dealers, and other functions. These individuals are participants in syndicated crime, yet their relationships may extend no further than this gambling establishment. The operator of this establishment, however, may allow a patron who is providing him with police protection to use his establishment as a base of passing counterfeit money to the customers. Thus when a gambling customer turns in his chips and is paid off he may have several counterfeit bills "slipped" to him. The patron himself may have obtained the counterfeit bills from a client who made an agreement to give him fifty percent of all he can pass. Here the gambling house owner will pay the patron in legitimate money the equivalent in amount of counterfeit bills he passed. Thus the only one who loses is the customer. If the customer later finds that he has been passed such a bill it is up to the owner to handle him. He may do so by giving him a legitimate bill and apologize, pretending that he doesn't know how it could have happened. On the other hand, he may tell the customer that he must have gotten the bill somewhere else. If the customer continues to insist, the owner may simply throw him out of the establishment and have his enforcers warn him that there will be "real trouble" if he doesn't quit bothering the boss.

Desiring to pass as much of the counterfeit money as he can the patron may use not only the services of the owner of the above mentioned gambling establishment, but he may use other owners of other gambling establishments for whom he is providing protection. One of these may also be a loan shark and offer to pass some of the money through the legitimate business place of one of his debtors, a request the debtor is in no position to refuse. Another of these owners, as a "big favor" to his patron, may offer to pass a large amount of it through one of his friends. In this case his friend may be a highly skilled confidence man who agrees to pass the money as payment for an expensive article. Later this confidence man fleeces another "mark" by selling this article to him at twice its value. He then gives his friend, the gambling house operator, the equivalent amount in legitimate money given him originally in counterfeit form and in turn himself keeps the extra he made from selling the article at twice its value. The gambling house owner in turn gives the money to his patron and thereby has done a favor in return for the continuing protection he receives. The patron in turn takes his fifty percent and gives the remainder to the original client who gave him the money to pass. This original person may have obtained the counterfeit money from a friend who smuggled it into the country as a favor to his patron who earlier was deported to the country where the counterfeit bills were originally manufactured.

In these enterprises, who belongs to what organization? Does the police official or politician who provides the protection for the patron's various clients belong? Do the dealers in the various gambling establishments belong? Does the confidence man belong? Does the deported patron in the country where the counterfeit money originated belong? Does the debtor who passed the money in his legitimate business establishment belong? A more significant question would be to ask what it is that they belong to.

Each of these participants engaged in the criminal activity basically for his own benefit. The patron wanted money and used his clients to achieve his end. The clients in turn want the patron's political protection for their enterprises and comply with his wishes. Some, who feel more obligated because of special favors they received from the patron or because they desire to endear themselves to him for future purposes, may be motivated to more creative and energetic methods of helping the patron. The debtor feels that if he helps his loan shark he may be given consideration in the event that he misses some of his payments. Or this activity may be accepted by the loan shark in lieu of one or several payments on the debt. The confidence man not only did a favor for his friend but also made himself a profit on the deal.

These individuals do not belong to an organization. Instead the structure of their relationships is predicated by the particular activity engaged in at any given time and the nature of the patron-client, friendship, and other forms of relationships motivating the participants. Rather than being a criminal secret society, a criminal syndicate consists of a system of loosely structured relationships functioning primarily because each participant is interested in furthering his own welfare. Since patron-client, friendship, and business-oriented relationships in syndicated activity are extremely flexible and constantly changing, it would be futile and unrealistic to attempt to chart or give limits or boundaries to the multitude and types of these relationships.

Also futile and unrealistic are the attempts to apply labels of "boss," "underboss," and others mentioned before. A "boss," which is really a term designating a patron status, may be a patron in one enterprise but a client in another. Since patron-client relationships constantly change in terms of their importance it is impossible and merely frustrating to attempt to designate them by rigid titles such as "underboss," "lieutenant," "soldier," and others. Patron-client relationships cannot be put on a chart of positions. Their many combinations and constantly changing nature make such positioning a contradiction of their nature. Add to these friendship, kinship, and other "contractual" types of social relationships and one begins to perceive the multitude of possible types of combinations of relationships among syndicate participants.

It is this aspect of syndicate crime that makes law enforcement efforts so frustrating. The conviction of a few top echelon participants only severs a partial system of relationships. Also, because of the many varieties of loosely knit combinations of criminal relationships, the work required to formulate legal cases against everyone involved in any one syndicate activity alone reaches phenomenal proportions. Yet because segments of the public and of law enforcement agencies believe in a neatly structured "Cosa Nostra" or "Mafia" organization, they are continuously puzzled about why such an organization isn't readily destroyed. One police official put it aptly: "It's because the public and some policemen themselves have bought this crap about the Mafia that makes our work twice as tough. They figure since they're organized, all we have to do is go out, get a couple of the big guys and the castle will come tumbling down."

Criminal syndicate structure varies with both the extent and nature of the activities in which its participants are involved. The number of participants is largely determined by the activity itself. Thus the structure of bookmaking enterprises in gambling involves a variety of functionaries including those who in New York—as in many other cities—are called "street agents, commissionmen or runners."[25] These do not "book" or take bets themselves but merely act as agents and take bets for a bookmaker on a commission basis. Another functionary is the bookmaker or "bookie" who actually takes the bets and incurs the losses or profits from the wins. This functionary generally has a front for his business often referred to as an "office."[26] As explained in Chapter 2, these fronts may be shops, restaurants, or other business places. Here he receives bets from street agents, runners and directly from bettors who call in their bets via telephone. A bookmaker with a large business may hire several telephone clerks to handle the large number of calls. He may hire several checkers to register the bets. The money is transacted through the runners or other agents working for the bookmaker rather than directly at the office. For the most part, unless they are under the protection of a patron, these bookmakers provide their own protection and in most cases that of their runners or street agents.

These bookmakers in turn use sources to lay off their bets. As explained earlier, this is the technique where the bookmaker attempts to guard himself against losses by placing some of his bets with another betting source. Thus if he has received a large number of bets on one horse in a given race, he must guard against the possibility of that horse winning. In order to do this, he himself places a portion of his bets on this horse with a lay-off source. If the horse wins, the lay-off source will pay him and in turn he can cover his own losses. These lay-off sources generally consist of syndicate participants who have the necessary capital to cover large amounts of bets of this type. Often this money is provided by several patrons of syndicated crime who take money made from their other enterprises and allow its use in this manner. The importance of the lay-off function is that large amounts of capital are necessary. For this reason only those patrons who have ready financial resources to spare from other enterprises can provide this service.

Gambling casinos, whether they be the small "backstore" operation or the large, plush ones, generally must be equipped with the necessary "dealers," "dice shooters" and other functionaries depending upon what types of games are played. The larger ones generally have bartenders, cooks, and waitresses to serve drinks and food, enforcers or bouncers to handle unruly customers, and a variety of others depending upon the size and type of operation.

"Floating" games, or those whose location changes frequently in order to avoid surveillance and raiding by police, generally have their dealers or shooters at the given location but add "steerers" or individuals who transport potential players to the location.

Slot-machine enterprises in those areas where they are illegal necessitate a number of functionaries. If the machines are manufactured out of state, some means of transporting them is necessary. Perhaps a trucker who owes money to a loan shark may be asked to use his truck to make such a delivery. The trucks of a legitimate firm under the control of a loan shark may be offered in return for some service the slot-machine enterpriser can offer.

Once the machines are ready to be placed, locations must be found. Here a panorama of kinds of arrangements emerge. Gambling casinos or other gambling locations operated by friends, patrons, or clients may be used. Machines may be placed in back rooms of legitimate business establishments on the basis that the owner will be paid a certain weekly or monthly sum per machine. A bar owner may allow machines to be placed in his establishment because their presence brings him more customers.

Some form of enforcement may be necessary to keep a rival syndicate member from "forcing" his machines into the area. Enforcers may be necessary should a gang or individual attempt to vandalize the machines or the places of business where they are located. Men capable of servicing such machines are also necessary.

Syndicate participants in narcotics require a rather extensive network of functionaries. Since narcotics generally have to be smuggled into countries where there is no internal source some form of contacts between syndicate participants in the country of export and the country of import have to be established. As in most other cases "The Mafia" and "La Cosa Nostra" have been cited as the major traffickers in this area. There is no doubt that relationships between syndicate functionaries in Sicily and Italy and functionaries in the United States exist. This is borne out not only by American law enforcement sources but by Italian governmental sources as well.[27] Rather than viewing these as "Mafia" or "Cosa Nostra" enterprises, for reasons we have already explained, it is more realistic to analyze these simply as relationships between participating syndicate functionaries in two or more different countries.

Smuggling of illicit goods into the United States dates back to the beginning of the country's history. Today, as always, smuggling necessitates the cooperation of syndicates in different countries. Which syndicates participate depends upon what is being smuggled. As Brean points out, in India the demand for gold is so great that millions of dollars worth are smuggled in each year.[28] In Italy, on the other hand, American and Swiss cigarettes, gasoline and coffee, all expensive products, are major items in the smuggler's trade.[29]

It is not always necessary to have the cooperation of two syndicates in different countries. A group of smugglers in Italy may go to Switzerland or to the United States and purchase as many cigarettes as they want since this is not illegal. The illegality of their activity lies in their bringing the goods into Italy without paying the necessary duty. Therefore, the syndicate participants must simply devise ways of getting the goods into the country and methods of distributing them on the contraband market.

When an American syndicate, however, is interested in obtaining opium from a country where its sale or use is illegal then there is obviously a need for the development of syndicates in that country to supply the illicit goods. Hence as O'Callaghan illustrates, in Lebanon where such is the case one important syndicate functionary and his participants established such a syndicate. He set up refining laboratories both there and in Syria to supply narcotics to syndicates in various parts of the world.[30] This individual provided for police and other forms of protection in Lebanon and had functionaries who delivered the drugs to syndicates outside the country. In one case a syndicate functionary from Lebanon was arrested after having made such a delivery to Detroit.[31]

When two syndicates in two different countries work together both usually develop and provide means by which the goods or products can be smuggled out of one country and into another. Their relationships are generally of a business nature since the nature and extent of their interaction doesn't permit the development of patron-client relationships. Although this interaction is on a business or contractual basis, it is true that over time some syndicate participants come to know and trust each other more than others and are therefore more amenable to extending favors that are mutually beneficial.

In the narcotics enterprises in the United States, syndicate functionaries may receive drugs directly from syndicates in other countries or they may receive them from syndicates in the United States. There is no doubt that one of the reasons for the assumption that an international "Mafia" is involved in drug traffic comes from the fact that many Italian and Sicilian syndicated criminals have been involved in narcotics traffic not only to the United States but to other parts of the world. There is also no doubt that many of the contacts between these and American syndicates were formulated by Italian-Sicilian syndicate criminals who were deported from the United States. The point is, however, that Italians and Sicilians are not the only criminals involved in this traffic. The literature shows involvement of syndicates in China, Corsica, France, Mexico, Algeria, Canada, Turkey, Egypt, Syria, Lebanon, and other countries. They all use the same methods. They are all selling and transporting the same product—narcotics. Why the need to see "The Mafia" as the so-called international criminal organization dealing in narcotics, when all of the above-mentioned syndicate relationships are obviously international in nature?

Syndicate functionaries in the United States who deal in narcotics receive their product either directly from syndicates in other countries or from syndicate functionaries in the United States. The extent of further involvement of syndicate functionaries depends upon whether the product is in raw or pure form. If it is raw, some means must be set up for its refinement. There is no doubt that syndicate functionaries who receive large amounts of unrefined narcotics must provide themselves with the necessary facilities for this purpose. Generally, according to police sources, these are not elaborate or large laboratories as is often portrayed by those writers who desire to overemphasize the clandestine. Quite often an ordinary house, inconspicuously located and equipped with a minimal amount of common pharmaceutical equipment and chemicals, is sufficient. As Siragusa notes those who do the refining are generally criminals who have learned the process.[32] One syndicate participant maintains that he did his own refining using ordinary household utensils.[33]

When the drugs are ready for sale, again a variety of outlets employing clients, friends, and outright buyers emerge. Narcotics enterprises function from the user to the original smuggling source because the individual participants are interested in making money. As usual, patrons only provide the money for purchase of the original source, while a variety of clients actually deal directly with the drugs. This, as in other enterprises, assures the patron insulation from arrest since, by the time the drug reaches the "pusher" on the street it has changed hands several times. A variety of terms such as "dealer," "wholesaler," "peddler," and others are used to describe the various levels of functionaries.

A basic distinction is generally made between those who actually deal directly with the user—the pushers—and those who provide the drugs to the pushers. Those above the pusher, generally called "wholesalers" obtain their supply from clients of syndicate patrons. In other words, these clients make their money by obtaining the drugs from their known syndicate sources and in turn sell them to the wholesaler, who then deals directly with the pusher. Agreements regarding protection, if they are made, are generally made only to the level of the syndicate functionary who is in a client position to an important patron. The wholesaler-client relationship, on the other hand, is generally viewed strictly as a business relationship, as is that of wholesaler and pusher. This means that the wholesaler is left on his own, to provide himself with protection. Occasionally, however, when arrested these individuals may turn against the syndicate client and use the threat of turning informant if help isn't given him. However, he can generally hurt only this client as he doesn't know who the client's sources are. The wholesaler provides his own form of protection, which generally consists of being extremely cautious in the methods he uses in getting the drugs to his pushers, and being careful not to accept pushers until he is certain they are not police "plants." Often pushers are themselves addicts and will protect their wholesaler out of personal rather than business needs.

Transportation of drugs from one area of the country to another necessitates the use of patron-client relationships. Again as in the case of slot-machines, a trucker in debt to a loan shark may be asked to carry a certain amount of drugs disguised as part of his regular cargo. A client may allow his bar to be used as an outlet for drugs. Another may allow the drugs to be stored in his place of business.

In narcotics as in most types of smuggling enterprises the most important function of syndicates is that they are the originators of the source of the product. Patron-level functionaries, because they have a network of existing patron-client relationships and because they are financially able to make the investments necessary to create the initial contacts in the countries where the product is located, are in a position to engage in and perpetuate these international enterprises.

One of the least complex enterprises in terms of the number of participants and equipment necessary to operate it is loan sharking. As for equipment, unlike gambling and narcotics where trucks, gambling devices, refining, and other equipment is needed, the loan shark needs none. One person can run a small loan sharking operation. Valachi, for example, did this.[34] In such cases all one needs is some capital to work with and the ability to use intimidation and force to get one's debtors to pay. In many cases one loan shark may get his capital by borrowing from another loan shark. Then by doubling his debtors' interest rate he can pay off his loan and make a profit for himself.

Large operations, however, are equipped with specialists who do the actual lending and collecting. Here the patrons do nothing more than make the money available to their clients, who in turn lend the money to the borrower at a specific rate of interest. These clients may themselves prefer to use the necessary intimidation and violence to collect their own loans. Or they may use others to do their collecting for them. In these types of relationships the patron has no contact with the borrower. The patron merely charges the client a low rate of interest, generally 1 to 5 percent, allowing the client to make money by in turn charging his debtor 20 percent or more. We should note here that sometimes, in cases of extended loans, these rates can go as high as 150 percent.

In many cases various levels of patron-client relationships may exist. A wealthy patron may lend a large sum to his clients at a rate of 1 percent interest. These clients then themselves serve as patrons to their clients by lending them the money at a rate of 5 percent interest. These clients then lend the money to customers at rates of 20 or more percent. These latter clients are the ones who must deal with the customer in terms of collecting, while the previous two levels simply make their money by virtue of having lent the money.

Loan sharking operations, then, take many forms. In a large number of cases as we explained previously loan sharks themselves are also involved in gambling enterprises from which they draw many of their debtors.

Along with gambling, narcotics, and loan sharking, syndicates in the United States provide a variety of illicit services. Despite the fact that there is no longer prohibition of liquor in the United States, the sale of illicit alcohol, as stated in Starr's work, has continued to be a lucrative enterprise.[35] New York State, since its tax increase on cigarettes in 1965, has become the market for a large traffic in "bootleg" cigarettes. Syndicate functionaries purchase cigarettes in North Carolina, which has no tax on its cigarettes, and transport them to New York where they are sold through a variety of fronts. Hijacking trucks delivering cigarettes and transporting the cargo to New York has also become a lucrative business for syndicate participants. The sale of these illicit cigarettes in New York costs the State a loss in tax revenue estimated to be in excess of fifty million dollars a year.[36]

Indications from both police and informants point out that hijacking currently seems to be becoming a larger and larger enterprise in the United States. This does not mean that hijacking has not always been part of the American criminal scene, nor does it mean that its proportions today equal those of the Prohibition era. Its increase seems to be explained by the fact that currently, hijackers are finding a greater number of outlets for their stolen goods. Whereas before, the hijacker was dependent upon a "fence" who could only handle a small amount of stolen goods, today syndicate functionaries are providing wider markets. We should point out that here the syndicate functionary, according to our definition, is not participating in syndicated crime since with only a few exceptions he is not offering a service to the public. He is offering a specific service to the hijacker. His services, according to our definition, could be classified as syndicated in nature only in those cases where the public demand for illicit goods is involved. Where it is not, the syndicate participant serves only as a patron to nonsyndicate criminal functionaries.

As a client to the syndicate patron, the hijacker has to make available only those goods which the patron is in the market for. Usually these are items for which there is a large demand on the legitimate market—clothing, color television, transistor radios, and other such items. The hijacker's job is to steal specific goods which later are to be sold through specific outlets. We note this point to show that hijackers do not simply pick any truck that happens to be coming down the road. Rather, selected items are hijacked on the basis of the demand for them and the feasibility of their quick sale through the prescribed outlets.

In order to accomplish their task, hijackers generally make use of an "inside man," someone working in the warehouse or factory from which the desired goods are shipped. The inside man manages to place himself in a position where he knows not only what each truck is carrying but its designated route. After the information is passed on to the hijacking crews, plans are made to stop the designated trucks at inconspicuous or isolated places along the routes where the hijacking takes place. Some hijacking crews, as one Boston police official told the author, use automobiles equipped with two-way radios through which they can readily transmit information pertinent to an effective execution of their task.

Once the goods have been hijacked, they are sold outright to the syndicate patron. From this point on the patron is the functionary through whom the goods are made available to the customer.

In most cases the syndicate patron sells the goods to his syndicate clients, who in turn sell them to appropriate outlets. In some cases these outlets consist of places where customers buy with the knowledge that these are stolen goods. In fact it is their demand for illicit goods at cheap prices that creates the market. In such cases we can argue that the syndicate patron is engaging in syndicated crime.

An example is the lucrative business of selling stolen women's clothing. The outlets are generally found in private residences. Here, customers, primarily middle class women, obtain expensive clothing at less than half the original cost. Yet because the outlet is not public the women can retain the pride of wearing expensive clothes without having it known that they in fact wear stolen goods. No doubt it is for this reason more than for protection from the law that these outlets for women's clothing are not public. These outlets are generally operated by women who buy the goods from the syndicate functionary.

Other goods, however, such as appliances, jewelry, and shoes, for the most part, are sold through public operating business establishments. Here the syndicate patron is merely interested in making a profit from the goods he bought at a cheap price from the hijacker. He is not interested in providing an illicit service to the customer. In this case, he is not participating in a form of syndicated crime but rather merely uses his patron-client relationships to achieve his end. Thus, as a favor, a friend who runs an appliance store may be asked to sell certain appliances. In return, he may be given a percentage for each item he sells plus the assurance of the patron's continuing friendship and its accompanying favors.

A loan shark may use as outlets his debtors who are in a variety of businesses. Having control of a certain percentage of a debtor's clothing business, the patron may demand that his hijacked clothes be sold there. Having almost complete control of a debtor's appliance store he can virtually turn this store into a regular outlet for hijacked appliances. The debtor in this case is made to continue operating the store under his name; thus in case of legal difficulties the patron's name is never involved.

Finally the patron may buy out or establish a business legitimately to be used as a source of declaring losses for tax purposes. This can also be used as an outlet.

We should briefly note further that along with providing outlets for hijacked goods, criminals do involve themselves in a variety of other nonsyndicated types of crime. Thus they often effect stock swindles, collect money from insurance firms for fires they themselves deliberately set, steal airline tickets for resale, and various other types of crime. Their involvement in cases of corruptive practices in labor unions is also well known. Here, however, we should stress, along with Saposs that "Contrary to popular belief, labor racketeering is primarily limited to specific industries, callings, and business, and thus is confined to a small number of unions."[37] We note also, along with former U.S. Secretary of Labor W. Willard Wirtz, that in most cases it was the unions themselves that "discovered the wrongdoing" and "submitted the case for proceedings under the law."[38]

An example of the varied nature of the activities of syndicate participants is that involving Sam Mannarino, brother of one of those present at the Apalachin meeting. A truck of a firm with which he was associated was used to transport guns to a plane bound for Cuba in 1958.[39] This venture was not successful; the pilot was arrested in West Virginia and the guns were confiscated. In the trial that followed "several Mannarino aides were found guilty of running guns to Fidel Castro in Cuba."[40]

Syndicate enterprises, as we have shown, vary both in types and in extent. Enterprises also vary from region to region. Hijacking and sale of cigarettes is a lucrative business in New York State where cigarette prices are high, but it is not in states where they are low or moderate. Narcotics traffic is high in New York and other urban centers of the United States, but as Rogovin and Higgins note, it is not a major syndicate enterprise in Boston.[41]

The format of syndicates then, rather than being prestructured in the sense of a bureaucratically and formally organized secret society, is instead structured according to the enterprises they are engaging in at a particular time and place. Sometimes these enterprises are initiated by syndicate functionaries who are in a client position. These may offer their patrons "a cut" of the business in return for the patron's political and police protection. In other cases, the patron may initiate the enterprise, thus involving a variety of clients and affording both the opportunity to further their ends.

In terms of their enterprises then, for the most part, syndicate criminals take advantage of rather than create needs. To do so, their structure must be flexible enough to allow adjustment to new public demands. A rigid formal organization does not allow flexibility as readily as a loosely structured system of patrons and clients. This loosely structured system, as we explained, also allows for relationships that reach into the legitimate areas of society. Although various syndicate functionaries on different patron-client levels make pay-offs, virtually every syndicate participant is a potential "corrupter." There seems to be an assumption on the part of those who ascribe to the *Evolutional-Centralization* thesis that all corruption takes the form of money. That is not true. A witness against an important syndicate figure may not be corruptible with money. He may become corruptible, however, when he learns that his brother is seriously in debt to a loan shark and that in exchange for his not testifying, his brother's loan will be cancelled. A witness who refuses to take a bribe may be ready to testify until she is reminded by an acquaintaince that if she does, something in her past of which she is ashamed will be revealed. She will not take money but her reputation is important enough to make her change her mind. These bases of corruption necessitate a variety of contacts and relationships outside the syndicate criminal's world. Again they lie in the realm of patron-client relationships that intersect the legitimate and illegitimate segments of society.

The structure of syndicated crime in the United States, as we have shown, is not confined to a rigidly organized group but rather has relationships drawn from a variety of sources, criminal and noncriminal. Its enterprises are generated at all levels of patron-client relationships and they are primarily held together by the fact that each participant is basically motivated by his own self interest. Power within the system depends upon the individual's rise in the number of significant patron-client relationships he is able to establish. So too, violation of agreements and the type of punishment meted out is dependent upon which patrons and clients are involved in the enterprise where the violation took place. Rather than the existence of "Mafia" or "Cosa Nostra" "courts" and "trials" as we are led to believe, violators and their infringements are discussed only among those patrons and clients whose enterprises the violator stands to threaten. The decision about what to do with him is not determined by any set rules or codes but primarily by how valuable and powerful the violator happens to be.

The same considerations apply when a functionary wishes to move from one enterprise to another or from one section of the country to another. As is true in legitimate society, it helps if he knows somebody. These functionaries know that they simply can't go to a city where several numbers enterprises exist and start their own enterprise the morning after they arrive in town. They know that they have to function through the existing network of relationships that has provided the necessary police protection. Here it helps if a participant's patron from the city where he formerly functioned makes a phone call to an important patron in the city to which he wishes to go and asks that "something be found" for him because he is a "good guy." The patron may agree to do so or he may say that he can't take anybody at the moment because "the heat is on" meaning that the law is presenting a situation where his enterprise may have to be temporarily terminated. If on the other hand, the participant's patron has been dissatisfied with his work he may simply tell the man "you're on your own," which means that he has to either seek out other patrons or friends who have an "in" in the city where he wishes to go or he will have to make his own contacts. This is also true of those functionaries who decide to "go straight," or get out of further syndicate participation. Whether or not they can do this depends upon their degree of involvement in various enterprises. If the individual is an unimportant functionary no one will miss him. On the other hand, since syndicate relationships are composed of vast networks of relationships, the individual may be so vital to a continuation of these relationships that extreme pressure may be brought to bear on him. Patrons of somewhat equal or higher status may

voice their displeasure with his action and although he may not
fear them he nonetheless doesn't wish to lose their friendship
since he someday may need it. Often functionaries of less importance cannot go straight because their particular skills have
become valuable to certain enterprises.

Struggles and conflicts between syndicates and among syndicate participants as illustrated throughout this work are motivated by a multitude of reasons including quest for power,
attempting to keep control over enterprises, personal reasons,
and sheer defiance of patron authority.

Rather than viewing syndicates then as standardized models
of bureaucracy whose structures and hierarchies always consist
of a commission, a boss, an underboss, lieutenants, and soldiers,
syndicates can only be adequately understood as systems of
relationships which not only vary with time and place but which,
above all, have no set limits to their composition. The power
and effectiveness of their functioning lies not in the fact that
they have a rigid bureaucratic structure but rather in the fact
that the number and types of possible variations in their structure is endless.

We bring this chapter to an end by noting the similarity
between syndicate structure in the United States and in Sicily.
These similarities are based, as we emphasized earlier, on the
fact that, both in Sicilian and in American society the activities
of syndicates are illicit in nature yet their services are desired by
segments of the society. The similarity of their formats is a
function of this illicit relationship to a legitimate social structure.
Secrecy, violence, and political protection in this relationship
become necessities to syndicate functioning. However, here the
similarities end and the differences begin. The Sicilian syndicate
structure, although employing the same methods as the American,
is nonetheless distinct from it in that it has developed and functions within the context of the entire Sicilian social structure.
Its enterprises and the nature of its patron-client relationships can be understood only within the context of the development of Sicilian society itself. To take them out of this system
as do those who argue the infusion of "The Mafia" into the

United States is merely to sever from Sicilian history and from the complex of Sicilian society itself a part which has meaning only within that context. Furthermore, to attempt to explain syndicated crime in the United States as a phenomenon infused from Sicily is to appreciate neither the differences between Sicilian and American history nor the differences between Sicilian and American society.

References

1 State of New York Commission of Investigation, *Report of an Investigation of Certain Crime Activities and Problems of Law Enforcement in Rochester, New York,* September, 1966, p. 19.

2 *Ibid.,* p. 24.

3 Charles Siragusa, *The Trail of the Poppy* (Englewood Cliffs: Prentice-Hall, Inc., 1966), p. 129.

4 Richard B. Stolley, "Deadly Items in a Crime Report," *Life* February 24, 1967, p. 23.

5 John Hobler, "Crimetown USA," *Saturday Evening Post,* March 9, 1963, p. 71.

6 New York State Commission of Investigation, *An Investigation of Law Enforcement in Buffalo, New York,* January, 1961, p. 47.

7 Mary Lorenz Dietz, "Violence and Control: A Study of Some Relationships of the Violent Subculture to the Control of Interpersonal Violence," (Unpublished Ph.D. dissertation, Wayne State University, 1968).

8 Gilbert Geis, "Violence and Organized Crime," *The Annals,* Vol. CCCLXIV (March, 1966), p. 87.

9 John D. Matthews, *My Name is Violence* (New York: Belmont Books, 1962), pp. 40–41.

10 *Ibid.*

11 New York State Commission of Investigation, *The Loan Shark Racket,* New York, April, 1965, p. 41.

12 Ray Brennan, "Weisphal Cites 5 as Tormentors," *Chicago Sun Times,* May 15, 1964, p. 3.

13 *Ibid.*

14 Norman Glubok, "N.Y.'s Juice Men Soft Pedal Violence," *Chicago Daily News,* June 9, 1964, p. 64.

15 *The Loan Shark Racket,* p. 41.

16 *Ibid.,* pp. 61–62.

17 *Ibid.,* p. 49.

18 Virgil W. Peterson, "Shades of Capone," *The Annals,* CCCXLVII (May, 1963), p. 33.

19 *Ibid.*

20 Gustav G. Carlson, "Number Gambling: A Study of a Culture Complex," (unpublished Ph.D. dissertation, University of Michigan, 1940), p. 48.

21 *Ibid.,* p. 54.

22 *Ibid.*

23 U.S. Congress, Senate, Committee on Government Operations, *Organized Crime and Illicit Traffic in Narcotics, Hearings,* before the permanent subcommittee on Investigations, United States Senate, 88th Cong., 1st sess., 1963, pt. 2, pp. 468–469.

24 *Ibid.*

25 New York State Commission of Investigation, *Syndicated Gambling in New York State,* February, 1961, p. 21.

26 *Ibid.,* p. 22.

27 Nucleo Centrale Polizia Tributaria della Guardia di Finanza, *Rapporto Penale di Denunzia,* Rome, June 6, 1961.

28 Herbert Brean, "Rich, Wild Racket: Smuggling," *Life,* January 18, 1960, p. 92.

29 *Ibid.,* p. 93.

30 Sean O'Callaghan, *The Drug Traffic* (London: Anthony Blond, Ltd., 1967), pp. 16–17.

31 *Ibid.*

32 Siragusa, *op. cit.,* p. 227.

33 John Starr, *The Purveyor* (New York: Fawcett World Library, 1962), pp. 185–186.

34 *Organized Crime in Illicit Traffic in Narcotics,* pt. 1, p. 267.

35 Starr, *op. cit.*

36 *The New York Times,* September 10, 1967, p. 56.

37 David J. Saposs, "Labor Racketeering: Evolution and Solutions," *Social Research,* XXV (Autumn, 1958), pp. 255–256.

38 W. Willard Wirtz, *Labor and The Public Interest* (New York: Harper and Row, Publishers, 1964), p. 87.

39 *Daily Dispatch* (New Kensington, Pennsylvania), June 6, 1967, p. 1.

40 *Ibid.*

41 Charles H. Rogovin and George V. Higgins, "Organized Crime in Massachusetts," in *Law and Order,* ed. by Bradbury Seasholes (Medford, Mass.: Lincoln Filene Center for Citizenship and Public Affairs, Tufts University, 1968), pp. 49–50.

8

The Life of the Syndicate Criminal: Some Social and Psychological Aspects

Our interest here is not to present a description of a type of individual which can be classified as a syndicate man. Rather our intent is to show that those who participate in syndicated crime have personality and social characteristics indicative of as much variation as that found among people in general society. The variations among syndicate criminals are basically those created by social class, ethnic, and other socialization backgrounds.

The impression is generally given that the syndicate criminal is a mentally deranged, sinister, gruesome character who goes up and down the street looking for someone to beat up or kill. This attitude is quite popular among those who have a need and desire to categorize syndicated crime and its participants as a phenomenon which is isolated from general society. This conception helps people to quickly compartmentalize the syndicate criminal as the evil-doer and the remainder of society as the victims. In our conception we have tried to show that syndicate crime transcends all segments of society. We wonder then who is more the evil-doer, the individual who looks for a place to gamble or the individual who provides it for him?

The tendency to view syndicated criminals as unique human beings generally follows from the belief in a criminal secret society. The reasoning involved in arriving at this conclusion is that if the secret society exists, it obviously must recruit only those who are evil by nature or training. Recruitment into syndicated crime in the United States, like its other aspects, also functions on the basis of friendship, kinship, contract, and patron-client relationships. A syndicate functionary may give his nephew an opportunity to get into a syndicate enterprise if the nephew shows both the interest and the desire to do so. If he needs any training, he can obtain it as he goes along, or if specific training is required, provisions may be made to have him work with someone who can teach him.

A boy may be given a job as a checker in a numbers house in return for a favor the owner owes his father. Specific skills such as those required of professional dealers in gambling casinos often are contracted and the individual paid a specific salary or a percentage. An enforcer may be recruited because he has specific skills such as those gained from having been a professional boxer. On the other hand a boy who has always been a good street fighter may slowly move into such a position because syndicate participants in his neighborhood "like the way he handles himself."

We must remember also that because of the flexibility of syndicate enterprises, recruitment does not imply membership or guaranteed participation in syndicate activity for any length of time. Rather than conceiving of recruitment as a process of entrance into an organization, we should think of it as a situation where an individual is placed into a position which more readily affords him the opportunity of establishing necessary patron-client relationships.

Advancement in the structure itself depends upon the individual's length of participation in various enterprises, his abilities, his motivation, and the nature and extent of the patron-client relationships he develops. Thus two of Chicago's most powerful syndicate figures of the prohibition era, Al Capone and Dion O'Bannion, began their careers as low status functionaries. Capone began as the operator and bouncer of the "Four

Deuces" nightclub in Chicago.[1] O'Bannion began as a hijacker.[2] Their success can be attributed to their ability to make political and underworld connections. This does not mean that every syndicate participant must begin as a low status functionary. Often a relative or friend of an important patron may have the necessary contacts allowing him an immediate position of power. Those familiar with the structure of syndicate crime are aware of how important contacts are to one's future welfare and success within that realm. As Spergel illustrates in his study, delinquents in a "racket subculture" viewed connections as the most important attribute in the process of "getting ahead."[3]

As is true in legitimate segments of society the process of attaining importance and power in syndicated crime has similar attributes and drawbacks. A person with ability may never achieve a status equal to his ability merely because he had misfortunes in many of his enterprises or simply never had the contacts that enabled others less capable than he to succeed.

Contrary to the literature of the *Evolutional-Centralization* approach, not all important syndicate figures are respected by those beneath them. They may be feared, but not necessarily loved and respected. We doubt that the two syndicate functionaries whose $30,000 in concession money was taken from them outright by Vito Genovese loved and respected him for it.[4] On the other hand, a syndicate figure who has always kept his word, has always treated his clients fairly, and has attempted to settle disputes in a manner agreeable to all concerned, will most probably have the respect and devotion of a far greater number of his fellow syndicate criminals.

Syndicate participants like other human beings vary in their personality characteristics. Some are quiet individuals, others boisterous. Some love a good fight and often go out of their way to get involved in one. Others, although unafraid of physical combat, view it as something one does only if one has to.

Many of the lower echelon participants come from lower class environments and their attitudes and norms are largely drawn from the value system of such settings. Thus masculinity means being able to "take care of yourself" in violent situations. The degree to which this is true is dependent not so much on class background as the status of the syndicate functionary. For the most part, a patron is not expected to fight; it is known that he has functionaries who "will take care of" the offending party.

One's sense of masculinity is also reinforced, as in legitimate society, by being seen with attractive women. Because a major form of recreation for syndicate participants centers around places of show business such as bars and nightclubs, the girls they go about with often come from occupations found there. They include singers, exotic dancers, go-go dancers, waitresses, hat-check girls, and prostitutes. This, however, does not mean that girls are selected only from these sources. The degree of involvement with these girls also varies as it does in general society. In some cases they are viewed purely as playthings while in others they become objects of serious attachment and marriage. In any relationship, particularly in marriage, the woman who is faithful and loving yet doesn't hang on to her boyfriend or husband, but allows him a great deal of freedom is generally the one who is viewed as being a good "old lady" or "old man."

In some cases girls are "kept"—that is, the syndicate figure pays for their apartment and much of their food and clothing along with giving them gifts on special occasions. This payment for rent, food, and other items is not viewed as payment in a business sense, but rather as a favor in exchange for the girl's affection and understanding. In most cases the girl with whom this type of relationship exists is expected to reserve her affection solely for her lover and generally must be available to him anytime he desires her company. Quite often, as expressed by one informant, the major difficulty these girls experience is the loneliness they feel when their boyfriends are out of town for long periods of time. As is true in general society, only those syndicate patrons who are financially able to afford this luxury have such relationships with women.

Syndicate participants, then, experience and engage in behaviors that have their parallels in the continuum of behaviors found in legitimate society. Some believe in God, some are agnostics, others are atheists. Often people wonder how it is possible for one to participate in syndicate crime with its violence, murder, and other illegal activities and yet participate in religious activities. Is this, however, so different from behavior found in the legitimate areas of society? How do whites who profess religious beliefs reconcile the fact that they refuse Blacks the opportunity to become members of their congregation? Is this behavior any less contradictory than that of the syndicate criminal?

So too with other behaviors: Some participants themselves are vehemently opposed to using narcotics and alcohol but have no qualms about engaging in the illicit sale of either. Arnold Rothstein, who in the 1920s participated in the sale of liquor and narcotics, never drank or smoked.[5] Whereas Jack "Legs" Diamond loved violence and often delighted in torturing his victims, Owen "Owney" Madden, although a firm and fearless man, used violence only when absolutely necessary.[6] Madden is an example of an underworld patron who worked toward attaining the respect of his underworld colleagues. During the 1920s he became one of the foremost syndicate figures in New York's underworld. Having himself come up in "Hell's Kitchen" and having served a prison sentence, his new position of power caused him to forget neither his former gang peers nor what it meant to be an ex-convict. In reference to the latter, he helped many ex-convicts to get work after release from prison. As Walker points out, Madden probably helped more ex-convicts "than all the social agencies put together."[7] Although himself involved in many illegal enterprises, Madden attempted to help these men not by exposing them to criminal ventures but rather by providing them with legitimate occupations. Contrary to the stereotype of the syndicate criminal as a vicious, hostile, and hardened person we find that Madden was an affectionate and sentimental person who "above all" loved pigeons.[8]

The Gallo Brothers, the group mentioned earlier in reference to the Gallo-Profaci war, in one instance made headlines when they rushed into a burning dwelling and saved six children from a fiery death. Once the children were safe, they emptied their pockets of all the money they had and gave it to the children's widowed mother.[9]

Al Capone was well known for his generosity. As Pasley relates, he always gave money to the street urchins who waited for him in crowds when they knew he was attending a boxing match.[10] At Christmas time he took great delight in passing out baskets filled with fruit, candy, turkeys, and other gifts to both the teachers and pupils at the school his sister attended.[11] Yet it was this same Al Capone, worth millions of dollars, who tried to cheat a bootlegger out of payment for fifty barrels of beer.[12]

To illustrate further the variation in the behavior of syndicate criminals we note the following extremes: Frank Gusenberg, one of the victims of the famous Chicago St. Valentine's Day Massacre, despite the fact that he knew he was dying, refused to reveal the identity of his killers to the police.[13] "Lucky" Luciano, on the other hand, in one instance made a deal with the legal authorities and revealed both the location of a large amount of narcotics as well as the names of its traffickers.[14] Luciano's behavior and its outcome illustrate that there are no absolutes in the realm of syndicate behavior. First, his action was a violation of the commonly accepted underworld norm of secrecy. Second, he never received any form of underworld retaliation for having committed this act.

Along with inconsistencies in the behavior of syndicate participants we also find among them the existence of idiosyncratic behavior such as that of Mickey Cohen who washed his hands "three or four times" after handling objects he thought "might be covered with germs."[15] This form of behavior has its counterpart in legitimate society; we note that one of Eliot Ness's select law enforcement agents, a member of "the secret six," was absolutely fearless until it came to germs.[16] This agent was deathly afraid of stepping into a bathtub in a hotel. In fact, he never did so until he had first scrubbed the bathtub clean with a solution of carbolic acid that he always carried in his suitcase when he travelled. He feared microbes. The basis of his fear—he "once read a book about microbes and it shook him up worse than pistols."[17]

Syndicate participants show as much variation in behavior as do individuals in general society. Their motivation, interests, fears, and other attributes differ as much as those of people in legitimate areas of society. Contrary to the view that the activity of syndicate participants is constantly directed by a central governing body of "The Mafia" or "Cosa Nostra," we find that much of this activity originates in the motivation of the individual himself. Hence in the literature we find constant mention of how Benjamin "Bugsy" Siegel was sent to California by the directors of some form of national syndicate in order to begin a branch of the organization there. Such statements are also found in regard to other syndicate functionaries. In most cases, such migrations are generally instigated by a patron who wishes to expand his enterprises and offers to provide financial and other support to a client or clients who are interested in participating in such a venture. In other cases the reason for the movement and the motivation itself stem from the individual functionary himself. Hence as Jennings explains, in the case of "Bugsy" Siegel "the decision to move to California was Siegel's own."[18]

Also found in the literature are numerous examples where, in an effort to support arguments for the existence of "The Mafia" or "Cosa Nostra," characteristics common to people of Sicilian-Italian backgrounds are cited as properties common only to these organizations. We are told for example that "The Mafia" or "Cosa Nostra" reinforces itself by having its member families marry into one another. Sondern lists seventeen such marriages.[19] These are marriages among Sicilian-Italian syndicate participants named in the 1958 Hearings before the Select Committee on Improper Activities in the Labor and Management Field.[20] The implication of these marriages for the *Evolutional-Centralization* advocates is that "The Mafia" or "Cosa Nostra" tries to reinforce its power by practicing endogamy. The added assumption is that this is the method "The Mafia" or "Cosa Nostra" uses to sustain itself as a secret society. These assumptions are at the outset refutable on the grounds of arguments we have presented in previous chapters. Furthermore, if this were true we would expect such a pattern to be uniform both in Sicily and in the United States. If this is truly a rigid, prescribed pattern of "The Mafia" or "Cosa Nostra" then all the participants should practice it. Otherwise it cannot be considered a rule and if it is not a rule, then this merely means that some syndicate participants, for reasons of their own, choose to marry into the families of other participants.

In the United States there is no evidence to show that the parents of contemporary important syndicate figures were themselves members of "The Mafia" or for that matter had any criminal involvements whatsoever. Nor as Prezzolini notes is there any evidence to show that the parents of important contemporary syndicate figures who immigrated to the United States from Sicily were themselves criminals in Sicily.[21] One would think that a secret society such as "The Mafia," which we are told has been in existence for centuries, would show quite a lineage based upon such inbreeding. We would not expect to find, as is true in Cleveland, the daughters of a prominent Italian-Sicilian syndicate figure there married to men of non-Italian-Sicilian backgrounds. Nor would we find that one of the foremost Prohibition era syndicate figures in Chicago, Johnny Torrio, acclaimed by many writers to be a "Capo-Mafia" was in fact married to an Irish woman.[22]

Rather than being a specific pattern of "The Mafia" or "Cosa Nostra," this is simply a custom found not only among Sicilian-Italian groups, but other ethnic groups as well. Considerations of propinquity, coupled with parental desire to have their siblings marry "someone who the family knows and trusts" often make for intermarriage within ethnic groups. The literature in marriage and the family shows this to be generally true of most ethnic groups. As accommodation and acculturation into American society takes place, however, these patterns change. This is illustrated by the following situation: A source familiar with a segment of the Sicilian community in Detroit was asked by the author to provide data concerning the number of endogamous and exogamous marriages in that segment. In providing the data, the source was asked to make certain not to include the names of any individuals who were known to be syndicate functionaries. Two samples were provided the author, one containing the ethnic origin of the mate of those members of the community who were born and raised in Sicily, and another containing the same information for those born and raised in the United States. Of the former, using a sample of 25 marriages, only 2 (8 percent) had married non-Sicilians. In the other sample consisting of 52 marriages of those born and raised in the United States, 19 (roughly 36 percent) had married mates from outside the Sicilian ethnic group. These findings are not surprising; as Campesi illustrates, many of the southern Italian family patterns undergo radical change as movement takes place from Italy to the United States and "accommodation" occurs from the first generation to the second.[23]

What we are saying then is that marriage among Italian-Sicilian syndicate participants in the United States merely reflects what is common to Italians and Sicilians in general. Since many of the contemporary older Sicilian-Italian syndicate figures are immigrants or come from first-generation backgrounds we can expect some of them to maintain the old traditions. We also find cases among Italian-Sicilian syndicate participants where marriages have in fact been arranged to better strengthen patron-client or business ties of the two participating functionaries. This, too, is not uncommon to the legitimate Italian-Sicilian community. When this occurs among the families of syndicate functionaries, it represents a continuation of an Italian-Sicilian custom rather than a unique practice of "The Mafia" or "Cosa Nostra." As is occurring among the second generation in the legitimate Italian-Sicilian community, we can expect a simultaneous decrease in this practice among future Italian-Sicilian syndicate functionaries of comparable generational origins.

It is interesting to note, based upon information given by informants, the variation in attitude toward this pattern expressed by the children of various Italian-Sicilian syndicate figures. Generally the attitude toward this pattern is directly related to the attitude which the sibling has toward his or her father's authority. In some cases there is outright resistance and refusal not only toward marrying the father's choice in a mate, but almost toward every request the father makes. This merely indicates, not surprisingly, that syndicate functionaries who are parents face the same types of problems as parents in general society. They, too, are faced with problems created by the "generation gap." Indeed some have sons who are "making the hippie scene." They, too, have sons and relatives who "get hooked" on dope. Like other parents, they are faced with the dilemmas their children's behavior frequently present.

In some cases, siblings adjust to their parents desires. One daughter of an important syndicate figure, for example, is in her late 20s and although very attractive has never been on a date. When asked how she felt about this an informant states she merely answered "Well I can't say I like it, but I happen to think the world of my dad and if he wants me to wait until he finds someone for me, that's what I'll do." In contrast to this, the daughter of another syndicate figure showed concern over the possibility that her father might select her spouse for her. As the informant who related this situation to the author put it, "If it happens, I don't know what she will do. I mean she's too 'Americanized' to go along with it, but yet she's too 'Italianized' to go against her dad."

Syndicate participants and their families are often viewed with suspicion by various segments of the community. As one individual who lived in the neighborhood inhabited by a number of prominent syndicate figures put it "They may be all right like some people say, but you can't trust them—after all they are gangsters." Quite often these negative feelings are expressed by more visible means. Thus in one case a sign was placed on the lawn of a syndicate functionary's home. It read "Gangster—Go Home." One neighbor referring to the family of a syndicate functionary living nearby indicated that she thought they were very nice people until a newspaper account revealed their involvement in drug traffic. From that time on she stated that she viewed them as "nothing more than animals."

The daily family life of syndicate criminals is similar to that of family life in general society. In the Italian-Sicilian home, in keeping with tradition, the wife does not involve herself with her husband's criminal or other activities. Generally her friends

are the wives and family members of other syndicate functionaries and her kin.

The nature and extent of relationships between kin who are
syndicate participants and those who are not reveal a great deal
of variation. Some relatives outrightly reject their kin who have
syndicate ties. Their common complaint is that they often become victims of prejudice and negative treatment as a consequence of the activities of their relatives. Others simply keep
their level of interaction on a kinship basis, never asking about
or involving themselves in the criminal affairs of their kin.

Relatives of syndicate criminals have indicated that family
gatherings that take place at the residence of their syndicate-
involved relatives are often dampened by police surveillance
activity and curiosity seekers. As one relative put it "It gets
pretty bad when you can't even have a birthday party without
police cars going back and forth taking down license numbers.
It seems like every time they see steaks being grilled on the
lawn, they think that somebody's having another Apalachin
meeting."

Another relative stated that her mother never uses the telephone to call her sister whose husband is a well-known syndicate
figure. "None of her sisters do. I mean like they will use the
phone maybe to get a recipe, but, if they want to discuss something about one of the kids or something like that, they can't
because they know the phone is tapped. I mean they aren't
discussing anything about the husband's business because they
don't know anything about it anyway. I'm talking about discussing a fight they had with one of the kids, they can't even
do that over the phone—they have to go to each other's house
in order to talk."

The differences in the behaviors, customs, and other aspects
of the lives of syndicate functionaries, aside from those behaviors necessary to their criminal functions, generally stem
from differences in the ethnic, social class, and other factors in
their background. Since there are a variety of ethnic groups
involved in syndicated crime, aspects of life will vary from group
to group. Hence it is meaningless and futile to try to describe a

"syndicate type" of personality. One is not put into a psychological or social vacuum merely by his entrance into syndicated criminal activity. With him come his fears, his prejudices, his hates, his habits, his mannerisms, as well as his goals and his motivation in achieving them.

In describing and attempting to understand syndicate criminals, then, one should look not for "a type" but rather for differences stemming from variations in psychological and social background. This approach helps overcome some of the useless controversies often encountered in the literature on syndicate crime. One such controversy surrounds the issue of whether or not the leaders of "The Mafia" or "Cosa Nostra" are referred to as "Dons." If we view this within the context of the Italian and Sicilian culture we find that in both Sicily and Italy the title "Don" is one generally given to Catholic priests. However, the title "Don" in some parts of Italy and Sicily and in Italian and Sicilian subcultures in America is often used to show respect to certain individuals. Generally when used in these contexts it is reserved for an older person who has done something of merit. Occasionally, however, the author has heard the title used to show respect to an elderly person who has achieved exceptional proficiency in a trade or profession. We emphasize again, however, that the use of this title varies extremely from region to region in Sicily and Italy and from subculture to subculture among Italians and Sicilians in the United States. For this reason we can also expect to find variation in the application and use of this title among Italian-Sicilian syndicate functionaries located in various parts of the United States. Again, when it is used here, its use is not meant as a title for a specific position in "The Mafia" or "Cosa Nostra." Rather, it merely reflects a customary usage among some Italian-Sicilian functionaries to show their respect to those individuals who have achieved the status of a patron.

The purpose of this chapter then has been not to describe the syndicate criminal as a "type," but rather to emphasize the fact that there is no such type.

References

1 Fred D. Pasley, *Al Capone* (Garden City: Garden City Publishing Company, 1930), pp. 10–11.

2 Edward D. Sullivan, *Rattling the Cup* (New York: The Vanguard Press, 1929), p. 10.

3 Irving Spergel, *Racketville, Slumtown, Haulburg* (Chicago: The University of Chicago Press, 1964), p. 37.

4 U.S. Congress, Senate, Committee on Government Operations, *Organized Crime and Illicit Traffic in Narcotics, Hearings,* before the permanent subcommittee on Investigations, United States Senate on S.R. 278, 88th Cong., 1st sess., 1963, pt. 2, pp. 366–367.

5 Russel Cromie, "The Murder of Arnold Rothstein: 1928" in *Sins of New York,* ed. by Milton Crane (New York: Grosset and Dunlap, Publishers, 1947), p. 185.

6 Stanley Walker, *The Night Club Era* (New York: Blue Ribbon Books, Inc., 1933), pp. 103, 123.

7 *Ibid.,* p. 122.

8 *Ibid.,* p. 124.

9 Jordan Bonfante, "Alright Already, The Mob Is Heroes," *Life* February 9, 1962, p. 48.

10 Pasley, *op. cit.,* pp. 90–91.

11 *Ibid.*

12 Roger Touhy (with Ray Brennan), *The Stolen Years* (Cleveland: Pennington Press, 1959), pp. 69–70.

13 Joseph Gollomb, *Crimes of the Year* (New York: Horace Liveright, 1931), pp. 296–297.

14 Sid Feder and Joachim Joesten, *The Luciano Story* (New York: David McKay Company, Inc., 1954), pp. 58–59.

15 Dean Jennings, *We Only Kill Each Other* (Englewood Cliffs: Prentice-Hall, Inc., 1967), p. 71.

16 Eliot Ness (with Oscar Fraley), *The Untouchables* (New York: Popular Library, 1960), p. 19.

17 *Ibid.*

18 Jennings, *op. cit.,* p. 36.

19 Frederic Sondern, Jr., *Brotherhood of Evil: The Mafia* (New York: Bantam Books, 1959), pp. 211–212.

20 U.S. Congress, Senate, Select Committee on Improper Activities in the Labor or Management Feld, *Investigation of Improper Activities in the Labor or Management Field, Hearings,* Senate on S.R. 74 and 22, 85th Cong., 2d sess., 1958, Exhibit 4.

21 Giuseppe Prezzolini, *I Trapiantati* (Milano: Longanesi and C., 1963), p. 169.

22 James O'Donnell Bennett, *Chicago Gangland* (Chicago: Chicago Tribune Publications, No. 35, 1929), p. 21.

23 Paul J. Campesi, "Ethnic Family Patterns: The Italian Family in the United States," in *Selected Studies in Marriage and the Family,* ed. by Robert Winch, Robert McGinnis, and Herbert Berreman (New York: Holt, Rinehart and Winston, 1962), pp. 176–180.

9

American Syndicated Crime: A Summary of Its Past, Present, and Future

In bringing this work to its conclusion we should like to offer some brief observations concerning past, present, and future aspects of syndicated crime in the United States.

The Past

We have already shown that this phenomenon is American in origin and its participants have been, at one time or another, representative of virtually every group—native and ethnic—in America. Its structure, like that of syndicated crime in many other countries, is largely influenced by the necessities of its illegal functioning. Since criminal syndicates provide illicit goods and services to segments of legitimate society over extended periods of time, its participants must provide themselves with some form of protection from legal interruption and disruption of their enterprises. In the United States we showed that this has been accomplished either by direct payment to police and politicians, by exchanging of favors with political machines, or by syndicate functionaries assuming political positions or public offices themselves.

Syndicated crime in the United States has functioned in the

same manner irrespective of the social and ethnic background or derivation of its participants. The basis of its historical change in the number and types of participants as well as in the enterprises it has engaged in is to be found both in the development of American technology and in an examination of the different types of illicit goods and services the American public has requested at various periods of its history. We have taken the position that the American public itself, in its demand for illegal products and services, instigates or offers the initial motivation for participants to meet that demand. These participants in turn can and do provide illegal goods and services to their customers, at the risk of varying forms of punishment by the law. Some agents of the law and the political system, to further their own interest, offer to lessen this risk for payment in money or favors. Syndicate functionaries, although protected by these brokers of the legal system, nonetheless cannot employ legal means to effect social control over or conformity among its participants. Hence these functionaries are forced to accomplish this by the use of fear and violence as well as attempting to recruit only participants who have displayed an acceptance of those underworld norms and values that are consonant with syndicate functioning within the social system.

In placing the base of origin and continuation of syndicate activity upon the need it satisfies for segments of the American public, we transfer its *raison d'être* away from that of a secret criminal society, variously called "The Mafia," *L'Unione Siciliana, La Mano Nera* and "Cosa Nostra," that "forced itself" upon America. We have illustrated that "The Mafia" and its synonymous terms are so indiscriminately used in the literature as to be absolutely meaningless. We showed historically that there is no evidence that "The Mafia" as a secret society ever existed in Sicily. We noted that lack of consistent use of the label "The Mafia" in Italian-Sicilian literature allows for no validation of such an organization's presence in Sicilian society. We specifically noted the frequent confusion among these writers of "The Mafia" with criminal societies known as *Fratellanze*, or brotherhoods, which had no political protection and thus were no more than criminal bands organized for the purpose of mutual aid.

Rather than a secret society we showed that, because of the emergence of the position of the *Gabellotto,* the constant threat of peasant revolts, and the unification of Italy—which placed this *Gabellotto* into the role of a "political broker"—after 1860 a system of relationships developed. It is this system—one involving a complex of patron-client relationships that intertwines the legitimate with the illegitimate social structure of Sicily, coupled with the need to settle and have settled through intermediation and violence all breeches of honor—that we refer to as *mafia.* As such, as we stressed, *mafia* is a system that, in terms of the conditions of its historical development and those which continue to sustain it as a system, is unique to Sicilian society.

Viewing *mafia* within this context, then, we argued the futility of attempting to trace its infusion into American society. We showed that the existence of "The Mafia" in the so-called Mafia incidents in New Orleans and its existence in other U.S. cities in the late 1800s was merely assumed, not proved. Again here, as in the Italian-Sicilian literature, we noted completely inconsistent descriptions of what this "Mafia" was. We concluded that, at most, what it consisted of was not an organization, but merely an assumption on the part of some American writers that wherever there are Sicilians, "The Mafia" will follow.

Our argument against the infusion of a "Sicilian Mafia" was further augmented by noting the existence of syndicated crime in the United States as basically a non–Italian-Sicilian phenomenon prior to the 1920s. Our explanation for this was centered around the fact that it was at this time that the Italians and Sicilians began to exert their influence as a political force in the American political machine. Prior to this, we noted it was primarily the Irish who had functioned in this capacity. We illustrated also, through an examination of the history of syndicated crime in the United States, that its method, incorporating the use of secrecy, violence, and political protection, was similar irrespective of whether it was in the hands of the Germans, the Irish, the Poles, the Chinese, or the Italians.

We further argue that the acceptance of the belief in the existence of a infused "Sicilian Mafia" was reinforced by the fact that the first congressional investigation of syndicated crime on a national basis, that of Senator Kefauver, came at a time when Italian-Sicilian functionaries were in the majority. For those already convinced of the existence of a mysterious "Mafia" in the United States, this was the final proof. Yet that very commission called before it scores of functionaries of non–Sicilian-Italian backgrounds. This contradiction of their relationship to a secret society defined as being exclusively Sicilian didn't seem to bother Kefauver nor did it alter his conclusions. As we indicated before, since Kefauver used as his basis of proof of "The Mafia" the fact that many Italian-Sicilian syndicate figures testified that they had never heard of it, then it is safe to assume that Kefauver had already accepted its existence. With this assumption then, to be an Italian or Sicilian syndicate figure who denied its existence was sure proof for Kefauver that such an individual was in fact a member of it. In this respect we agree wholeheartedly with Gordon Hawkins, who in a very thought-provoking article points out that many of the arguments offered as proof for the existence of "The Mafia" are in fact similar to those offered as proof of the existence of God.[1]

In praise of Kefauver, however, we add that his hearings did serve a vital function in providing a wealth of information concerning the interstate relationships among syndicate functionaries.

Immediately following the Kefauver Hearings, the American public was treated to a series of books that sought at all costs to find some form of relationship between syndicate crime in the United States and its supposed source—the Sicilian Mafia. We need not repeat the quality of the information or the oversimplified explanations that were offered as proof.

Reinforced by the constant yet inconsistent daily use of the term "Mafia" by the press and other media, and convinced that it existed in the form of a secret society, the public in 1963 was ready for Joseph Valachi. Presented as a revealer of the life and secrets "inside" the organization now called "La Cosa Nostra," Valachi's testimony has since then been accepted not only by segments of the American public but by many governmental agencies as the most vital information available on the national secret society. Valachi stated that he had never heard of the organization referred to as "The Mafia," but here others didn't need his information—they were convinced that "Cosa Nostra" and "Mafia" were one and the same.

We noted the inconsistencies in Valachi's testimony. We are not blaming Valachi as much as those who did not recognize him simply as one informant with his own version or understanding of the criminal phenomenon of which he was a participant. Nor can we criticize Valachi for the various conclusions drawn without substantiation from his and other testimony during the hearings. Mr. Valachi, as we stated before, did not describe a formally organized secret criminal society; rather, he in fact described the exact opposite—a system of relationships rather than a bureaucratically structured organization.

We wonder how segments of the public and writers can continue to speak of a secret society when daily the names of the so-called bosses, lieutenants, and others are published openly in newspapers across the country. What then is the secret? It appears that the real secret is the one that those who believe in a secret society themselves without realizing it help to perpetuate —the secret that syndicated crime is not only a part but a desired part of American society.

Our contention, then, is that syndicates are systems of patron-client relationships that have no set limits in the sense of membership. They are composed of participants who interact at various levels for varying lengths of time depending upon their function within the enterprise. Participants in syndicated crime, then, can and do simultaneously work in a variety of enterprises. The number and types of participants involved in each enterprise is directly related to the nature of the enterprise itself. Some syndicates involve participants confined to a relatively restricted area. Others involve participants not only in other states but in other countries. Of major importance in the structure of syndicates are the interrelationships that exist between patrons and clients. It is this relationship that is often referred to as the "feudal" structure of syndicated crime.

Viewing syndicates and their participants in this way, we can better appreciate the flexibility they have in moving from enterprise to enterprise as well as the complexity of the many possible variations that exist between syndicates. Each syndicate must be studied and understood in terms of the development and existing structure of all its patrons and clients. Along with an understanding of the relationships among the syndicate participants themselves, we must add also the relationships between them and the "political and police patrons" who provide them with protection.

With an appreciation of the many and varied forms these relationships can take we can begin to appreciate the real complexity of syndicated crime. It is this nature coupled with the fact that segments of society demand its services that make it a difficult phenomenon to understand and eliminate.

We realize that our conceptualization of the nature and structure of syndicates may not be as appealing as that given by the *Evolutional-Centralization* advocates. After all they provide an explanation that has definite categories, titles for positions, and a complete bureaucratic arrangement of the so-called levels of the organization. Yet as we saw earlier it is this attempt at a rigid explanation by these advocates that creates the many inconsistencies found in the very material which they present as proof of their own thesis. There is no doubt that the more simple explanations in life are always the more appealing. The question here is, are we interested in the most appealing explanation or the more realistic one.

Our approach suggests that syndicates, in order to be completely understood, must be viewed as systems whose structure is not set by a given format, but rather varies according to the nature of the enterprise, the number and types of participants involved, the spatial or regional distribution of patron-client and patron-patron contacts, and the number and types of relationships employed to secure the necessary legal protection. Viewed this way, syndicates become a series of very complex and interwoven relationships. For this reason we have not and cannot offer a model or format of any set structure. To do so would be to describe only one syndicate form. What we have tried to do is to give examples of various forms these relationships take purely as examples, not as models describing a set type.

The Present

Looking at the present situation in syndicated crime in the United States we note that while many of its functionaries are of Italian-Sicilian and Jewish backgrounds, virtually every ethnic group is represented. It must be remembered, too, that the larger representation of these two ethnic groups in syndicate crime comes from the fact that most of the powerful syndicate figures today rose through the patronage of Italian, Sicilian, and Jewish patrons who themselves were established during the Prohibition era. Contrary to popular belief, however, the literature indicates that with the Italian-Sicilian and Jewish functionaries rose other functionaries representing a variety of ethnic and native groups.

Along with the material found in the Kefauver and McClellan Hearings one need only examine the 1957–1959 *Report on Organized Crime in California*[2] to note the number of syndicate figures who began their careers in the 1920s and early 1930s. One need only further examine the associational charts and arrest records in this report to observe the variation in the ethnic backgrounds of these participants.

Future Prospects

Serving as patrons with their established avenues of political and other protection there is no doubt that those holding these power relationships at the present time will continue to do so. However there are various changes taking place which will have an affect upon the future of syndicated crime. It is difficult not to concede the fact that syndicated crime in the United States has been and continues to be the avenue of upward mobility for those groups and individuals who occupy minority or lower class status. In fact syndicated crime and the political machine have both spawned, in some cases simultaneously, the rise of many wealthy syndicate figures and politicians. Within the patron-client relationship of syndicated crime itself we find that clients are generally drawn from the lower classes. As a minority group loses its minority status, members of this group obviously find more legitimate channels of upward mobility thereby effecting a decline in the number of individuals among this minority group who desire to serve as syndicate clients. With time then the patrons who came from this minority group must accept members of other minority groups who, like their predecessors, view syndicated crime as an avenue of success.

Since Italians and Jews have slowly lost their minority group status and now have legitimate pathways to upward mobility we can expect a gradual decline in their participation in syndicated crime. Obviously the rate and rapidity of this decline will vary from place to place and is largely dependent upon the nature of the patron-client relationships in the various syndicates as well as the nature of the enterprises which they are engaged in. As contemporary patrons die off, their clients will assume their function. With time, however, members of contemporary minority groups, some of whom already have established client relationships within syndicates, will begin moving into patron positions. Like many of the Italian, Sicilian, Jewish, and other functionaries who moved up from positions like hijacker, muscleman, and other client positions to their contemporary patron status, so too lower class and minority group functionaries will themselves develop clients, who will then place them into influential positions. With time they will move into the positions of power held by the contemporary syndicate patrons.

Obviously the minority or lower class group that moves up through this system in the future will depend again upon the location of the syndicate and what groups have a minority status in that area. Needless to say, we are not overlooking the fact that because minority groups differ in terms of their value systems, they will also differ in their degree of condemnation or approval of their members participating in syndicated crime.

One group that certainly will continue to become more and more influential in future syndicated crime will be the Blacks.

Ralph F. Salerno, refers to this process as the coming of a "Black mafia."[3] Black functionaries as we noted before have and continue to participate in a variety of syndicate enterprises. As noted by the recent election of several Black mayors and other public officials across the nation, this group is becoming a powerful political force. As such, like the Irish, Germans, and Italians, who preceded as power forces in the political machine, so too Blacks will probably become political or vote brokers for the machines of the future. In this respect, we should note that this will obviously be true only in those cities where powerful machines and bosses continue to exist. Since machine politics is declining in the United States, Blacks and other minority groups will not be afforded the use of this mechanism of upward mobility to the same extent as their forerunners. There is no doubt, as Cornwell illustrates, that political machines will continue to offer Blacks and other minority groups various forms of representation,[4] but not, however, on the same scale as was true in the past. Also in some cases, old machines may be replaced by new ones. Thus, as Sexton observes, in East Harlem, Blacks and Puerto Ricans have not as yet found or developed an organization equivalent to that of the "old Italian" political machine.[5]

As has increasingly become the case with contemporary syndicates, political protection for future syndicate participants will most likely be more frequently obtained through direct pay-offs to police and through contributions to the election campaigns of cooperating candidates rather than through the mechanism of the political machine.

We should call attention to the fact that Black client syndicate functionaries in various cities have begun to use intimidation and violence against their white patron syndicate participants. In several cities, for example, various lower echelon Black syndicate functionaries have begun the practice of kidnapping important white syndicate figures and holding them for ranson. In one case, as one police source told the author, the payment demanded for the return of the victim was that of being given control of part of a numbers operation. In other cases the payment is in the form of ransom money. According to one account, white syndicate participants in New York thus far have paid approximately one quarter of a million dollars for the return of kidnapped victims.[6]

Extortion-oriented crimes directed at Black merchants also seem to be becoming prevalent in the Black community. Several police officials in various cities told the author that gangs of Blacks were beginning to request regular payment of protection money from Black merchants. Although these gangs told merchants that this money was to be used to finance Black revolutionary causes, police felt that although perhaps true in some cases, these gangs were primarily interested in their own financial aggrandizement.

So long as American society retains its present legal and social structure, we can expect syndicates and their participants to continue their task of offering illicit goods and services whatever these may be in terms of future demands. The background of those individuals who participate in the future will most probably continue to be derived primarily from lower class and minority group segments of American society. These too, unless syndicate structures change radically, like their forerunners will rise through the structure of syndicate patron-client relationships.

Although legalization of enterprises may be considered as a means of curbing and eliminating syndicated crime in the future, it must be remembered that this can be accomplished only if the legal service or goods offered the customer by the legal source is equal to that offered him by the syndicated criminal. Hence, a legal state lottery does not offer syndicate customers an important benefit—not paying income tax on his winnings.

We hope we have given the reader a better understanding of what syndicated crime consists of in the United States. We hope that his work will help eliminate the use of the terms "Mafia" and "Cosa Nostra" from future books, newspapers, and magazines since all these terms serve to do is obliterate the reality of American syndicated crime—the reality that it belongs to America.

References

1 Gordon Hawkins, "God and the Mafia," *Public Interest*, No. 14 (Winter, 1969), pp. 24–51.

2 *Organized Crime in California*, Report of the Subcommittee on Rackets of the Assembly Interim Committee on Judiciary, Sacramento: Assembly of the State of California, 1959.

3 Pat Sealey, "Negroes Get Rung on Mafia Ladder," *The Miami Herald*, March 12, 1968, p. 1.

4 Elmer E. Cornwell, Jr., "Bosses, Machines and Ethnic Groups," *The Annals*, CCCLIII (May, 1964), pp. 27–39.

5 Patricia Cayo Sexton, *Spanish Harlem*, Harper Colophon Books (New York: Harper and Row, Publishers, 1965), p. 122.

6 *The Michigan Chronicle*, March 23, 1968, Section F, p. 1.

Bibliography

Abbott, John S. C. *Italy and the War for Italian Independence.* New York: Dodd, Mead and Co., 1882.

Adamic, Louis. *Dynamite.* New York: The Viking Press, 1934.

Adams, Brewster. "The Street Gang as a Factor in Politics." *The Outlook.* August 22, 1903, pp. 985–988.

Adams, Graham, Jr. *Age of Industrial Violence, 1910–15.* New York: Columbia University Press, 1966.

Agnew, Arnold. "Cyprus—A Challenge to the Art of Keeping the Peace." *Detroit's Daily Express.* November 28, 1967.

Alastos, Doros. *Cyprus Guerrilla.* London: William Heineman, Ltd., 1960.

Alessandro, Enzo d'. *Brigantaggio e Mafia in Sicilia.* Firenze: Casa Editore G. D'Anna, 1959.

Allen, Douglas M. "The Gangs of New York." *Newsweek,* September 14, 1959, pp. 53–55.

Allen, Edward J. *Merchants of Menace.* Springfield, Ill.: Charles C. Thomas, 1962.

Allen, Robert S. *Our Fair City.* New York: The Vanguard Press, Inc., 1947.

Allsop, Kenneth. *The Bootleggers and Their Era.* Garden City, N.Y.: Doubleday and Co., Inc., 1961.

Alongi, G. *La Mafia.* Milano: Remo Sandron, 1904.

Anderson, Robert T. "From Mafia to Cosa Nostra." *The American Journal of Sociology.* LXXI (November, 1965), 302–310.

Anslinger, Harry J., and Will Oursler. *The Murderers.* New York: Avon Books, 1961.

Anslinger, Harry J., and William F. Tompkins. *The Traffic in Narcotics.* New York: Funk and Wagnalls Co., Inc., 1953.

Antiochia, Corrado. "Gli studenti di Alcamo fra mafia e autonomia." *La Critica Sociologica.* Winter, 1967, 140–146.

"Antitrust Enforcement by Private Parties: Analysis of Developments in the Treble Damage Suit." *The Yale Law Journal.* LXI (June–July, 1952), 1010–1065.

331

Arm, Walter. *Pay-Off.* New York: Appleton-Century-Crofts, Inc., 1951.

Asbury, Herbert. *The Gangs of New York.* New York: Garden City Publishing Co., Inc., 1927.

Asbury, Herbert. *The Barbary Coast.* New York: Garden City Publishing Co., Inc., 1933.

Asbury, Herbert. *The French Quarter.* New York: Garden City Publishing Co., Inc., 1938.

Asbury, Herbert. *Sucker's Progress.* New York: Dodd, Mead and Co., 1938.

Asbury, Herbert. *Gem of the Prairie.* Garden City, N.Y.: Garden City Publishing Co., Inc., 1942.

Balakrishna, Kulamarva. *A Portrait of Bombay's Underworld.* Bombay: P. C. Manaktala and Sons Private, Ltd., 1966.

Banfield, Edward C. *Urban Government.* New York: The Free Press of Glencoe, 1961.

Banfield, Edward C., and James Q. Wilson. *City Politics.* Cambridge: Harvard and the M.I.T. Press, 1963.

Barker, Dudley. *Grivas, Portrait of a Terrorist.* New York: Harcourt, Brace and Co., 1959.

Barnes, Harry Elmer, and Negley K. Teeters. *New Horizons in Criminology,* 3rd ed. Englewood Cliffs, N.J.: Prentice-Hall, Inc., 1959.

Barzini, Luigi. *The Italians.* New York: Bantam Books, Inc., 1965.

Barzini, Luigi, Jr. "The Real Mafia." *Harper's Magazine.* June, 1954, pp. 38–46.

Bell, Daniel. *The End of Ideology.* New York: Collier Books, 1962.

Bennett, James O'Donnell. *Chicago Gangland.* Chicago: Tribune Publications, No. 35, 1929.

Bent, Silas. "Newspapermen—Partners in Crime?" *Scribner's.* November, 1930, pp. 520–526.

Bergler, Edmund. *The Psychology of Gambling.* New York: Hill and Wang, 1957.

Blasio, A. de. *Usi e Costumi dei Camorristi.* Napoli: Luigi Pierro, Editore, 1897.

Bloch, Herbert A. "The Sociology of Gambling." *The American Journal of Sociology.* LVII (November, 1951), 215–221.

Bloch, Herbert A. "The Juvenile Gang: A Cultural Reflex." *The Annals.* CCCXLVII (May, 1963), 20–29.

Bloch, Herbert A., and Arthur Niederhoffer. *The Gang.* New York: Philosophical Library, 1958.

Blok, Anton. "Land Reform in a West Sicilian Latifondo-Village: The Persistance of a Feudal Structure." *Anthropological Quarterly.* XXXIX (January, 1966), 1–16.

Blok, Anton. "Peasants, Patrons and Brokers in Western Sicily." *Anthropological Quarterly.* XLIII (July, 1969), 159–170.

Boissevain, Jeremy. "Patronage in Sicily." *Man.* I (March, 1966), 18–33.

Bonfante, Jordan. "Alright, Already, The Mob Is Heroes." *Life.* February 2, 1962, pp. 43–48.

Borkin, Joseph. *The Corrupt Judge.* New York: Clarkson N. Potter Inc., 1962.

The Boston Globe. July 9, 1968.

"Bovini infetti nella Fiera di Palermo." *L'Unita.* June 2, 1963.

"The Break O'Days." *Detroit Post and Tribune.* January 27, 1876.

Brean, Herbert. "Rich, Wild Racket: Smuggling." *Life.* January 18, 1960, pp. 92–106.

Brean, Herbert. "Men of Mafia's Infamous Web." *Life.* February 1, 1960, pp. 58ff.

Brennan, Bill. *The Frank Costello Story.* Derby, Connecticut: Monarch Books, Inc., 1962.

Brennan, Ray. "Weisphal Cites 5 as Tormentors." *Chicago Sun Times.* May 15, 1964.

Bright, John. *Hizzoner Big Bill Thompson.* New York: Jonathan Cape and Harrison Smith, 1930.

Bruno, Cesare. *La Sicilia e la Mafia.* Roma: Ermanno Loescher e Co., 1900.

Burns, Walter Noble. *The One-Way Ride.* Garden City, New York: Doubleday, Doran and Co., 1931.

Buse, Renée. *The Deadly Silence.* Garden City, N.Y.: Doubleday and Co., Inc., 1965.

Byford-Jones, W. *Grivas and the Story of EOKA.* London: Robert Hale Limited, 1959.

Cain, Stephen. "Youngsters Taking LSD Trips Tax Treatment Centers Here." *The Detroit News.* December 8, 1968.

Caldwell, Earl. "Angry Panthers Talk of War and Unwrap Weapons." *The New York Times.* September 10, 1968.

Caldwell, Robert G. *Criminology,* 2nd ed. New York: The Ronald Press Co., 1965.

Campbell, J. K. *Honour, Family and Patronage: A Study of Institutions and Moral Values in a Greek Mountain Community.* Oxford: Clarendon Press, 1964.

Campesi, Paul J. "Ethnic Family Patterns: The Italian Family in the United States," in *Selected Studies in Marriage and the Family.* Edited by Robert Winch, Robert McGinnis, and Herbert Berreman. New York: Holt, Rinehart and Winston, 1962.

Candida, Renato. *Questa Mafia,* 3rd ed. Roma: Salvatore Sciascia Editore, 1964.

Caplow, Theodore. *Principles of Organization.* New York: Harcourt, Brace and World, Inc., 1964.

Carlson, Gustav G. "Number Gambling: A Study of a Culture Complex." Unpublished Ph.D. dissertation, University of Michigan, 1940.

Cavan, Ruth Shonle. *Criminology*, 3rd ed. New York: Thomas Y. Crowell Co., 1962.

Chafetz, Henry. *Play the Devil*. New York: Clarkson N. Potter, Inc., 1960.

Chalmers, David M. *Hooded Americanism*. Garden City, N.Y.: Doubleday and Company, Inc., 1965.

Chamberlain, Henry Barrett. "Some Observations Concerning Organized Crime." *Journal of Criminal Law and Criminology*. XXII (January, 1932), 652–670.

Civil Liberties. September, 1968.

Coblentz, Stanton A. *Villains and Vigilantes*. New York: Thomas Yoseloff, Inc., 1936.

Cohen, Albert H. *Delinquent Boys: The Culture of the Gang*. Glencoe, Ill.: The Free Press, 1955.

Coles, Robert. "Danilo Dolci: The Politics of Grace." *The New Republic*. August 19, 1967, pp. 23–25.

Combating Organized Crime. Report of the 1965 Oyster Bay, New York, Conferences on Combating Organized Crime. Albany, N.Y.: Office of the Counsel to the Governor, 1965.

Commonwealth of Massachusetts, Senate. *Report of the Special Commission revived and continued for the purpose of Investigating Organized Crime and other related matters*. April, 1957.

Cook, Fred J. *The Secret Rulers*. New York: Duell, Sloan and Pearce, 1966.

Cook, Frederick Francis. *Bygone Days in Chicago*. Chicago: A. C. McClurg and Co., 1910.

Cooper, Courtney Ryler. *Here's to Crime*. Boston: Little, Brown and Co., 1937.

Cornwell, Elmer E., Jr. "Bosses, Machines and Ethnic Groups." *The Annals*. CCCLIII (May, 1964), 27–39.

Coxe, John E. "The New Orleans Mafia Incident." *The Louisiana Historical Quarterly*. XX (January–October, 1937), 1067–1110.

Crawford, Francis Marion. *Southern Italy and Sicily and the Rulers of the South*. Vol. 2. New York: The Macmillan Co., 1907.

Cressey, Donald R. "Methodological Problems in the Study of Organized Crime as a Social Problem." *The Annals*. CCCLXXIV (November, 1967), 101–112.

Cressey, Donald R. "Organized Crime as a Social System." *Law Enforcement Science and Technology*. Vol. I. Washington: Thompson Book Co., 1967.

Cressey, Donald R. *Theft of the Nation*. New York: Harper and Row, Publishers, 1969.

Cromie, Russel. "The Murder of Arnold Rothstein: 1928." *Sins of*

New York. Edited by Milton Crane. New York: Grosset and Dunlap, Publishers, 1947.

Cutrera, Antonino. *La Mafia e I Mafiosi.* Palermo: Alberto Reber, 1900.

Daily Dispatch (New Kensington, Pennsylvania). June 6, 1967.

Davis, Richard (Dixie). "Things I Couldn't Tell Till Now." *Collier's.* August 5, 1939, pp. 12–13ff.

Dedmon, Emmett. *Fabulous Chicago.* New York: Random House, 1953.

Demerath, H. J., III, and Richard A. Peterson. *Systems, Change and Conflict.* New York: The Free Press, 1967.

Detroit American. June 28, 1968.

The Detroit Journal. November 11, 1908.

Detroit's Daily Express. January 8, 1968.

Dewees, F. P. *The Molly Maguires.* New York: Burt Franklin, 1877.

Dietz, Mary Lorenz. "Violence and Control: A Study of Some Relationships of the Violent Subculture to the Control of Interpersonal Violence." Unpublished Ph.D. dissertation. Wayne State University, 1968.

Dillon, Richard H. *The Hatchet Men.* New York: Coward-McCann, Inc., 1962.

DiSalle, Michael V. *The Power of Life or Death.* New York: Random House, 1965.

Dorr, Rheta Childe. "The Other Prohibition Country." *Harper's.* September, 1929, pp. 495–504.

Doumas, Christos Leonida. "The Problem of Cyprus." Unpublished Ph.D. dissertation. University of California, Los Angeles, 1963.

Drake, St. Clair, and Horace Cayton. *Black Metropolis.* New York: Harcourt, Brace and Company, 1945.

Duffy, William J. "Organized Crime—Illegal Activities." *Law Enforcement Science and Technology.* Vol. I. Washington, D.C.: Thompson Book Co., 1967.

Durkheim, Emile. "On the Normality of Crime." *Theories of Society.* Edited by Talcott Parsons, Edward Shils, Kaspar D. Naegele, and Jesse R. Pitts. New York: The Free Press, 1961.

Elliott, Mabel A. *Crime in Modern Society.* New York: Harper and Brothers, 1952.

Ellison, E. Jerome, and Frank W. Brock. *The Run for Your Money.* New York: Dodge Publishing Co., 1935.

Epstein, Abraham. "The Insurance Racket." *The American Mercury.* September, 1930, pp. 1–10.

Etzioni, Amitai. *Modern Organization.* Englewood Cliffs, N.J.: Prentice-Hall, Inc., 1964.

Farjeon, Jefferson. *The Compleat Smuggler.* New York: The Bobbs-Merrill Co., 1938.

Feder, Sid, and Joachim Joesten. *The Luciano Story*. New York: David McKay Co., Inc., 1954.

Feldman, Justin N. "How Tammany Holds Power." *National Municipal Review*. XXXIX (July, 1950), 330–334.

Ferrarotti, Franco. "La Mafia di Sicilia come probema dello sviluppo nazionale." *La Critica Sociologica*. Winter, 1967, pp. 127–139.

Fiaschetti, Michael. *You Gotta Be Rough*. New York: Doubleday, Doran and Co., Inc., 1930.

Foley, Charles, editor. *The Memoirs of General Grivas*. New York: Frederick A. Praeger, Publishers, 1965.

Fox, Sylan. "Many Police in City Leaning to the Right." *The New York Times*. September 6, 1968.

Fraley, Oscar. *Four Against the Mob*. New York: Popular Library, 1961.

Franchetti, Leopoldo, and Sidney Sonnino. *La Sicilia Nel 1876*. Vol. I. Firenze: Vallecchi Editore, 1925.

Frasca, Dom. *Vito Genovese: King of Crime*. New York: Avon Books, 1963.

The Free Press (Detroit). November 27, 1968.

Friedman, F. G. "The World of 'La Miseria'." *Partisan Review*. XX (March–April, 1953), 218–231.

Friedman, Gene. "Crime Fighters Zero In On Us." *Reading Times*. May 15, 1967.

Frost, Thomas. *The Secret Societies of the European Revolution, 1776–1876*. London: Tinsley Brothers, 1876.

Fuller, John G. *The Gentlemen Conspirators*. New York: Grove Press, Inc., 1962.

Gaja, Filippo. *L'escrito della Lupare*. Milano: Area Editore, 1962.

"Gamblers Evade Ban in Singapore." *The New York Times*. January 5, 1968.

Gardiner, John A. "Public Attitudes Toward Gambling and Corruption." *The Annals*. CCCLXXIV (November, 1967), 123–134.

Gardiner, John A. "Wincanton: The Politics of Corruption." *Task Force Report: Organized Crime*. Washington, D.C.: U.S. Government Printing Office, 1967.

Garrett, Charles. *The LaGuardia Years*. New Brunswick: Rutgers University Press, 1961.

Geis, Gilbert. "Violence and Organized Crime." *The Annals*. CCCLXIV (March, 1966), 86–112.

Gentry, Curt. *The Madams of San Francisco*. New York: The New American Library of World Literature, Inc., 1964.

Gillette, Paul J., and Eugene Tillinger. *Inside the Ku Klux Klan*. New York: Pyramid Books, 1965.

Glubok, Norman. "N.Y.'s Juice Men Soft Pedal Violence." *Chicago Daily News*. June 9, 1964.

Gollomb, Joseph. *Crimes of the Year*. New York: Horace Liveright, 1931.

Gong, Eng Ying, and Bruce Grant. *Tong War*. New York: Nicholas L. Brown, 1930.

Gosling, John, and Dennis Craig. *The Great Train Robbery*. New York: The Bobbs-Merrill Company, Inc., 1965.

Gowen, Emmett. *A True Expose of Racketeers and Their Method*. New York: Popular Book Corporation, 1930.

Graham, Phillip L. "High Cost of Politics." *National Municipal Review*. XLIV (July, 1955), 346–351.

Greer, Scott A. *Social Organization*. New York: Random House, 1955.

Gregorio, John di. "Mussolini and the Mafia." *The Nation*. March 7, 1928, pp. 263–265.

Gruntzner, Charles. "Mafia Violence Brings Fear of Open Gang Warfare." *The New York Times*. April 28, 1968.

Gunther, John. "The High Cost of Hoodlums." *Harper's*. October, 1929, pp. 529–540.

Gurfein, Murray I. "Racketeering." *Encyclopedia of the Social Sciences*. Vol. XIII.

Hales, E. E. Y. *Mazzini and the Secret Societies*. London: Eyre and Spottiswoode, 1956.

Haney, Lewis H. *Business Organization and Combination*. New York: The Macmillan Company, 1922.

Hansl, Proctor W. *Years of Plunder*. New York: Harrison Smith and Robert Haas, 1935.

Harney, Malachi L., and John C. Cross. *The Informer in Law Enforcement*, 2nd ed. Springfield, Ill.: Charles C Thomas, 1968.

Hartung, Frank E. "White-Collar Offenses in the Wholesale Meat Industry in Detroit." *The American Journal of Sociology*. LVI (July, 1950), 25–34.

Hawkins, Gordon. "God and the Mafia." *Public Interest*. No. 14 (Winter, 1969), 24–51.

Heberle, Rudolf. *Social Movements*. New York: Appleton-Century-Crofts, Inc., 1951.

Heckethorn, Charles William. *The Secret Societies of All Ages and Countries*. 2 Vols. London: Richard Bentley and Son, 1875.

Heckethorn, Charles William. *The Secret Societies of All Ages and Countries*. I. New York: University Books, 1965.

Hill, Sir George. *A History of Cyprus*. Vol. IV. Edited by Sir Harry Luke. Cambridge: The University Press, 1952.

Hilton, David. *Brigandage in South Italy*. 2 Vols. London: Sampson, Low, Son and Marston, 1864.

Hines, Joseph S. *The Study of Sociology*. Glenview, Ill.: Scott, Foresman and Co., 1968.

Hobsbawm, E. J. *Primitive Rebels*. Manchester, England: University of Manchester Press, 1959.

Hood, Alexander Nelson. *Sicilian Studies*. New York: Dodd, Mead and Co., 1916.

Horan, James D. *The Mob's Man*. New York: Crown Publishers, Inc., 1959.

Horan, James D. *The Pinkertons: The Detective Dynasty That Made History*. New York: Crown Publishers, Inc., 1967.

Hostetter, Gordon L., and Thomas Quinn Beesley. *It's A Racket*. Chicago: Les Quin Books Inc., 1929.

Howe, Mand. *Sicily in Shadow and in Sun*. Boston: Little, Brown and Co., 1910.

Hughes, H. Stuart. *The United States and Italy*. Cambridge: Harvard University Press, 1965.

Hughes, Rupert. *The Story of Thomas E. Dewey*. Grosset and Dunlap, 1944.

Inner City Voice. April, 1968.

"The Inside of the Testimonial Racket." *Advertising and Selling*. January 7, 1931, pp. 20–21ff.

The Italian "White Hand" Society in Chicago, Illinois; Studies, Actions, and Results. Chicago, 1908.

Jackson, Kenneth T. *The Ku Klux Klan in the City, 1915–1930*. New York: Oxford University Press, 1967.

"Japan: The Way of Chivalry." *Newsweek*. September 14, 1964, p. 42.

Jennings, Dean. *We Only Kill Each Other*. Englewood Cliffs, N.J.: Prentice-Hall, Inc., 1967.

Johnson, Earl Jr. "Organized Crime: Challenge to the American Legal System." *Journal of Criminal Law, Criminology and Police Science*. LIII (December, 1962), 399–425.

Johnson, Elmer Hubert. *Crime, Correction and Society*. Homewood, Ill.: The Dorsey Press, 1968.

Johnston, R. M. *The Napoleonic Empire in Southern Italy and the Rise of the Secret Societies*. London: Macmillan and Co., Ltd., 1904.

Kefauver, Estes. *Crime in America*. Garden City, N.Y.: Doubleday and Co., Inc., 1951.

Kendall, John S. "Who Killa de Chief?" *The Louisiana Historical Quarterly*. XXII (January–October, 1939), 492–530.

Kennedy, Robert F. "The Baleful Influence of Gambling." *The Atlantic Monthly*. April, 1962, pp. 76–79.

Kenny, Michael. *A Spanish Tapestry*. London: Cohen and West, 1961.

King, Bolton, and Thomas Okey. *Italy To-Day*. London: James Nisbet and Co., Ltd., 1901.

Kobler, John. "Crimetown USA." *Saturday Evening Post*. March 9, 1963, pp. 71–76.

L. B. "Camorra in Calabria." *Archivio di Psichiatria, Scienze Penali ed Antropologia Criminale.* Vol. IV. Roma: Fratelli Bocca, 1883.

Landesco, John. *Organized Crime In Chicago.* Chicago: Illinois Association for Criminal Justice, 1929.

"The Landlady Racket." *The Literary Digest.* March 7, 1931, p. 11.

Lestingi, F. "L'Associazione della Fratellanza nella provincia di Girgenti." *Archivio di Psichiatria, Scienze Penali ed Antropologia Criminale.* Vol. IV. Roma: Fratelli Bocca, 1884.

Lewis, Arthur H. *Lament for the Molly Maguires.* New York: Harcourt, Brace and World, Inc., 1964.

Lewis, Norman. *The Honored Society.* New York: G. P. Putnam's Sons, Inc., 1964.

Life and Writings of Joseph Mazzini. London: Smith, Elder, and Co., 1890.

Linares, Vincenzo. *Racconti Popolari.* Palermo: Luigi Pedone Lauriel, Editore, 1886.

Lincoln, Eric C. "On the Black Muslims." *The Sociological Perspective.* Edited by Scott G. McNall. Boston: Little, Brown and Co., 1968.

Lindesmith, Alfred R. "The Nature of Organized Crime." *Criminology.* Edited by Clyde B. Vedder, Samuel Koenig, and Robert E. Clark. New York: Holt, Rinehart and Winston, 1953.

Lippman, Walter. "The Underworld: Our Secret Servant." *Forum.* January, 1931, pp. 1–4.

Lipset, Seymour Martin. "An Anatomy of the Klan." *Commentary.* October, 1965, pp. 74–83.

Littlefield, Walter. "Camorra." *Encyclopedia of the Social Sciences.* Vol. III.

London, Geo. *Deux Mois avec les Bandits de Chicago.* Paris: Editions des Portiques, 1930.

Lo Schiavo, G. "La Mafia e il Reato di Associazione per Delinquere." *Antologia della Mafia.* Palermo: Il Punto, edizioni, 1964.

Loschiavo, Giuseppe Guido. *Piccola Pretura.* Roma: Colombo, 1948.

Loth, David. *Public Plunder.* New York: Carrick and Evans, Inc., 1938.

Lowe, David. *Ku Klux Klan: The Invisible Empire.* New York: W. W. Norton and Co., Inc., 1967.

Lowell, Lawrence A. *Public Opinion and Popular Government.* New York: Longman's, Green and Co., 1913.

Lundberg, Ferdinand. *The Rich and the Super-Rich.* New York: Bantam Books, Inc., 1969.

Luzio, Alessandro. *Giuseppe Mazzini, Carbonaro.* Torino: Fratelli Bocca, Editori, 1920.

Lynch, Denis Tilden. *Criminals and Politicians.* New York: The Macmillan Co., 1932.

Maas, Peter. *The Valachi Papers*. New York: G. P. Putnam's Sons, 1968.

McClellan, John L. *Crime Without Punishment*. New York: Popular Library, 1963.

McConaughy, John. *From Cain to Capone*. New York: Brentano's, 1931.

MacDonald, John C. R. *Crime Is a Business*. Stanford, California: Stanford University Press, 1939.

MacDougall, Ernest D. "Report of Committee on Mercenary Crime." *Journal of Criminal Law and Criminology*. XXVI (May–June, 1932), 94–100.

McKean, Dayton. "Who Gets the Billion Graft." *National Municipal Review*. XXXVIII (December, 1949), 546–550.

Mackenzie, Frederick A. "Killing by Proxy: 1912." *Sins of New York*. Edited by Milton Crane. New York: Grosset and Dunlap, Publishers, 1947.

McManis, John. "Murder Tieup Recalls Purple Rule of Terror." *The Detroit News*. January 14, 1945.

MacNamara, Donal E. J. "Criminal Societies." *Encyclopedia Americana*. Vol. XIII, 1963.

McNeish, James. *Fire Under the Ashes*. London: Hodder and Stoughton, 1965.

"The Mafia: A Criminal Phenomenon." *International Criminal Police Review*. XXI (1966), 94–98.

Maharry, Michael. "Klan Wizard Due Here for Cheers, Cash." *The Detroit News*. April 27, 1967.

Marshall, Constance. "Racketeering in Vice." *The Woman's Journal*. May, 1931, pp. 18–19ff.

Martin, Edward Winslow. *The History of the Great Riots*. Philadelphia: The National Publishing Co., 1877.

Martin, John Bartlow. *Butcher's Dozen and Other Murders*. New York: Harper and Brothers, 1950.

Martin, Raymond. *Revolt in The Mafia*. New York: Popular Library, 1964.

Matthews, John D. *My Name Is Violence*. New York: Belmont Books, 1962.

Maxwell, Gavin. *Bandit*. New York: Harper and Brothers, 1956.

Maxwell, Gavin. *The Ten Pains of Death*. New York: E. P. Dutton and Co., Inc., 1960.

Mays, John Barron. *Crime and the Social Structure*. London: Faber and Faber, Ltd., 1963.

Merlino, S. "Camorra, Maffia and Brigandage." *Political Science Quarterly*. IX (September, 1894), 467–485.

Merton, Robert K. *Social Theory and Social Structure*. Glencoe, Ill.: The Free Press, 1957.

Messick, Hank. *The Silent Syndicate*. New York: The Macmillan Co., 1967.

The Michigan Chronicle. March 23, 1968.

Migliorini, Bruno, and T. Gwynfor Griffith. *The Italian Language*. London: Faber and Faber, 1966.

Miller, Walter B., Hildred Geertz, and Henry S. G. Cutter. "Aggression in a Boys' Street-Corner Group." *Psychiatry*. XXIV (November, 1961), 283–298.

Mitgang, Herbert. "The Black Hand of Disaster in Sicily." *The New York Times*. January 21, 1968.

Mockridge, Norton, and Robert H. Prall. *The Big Fix*. New York: Henry Holt and Co., 1954.

Monroe, Will S. *Sicily*. Boston: L. C. Page and Co., 1909.

Montalbano, Giuseppe. "La Mafia." *Nuovi Argomenti*. V (November–December, 1953), 165–204.

Mori, Cesare. *The Last Struggle with the Mafia*. London: Putnam, 1933.

Morris, Robert P. "An Exploratory Study of Some Personality Characteristics of Gamblers." *Journal of Clinical Psychology*. XIII (January, 1957), 191–193.

Mosca, Gaetano. "Mafia." *Encyclopedia of the Social Sciences*. Vol. X.

Murphy, Arthur M. "Small-Loan Usury." *Crime for Profit*. Edited by Ernest D. MacDougall. Boston: The Stratford Co., 1933.

Musmanno, Michael A. *The Story of the Italians in America*. Garden City, N.Y.: Doubleday and Co., Inc., 1965.

Myers, Gustavus. *The History of Tammany Hall*. New York: Published by the author, 1901.

Myers, Gustavus. *History of the Great American Fortunes*. Vols. II and III. Chicago: Charles H. Kerr and Company, 1910.

National Commission on Law Observance and Enforcement. *Report on Crime and the Foreign Born*. 1931.

Nelli, Humbert S. "Italians and Crime in Chicago: The Formative Years, 1890–1920." *The American Journal of Sociology*. LXIV (January, 1969), 373–391.

Ness, Eliot (with Oscar Fraley). *The Untouchables*. New York: Popular Library, 1960.

"Never Sold Any Bibles." *Time*. November 28, 1949, pp. 15–17.

Neville, Robert. "The Mafia is Deadlier." *The New York Times Magazine*. January 12, 1964.

"New Gang Methods Replace Those of Eastman's Days." *The New York Times*. September 9, 1923.

New York State Commission of Investigation. *An Investigation of Law Enforcement in Buffalo*. New York, January, 1961.

New York State Commission of Investigation. *The Loan Shark Racket*. New York: April, 1965.

New York State Commission of Investigation. *Syndicated Gambling in New York State*. New York: February, 1961.

The New York Times. May 3, 1959.

The New York Times. September 10, 1967.

The New York Times. October 29, 1967.

Newsweek. August 19, 1963, p. 27.

Nicotri, Gaspare. *Rivoluzioni e Rivolte in Sicilia*. Palermo: Alberto Reber, Editore, 1909.

Nucleo Centrale Polizia Tributaria della Guardia di Finanza. *Rapporto Penale di Denunzia*. Rome: June 6, 1961.

O'Callaghan, Sean. *The Drug Traffic*. London: Anthony Blond, Ltd., 1967.

O'Connor, John. *Broadway Racketeers*. New York: Horace Liveright, 1928.

O'Connor, Richard. *Hell's Kitchen*. New York: J. B. Lippincott Co., 1958.

"Old-Style Mafia and Its Heirs, the Calculators." *Life*. February 23, 1959, pp. 19–26.

Ontario Police Commission. *Report to the Attorney General for Ontario on Organized Crime*. Toronto: 1964.

Organized Crime in California. Report of the Subcommittee on Rackets of the Assembly Interim Committee on Judiciary. Sacramento: Assembly of the State of California, 1959.

Pantaleone, Michele. *The Mafia and Politics*. New York: Coward-McCann, Inc., 1966.

Pasley, Fred D. *Al Capone*. Garden City, N.Y.: Garden City Publishing Co., 1930.

Paton, William Agnew. *Picturesque Sicily*. New York: Harper and Brothers, 1900.

Pearson, Drew. "Racketeer Details His Aid to Nixon." *The Free Press* (Detroit). October 31, 1968.

Pecorini, Giorgio. "Chiesa e mafia in Sicilia." *Comunita*. January–April, 1967, pp. 49–68.

Peel, Roy V. *The Political Clubs of New York City*. New York: G. P. Putnam's Sons, 1935.

Pesce, Livio. "I segreti della Mafia." Part 2. *Epoca*. December 10, 1967, pp. 126–129.

Peterson, Virgil W. *Barbarians in Our Midst*. Boston: Little, Brown and Co., 1952.

Peterson, Virgil W. "Shades of Capone." *The Annals*. CCCXLVII (May, 1963), 30–39.

Pileggi, Nicholas. "The Mafia Is Good For You." *The Saturday Evening Post*. November 30, 1968, pp. 18–21.

Pitré, Giuseppe. *Biblioteca della Tradizioni Populari Siciliane*. Vol.

XV. *Usi e Costumi, Credenze e Preguidizi.* Palermo: Libreria L. Pedone Lauriel di Carlo Clausen, 1889.

Pitré, Giuseppe. *Biblioteca della Tradizioni Populari Siciliane.* Vol. XXII. *Studi di Leggende Popolari in Sicilia.* Torino: Carlo Clausen, 1904.

Porter, Sylvia. "On Wall Street." *Organized Crime in America.* Edited by Gus Tyler. Ann Arbor: The University of Michigan Press, 1962.

Poston, Ted. "The Numbers Racket." *Organized Crime in America.* Edited by Gus Tyler. Ann Arbor: The University of Michigan Press, 1962.

The President's Commission on Law Enforcement and Administration of Justice. *Task Force Report: Organized Crime.* Washington, D.C.: Government Printing Office, 1967.

Presthus, Robert. *The Organizational Society.* Vintage Books. New York: Random House, 1962.

Prezzolini, Giuseppe. *I Trapiantati.* Milano: Longanesi and Co., 1963.

The Professional Thief. Annotated and Interpreted by Edwin E. Sutherland. Phoenix Books. Chicago: The University of Chicago Press, 1965.

"Prohibition Produces a New Crop of Vikings in Norway." *The Literary Digest.* September 18, 1920, p. 69.

The Providence Journal. May 20, 1967.

Puffer, Adams. *The Boy and His Gang.* Boston: Houghton Mifflin Company, 1912.

Puglia, G. M. "Il 'Mafioso' non è Associate per Delinquere." *Antologia della Mafia.* Palermo: Il Punto, edizioni, 1964.

"The Rackets of New York." *The New Statesman.* December 6, 1930, pp. 262–264.

Radzinowicz, Leon. *Ideology and Crime.* New York: Columbia University Press, 1966.

Reid, Ed. *Mafia.* New York: The New American Library of World Literature, Inc., 1964.

Reid, Ed. *The Shame of New York.* Scranton: The Haddon Craftsmen, Inc., 1953.

Report of the Honourable Mr. Justice Wilfrid D. Roach. Toronto: March 15, 1963.

Reynolds, Frank, and Michael McClure. *Freewheelin' Frank.* New York: Grove Press, Inc., 1967.

Rogovin, Charles H., and George V. Higgins. "Organized Crime in Massachusetts." *Law and Order.* Edited by Bradbury Seasholes. Medford, Mass.: Lincoln Filene Center for Citizenship and Public Affairs, Tufts University, 1968.

Romano, Salvatore Francesco. *Momenti del Risorgimento in Sicilia.* Firenze: Casa Editore G. D'Anna, 1952.

Romano, Salvatore Francesco. *Storia della Mafia.* Milano: Sugar Editore, 1963.

Root, Jonathan. *One Night in July.* New York: Coward-McCann, Inc., 1961.

Runciman, Steven. *The Sicilian Vespers.* Cambridge: The University Press, 1958.

"Runners Haul Liquor Across Frozen River." *The Detroit News.* February 12, 1930.

Russo, Giovanni. "Piety and Poverty in Sicily." *Atlas.* X (August, 1965), 91–95.

Sait, Edward McChesney. "Machine, Political." *Encyclopedia of the Social Sciences.* Vol. IX.

Saposs, David J. "Labor Racketeering: Evolution and Solutions." *Social Research.* XXV (Autumn, 1958), 353–370.

Savage, Marion Dutton. *Industrial Unionism in America.* New York: The Ronald Press Co., 1922.

Sax, Joseph L. "Civil Disobedience: The Law Is Never Blind." *Saturday Review.* September 28, 1968, pp. 22–25ff.

Schelling, Thomas C. "Economics and the Underworld of Crime." *Law Enforcement Science and Technology.* Vol. I. Washington, D.C.: Thompson Book Co., 1967.

Schermerhorn, Richard A. *Society and Power.* New York: Random House, 1961.

Schiavo, Giovanni. *The Italians in Chicago.* Chicago: Italian American Publishing Co., 1928.

Schiavo, Giovanni. *The Truth About the Mafia.* New York: The Vigo Press, 1962.

Schneider, Jane Catherine Thompson. "Patrons and Clients in the Italian Political System." Unpublished Ph.D. dissertation. The University of Michigan, 1965.

Schur, Edwin M. *Crimes Without Victims.* Englewood Cliffs, N.J.: Prentice-Hall, 1965.

Sciascia, Leonardo. *Mafia Vendetta.* New York: Alfred A. Knopf, 1964.

Sealey, Pat. "Negroes Get Rung on Mafia Ladder." *The Miami Herald.* March 12, 1968.

Sedwick, H. D., Jr. "Musolino the Bandit." *The Outlook.* LXXI (August, 1902), 1057–1060.

Sellin, Thorsten. *Culture Conflict and Crime.* New York: Social Science Research Council, 1938.

Sellin, Thorsten. "Organized Crime: A Business Enterprise." *The Annals.* CCCXLVII (May, 1963), 12–19.

Sexton, Patricia Cayo. *Spanish Harlem.* Harper, Colophon Books. New York: Harper and Row, Publishers, 1965.

Shepperd, William G. "What's The Racket?" *Collier's.* April 11, 1931, pp. 10–11ff.

"Sicilian Vespers." *Chamber's Encyclopaedia.* Vol. IX. New Edition. London: W. & R. Chambers Limited, 1927.

Silverman, Sydel F. "Patronage and Community-Nation Relationships in Central Italy." *Ethnology.* IV (April, 1965), 172–189.

Siragusa, Charles. *The Trail of the Poppy.* Englewood Cliffs, N.J.: Prentice-Hall, Inc., 1966.

Sladen, Douglas. *Sicily.* New York: E. P. Dutton and Co., 1907.

Smith, Alson J. *Syndicate City.* Chicago: Henry Regnery Co., 1954.

Smith, Dennis Mack. "The Mafia in Sicily." *Atlas.* III (June, 1962), 437–441.

Smith, Sandy. "The Mob." *Life.* September 1, 1967, pp. 34–43.

Smith, Sandy. "You Can't Expect Police on the Take to Take Orders." *Life.* December 6, 1968, pp. 40–42.

Sola Pool, Ithiel de, and Irwin Shulman. "Newsmen's Fantasies, Audiences and Newswriting." *Public Opinion Quarterly.* XXIII (Summer, 1959–60), 145–158.

Sondern, Frederic, Jr. *Brotherhood of Evil.* New York: Bantam Books, 1960.

Sparkes, Boyden. "The Club Racket Has You." *Nation's Business.* September, 1930, pp. 44–47.

Spergel, Irving. *Racketville, Slumtown, Haulburg.* Chicago: The University of Chicago Press, 1964.

Sprigle, Ray. "East End 'Fix' Gives Numbers Mobs Free Rein." *Pittsburgh Post-Gazette.* July 12, 1950.

Sprigle, Ray. "It Isn't the Original Cost, It's the Cops' Upkeep That Keeps the Poor Racketeer 'Broke'." *Pittsburgh Post-Gazette.* August 4, 1950.

Sprigle, Ray. "Numbers Take $50,000,000 Yearly in City." *Pittsburgh Post-Gazette.* July 10, 1950.

Sprigle, Ray. "Roll Call of Democratic Chairmen in Racket Wards Shows Good Jobs Go Hand-in-Hand with Vote Power." *Pittsburgh Post-Gazette.* August 5, 1950.

Starr, John. *The Purveyor.* New York: Fawcett World Library, 1962.

State of New York Commission of Investigation. *Report of an Investigation of Certain Crime Activities and Problems of Law Enforcement in Rochester, New York.* September, 1966.

Steffens, Lincoln. *The Shame of the Cities.* New York: Peter Smith, 1948.

Stolley, Richard B. "Deadly Items in a Crime Report." *Life.* February 24, 1967, pp. 23–29.

Storer, Norman W. *The Social System of Science.* New York: Holt, Rinehart and Winston, 1966.

Sullivan, Edward D. *Rattling the Cup.* New York: The Vanguard Press, 1929.

Sutherland, Edwin H., and Donald R. Cressey. *Principles of Criminology,* 7th ed. New York: J. P. Lippincott Co., 1966.

Sylos-Labini, Paolo. "Problems of Sicilian Economic Development Changes in Rural-Urban Relations in Eastern Sicily." *Mediterranean Social Sciences Research Council.* General Assembly. Catania. October 30–November 4, 1961.

Taft, Donald R., and Ralph W. England, Jr. *Criminology,* 4th ed. New York: The Macmillan Co., 1964.

Temporary Commission of Investigation of the State of New York. *Summary of the Activities During 1963.* March, 1964.

Terrett, Courtenay. *Only Saps Work.* New York: The Vanguard Press, 1930.

"Testimonianza Resa della Commissione parlementare d'inchiesta sul fenomena della mafia in Sicilia nella seduta 22 Febbraio 1967" (trascrizione verbatim). *La Critica Sociologica.* Summer, 1967, pp. 12–16.

Thayer, Charles W. *Guerrilla.* New York: The New American Library, 1963.

Thompson, Craig, and Raymond Allen. *Gang Rule in New York.* New York: The Dial Press, 1940.

Thompson, Victor A. *Modern Organization.* New York: Alfred A. Knopf, 1961.

Thrasher, Frederic M. "Gangs." *Encyclopedia of the Social Sciences.* Vol. VI. New York: The Macmillan Company, 1933.

Thrasher, Frederic M. *The Gang.* Chicago: The University of Chicago Press, 1927.

Time. October 18, 1968, p. 26.

Touhy, Roger. (with Ray Brennan). *The Stolen Years,* Cleveland: Pennington Press, 1959.

Train, Arthur. *Courts, Criminals and the Camorra.* New York: Charles Scribners' Sons, 1912.

Train, Arthur. "Imported Crime: The Story of the Camorra in America." *McClure's Magazine.* May, 1912, pp. 83–94.

Turkus, Burton B., and Sid Feder. *Murder, Inc.* Garden City, N.Y.: Permabooks, 1952.

Turner, Wallace. *Gambler's Money.* Signet Books. New York: The New American Library, 1966.

Tyler, Gus. "The Roots of Organized Crime." *Crime and Delinquency.* VIII (October, 1962), 325–338.

Tyler, Poyntz. Editor. *Immigration and the United States.* New York: The H. W. Wilson Company, 1956.

U.S. Congress. House. *Reports of the Industrial Commission on Immigration.* H. Doc. 184, 57th Congress, 1st Sess., 1901.

U.S. Congress. Senate. Committee on Government Operations. *Organized Crime and Illicit Traffic in Narcotics, Hearings* before the permanent subcommittee on Investigations. United States Senate, 88th Cong., 1st sess., 1963, pt. 1, pt. 2 and pt. 3.

U.S. Congress. Senate. Report of the Committee on Government Operations. *Organized Crime and Illicit Traffic in Narcotics.* Senate Report No. 72, 89th Cong., 1st sess., 1965.

U.S. Congress. Senate. *Reports of the Immigration Commission.* S. Doc. 747. 61st Cong., 3d sess., 1911.

U.S. Congress. Senate. *Reports of the Immigration Commission.* S. Doc. 750. 61st Cong., 3d sess., 1911.

U.S. Congress. Senate. Select Committee on Improper Activities in the Labor and Management Field. *Investigation of Improper Activities in the Labor and Management Field, Hearings.* Senate, on S.R. 74 and 22. 85th Cong., 2d sess., 1958.

U.S. Congress. Senate. Special Committee to Investigate Organized Crime in Interstate Commerce. *Investigation of Organized Crime in Interstate Commerce, Hearings.* Senate. S. Res. 202. 81st Cong., 2d sess., 1951.

Valentine, Lewis J. *Night Stick.* New York: The Dial Press, 1947.

VanCise, Phillip S. *Fighting the Underworld.* Boston: Houghton Mifflin Co., 1936.

Vanzi, Max. "Tokyo Gangster Describes His Work, Philosophy." *Columbus Dispatch.* December 10, 1967.

Varna, Andrew. *World Underworld.* London: Museum Press Ltd., 1957.

Vecoli, Rudolph J. "Chicago's Italians Prior to World War I: A Study of Their Social and Economic Adjustment." Unpublished Ph.D. dissertation. University of Wisconsin, 1962.

Vedder, Clyde B., Samuel Koenig, and Robert E. Clark, editors. *Criminology.* New York: Holt, Rinehart and Winston, 1953.

Vizzini, A. *La Mafia.* Roma: Tipografia Artero e Comp., 1880.

Vold, George B. *Theoretical Criminology.* New York: Oxford University Press, 1958.

Waggoner, Walter H. "Jersey Jury Inquiry Asked on Mafia-Legislator Links." *The New York Times.* December 18, 1968.

Walker, Stanley. *The Night Club Era.* New York: Blue Ribbon Books, Inc., 1933.

Waller, George. *Saratoga, Saga of an Impious Era.* Englewood Cliffs, N.J.: Prentice-Hall Inc., 1966.

Wendt, Lloyd, and Herman Kogan. *Lords of the Levee.* Garden City, N.Y.: Garden City Publishing Co., Inc., 1944.

Weyl, Nathaniel. *Treason.* Washington, D.C.: Public Affairs Press, 1950.

Whyte, William Foote. "Sicilian Peasant Society." *American Anthropologist.* XLVI (1944), 65–74.

Whyte, William Foote. *Street Corner Society.* Chicago: The University of Chicago Press, 1965.

Wiebe, G. O. "Responses to the Televised Kefauver Hearings: Some Social Psychological Implications." *Public Opinion Quarterly.* XVI (Summer, 1952), 179–200.

Wiley, Norbert F. "The Ethnic Mobility Trap and Stratification Theory." *Social Problems.* XV (Fall, 1967), 147–159.

Wirtz, W. Willard. *Labor and the Public Interest.* New York: Harper and Row, Publishers, 1964.

Wiseman, H. V. *Political Systems.* New York: Frederick A. Praeger, 1967.

Wolf, Eric R. "Aspects of Group Relations in a Complex Society: Mexico." *American Anthropologist.* LVIII (December, 1956), 1065–1078.

Wolf, Eric R. "Kinship, Friendship, and Patron-Client Relations in Complex Societies." *The Social Anthropology of Complex Societies.* Edited by Michael Banton. New York: Frederick A. Praeger, Inc., 1966.

Wolff, Kurt H. Editor. *The Sociology of Georg Simmel.* New York: The Free Press, 1964.

Wosgian, Daniel S. "Turks and British Rule in Cyprus." Unpublished Ph.D. dissertation. Columbia University, 1963.

Wuorinen, John H. *The Prohibition Experiment in Finland.* New York: Columbia University Press, 1931.

Author Index

Adams, Graham, Jr., 41
Allen, Edward J., 4, 109
Allsop, Kenneth, 7
Alongi, G., 117, 118
Anderson, Robert T., 172, 175–176
Anslinger, Harry J., 2–3
Antiochia, Corrado, 144
Asbury, Herbert, 159–162, 163, 178, 179–180, 181–183, 185, 199–200

Banfield, Edward C., 73–74
Barker, Dudley, 43
Barnes, Harry Elmer, 25, 26, 27
Barzini, Luigi, 122
Beesley, Thomas Quinn, 30
Bell, Daniel, 3
Bent, Silas, 32
Bloch, Herbert, 22–23, 26, 59–60
Blok, Anton, 111, 139, 140
Boissevain, Jeremy, 110–111, 138
Borkin, Joseph, 76
Brean, Herbert, 91
Brennan, Bill, 157–158, 248
Brock, Frank W., 30
Bruno, Cesare, 92, 103, 114
Buse, Renée, 2

Caldwell, Robert, 24–25, 26, 27, 33
Campbell, J. K., 110
Campesi, Paul J., 313
Candida, Renato, 91, 100, 112
Caplow, Theodore, 35, 36
Carlson, Gustav C., 59, 66–67, 75, 278, 279
Cavan, Ruth S., 25–26, 27, 28, 33
Cayton, Horace, 59

Chafetz, Henry, 186–187
Chalmers, David H., 40
Chamberlain, Henry Barrett, 77
Cohen, Albert E., 46
Cook, Fred J., 7, 201, 247–248
Cooper, Courtney Ryley, 8, 56
Cornwell, Elmer E., 327
Coxe, John E., 162, 163, 165
Craig, Dennis, 33
Crawford, Francis Marion, 94
Cressey, Donald R., 11, 28, 33, 62, 176, 238, 242–243, 249, 250–255, 264
Cross, John C., 225–226
Cutler, Henry S. G., 47
Cutrera, Antonino, 100, 112, 114, 118

Davis, J. Richard "Dixie", 244
DeBlasio, A., 120, 121
deSola Pool, Ithiel, 86
Dedmon, Emmet, 184
Demerath, H. J. III, 13
Dietz, Mary Lorenz, 272
DiGregorio, John, 140
Dillon, Richard H., 8, 190
Dolci, Danilo, 109
Drake, St. Clair, 59
Duffy, William J., 61
Durkheim, Emile, 9–10

Elliott, Mabel, 23–24
Ellison, E. Jerome, 30
England, Ralph W., 27
Epstein, Abraham, 31–32
Etzioni, Amitai, 35, 36

Feder, Sid, 6, 7, 70, 125, 141, 158, 244
Ferrarotti, Franco, 143–144
Fiaschetti, Michael, 195–196
Fiddle, Seymour, 58
Finestone, Harold, 58
Franchetti, Leopoldo, 122, 192
Friedman, F. G., 108–109
Fuller, John G., 34

Geertz, Hildred, 47
Geis, Gilbert, 273
Gillette, Paul J., 40–41
Gong, Eng Ying, 190
Gosling, John, 33
Gowen, Emmett, 30
Graham, Philip L., 71, 72
Grant, Bruce, 190
Greer, Scott A., 35
Gunther, John, 29, 30
Gurfein, Murray I., 29–30

Haney, Lewis H., 31
Harney, Malachi L., 225–226
Hartung, Frank E., 48
Hawkins, Gordon, 322
Heckethorn, Charles William, 99–100, 113, 116, 117, 119, 120, 142, 171
Higgins, George V., 299
Hill, Sir George, 43
Hilton, David, 119, 142
Hobsbawm, E. J., 89, 104, 114, 123
Horan, James D., 164–165
Hostetter, Gordon L., 30
Hughes, Rupert, 76

Jackson, Kenneth T., 40
Joeston, Joachim, 6, 125, 141, 158
Johnson, Earl, Jr., 65–66
Johnson, Elmer H., 24

Kefauver, Estes, 3, 210
Kendall, John S., 165
Kennedy, Robert F., 60, 241
Kenny, Michael, 110
King, Bolton, 123

Landesco, John, 191, 207
Lestingi, F., 113–114, 117
Lewis, Norman, 7–8, 92, 195
Lewis, Oscar, 109

Linares, Vincenzo, 116
Lincoln, C. Eric, 59
Lindesmith, Alfred, 27
Lippmann, Walter, 66
Lipset, Seymour Martin, 40
London, Geo., 55
LoSchiavo, G., 123
Lowe, David, 72
Lowell, A. Lawrence, 70
Lundberg, Ferdinand, 72
Luzio, Alessandro, 100

Maas, Peter, 238, 249
McClure, Michael, 33
McConaughy, John, 29
MacDonald, John C. R., 28
MacDougall, Ernest, 45
McKean, Dayton D., 74
Marshall, Constance, 30–31
Matthews, John D., 76, 273
Maxwell, Gavin, 5, 108
Mays, John Barron, 57
Merlino, S., 119
Merton, Robert K., 10
Messick, Hank, 5
Miller, Walter B., 47
Mockridge, Norton, 209–210
Monroe, Will S., 123
Montalbano, Giuseppe, 113, 118
Mori, Cesare, 140
Mosca, Gaetano, 92
Musmanno, Michael A., 102
Myers, Gustavus, 31, 181

Niederhoffer, Arthur, 26

O'Connor, John, 30
O'Connor, Richard, 179, 180–181
Okey, Thomas, 123

Pantaleone, Michele, 5, 129, 130, 131
Pasley, Fred, 7
Paton, William Agnew, 128
Pecorini, Giorgio, 144
Pesce, Livio, 140
Peterson, Richard A., 13
Peterson, Virgil W., 71, 177, 178–179, 184, 276
Pileggi, Nicholas, 61–62, 66
Pitrè, Giuseppe, 98, 103–106, 109
Porter, Sylvia, 34

Post, Melville, 93
Prall, Robert H., 209–210
Presthus, Robert, 35
Prezzolini, Giuseppe, 5, 312
Puffer, J. Adams, 33, 47
Puglia, G. M., 123

Radzinowicz, Leon, 131–132
Raymond, Allen, 6, 206, 244
Reid, Ed, 3–4, 6, 71, 93–94, 96, 97,
    112–113, 195
Reynolds, Frank, 33
Rogovin, Charles H., 299
Runciman, Steven, 95, 96–97, 99
Russo, Giovanni, 112

Sait, Edward McChesney, 72
Sax, Joseph L., 39
Schelling, Thomas C., 65
Schermerhorn, Richard A., 70
Schiavo, Giovanni, 6–7, 105–106, 125,
    206–207
Sellin, Thorsten, 39, 77, 123
Shepherd, William G., 30
Shulman, Irwin, 86
Smith, Alson, 5
Smith, Dennis Mack, 122
Sondern, Frederic, Jr., 4–5, 6
Sonnino, Sidney, 122, 192
Sparkes, Boyden, 32
Sprigle, Ray, 66, 74

Steffens, Lincoln, 199
Storer, Norman W., 13
Sutherland, Edwin E., 26, 28, 33
Sylos-Labini, Paolo, 130–131

Taft, Donald R., 27
Teeters, Negley K., 25, 26, 27
Terrett, Courtenay, 29
Thompson, Craig, 6, 206, 244
Thompson, Victor A., 35
Thrasher, Frederic M., 26, 47
Tillinger, Eugene, 40–41
Train, Arthur, 170–171
Turkus, Burton B., 6, 7, 70, 244
Turner, Wallace, 71
Tyler, Gus, 22

VanCise, Phillip S., 46
Varna, Andrew, 2, 6, 125
Vecoli, Rudolph J., 175, 208
Vizzini, A., 99–101
Vold, George B., 28

Walker, Stanley, 309
Weyl, Nathaniel, 38–39
Whyte, William Foote, 98
Wiebe, G. D., 84
Wilson, James Q., 73–74
Wirtz, Willard W., 299
Wiseman, H. V., 13
Wolf, Eric R., 10, 110–111

Subject Index

Accardo, Tony, 276
Amoroso, Fratelli, 118
Apalachin Meeting, 245–246, 247–250
Axler, Abe, 204

Becker, Charles, 198–199
Black Hand, 6–7, 11–12, 25, 191–195
Black Panthers, 39
Bribery, 67–68, 69–71, 75–77
Brokers, 10
Brown, John, 38–39
Buchalter, Louis "Lepke," 65, 201, 209

Camorra, 6, 119–122, 142–143, 170–173, 174–175, 177, 242
Capone, Alphonse, 7, 8, 64, 71, 72, 158, 201, 204–205, 207, 208, 212, 306–307, 309–310
Carbonari, 100–101
Chicago, history of syndicated crime in, 177–179, 183–186
Client, function of, 63–64
Cohen, Mickey, 71, 310
Colosimo, James "Big Jim," 197, 212
Corruption, 67–68
Corruption, political, 70–74
Cosa Nostra, 6, 10, 174–175, 176, 223–258, 320, 323
Costello, Frank, 201, 210, 230, 255
Coughlin, "Bathhouse John," 197, 205
Curran, One-Lung, 180–181

D'Andrea, Anthony, 207
Diamond, Jack "Legs," 309
Drucci, Vincent "Schemer," 205
Dwyer, William "Big Bill," 201, 206

Enosis movement, 42–45

E.O.K.A., 43–45
Esposito, Giuseppe, 165–166

Flegenheimer, Arthur "Dutch Schultz," 70, 206, 209
Fletcher, Eddie, 203, 204
Fratellanza, 112, 114
Fratellanze, 90, 112–119, 320

Gabellotto, 127–134, 137, 321
Gallo brothers, 309
Gambling, 58–60, 289–291
Gambling, numbers, 59, 278–283
Gang, definition of, 33–34
Genovese, Vito, 64, 238, 307
Giuliano, Salvatore, 114–115
Gordon, Waxey, 201, 206
Grivas, George, 42–45
Gusenberg, Frank, 310

Hennessy, David C., 159–167
Hijacking, 296–299
Hines, Jimmy, 70–71

I Beati Paoli, 116–117
Immigration of Italian criminals, 167–170

Kastel, Dandy Phil, 201
Kenna, "Hinky Dink," 197, 205
Keywell, Harry, 204
Ku Klux Klan, 39–41, 72

Labor Unions, as political-social organized crime, 41–42
Latifondo, 127–128, 129
Liquor enterprises during Prohibition, 200–201
Loan-sharking, 60–62, 274–276, 295–296

Lombardo, Antonio, 207
Luchese, Thomas "Three-Finger Brown," 71
Luciano, Charles "Lucky," 2, 7–8, 64, 141, 158, 201, 206, 209, 238, 243–245, 246, 310

McCarren, Pat, 71
MacDonald, Mike, 183–186
Madden, Owney, 201, 206, 309
Mafia, 1–7, 9, 10, 25
  definition of, 83–89
  history of term, 91–107
  in Sicily, 89–145, 321–322
  in United States, 153–177, 320
Mafioso, role of, 157
Makarios III, Archbishop, 43–44
Mala Vita, 171–172
Mazzini, Giuseppe, 99–102
Merlo, Mike, 206, 207
Milberg, Irving, 204
Miller, "Honey Boy," 204
Millman, Harry, 204
Molly Maguires, 41–42
Moran, George "Bugs," 201, 205
Morrissey, John, 186–189

Narcotic drugs, 58, 291–295
Newspapers and syndicated crime, 68–69, 175
New York City, history of syndicated crime in, 180–183, 186–189

O'Banion, Dion, 32, 201, 205, 306–307
Oblonica, 99–101
O'Dwyer, William, 71
Omerta, 107–110
Organized crime, clarification of meaning, 21–22
  defined, 37–38
  in-group-oriented, 46–47
  mercenary, 45–46
  political-social, 38–46
  structure of, 23–28, 35–49

Patron-client system, 110–112, 264–303
Pearson, Drew, 71
Petrosino, Lt. Joseph, 195–196
Plant, Roger, 178

Prohibition of alcoholic beverages, 57–58
Purple Gang, 202–204

Racket, definition of, 29–35
Rosenthal, Herman, 198
Rothstein, Arnold, 196, 309

Sage, Russell, 31
Saietta, Ignazio, 157, 158
Salerno, Ralph E., 327
Saltis, Joe, 201
Shapiro, Gurrah, 201, 209
Shelton Gang, 201–202
Sicilian Vespers, 93–99
Siegel, Benjamin "Bugsey," 9, 201, 311
Smuggling, 292–293
Stuppagghiari, 112, 113–114
Syndicate criminal, functions of, 64–66, 77–78, 154–155, 273–278
  socio-psychological aspects of, 305–316
Syndicated crime, 1, 9–10, 47–48, 319–328
  developmental-associational conception, 155–156
  evolutional-centralization conception, 155–156, 167, 175, 211–212, 221, 223, 225, 226–227, 257, 267, 284, 300, 307, 311, 324
  structure of, 55–63, 77–78, 155, 176–177, 263–303, 319–324

Tennes, Mont, 197
Thompson, William "Big Bill," 71
Tongs, 8, 190–191
Torrio, Johnny, 205, 312
Tweed, Boss, 188

Unione Siciliano, 6–7, 157, 158, 159, 206–208, 244, 320

Valachi, Joseph, 6, 223–232, 234–241, 243, 246, 250, 256, 322–323
Varnell, Harry, 184

Wire service, 270–271

Young Italy, 101–102

Zwillman, Longy, 201